Gregory Clancey · EARTHQUAKE NATION

The Cultural Politics
of Japanese Seismicity, 1868–1930

University of California Press

Berkeley   Los Angeles   London

University of California Press, one of the most distinguished
university presses in the United States, enriches lives around the
world by advancing scholarship in the humanities, social sciences,
and natural sciences. Its activities are supported by the UC Press
Foundation and by philanthropic contributions from individuals and
institutions. For more information, visit www.ucpress.edu.

University of California Press
Berkeley and Los Angeles, California

University of California Press, Ltd.
London, England

Library of Congress Cataloging-in-Publication Data
Clancey, Gregory K.
   Earthquake nation : the cultural politics of Japanese seismicity,
1868–1930 / Gregory Clancey.
      p.   cm.
   Includes bibliographical references and index.
   ISBN 0-520-24607-1 (cloth : alk. paper)
   1. Japan—Civilization—1868–1945.   2. Earthquakes—Japan—
Psychological aspects.   3. Earthquakes—Japan—Social aspects.   I.
Title: Cultural politics of Japanese seismicity, 1868–1930.   II. Title.
DS822.3.C46   2006
624.1'762095209034—dc22   2005028159

Manufactured in the United States of America
15   14   13   12   11   10   09   08   07   06
10   9   8   7   6   5   4   3   2   1

This book is printed on New Leaf EcoBook 50, a 100% recycled fiber
of which 50% is de-inked post-consumer waste, processed chlorine-
free. EcoBook 50 is acid-free and meets the minimum requirements of
ANSI/ASTM D5634-01 (Permanence of Paper). ⊚

To my son, Kenta,
who grew up with this book

CONTENTS

ILLUSTRATIONS

ACKNOWLEDGMENTS

This project began at the Science, Technology, and Society program at the Massachusetts Institute of Technology, where my three principal advisors, Merritt Roe Smith, John Dower, and Peter Perdue, each excelled in their roles. I was also skillfully advised by Michael M. J. Fischer and Pauline Maier and received valuable comments from Deborah Fitzgerald, Hugh Gusterson, Harriet Ritvo, Jessica Riskin, Joe Dumit, and Jed Buchwald.

My initial Japanese research was generously funded by a Fulbright scholarship, and I thank both the Institute of International Education, which oversees this program, and the Japan-United States Educational Commission (JUSEC), which administers it in Japan. Samuel Shepherd, director of the JUSEC, and Jinko Itō, who handled all the details of my residency in Tokyo, deserve special thanks.

Suzuki Hiroyuki invited me into his *kenkyūshitsu* at the University of Tokyo on the strength of a single meeting, and has since been infinitely gracious with his time and good advice. Among the many other Japanese scholars who have been generous with their support these past years, I must single out Shimizu Keiichi of the National Science Museum; Nakatani Norihito of Waseda University (now at Osaka City University) and the members of his *Meiji zemi;* Fujimori Terunobu, Hashimoto Takehiko, and Fujii Keisuke of the University of Tokyo; Fujita Fumiko of Tsuda College; Chiku Kakugyō of the Kanazawa Institute of Technology; Yamazaki Kanichi; Ōhashi Ryūta; Yamaguchi Hiroshi of Nihon University; the late Endō Akihisa of the Hokkaido Institute of Technology; the late Itō Heizaemon of

Chūbu University; Uchida Seizō of Bunka Women's College; and Murao Kinichi of Niigata Polytechnic College. Kasuya Akira provided me with many valuable clippings.

Tokyo *miya-daiku* Mochizuki Kenichi taught me what I know of Japanese carpentry and gave me many valuable gifts, from physical ones such as *kiku-jutsu-sho* (carpenters' geometry books) to the intangible ones of his memory and wit.

Among graduate student colleagues (now all teachers themselves) who I met at Japanese and American institutions, many of whom provided books, advice, leads, and good company, I must particularly thank Makita Tomoko, Alice Tseng, Don Choi, Shigeatsu Shimizu, Ken Tadashi Oshima, Sara Wermiel, Amy Slaton, and Emily Thompson.

Cherie Wendelken of Harvard University and James Bartholomew of Ohio State University both read early drafts of this manuscript and have aided and inspired my work in other ways.

My initial draft was written at the Dibner Institute for the History of Science and Technology in Cambridge, Massachusetts, which provided me a generous stipend and good fellowship in addition to office space. My thanks to Evelyn Simha and her staff. Three Dibner Fellows in particular—Rebecca Herzig, Slava Gerovitch, and Karen Ellison—shared my writing struggles and relieved them at the same time. I was also helped in this period by Umezu Akiko and Akiko Takenaka-O'Brien.

At an early stage in my research I received a grant from the Hakodate Kara Foundation in Hakodate, Japan, thanks to architect Yanagida Ryōzō of Yanagida, Ishizuka, and Associates and Morishita Mitsuru of Hokkaido University, who also provided my first real introduction to Meiji-period architecture.

While conceptualizing this project I spent a season at the Department of the History of Science and Technology at the Royal Institute of Technology in Stockholm, Sweden, as a Lars Hierta Fellow, courtesy of Svante Lindqvist. I have not the space to name the many people I met and shared ideas with in Sweden (and Norway, where I traveled through the generosity of the institute), but I must particularly thank Ulf Larsson, Nina Wormbs, and Arne Kaijser.

At the National University of Singapore (NUS), where I carried out the final phase of research and writing, I've also received much help. A grant from the Toshiba International Foundation paid for a last research trip to Japan, and a writing fellowship from the Asia Research Institute let me complete the penultimate draft. Among members of the NUS Faculty (permanent and visiting) who have given their advice or comments are Paul Kratoska, Barry Steben, Timothy Tsu,

James Warren, and Anthony Reid. I'm also grateful for the institutional support of Tan Tai Yong, Alan Chan, and the NUS Faculty of Arts and Social Sciences.

Other scholars with whom I've profitably discussed this project since coming to Singapore include Henry D. Smith II of Columbia University, Charles Schencking and Janet Borland of the University of Melbourne, Jonathan Reynolds of the University of Southern California, Kerry Smith of Brown University, Gregory Bankoff of the University of Auckland, and Tsukahara Togo of the University of Kobe.

My graduate student Elizabeth P. Y. Chee helped check, correct, and otherwise wrestle this manuscript into final form. Yasuko Kobayashi provided invaluable assistance in helping me to revise the fifth chapter, including some translation work. The other translations from Japanese to English in this chapter and throughout the book are my own.

I'm indebted in many ways to Jordan Sand of Georgetown University, but particularly for his close and wise reading of my final draft. Thanks also to my second, anonymous reviewer.

Some of the themes developed in this book, particularly those dealing with carpenters and architects, were formed a very long time ago. I thus have to go a bit further back in time to thank those who helped shape those interests, especially Earle G. Shettleworth, Jr., Richard Candee of Boston University, Dave Adams, Steve Roy, the late Morgan Phillips, John Leeke, Roger Reed, and the late Arthur Gerrier.

Dissertations are largely crafted in libraries. Of the many remarkable libraries I have had the privilege of inhabiting these last few years, I'd like to single out the Humanities, Dewey, Rotch, and Retrospective libraries at the Massachusetts Institute of Technology; the Widener, Yenching, Loeb, Kummel, Cabot, Littauer, Lamont, and Pussey libraries at Harvard University; the University, School of Architecture, and Earthquake Research Institute libraries at the University of Tokyo; the National Diet Library in Tokyo; the Nakano-ku Minami-dai branch of the Tokyo Municipal Library System; the Ichinomiya City Toshima Library (Aichi prefecture); the Nagoya City Library; the Burndy Library at the Dibner Institute; the History of Science and Technology Library at the Royal Institute of Technology in Stockholm; the Bangor (Maine) Public Library; and the Main Library of the National University of Singapore. Thanks also to the staff of the Nagoya City Museum for allowing me to reproduce a number of images from their collection.

I've saved the most important thanks for last. This book belongs to Kasuya Chiyuki, my wife, as much as to myself.

Introduction

The story of the Great Nōbi Earthquake has a long history of narration in Japanese, particularly by architects and their historians.[1] It has not, as far as I know, ever been told in English.[2] Allowing for variations, the rudiments of the story go something like this: beginning in the 1870s, shortly after the Meiji Restoration, foreign teachers were brought to Japan to train the first generation of architects and engineers. The foreign (mostly British) architects taught Japanese to build in brick and stone, and the engineers demonstrated how to string telegraph wires, lay railroads, and span rivers with iron truss bridges. It was a classic example of "technology transfer," except that the object transferred was not so much machinery or material, but embodied knowledge. Masonry also laid up "culture" in the form of buildings indistinguishable from those lining the streets of London or Manchester. Bricks and pieces of stone became the smallest and most basic material units in the general technocultural adornment of a young, nervous, and radical regime.

Wooden-country Japan, it was decided, would be rebuilt in masonry and iron. The existing Japanese landscape—the temples, houses, and arched timber bridges—became the object of elaborate denigration (sometimes coded, sometimes bald) by foreign teachers and their Japanese pupils alike. The reigning metaphor was strength. Everything in and about Japan seemed, in comparison to Europe and the United States, fragile. This fragility made Japan seem feminine to foreign eyes, but sometimes made it beautiful.

Then, on October 28, 1891, one of the most powerful earthquakes in modern Japanese history, centered on the Nōbi Plain just north of Nagoya, rocked the main island of Honshu from Tokyo to Osaka. Large iron bridges and the walls of brick factories and post offices came crashing down, while Japanese temples, pagodas, and architectural monuments such as Nagoya Castle seemingly escaped unharmed. In the aftermath of the great earthquake, Japanese architects and engineers were forced to question foreign knowledge, and the foreign teachers began even to question themselves. Tokyo University lecturer Josiah Conder, an English architect, advised his students to reexamine the methods and practices of Japanese carpenters *(daiku)*. The generation who lived through the Nōbi earthquake now took on the task of adapting foreign knowledge to Japanese nature and marrying the knowledge of the present to the knowledge discovered by their countrymen long ago. This task would preoccupy many of the best professional minds well into the twentieth century.

When I first heard this story of the Nōbi earthquake (or, rather, began piecing it together from many mouths and texts), it seemed the mirror-image twin to classical histories of Japanese technology and industrialization. Many stories of Japanese technical change begin much like the one I've told above (with the arrival of foreign teachers) but continue the way they begin, with Japan henceforth a pupil nation and the West a teacher culture. The most sensitive historians complicate this text by cultivating continuity between the Edo and Meiji periods (showing Japan to have been unusually "well prepared" to learn), emphasizing the speed with which foreign teachers were replaced by their Japanese pupils, or highlighting indigenous adaptation and innovation. Others point out the brutal human and natural costs of all that rapid learning. But rarely in the existing historiography of modern Japanese change does foreign knowledge itself so badly stumble (let alone come crashing down) as in the Japanese narrative of the Great Nōbi Earthquake.[3]

Why has the story of Nōbi failed to attract foreign narrators? It is—is it not?— a good story, and portions of it have been well documented in Japan for some time. One practical answer (we will encounter others less practical) is that it has mainly been told in a theater that few Western scholars of Japanese technopolitical change regularly enter: Japanese architectural history. In Europe and the United States, the Modern movement in architecture notwithstanding, the history of science and technology is considered far from architectural history and an ocean away from the history of art.[4] In Japan, however, where the word for technology *(gijutsu)* sounds more like the word for art *(bijutsu)* than the word for science *(kagaku)*, where nearly all architects are first trained as engineers, and where chief carpenters are licensed architects, it is not so odd to find earthquake-resistant engineering in books that are also about Buddhist temples and Le Corbusier. It is Japanese architectural history, rather than the history of Japanese science and technology, which includes in its domain the most elaborate and complex *gijutsu* of the period before foreigners arrived.[5]

Even when Japanese architectural historians talk about art and architecture in their pure forms, however, that is with nature or technology as context rather than content, European and American scholars have only infrequently listened. It is not just a language barrier. Since the nineteenth century, architects and artists in Europe and the United States have cultivated direct experience of the history of Japanese art and architecture (and that of many other non-Western peoples) through photographs and site visits. They have had less interest in retaining local guides, convinced that art and architecture are embodied in objects they can see, touch, and enter, rather than stories about those objects.[6] In any case, earthquakes are just as far from art in Europe and the United States as art is from technoscience.

On the other hand, architectural historians in every country have certain things in common. One is an uneasy relationship with narratives of progress, which began well before the term *postmodernity* was coined among them to describe a shift in design theory. In Japan, where all architectural historians are first trained as engineers, and then as architects, and finally as historians, the unease has arguably been less strong than in the West. Yet it still exists. On faculties of engineering at Japanese universities, Japanese architectural historians find themselves the only humanists, and perhaps the only group that does not wholeheartedly embrace the vision of unilinear progress notoriously common among engineers of all nationalities. "Progress" has often been viewed with suspicion in the cosmopolitan world of art (it is arguably one of the ideas that that world first constructed itself against) and this is also the inheritance of Japan's architects and, even more, their historians, many of whom study and admire ancient buildings. The story of Nōbi has progressive elements—the move away from received foreign authority is also one toward self-sustaining Japanese discovery—but its central trope, the need to discover a local style synthesizing past and present, is more typical of art historical narratives than technoscientific ones.[7]

Nonetheless, a Japanese architectural historian I know refers to the Nōbi earthquake using a term from cosmology: the Big Bang.[8] This perfectly captures the sense of the Nōbi earthquake as a moment of violent creation, infinitely expansive. Before the Big Bang, Japanese merely absorb foreign knowledge. Nature itself then intervenes—a peculiarly Japanese sort of destructive nature—and sets the nation on a knowledge-producing quest at once "Western" yet all its own (or as a later generation would have it, "modern"). The political and gender relations between foreign knowledge and Japanese nature reverse overnight. Japan is no longer fragile. Its beauty, once considered refined, is now sublime, powerful. The Western factories and bridges now embody vulnerability rather than strength. They require an act of rescue.

It cannot be coincidence, however, that this story of the Nōbi earthquake evokes a moment—circa 1890—that historians have identified as a watershed in Japanese nationalism. Foreign knowledge is humbled on the Nōbi Plain at the very time it was being questioned at a whole range of other sites, and in a range of ways.[9] Any sense of mystery in this convergence between nature and nation disappears once we accept the science-studies lesson that nature is inevitably spoken for—even manifestations of nature as loud and unmistakable as earthquakes.[10] Indeed, while certain strands in the story were crafted in the disaster's immediate aftermath, others predated it—receiving sudden amplification in the theater provided by the ruins of Nagoya—and still others have been influenced by subsequent events. The idea that Japanese cultural nationalism is bound up with stories about nature is hardly new or surprising.[11] But that nationalism can also be bound up with natural catastrophe may be a more novel contention.

Although earthquakes are normally treated as a footnote to modern Japanese history, late Meiji and Taishō were periods of unusually strong and frequent seismic activity, climaxing with the destruction of Tokyo itself in 1923. Seismicity was in this sense a constant, catastrophic undercurrent to the Japanese nation-building project, one that not only dogged it, but in some sense produced it. We are used to the idea that accidents and disasters expose previously unimagined vulnerabilities, and this has certainly been true in modern Japan. Less self-evident is the way political actors (including scientists, architects, and other state-credentialed professionals) craft advantage from these same phenomena. How the unexpected natural disaster and the normative machinery of governance intertwine, creating not only states of emergency but emergency-oriented states, is a topic we have only begun to explore despite a plethora of intriguing evidence.[12] Japan—where catastrophe not only has been regular and consequential over so long a period of time but also has left such a rich documentary record—is an excellent place to pursue such inquiries.[13]

What I am after in the pages that follow, however, is not the political or social history of earthquakes per se, but their emergence as objects of Meiji-period knowledge-making. The mastery of new and foreign knowledge was, after all, a major component in the charisma of the Imperial state. The phenomena of seismicity would prove unexpectedly problematic, however, both to the Japanese project of "Western learning" *(yōgaku)* and Western efforts—often initiated by expatriates—at characterizing Japan as landscape and culture. Tracing the construction of knowledge is normally a matter of choosing a discipline, describing its discourse and practices, and locating it within discrete institutions. I will be more interested in the way an emerging problem—in this case seismicity—restructured disciplines, institutions, and individual careers around itself, and sometimes set them in conflict. I am not suggesting that earthquakes have agency in the sense of making choices about how groups and individuals choose to confront them. In fact, experts, institutions, and specialized equipment proved necessary, as we will see, in order that seismicity even be isolated and named. Earthquakes did have a certain agency, however, in refusing to become stable "knowledge objects." This force of Japanese nature was important and intractable enough to reorder academic discourses and practices imported from locations such as Britain and Germany, where the earth does not move with such destructive consequences. Thus did the science and architecture of earthquakes become internationally recognized Japanese specialties by the beginning of the twentieth century, although efforts to sustain that achievement would prove more than mercurial.

My account opens with the arrival of foreign (mostly British) professors at Tokyo's College of Technology (Kōbudaigakkō) in the middle 1870s. It first follows a particular college course, architecture, which in Japan was also a new word, practice, substance, and type of calling. Anglo-Japanese architecture is historicized in a matrix that includes *daiku* (traditional Japanese architect-carpenters), engineering (the unifying principle of the College of Technology), and art (something that was not engineering, but maybe architecture, and maybe even *daiku*-work). My own uncertainty about some of these words and their meanings is not an attempt to be coy, but to preserve and report uncertainty or contingent usage among my initial subjects—British men for whom Japan, by a certain metaphorical logic, was sometimes "the Britain of the East." I construct solid materials—stone, brick, wood, and eventually concrete—into my narrative at the same time, inscribed in all sorts of ways by their foreign and Japanese handlers. What I am aiming for in these early sections is the design of "Japan" and "the Japanese" by Anglo-Japanese architecture, and the simultaneous erection by that same nascent discipline of "the West" in Japan itself. As I demonstrate in the second chapter, earthquakes were a central concern and opportunity in the construction of this Far-Easterly Britain.

The account of the Nōbi earthquake with which I began was crafted in its original form not by architects, but members of a second discipline even closer to the phenomena of earthquakes: seismology. Despite having European roots, seismology's development as a modern science—one with its own institutions, diplomas, instruments, publications, and so on—occurred largely on Japanese soil in this same period. Bringing seismologists onto the stage, which I do in the third chapter, reworks the standard narrative in fundamental ways. It demonstrates, for example, that foreign knowledge of Japanese nature prior to the Big Bang was not monolithic or uncontested, even among foreign professors. In fact a bitter disagreement broke out at Kōbudaigakkō itself about how the events of Japanese nature and the materials of Japanese culture intertwined, even about where (and if) lines should be drawn between them. At the center of this contest were two Englishmen, Josiah Conder, "the father of modern Japanese architecture," and John Milne, the founder of "Anglo-Japanese seismology." Disputes over earthquakes and *daiku* merged with disputes over the relandscaping of Japan, the relandscaping of Britain, the knowledge-practices of different sciences and arts, portrayals of race and gender, and how to properly map Eurasia and the world. When disaster was finally visited on central Japan in 1891, all parties flocked to the ruins in order that longstanding scientific and cultural disputes might be settled. One result of that settlement was the emergence of Japanese seismology as a global science, and one full of insights for a receptive West.

In later chapters, I shift attention from the teachers to their pupils, the first generation of Japanese architects and seismologists, who were deeply affected by lessons learned on the Nōbi Plain. Following the careers of scientists such as Ōmori Fusakichi and Sekiya Seikei and architects such as Tatsuno Kingo, Itō Tamekichi, and Sano Toshikata, I trace how foreign knowledge about Japan changed (and other times remained stubbornly fixed) as Japanese themselves gained access to its productive machinery. Well initiated into European and American professional practices and personas, Ōmori, Itō, and their colleagues still constructed different relations with the West-centered disciplines than had their teachers. Japanese seismologists—practitioners of a "Western" science born and principally nurtured in Japan itself—negotiated knowledge production with the European powers as citizens of an "earthquake nation."[14]

Analyzing earthquakes discursively need not lesson their reality as physical events and human catastrophes. A large swath of Japan moved in October 1891 like waves move on the ocean (for those who have never experienced a major earthquake, I am not taking license). Tens of thousands died or were injured, and hundreds of thousands lost their homes. Great British-built bridges and factories indeed came crashing down. Foreigners and Japanese alike were shaken in every sense, and searched for cogent things to say. It was a traumatic event, for all its subsequent malleability. My own text, in staying relatively close to academic discussions, cannot do full justice to the social histories of this and other disasters nor trace the plight of victims. I do, however, have something to say about their manipulation. Others have argued before me that the traumatic events we call natural catastrophes are excellent sites at which to see social, cultural, and political processes revealed. As I hope this fine-grained study demonstrates, however, the anxieties and opportunities that disasters evoke have themselves been destabilizing to processual notions in the physical and social sciences both. In objectifying seismicity and seeking to inscribe it onto paper with machines, nineteenth-century science did its best to make the sudden and sublime into the gradual, regular, and, above all, understandable. At the end of the day, however, it could not save modern Tokyo. Nor could it fully save itself—as theory, method, or even community—from the consequences of the unanticipated event.

Although I leave the words *foreign* and *knowledge* to be defined by historical actors, the text will, I hope, make the phrase "technology transfer" even less tenable than it currently is as a description of how objects and practices come to be constructed across different geographies. An artifact of modernization theory—a colonizing project whose effect on histories of Japan has been particularly obscuring—the metaphor of packing and shipping does not describe very well the action in the pages that follow, even if it animates some of the historical discourses I trace.[15] I have used linguistic metaphors such as "translation" and "pidgin" in places where they seem to fit, but have relied more heavily on the notion of "inscription," which evokes the physical and material part of the act of writing, is well grounded in the instrumental sciences (such as seismology), and is slightly less laden with communicativeness. The characters in my account are not always mimicking language as they inscribe objects and practices with properties and meanings. The Earth is also a character that inscribes—rearranges technical and cultural objects into patterns—but one that never "speaks for itself."

Neither do all of the human actors in this book have equal voice, particularly *daiku* (Japanese architect-carpenters), who, as much as earthquakes, are central to most of the stories I tell. *Daiku* are sometimes quoted directly, but, like the Earth, more often are spoken about and for. Although I am sympathetic to the social-history ideal of giving voice to the voiceless, this text is especially concerned with the practice of disciplinary ventriloquism. Subaltern figures such as *daiku* (and, more generally, "artisans") have been regularly animated in the writings of architects and other elite professional groups, including their historians. With a few notable exceptions, however, their own testimony is largely lost to us. We can still accord the voiceless a measure of justice, however, by being precise about who is speaking for and about them and why, by segregating them from their spokesmen and specters to the degree that they regain the respect we reserve for the unknowable.

This book is a work of history, but one that attempts to be faithful to transdisciplinarity, as one step toward an academy less disciplined against (and more nurturing toward) studies that cross multiple borders. My research has required extended stays and the forging of friendships across a number of disciplinary realms. It has also involved shuttling between disciplinary libraries, which, both in Tokyo and Cambridge, Massachusetts, organize their books so that architectural students will never encounter biologists, seismologists will be shielded from what artists said, and Japanese carpenters and English botanists seem as different as the Sun and an octopus. In order to follow the actors across the field, however, we have sometimes to follow them into the woods. The book is partly a plea to "retie the Gordian knot," as Bruno Latour puts it, "by criss-crossing as often as we have to, the divide which separates exact knowledge and the exercise of power."[16] In this case it is not only science and power that have had to be criss-crossed to follow the action, but physics, carpentry, and art; Japan, Italy, and California; race, generation, and gender; and so forth. Such crossings not only leave each category less discrete and bounded, but trace out a landscape in which catastrophic events (and their threat) require a feverish repair and reconstruction often missing in classical accounts of knowledge-making.

Recognition of fragmented identity among my characters and myself has led me to adopt, for the majority of this text, the narrative form. One can only arrange a text analytically if speaking to an audience that accepts the terms of an analysis and owns common analytical tools. The way scientists and architects, science-studies scholars and Japan specialists, historians of technology and art, or Americans and Japanese, write, are inevitably far apart. One of the Japanese characters in this story, self-styled "American Architect" Itō Tamekichi, dealt with a similar problem by writing separate chapters, in one of his later books, for each intended audience. He would begin each chapter, "I am an old X, like yourself."[17] The danger, of course, is that each X will read only chapter X, concluding "as I thought!" It was indeed Itō's hope to become X (to the 10th power). I have no such interests or illusions.

The narrative form, as every novelist knows, lets everyone and everything ascend the stage as they do in real time. Chisel-wielding Japanese carpenters can burst into a meeting of seismologists examining seismograms, architects may find themselves dancing with politicians at a costume ball, zoologists can declare themselves to be architectural historians, and seismologists turn out to be ethnographers. All of these things occur in the following text, at least metaphorically. Actors were not only uncertain about where they are going, but whom they are going there with, and sometimes who they themselves were. It strikes me as important to emphasize uncertainty and liquidity in a time and place—Meiji Japan—where they extended even to the ground beneath one's feet.

Because I approach architecture and science through their relationship with destructive earthquakes—and hence with each other—there is necessarily much in the life of Meiji-period architects and scientists I have not discussed, and which specialists in one or the other field might wish that I had. Architects, for example, were more concerned on a regular basis with floor plans, elevations, ornament, and style than with earthquakes. Seismologists spent more time pouring over seismograms and mapping fault lines than considering how buildings performed in the face of seismic waves. From the perspective of some disciplinary scholarship, the issues at the center of my account might thus be interpreted as exceptional rather than the normative. As we shall see, however, architects and scientists in Japan could scarcely remain for long on one side of that equation. While necessarily selective, my accounts of Japanese architecture and geophysics are certainly no more so than histories of design organized by style, or of seismology organized around instruments or theories. I recognize my debt, however, to scholars working across a range of methodologies, and beg their indulgence as I organize often-familiar material in unfamiliar ways.

Aside from issues of methodology and textual crafting, this study will, I hope, invite new questions about how "Western learning" was defined, interpreted, transformed, and made use of not only in Meiji Japan but at other sites around a colonized world. When we abandon the metaphor of "transfer" for more fine-grained accounts of how technoscientific objects were formulated, knowledge-making emerges as less unidirectional, and ultimately more believable in its chaos and partiality. Storytelling about how smoothly things and behaviors were reestablished across cultural boundaries made a certain strategic sense to the first generations of non-Western scientists, engineers, architects, anthropologists, and so forth whose careers depended on their apparent synchronization with distant knowledge-producing centers. This makes less sense, however, in the retelling, especially when it obscures a more subtle but revealing dissonance. As we will see in the case of the first Japanese scientists and architects, narratives of resistance or correction were often woven into texts that still sought sympathetic readership in Europe and the

United States. We cannot continue to see non-Western scientists, architects, and other professionals, then or now, as universally content to gather data for foreign interpretation or infinitely to replicate foreign forms, even when they tell us, in many instances, that that is mainly what they are doing.

Most of the figures encountered in the following pages, despite frequent reverses and failures, arguably had greater faith than our own contemporary experts (and citizens) in their ability to confront and contain destructive nature. Their naming of Japan as a nation of earthquakes was no simple exercise in natural description, and was certainly no surrender to pessimism. An age-old source of catastrophe became in the Meiji period a new sort of problem, but also something of an opportunity. Only in the Taishō period would seismicity become a subject virtually anathema to processual narratives, a status it arguably retains today. In traveling this peculiar arc, earthquakes shaped Japan materially and symbolically as deeply as Japan shaped the arts and sciences of natural disaster. Contemporary accounts of modern Japanese change cannot forever avoid their rumbling presence.

ONE · Strong Nation, Stone Nation

KŌBUDAIGAKKŌ
(THE COLLEGE OF TECHNOLOGY)

The emergence in Meiji Japan (1868–1912) of a coterie of new, westernizing identities among the former samurai class remains strangely under-problematized. Despite much biographical information about the first Japanese to call themselves scientists, engineers, architects, attorneys, and so forth, few scholars, either Japanese or foreign, have asked what it meant to thus name oneself: to occupy, develop, and alter roles originally written for a distant stage.[1] Some Western professional roles conveniently overlapped with existing Japanese ones; for example, there had always been Japanese doctors, who commanded roughly the same respect as their Western counterparts. Architecture offers the opposite example. The samurai of Tokugawa Japan had little direct experience with constructing space and matter, and possessed few sets of actions, words, or concepts that could have aided in the transition to the Western role of architect.[2]

"Architecture" and "building" were not separately named or embodied in pre-Meiji Japan as they were in Europe and the United States, and did not readily map onto existing Japanese understandings. Buildings, like every other Japanese object, were made by specialized artisans who designed and executed in a process so continuous that "design" and "execution" were not marked or named. In a culture that for more than two hundred years made no military engines or deep-ocean ships,[3] no other producer marshaled equivalent resources or created such dramatic effects.[4] The term "great" or "chief" artisan *(daiku)*, originally designating mastership in any art, came to be used during the Edo period (1600–1868) exclusively for those who made buildings.[5]

Daiku were not a small artisanal elite; they constituted one-third of all artisans in Edo (Tokyo) in the Tokugawa period, a population five times that of the next two largest artisanal groups, *tatami-ya* (tatami makers) and *sakan* (plasterers), both of whom were dependent on *daiku* patronage and thus captive to the larger occupation.[6] The term *daiku* was further modified by prefixes according to specialty: *miya-daiku* made urban temples and shrines; *sukiya-daiku*, the tea-houses and residential buildings of the upper samurai; *machi-daiku*, regular urban houses; and (un-prefixed) village *daiku*, who oversaw what were largely communal building processes. Besides the use of the term *daiku*, all of these artisans had in common the practice of framing in wood. Although stone-masonry had been practiced in Japan in antiquity, it survived into the Edo period only in the parabolic retaining walls for castle and palace moats, and as a minor tradition of bridge-making in the far west.[7] Japan was, overwhelmingly, a wooden country.

Under the Meiji government, which scrutinized every available detail of Euro-American life, differences between Japanese *daiku shoku* (literally, *daiku*-work) and Western architecture became one of many gaps targeted for closure. As early as 1872, following the destruction of a section of Tokyo by fire, the Dajōkan (Council of State) instructed the Tokyo government that not only the burned section, but the entire city would be rebuilt in brick and stone, materials emblematic of European architecture. "No matter how much money it costs," said oligarch Saigō Takamori, "we should do it, for the sake of our honor."[8] The physically modest but archi-technically ambitious result was the Ginza, a wide-columned neighborhood of brick shops designed by the Irish architect Thomas Waters and set into dense, wooden Tokyo as a model of things to come.[9]

The Meiji oligarchs were themselves foreigners in Tokyo (the new post-revolutionary name for Edo), a city greatly depopulated after 1868 by politically inspired out-migration.[10] British architecture (and technology) was not completely foreign, however, to the Sat-Chō faction—samurai from the far western domains of Satsuma and Chōshū—who constituted the oligarchy's core. English-style brick textile mills and warehouses were part of Satsuma's landscape even prior to the Meiji Restoration; architect Waters was brought to Tokyo largely as a functionary of the Satsuma clan. A group of young Chōshū samurai, including Itō Hirobumi (future prime minister) and Yamao Yōzō (future minister of Public Works) had even been secreted to Britain during the Bakumatsu (late Tokugawa period) in order to learn about Western technology. Yamao worked with his hands in a Glasgow shipyard and took engineering classes at night.[11] He and other future oligarchs were building on the late Tokugawa experience of "Dutch learning," through which images of Western material culture—including brick and stone walls—had been rendered familiar to an educated elite even prior to the arrival of American commodore Matthew Perry.[12]

Beginning about 1870 (two years after the Restoration), the government began hiring foreign experts *(yatoi)* to staff technical positions in the new ministries and teach at the newly created College of Technology (Kōbudaigakkō) in Tokyo. The regime would employ over three thousand foreigners in the course of the Meiji period, most of them in its initial two decades. Kōbudaigakkō, conceived and planned by Itō and Yamao, was staffed by young British scientists and engineers under a twenty-four-year-old Scottish principal, Henry Dyer. Dyer and Yamao had sat in the same night-school classroom at Anderson's College in Glasgow. Kōbudaigakkō was to be the training school for Yamao's powerful Ministry of Public Works (Kōbushō), sometimes translated as "the Ministry of Technology," the prime mover in the government's early attempts to enlist "Western learning" *(yōgaku)*.[13]

Among the college's seven original departments was *zōkagaku* (architecture), which from 1877 was in the charge of English architect Josiah Conder.[14] Conder ended up staying in Japan for the rest of his life, long enough to be named by a later generation as "the father of modern Japanese architecture." His bronze statue now stands before Tokyo University's Faculty of Engineering (the successor to Kōbudaigakkō), and matriculating architectural students still take group photographs at its base.

Kōbudaigakkō was established not to educate the sons of *daiku* or other artisans, but those of samurai.[15] Conder's *zōkagaku* course was intended to produce British-style architects, just as British-style engineers and scientists were simultaneously under production in other Kōbudaigakkō departments. All instruction was in English, and the students ate at least one English meal per day. The better students would end up spending extended periods abroad at European and American universities. The curriculum was built around the Western system of drawing plans and elevations on paper, to be transmitted as instructions to tradesmen who would execute each drawing in three dimensions. Although various types of line drawings and sketches were in use by *daiku,* the technique of "measured drawing"—graphic microinstructions from architects to anonymous tradesmen—was unknown in Japan, as were "architects," "tradesmen," and the materials, systems, and forms that the students drew. The principal consumer of such plans was to be the revolutionary government, then intent on commissioning large brick and stone ministerial buildings (including industrial ones) in European styles, essentially realizing the Ginza on a national scale.

The *zōka* course was organized around a uniquely European series of dualisms, beginning with "architecture and building." Lectures were split into two divisions, themselves constituting pairs: "The History and Art of Architecture" and "The Qualities of Materials and Principles of Building Construction." Each history and art lecture described one of sixteen "national architectures," grouped into two sets. The first six lectures mapped out Asia from west to east (Egyptian, Assyrian, Persian, Indian, Chinese, and Japanese). The subsequent ten lectures moved through Europe, more chronologically than geographically, beginning with "Grecian Architecture" and ending with "Late Gothic," followed by the "Modern Architecture of Europe." This last lecture emphasized the revival of historic styles, or the contemporary mastery and synthesis, by Europeans, of everything that had come before.[16]

The "Building Construction" *(kaoku kōzō)* lectures centered on masonry, a material/technology largely alien to Japanese building practice, yet typical of the other fifteen "national architectures" the students learned. There were also lectures on carpentry, but these discussed only the roofs, floors, and staircases of masonry buildings, not the construction of wooden ones. Even wooden houses were outside the training of a *zōkagaku-shi* (the initial term for "architect"), as Japanese domestic architecture was expected, in future, to be of brick and stone. One of the multiple-choice questions on the 1879 examination for diploma makes the issue of materials relatively clear: "Considering the climate of this country and the pursuits and habits of the people generally, also bearing in mind the serious destruction of wooden cities by fire; what suggestions would you make for the future of Domestic Architecture for Japan?" A drawing exercise on the same examination gave the student the choice of these materials: "either brick and stone, brick and terracotta, entirely brick, or entirely stone."[17]

MASONRY AND CIVILIZATION

British architecture and civil engineering in the 1870s were synonymous with brick and stone. It was not just that everything architects and civil engineers had been taught was predicated on their manipulation. Masonry was the very identity of both professions. Architects of nineteenth-century Europe traced the origins of their profession to the builders of Greek temples, Roman villas, and medieval cathedrals, that is, to stonemasons. Brick and stone in the cultures of both professions were penultimate materials: hard, weighty, strong, and durable—the very metaphors that architecture had always employed to portray kingship and the nation-state in Europe, and expected to do in Japan as well.

Stone and brick were also actors in a story about change, which was also the story of "civilization" (*bunmei* in Japanese, which in the Meiji period was commonly used synonymously with Western civilization).[18] Masonry was perceived to have replaced wood (to have driven carpentry up into the roof or down into the floor) wherever civilization occurred.[19] Indeed, the presence or absence of civilization in European eyes was marked not only by the presence or absence of agriculture, but by masonry, and more especially by ruins.[20] As Michael Adas has pointed out, the paucity of stone ruins in sub-Saharan Africa helped construct for Europeans the "dark" continent and black Africans as technologically backward. The discovery of the stone city of Zimbabwe was sufficiently unsettling to the nineteenth-century conjunction of civilization, race, and masonry that European archaeologists assigned its construction to Arabs.[21]

The "advance" of masonry on wood, of the "permanent" on the "temporary," was by the middle of the nineteenth century no longer considered a matter of ebb and flow (the cyclical "rise and fall of civilizations") but a unidirectional and world-historical process. In the time-line of European architecture, it began with the Greeks replacing wooden temples with stone ones, and continued through the rebuilding of wooden London in stone following the Great Fire of 1666, a project overseen by the father of English architecture, Sir Christopher Wren. It continued into the nineteenth century with what was seen from Europe as the American maturation from log cabins to masonry cities.[22]

This concept of an evolution from wood to masonry had even begun to erode (and this in the age of Charles Darwin) in favor of a theory of epistemic break. In his *Discourses on Architecture* of 1863, the French gothicist Eugène-Emmanuel Viollet-le-Duc endeavored to prove that Greek temples were not "copied from the wooden hut" (nor medieval cathedrals "from the forests of Gaul or Germany") but constituted a uniquely European alliance between stone and reason. As evidence that Greek architecture did not derive from carpentry practice, Viollet-le-Duc contrasted it with dozens of details from the masonry traditions of Asia (primarily India and the Muslim countries), which he endeavored to prove clearly did. While architects in "the immense continent from China to the Caspian, from the Black Sea to the Persian Gulf" had worked out their structural principles in forests, he argued, Greek architects had worked out theirs in quarries. European architecture, he concluded, "does not receive its inspiration from natural objects, but follows laws established to meet certain necessities. These laws are the result of reasoning."[23]

Thus was masonry nearly the analog, in the world of architecture and civil engineering, of metal in the world of mechanical engineering and industry. Although stone and metal were both dug from the earth, in European culture their connection with nature had nearly been severed in a way that wood had not.[24] There was the binarism "organic" and "inorganic" (or, as translated in architectural language, "ligneous" and "lithic"), which placed wood among living things (and hence things that age, decay, burn, and otherwise change). In Japan, deeply informed by the animistic religion of Shinto, the difference between a stone and a tree was not so marked. A stone could be the container of spirit, and in that sense alive.

Even in the West, some bits of living nature, such as rubber, resin, and tallow, lay ambiguously between the natural and artificial. The location of a substance along a nature/culture continuum was not simply a matter of scientific classification, but was related to who had inscribed their knowledge/practice onto it and how. While wood was widely used by European civil engineers and architects, it was perceived to be equally within the domain of knowledge and practice of native (domestic) carpenters and native (foreign) peoples. "Nativeness" at home and abroad was commonly constructed of animate substances. Stone, on the other hand, was more actively handled (and hence more intimately known) by a nexus of important European professions, including not only architecture and civil engineering, but crucially, geology. Lectures on the new science of geology were an important component of Kōbudaigakkō's architecture curriculum.[25]

Thus in his graduation thesis of 1879, Sone Tatsuzō, one of the first four Japanese enrolled in the *zōkagaku* course, would write that contemporary Japan was home to five architectural styles: "native, semi-European, European wooden, brick, and stone." The list begins with ethnography and ends with geology. In between are two terms suggesting a cultural passage, whose difficulty and danger Sone underlines by telling us, a few lines later, that "semi-European" is "tasteless and contemptible." "Semi-European" referred to *daiku* attempts to strike a compromise between their own design sensibilities and those of European and Europeanizing clients, a phenomena dealt with at length in the following section.[26] Sone's list is also a chronology. As Satachi Shichijirō, another of the original *zōkagaku* students, would write in his own graduation thesis: "The prevailing style of Japan has begun to deteriorate by the encroachment of the foreign style and the new style begins to rise. Now it is in a transitional period, turning into brick and stone architecture." Sone, Satachi, and the other young architects in the *zōkagaku* course were to be instruments for accomplishing this evolution/revolution in Japanese material culture: the replacement of a "native" landscape with one that marked Japanese participation in the global culture of the nation-state. The architecture they produced would serve partly as crystallized diplomacy, an argument toward accomplishing the principal goal of the first generation of Meiji politicians: revision of the hated Unequal Treaties.

The native tradition of Japanese carpentry even imposed on Japanese architects a special burden. Wooden Japan presented the paradox, to many late-nineteenth-century Europeans, of an ancient culture that had not "permanently" inscribed itself onto its own landscape through the use of stone building techniques. It differed in this respect from the Arab lands, from India, from China, and from the sixteen "national architectures" taught in the *zōkagaku* course. Japan's thorough-going woodenness struck many Europeans as insubstantial, combustible, and paper thin, and could even interfere with the contemplation of the beautiful. "My feelings," wrote Kōbudaigakkō professor of engineering George Cawley in 1878, "are that the structural material of which the native temples are formed detracts in some degree from their beauty, because of its comparative want of durability; for the sentiment arising in the mind from the contemplation is tinged with sadness by notions of decay."[27]

Decay was of course characteristic of stone buildings as well (hence the production of "ruins"), but decay in wood promised eventual disappearance. The very word *refinement*, so often chosen as a description for things Japanese, hints at this phantom quality of vulnerability, lightness and, ultimately, femininity that foreigners so often pointed to in the culture of the late Edo and early Meiji periods. Japan's lack of masonry ruins was, among other factors, equated with an absence of memory, a contempt for the serious, a disregard of the solid.

The centuries-long accumulation of Japanese temple, shrine, and palace-building melted so thoroughly into nature for many foreign observers as to approach the invisible. "The slightness of the [Japanese] buildings," wrote an American architect in 1876, "is perhaps reason enough for their attracting so little attention."[28] As late as 1905, well after Nikkō had become an important tourist destination and the Phoenix Pavilion had been viewed by thousands at the 1893 Columbian Exposition in Chicago, another American architect (the Japanophile Ralph Adams Cram) could still write: "Japanese architecture is undoubtedly less well known and less appreciated than the architecture of any other civilized nation. . . . In nearly every instance those who have written most intelligently of

FIGURE I

Tanabe Sakurō, an engineering graduate of Kōbudaigakkō (College of Technology), circa 1883. Tanabe's Western clothing and hairstyle befit his training and status. Like nearly all of his classmates, he would pursue a career in government service. (Courtesy of the National Science Museum, Tokyo.)

Japan and her art have shown no rudimentary appreciation of her architecture. It is dismissed with a sentence. To the western traveler it seems fanciful and frail, a thing unworthy of study."[29]

Cram was criticizing a failure of insight he mainly associated with Europeans, and those Americans who unreflexively adopted European standards. The United States after all shared with Japan a living tradition of wooden architecture that would never be entirely displaced or marginalized by industrial development and the greater use of brick and stone. The foreign architects and engineers in Meiji Tokyo, however, were overwhelmingly from Britain, where even American examples of modern architecture in wood would likely have seemed exotic. Wood helped construct for Englishmen and many other Europeans, as Cram must have known, the greater naturalness and ephemerality of not only the Japanese landscape, but the American one as well.

That Japan was thus destined to become a nation of stone and brick was unquestioned by *yatoi* architects and engineers and the Japanese architects and engineers they initially trained. All that *daiku* had done in the past, and might do in the future or present, was reclassified as "temporary."[30] As an anonymous Japanese author put it in the architectural journal *Kenchiku zasshi* in 1888: "Gradually, we should make every building in Japan completely brick or stone. Academically trained people should be in charge of this, and architectural regulations should be set. This is the basis of a strong nation."[31]

ARCHITECTNESS AT KŌBUDAIGAKKŌ

Looking at either the drawings or buildings produced by the first generation of Japanese architects, it is easy to believe that Kōbudaigakkō transferred European architecture to Japan only too well. In the decade following the graduation of Conder's first four students (Tatsuno Kingo, Katayama Tōkuma, Sone Tatsuzō, and Satachi Shichijirō) in 1879, Japanese architects largely replaced foreigners as the designers of monumental buildings for the ministries and large industrial concerns (*zaibatsu*). Their handling of *yōfū* (Western-style) architecture was almost indistinguishable from its handling by Westerners in Japan or abroad. Such indistinguishability was indeed the treasured goal of both the first generation of *zōkagakushi* and their ministerial, commercial and industrial patrons.

The convincing Europeanness of Meiji architecture (and the rest of the Meiji object-world) even now stands as a sort of wall against understanding its production and locatedness in Japan, and understanding "Japan" as its product. *Yōfū* facades, however, are only one layer of an architectural stratigraphy that, when fully excavated, is less transparently European. Conder taught Japanese students to use English instruments and techniques in order to design English-looking structures, but the identity "architect" and the knowledge-realm "architecture" were not unproblematically translated across the breadth of Eurasia. Part of it was the strangeness of the European concept "architecture" in Japan, but part of it was the strange "Europe" created in Japan at Kōbudaigakkō.

When the president of the Royal Institute of British Architects (RIBA) came to Japan in 1964, he was pleased and surprised to learn that Japanese architectural training had been founded a century before "on the model of the existing English schools."[32] But the system of state schooling that was intended to replicate British architects (and British scientists and engineers) in Japan had no real model in Britain itself.[33] English architects of the 1870s, including Conder, were still apprenticed and self-titled, although an elite achieved special recognition through membership in the Royal Institute.[34] Regular college schooling of architects in Britain began two decades later than it did in Japan, and even then was not fully institutionalized until after World War II.[35]

Although schools of architecture then existed in France, the United States, and elsewhere, this training and titling of architects by the Japanese state was a situation new in world history.[36] The title zōkagaku-shi derived from the name of the course of study at Kōbudaigakkō (later the Imperial University), the only place architects were produced in Japan for the next thirty years. While British architects had a large range of backgrounds and competencies, Japanese ones were all classmates, their exclusivity reinforced by their small numbers. Conder trained only twenty-three students in his eight years of full-time teaching.[37] In 1897, almost thirty years after the founding of the zōka course, there were only about forty-five zōkagaku-shi in all of Japan.[38] In Britain at roughly the same time (the gathering of the 1901 census) 10,781 men called themselves "architect."[39]

In Britain the Royal Institute painstakingly cultivated the identity "professional," on the model of lawyers and physicians (and in a more root sense, the clergy).[40] Kōbudaigakkō trained zōkagaku-shi to be servants of the Meiji state. Students were called cadets and wore military-style uniforms. Graduates were required to serve in the Ministry of Public Works (Kōbushō) for at least seven years after receiving their diploma, and the majority remained in government for the rest of their careers. Of the forty-five zōkagaku alumni in 1897, thirty were in state service (including those who taught at the Imperial University), seven worked for large companies, and only two were in private practice.[41] Although the proportion of graduates in state positions would begin to decline at the end of the nineteenth century, professors and bureaucrats still constituted the largest and most influential group of Japanese architects as late as World War II.[42] Even radically "modern" architects of the 1920s were employees of the state; the center of the avant-garde Succession movement was the design department of the Ministry of Communications.[43]

While in Britain, "Royal" institutes, institutions, and societies lifted ambitious commoners closer to kingship and the nobility, most of the Japanese students at Kōbudaigakkō were already well-born (of samurai background).[44] Conder and his fellow Royal Institute architects had the problem of distinguishing themselves from thousands of non-Royal Institute architects, many of whom were aspiring tradesmen or builders. *Zōkagaku-shi*, who were already just such a small and distinguished group, had nearly the opposite problem: how to associate themselves with, and gain some type of mastery over, the process of material/cultural production that for centuries had been under the guidance or control of *daiku*. It was not initially apparent how *zōkagaku-shi* and *daiku* would (and would not) interact, both practically and discursively. In order to be and act as "architects," *zōkagaku-shi* had first to teach *daiku* and many other groups of Japanese the utility and meaning of that role.

As Conder told his students in the second decade of the *zōkagaku* project (1886), "The Japanese public are not yet capable of appreciating the different status of a profession and a trade . . . popular opinion in Japan requires education in order to appreciate the status of different occupations. You are not, therefore, called upon to accept the public idea of the position of an architect or of the practice of architecture."[45] The "public idea," to read between the lines of this and similar passages, was that an architect was a sort of *daiku* of brick and stone—a man who "made," in the holistic sense of that term, masonry buildings rather than wooden ones. *Zōkagaku-shi*, however much they were taught about architecture as a transcendent knowledge-realm, faced daily the separation of a few large masonry and European-like buildings erected under their own guidance from an immense number of still-normative wood-framed buildings erected by *daiku*. In the public mind, if not their own, the *zōkagaku-shi* was a producer of one object and the *daiku* of another. What made this situation all the more precarious, as architecture student Satachi Shichijirō wrote in his 1879 graduation exercise, was that "at the present day the people do not understand the advantages of the brick buildings."[46]

The problem of how to make architecture a knowledge-realm—a something to be "professed" rather than sold; a center from which to speak authoritatively about peripheral objects; a way to control without touching (e.g., through inscribing messages onto paper)—was evident even in the initial attempts to translate that word *(architecture)*. As Nakatani Norihito has pointed out, the term *ƶōkagaku* was coined inside the Kōbushō in the early 1870s, prior to the arrival of the foreign teaching staff. The root *ƶōka* was selected from a number of new two-character combinations that, since at least the 1860s, had competed to translate the "architecture" concept. Separately, each character was evocative of *daiku*-work, *ƶō* meaning large-scale construction, and *ka* being roughly "house" (although this applied to more than just residences). *Zōka* was necessarily imprecise, however, because there was no one Japanese word that inclusively described "buildings," or even the act of making buildings in all instances. The suffix *gaku* meant "learning," so that from the beginning "architecture" was also marked in Japan as a product of academic instruction.[47]

That the term *ƶōkagaku* combined characters for "construction," "house," and "learning" would make it an embarrassment to the second generation of Japanese architects, who had come to understand that architecture in the West was set more or less against each of those things. "Construction," in English usage, was the instrumentality of architecture, not architecture itself.[48] "House" was the type or class of building least within the domain of architectural interest or control. "Learning" in Euro-American usage was increasingly set in contrast with art, which, according to influential architects, could not be taught or learned, but only developed or cultivated from natural talent.[49]

In the later 1890s the term *ƶōkagaku* was therefore replaced with *kenchiku*, which is still the accepted translation for "architecture." *Kenchiku* was not more philologically precise, but simply different. Like *ƶōka*, it was also pieced together from characters rooted in *daiku* usage (it is an inversion of the pre-Meiji term *chiku-ken*, whose meaning was virtually the same as *ƶōka*). *Kenchiku* came to be "architecture" mostly because of what it eliminated (the characters for "house" and "learning").[50] The term *kenchiku-gaku* was still sometimes used, but it now referred to "architectural learning" rather than architecture itself.

Yet even as the term *kenchiku* strove for the status of "architecture," it never fully expressed that yearning for transcendence—the separation from "building," the building site, and people who built—crucially embodied in the Western term. *Kenchiku* was first deployed in the title of a magazine (*Kenchiku ƶasshi*, or Architecture Magazine) in 1887, in order to invite a larger readership and contributor base than could be attracted by use of the term *ƶōkagaku*.[51] *Kenchiku* was born, in other words, from a need to expand the jurisdiction of architecture rather than the instinct to conserve it typical of the Anglophone West; from a desire to seize leadership from above rather than to simply hover there. Japanese architects began speaking of a *kenchiku sekai* (architectural world), by which they meant potentially everyone who contributed to building Japan under their own leadership.[52] The construction "architectural world" is odd in English, where even the phrase "vernacular architecture" preserves the exclusivity of the second word.[53]

In the preface to *Nihon kenchiku ji* (1904), the first Japanese architectural dictionary, Conder's student Nakamura Tetsutarō described "architectural learning" this way:

> *Kenchiku-gaku* is an extremely broad area, but the truth of what it is, its actual face, is not well-known anywhere in the world. Ideally, the *kenchiku-shi* [architect] should be both *jōgo* [those who love sake] and *geko* [those who can't drink at all]. That is to say, who know art well and are at the same time good at mathematics. But generally speaking, it is the case that if someone is good at one thing, he's not good at the other thing. Those who are good at both are extremely rare, like Venus [the star].[54]

Nakamura reproduces the dualism "art" and "building" (or in this case "mathematics") within both the Japanese body and the body of Japanese architecture. The Western dyad is presented as the most mundane of Japanese distinctions, between the drinker and nondrinker. This nativization operates two ways—using an everyday dichotomy to ease the acceptance of the more abstract and foreign one, but at the same time making it so concrete and embodied as to subvert its power as abstraction.

"Architecture" was rendered no more translatable by defining it, as Conder often did, as "an art and a science," equally foreign concepts that had required the coining of additional two-character words *(bijutsu* and *kagaku)*. Kōbudaigakkō made the "art" part of architecture more concrete by attaching a school of painting and free-hand drawing, under Italian teachers, to the *zōkagaku* course. European architects then considered painting an "allied art" inherently related to their own education and development as artists. The term "allied," however, belied a contested hierarchal relation. Painting, sculpture, and so forth were spoken of in Europe as "fine" arts and architecture as an "applied" one. Conder accepted and taught this distinction, yet subverted it with the additional teaching (common within his profession) that architecture was the "mother" of all other arts. When writing of Japanese painting, however, or any other of the Japanese arts, he did not classify them as "fine," but, like architecture, "applied."[55]

The cultural status of British architecture depended on its closeness to fine arts and its distance from rude ones; on avoiding overly direct contact with building processes from construction to calculation. The phrase "gentleman in charge of building" evoked a stratigraphic layering of other occupations—surveyors, general contractors, and tradesmen—between the architect and the physicality of the building materials and production process.[56] "Architecture" in the British model was both the product of this system of layered roles (i.e., "pieces of architecture" or "examples of architecture"), and the complex of language, practice, and behavior that held that stratigraphy in place. English architects had earned what respect they had, Conder told his Japanese students in 1886, by "refus[ing] to contaminate their fingers with contractor's details."[57]

That a foundational relationship existed between makers of buildings and makers of paintings, however, was far from natural to the Japanese, and was the first of many European alliances that began to come unstuck on the other side of Eurasia. Kōbudaigakkō's art school, after encountering its own difficulties with supporters of traditional Japanese painting, was closed by the ministry in 1882, and the Italian instructors let go. *Zōkagaku* students continued to be taught free-hand drawing and painting, but the relationship between architecture and fine art—and the architect's identity as "artist"—would by this and other events (traced in subsequent chapters) come to be de-essentialized, although never completely severed. It is telling that architecture student Satachi Shichijirō chose to make a long defense of sketching in his 1879 thesis not on artistic grounds, but military ones. It was "by the knowledge of this art that many military men have first gained the distinction and notice which have led to future fame and fortune," he wrote, naively perhaps but demonstrative of the contemporary hierarchy of Japanese values.[58]

As the alliance between architecture and art loosened on Japanese soil, the space that had been created in Europe between architecture and technicity began to close. Conder had spoken of fingers contaminated by contractor's details. For his Japanese students, however, such details were not only unavoidable, but not necessarily contaminative in the European sense. Masonry and architectural drawing were equally "Western learning"; each needed to be intensely learned in foundational ways. Yet "knowing" masonry, for Japanese architects, could not be just a matter of learning what their Western counterparts already knew. In truth, Western architects had relatively little of the tacit knowledge necessary to command an entire building into reality, because they were specialists in the art of drawing. Thus did a largely unstated gap emerge between what Western architects knew and what Japanese ones felt they needed to learn in order to fully perform architecture. Understanding the micro-technics of wall construction, for example, at least to the point where one could direct or even teach it oneself, was outside the domain of British architecture as professional performance. More precisely, British architects had long had a technological and human buffer between themselves and actual stone walls in the form of masons. It was the existence of this class of "tradesmen" (traders of artisanal knowledge as well as labor) that allowed British architects to draw elevations and floor plans, and leave others to worry about how to lay up heavy pieces of stone in such a way as to make the drawings into physical objects. In Japan, where initially there were no masons, each motion in the new architectural process—from the movement of the architect's drawing pencil to the wielding of a trowel—thus came to be reconceptualized as a sort of continuous flow of necessary knowledge, responsibility, and concern, the type of flow, incidentally, characteristic of the work of *daiku*. Thus would *zōka* student Satachi note, in his 1879 graduation essay, not only the location of every provincial stone quarry in Japan, but go on to describe and rate their products in detail.[59]

The need to reproduce English architecture materially in Japan thus undermined, in some sense, its reproduction as social organization and cultural performance, an irony that Conder sensed. The "English system" of architectural practice, he told his students in 1886, was, for the short term, "out of the question for this country." It was not yet certain who would play the part of tradesman, and what would be the nature and the order of the trade. The equally crucial part of general contractor—who in England was a sort of white glove between the architect and the trades—was also without obvious candidates.[60] In the short term, he wrote, Japanese architects would have to model themselves after those of France, who dealt directly (bodily) with various artisans and closely coordinated their several movements.[61]

Kōbudaigakkō was not, however, the École des Beaux-Arts. Its unifying idea was engineering *(kōgaku)*. In Britain and the United States, architecture and engineering were already distinct cultures in the 1870s, and would become increasingly more so, even (perhaps most of all) when located on the same university faculties.[62] The formation by Japanese students in 1886 of a Zōka-gakkai (Architecture Institute) as a breakaway group from the Kō-gakkai (Engineering Institute) indicates they understood and sought, to some degree, to replicate this distinction. But in early Meiji Japan, *kō* was a much stronger and better-known identity than *zōka*. In Japan it was engineering that had the higher epistemological status. Architects thus identified themselves in print and other public venues not as *zōkagaku-shi* but *kōgaku-shi* (engineers), which they were entitled to use as graduates of an engineering college.[63]

Anglo-Japanese architecture (soon to become just Japanese architecture) was thus shaped not only by preexisting differences between Japan and Britain, but by differences between Kōbudaigakkō—as the model "Britain"—and the motherland itself. Objects and practices that in Britain and the United States were painstakingly inscribed with difference, according to whether they were "art," "science," or "technology"; "fine"/"pure" or "applied"; "the practice of . . ." or "the principle of . . ." and so forth, tended at Kōbudaigakkō to be reinscribed with commonality, or to have their inscriptions shift in subtle ways. That each Kōbudaigakkō course had a single professor, isolated often by the breadth of Eurasia from colleagues in the same discipline; that students moved easily between teachers, especially for the first two years; and that the college had been designed specifically to teach knowledge in an applied rather than pure-bred form, encouraged the fashioning of common and often local object-worlds by both professors and students. Trusses and telegraphs, brick walls and the periodic table of elements, agricultural implements and dynamos—objects that in the West felt and tasted different even as words on the tongue—became in Japan coequal elements of Western learning, unified even further by the concept "science." If locomotives and steam engines were suitable for Japan, argued architecture student Funakoshi Kinya in his 1883 graduation thesis, why not Western buildings?[64]

For these and other reasons we have yet to explore, zōkagaku-shi, at least by the commencement of a new government building program in the 1880s, had developed a different relationship with the technomateriality of architecture than their British counterparts. What in Conder's Britain was an unproblematic artisanal tradition reproduced as an item of trade, was to his students highly problematic Western science embodied, for the moment, in themselves. As it was put in a widely read 1890 Japanese textbook by zōkagaku-shi Taki Daikichi: "Architecture is the study of how to use natural and artificial materials and make them good looking, strong, and efficient. You need to study physics, chemistry, and mathematics, so it is a rather difficult thing."[65] Architect Itō Tamekichi also described "the buildings of today [i.e., European-style], as opposed to those of long ago [i.e., Japanese-style]," as being "chemical inventions."[66] The "chemistry" of Anglo-Japanese architecture principally referred to the composition and setting of lime and cement-based mortar, materials entirely unknown to Japanese artisanal tradition. In Europe, mixing mortar was as ancient as brick- and stone-masonry itself, and the recipes were generally within the discretion of masons. But zōkagaku-shi were taught the "practice" of making mortar, as the application of "chemical principles." In Europe, this would have been understood merely as the rational explanation for artisanal practice, as in Denis Diderot's *Encyclopédie*. In Japan, however, European artisanal or trade practice did not initially exist outside the rubric of scientific instruction.

The vocabulary provided by chemistry could give further meaning, in other passages, to the insubstantiality of wood. Wrote student Sone Tatsuzō: "We are deeply regretful for the perishable nature of wooden buildings and their liability to catch fire. Chemical change can operate on them with ease." In apologizing for Japanese flammability, Sone's essay moved easily between chemistry and political economy, invoking in the same paragraph "the feudal system," "the long exclusion of foreigners," the country's existence "in a sleepy state," and the inclination "to retain old conditions and to live quietly in any way" as explanations for why Japanese had not independently discovered the virtue of masonry. With the new regime came the new architecture. Remaining with the theme of fire, Sone concluded with the statement that Japanese "are in a burning emotion to rank equally with the most cultivated nations."[67]

The "physics" of architecture, to return to Taki's description, referred principally to the construction of arches and "the application of Euclid's seventh proposition," as Conder once described to his students the arrangement of wooden members in the form of roof trusses. Trussing had likewise been part of English carpentry practice since medieval times, well before the rediscovery of Euclid. In the late nineteenth century the ability to make trusses was widely dispersed among the carpenters of even small British and American towns, where it went on daily without reference to physics or higher mathematics.[68] In Japan, however, such techniques were unknown in *daiku* practice, and thus arrived as a form of higher, mathematical learning monopolized by graduates of the *zōka* course.

Even stone came to be more deeply inscribed with "science" at Kōbudaigakkō than in the pages of Viollet-le-Duc. Though *zōka* students might have come to understand the "weight of history" that Europeans had invested in the concept "stone," texts foundational to an understanding of monumentality, such as John Ruskin's *Stones of Venice*, were not part of the curriculum. The technoscientific bias of Kōbudaigakkō and the mining centeredness of the new industrial economy it served tended to make its professors and students favor geological descriptions of stone over ones more obviously cultural-laden. Thus in the architectural materials section of the textbook *Kenchikugaku kōhon* of 1905, masonry is taught as "chemical composition," "physical structure," and "mechanical and chemical agents." Architects are introduced to "crusting and transverse strength" of stone, after the manner of mining engineers. There is, incidentally, no mention in the architectural materials section of this textbook of carpentry or wood.[69]

Inscribing "science" across the breadth of the new Meiji object-world would have important, long-term consequences in how certain Western roles were performed in Japan, as opposed to anywhere in the West itself. *Zōkagaku-shi* competed with one another to be skilful in truss calculation, for example, at the very time when British and American architects were retreating from mathematics and material science under the slogan "fine art," and through ever greater indulgence in the practice of drawing. From 1887 to 1893, the amount of lecture time in the *zōkagaku* course (i.e., note-taking) increased at the expense of drafting or design time (drawing), the very reverse of the trend at American architectural schools.[70]

DAIKU

Histories of *daiku* normally serve as a prelude to histories of Japanese architects. By beginning them in the opposite order, I mean to underline that *daiku* became the objects of descriptive narrative only as architecture developed a subject position within Japan. *Daiku* do not precede architects in ancestral fashion; the two groups coexist and coproduce one another arguably to this day. There is no written history of *daiku* that is not also a constituent part of professional architecture itself. There are few places "before" or "outside" architecture where we can throw off professional guides and be alone with the *daiku* of the past. We will not want to "throw off" professional interpreters, however, if we take the relation of *daiku* to *zokagaku-shi* as constituting our real subject.

Although "architecture" was eventually extended to the work of *daiku* as an honorific, using the term (or "science" or "art" or "technology") unreflexively from the beginning masks the very historical process we need to trace. I will continue for the same reason to use *daiku* rather than "carpenter," its accepted English translation, because this naming was itself a product of the new disciplinary regime. At the beginning of the Meiji period, *daiku* performed roles that, in Britain and the United States, were parceled out among architects, general contractors, and carpenters/masons (roles themselves emergent, ambiguous, and contested at their point of origin). The choice of the designation "carpenter" reduced *daiku* to only one of these positions—the least powerful one.

In Europe "carpenter" formed a pairing with "mason," designating competencies with the two most important (and age-old) building materials. Yet as we saw in the previous section, Europeans inscribed different meanings onto wood and stone, and this effected the status of their handlers. "Mason" (used in an historical sense) held discursive superiority even in areas of the European diaspora where few real masons lived. The American architectural profession, for example, whose founders were almost all trained as carpenters, had embraced the European mason (the medieval "master-builder") as its principal ancestral figure by the last quarter of the nineteenth century. That the term "architect" was derived from the Greek *archos* (chief) and *tekton* (carpenter) was by the mid-nineteenth century an etymological curio—an alternative origin story rarely deployed in Britain or the United States and never in Meiji Japan.

To write that *daiku* performed as "architect," "builder," and "carpenter" is not to reduce them, however, to the sum of this foreign stratigraphy. The Japanese building process was also marked by successive religious ceremonies in which *daiku* assisted, or took on the functions of, Shinto priests. Ceremonies for groundbreaking *(jichinsai)*, ridge-raising *(jōtōshiki)*, and completion *(rakuseishiki)* all had Euro-American equivalents. But in late Edo and early Meiji Japan, building-site ceremony was particularly elaborate and politically constitutive, requiring not only special costume but a detailed knowledge of performative scripts. Possessing costume and script-knowledge was as essential to the identity *daiku* as possessing woodworking tools, books, patrons, and so forth. It measured their distance from (and authority over) other classes of building artisans, who had peripheral ceremonial roles. It also acted out *daiku* closeness to Shinto and its priesthood, a religion deeply entwined with forests and trees.[71] To this day Shinto shrines are nearly always wooden and *daiku*-built, while Buddhist temples, since the second quarter of the twentieth century, are allowably built in a range of materials including ferroconcrete.[72] Before the Meiji restoration, however, Buddhist temple architecture had always been the locus of *daiku* technique. Major artisanal schools *(ryū)* or dynasties were nurtured within temple complexes, sites needful of monumental expression and periodic expansion. From the introduction of Buddhism as religion and artisanal practice in the sixth century, designing and constructing temples (including pagodas) defined the apex of *daiku* skill. When previously secret (hereditary) *daiku* literature began to be widely diffused in the seventeenth century through wood-block printing, its focus was on how to construct temples and shrines, particularly their parabolically curved roofs. There was no equivalent writing on, for example, house construction, even though that was what the majority of *daiku* did.[73]

Much has been taught and learned in architectural writing since the Meiji period about the relationship between *daiku* and their tools *(dōgu)*. This is partly because the tools were important, but also because they are collectable and easily arranged and illustrated. The literal translation of *dōgu* is "tools of the Way"; thus *daiku*

FIGURE 2

Tateishi Seijyū, *miya-daiku* (temple and shrine builder), circa
1885. Tateishi designed one of Japan's earliest and most ambitious "Western-style" schoolhouses in Nagano prefecture in
1876. He retains traditional dress, footwear, and hairstyle in this
portrait, but poses before Western-style wall molding. (Courtesy
of the National Science Museum, Tokyo.)

dōgu were "tools of the Way of *daiku*." Architect Kiyoshi Seike points out that among the tools of building-related artisans, only those of *daiku* were called *dōgu*, a distinction they shared with the instruments of tea masters. There was not, for example, a "Way of *tatamiya*" (tatami makers). The spirituality thought to be embodied in *daiku* tools helped elevate their users above other artisans, and closer to tea masters and priests, in much the same way as building-site ritual. Displaying special, elaborately crafted·tools was also a central part of site-related ceremonies.[74]

Much less has been taught and learned through architectural literature about *daiku* books. Like Western architects (and carpenters), *daiku* had written language; they inherited and reproduced into the Meiji period a large and differentiated body of technical literature, large enough by late Edo to spawn its own publishing houses. *Daiku* books of the Edo and early Meiji periods were very graphic and often beautiful, so that their having been written in Japanese does not explain why, in comparison to tool and ritual, they have remained comparatively underdisplayed, even (or especially) by Japanese architects. Displaying *hinagata* or *kiku-jutsu-sho* shows *daiku* designing (like architects) and calculating mathematically (like engineers). It shows them to be a community that inscribed knowledge on paper as well as wood.[75]

When they are known primarily through tool and ritual, *daiku* become art (and ethnographic) figures rather than historical actors—another native people sadly (but necessarily) displaced by modern change. Yet there is a different and parallel architectural narrative in which (some) *daiku* act in the modern space of time. This move into historical time, however, calls into question their very discursive status, at least in architectural texts, as *daiku*.

In the twenty years between the opening of the first treaty ports in 1858–1859 and the graduation of the first *zōkagaku-shi* in 1879, *daiku* culture and practice did not stand still. *Daiku* in many parts of Japan began designing and constructing what Japanese architectural historians now call *wayō setchū* (Japanese-Western compromise) architecture.[76] This phenomenon encompassed private houses and the largest structures of the new state. New materials (including brick and stone) were handled and molded, new forms worked out, and new programs satisfied all within the rubric of *daiku*-work. *Wayō setchū* was a form of pidgin, the equivalent of the other pidgins constructing and regulating the daily existence of Yokohama and the other treaty ports. Compromise *(setchū)* occurred in different ways and at various places within and around each project, most obviously in forms and surfaces, where Japanese and foreign elements were created and mixed into appearances foreign (yet recognizable) to both cultures. Compromise was also possible, however, between this publicly visible form/surface and the hidden form of the building's wooden frame. Even the most externally derivative *wayō* buildings usually (although not invariably) had Japanese guts.[77] The wall surface had never been the primary carrier of meaning in *daiku*-work, which usually lacked walls altogether. Surface as material and surface as meaning were in that sense coproduced. On the other hand, the reservoirs of knowledge, practice, and ritual already pooled in wooden frames remained there for some time after such frameworks were masked by the birth of the wall. The wooden frame remained the technosocial frame for the process of building itself, the space within which *daiku* organized not only their own labor but that of captive artisans.

Edo *daiku* families such as the Shimizu and Kajima, who were building temples and shrines at the time of Perry's arrival, opened branches in Yokohama in the early 1860s and began engaging in *wayō setchū* with foreign and Japanese clients. The Takenaka family did the same in Nagoya and later Kobe. We know a great deal about these particular three because they are currently among the "big six" Japanese construction companies, among the largest building firms in the world.[78] Takenaka in particular makes much of its *daiku* origins, displaying photographs of the family's pre-Meiji shrines in company literature and operating a carpentry-tools *(daiku no dōgu)* museum in Kobe.[79]

Organizing new artisanal networks around important government and/or *zaibatsu* connections and contracts, *daiku* such as the Shimizu, Kajima, and Takenaka families became *ukeoi-shi* (the literal translation is "contractor"), eventually abandoning any direct connection with woodworking, which was parceled out to subcontractors (smaller *daiku*). Yet to say that these families/companies ceased to be *daiku*, at least in early to mid Meiji, privileges the translation "carpenter"—its sense of hands working wood with tools—while taking "contractor" too literally.[80] Not only was the contract itself a problematic object in early Meiji Japan, but *ukeoi-shi* long retained, within their new capitalist organizations, the customary responsibilities and control of *daiku tōryō* (masters). They were not "general contractors" or "builders" in the Anglo-American sense because they never surrendered to architects the act of design. Rather, Shimizu-gumi and its competitors instituted a policy of hiring architect-graduates of the *zōka* course to staff design departments, accepting plan-drawing as a distinct process but reintegrating it into a design/build system *(sekkei-sekō)*.[81] Other functions traditional to *daiku*, including the performance of building-site rituals, were compartmentalized or bureaucratized as each company grew.[82] Even now the big six perform a range of Shinto site ceremonies, at which noncompany architects (if involved at all in a company project) play a distinctly subsidiary role.[83]

This phenomenon of *daiku*-turned-*ukeoi-shi* directly employing *zōkagaku-shi* was another deviation from the performed stratigraphy of British architecture, despite its apparent replication of the "architect" and "general contractor" roles. "The custom . . . that generally prevails in England," Conder had told his graduate students in 1886, is that the architect "must not in any way put himself under the power of the general contractor."[84] Architects under the power of carpenters was even less customary. That Shimizu hired Conder's student Sakamoto Naomichi, one of the earliest graduates of the *zōka* course, testifies to the contradictions of "architect" and "carpenter" at their Japanese point of origin. Henceforth Sakamoto's position in Shimizu-gumi would always be held by a Kōbudaigakkō (and later, Imperial University) man, and the large construction companies would eventually employ nearly as many Japanese architecture-school graduates as the state.[85]

The Sakamoto hiring was not a simple case, however, of the subordination of a *zōkagaku-shi* to a *daiku*, which would likely have constituted an impermissible crossing of class barriers. The Shimizu family had long been *daiku*, but Shimizu Manautsuke, in charge when Sakamoto was hired, was himself of samurai origin, having taken over the family name through marriage.[86] The ability of a *daiku* family to hire samurai (in the form of a *zōkagaku-shi*) may have depended on the prior ability to intermarry with that class based on the accumulation of wealth and political connections, with the foreignness of the new identity *ukeoi-shi* perhaps aiding this social compromise.[87]

While some *daiku* made the transition to the rituals and tools of capitalism (a capitalism constructed by *daiku* rituals and tools), others became officials in the Meiji state. When Conder arrived to teach at Kōbudaigakkō, *daiku* already held positions of authority in the Kōbushō itself. Some of these men had worked in a similar capacity under the Tokugawa regime, which had long reserved certain bureaucratic offices for *daiku*. The ministry's Eizen-ryo (Construction Bureau) was initially staffed by former *daiku* Asakura Seiichi and Tachikawa Tomokata, who had worked on the construction of the French-engineered Yokosuka Navy Yard and Iron Works under the Tokugawa regime. The bureau was headed from 1874 onward by Hayashi Tadahiro, another former *daiku* who had not only worked at Yokosuka but, like Shimizu and Kajima, had practiced *wayō setchū* in Yokohama. Before Conder's students began restaffing ministerial *eizen* bureaus in the 1880s, Hayashi was designing and executing convincing "Western" government buildings in a neo-Palladian British colonial style, ultimately producing over thirty structures for the Kōbushō and five for the Navy ministry, some in brick, but others framed in wood and then covered with stucco and given stone quoins (corners) to make them appear to be masonry.[88]

State *daiku* (called *sakujikata*) were often from old and high-status artisanal families. Tachikawa was sixth generation, and Ōshima Mitsumoto, who was initially in charge of construction for the Railroad Bureau (Tetsudō-ryō) at the Kōbushō, was from the Koura, one of the oldest and most powerful of the court *daiku* families under the Shogunate.[89] Knowledge of Western forms, techniques, and practices learned at sites like Yokosuka and Yokohama was in their case added to inherited knowledge/practice, and did not necessarily supplant it. Another large group of state *daiku* worked in the Imperial Household Agency, housing the Emperor and Imperial court. Members of both groups would mount challenges to the authority of "architecture" into the 1890s.[90]

A differently constructed site of *wayō setchū* was Hokkaido. The colonization of the northern island began in earnest during the 1870s under the Kaitakushi (Colonization Ministry), which hired civil engineers and agriculture specialists from the United States to work with Tokyo *daiku* like Adachi Yoshiyuki in constructing Sapporo and other new inland centers. The American advisors, being from a carpentry culture, expected from the beginning that Sapporo would be a largely wooden, New England–like town, dependent on an infrastructure of carpenters and sawmills. Hokkaido, like Yokohama, became a training ground in Western (mostly American) design for *daiku* from various parts of Japan. As early as 1873, *daiku* working with American engineers had produced one of the largest buildings in the country, the prefectoral legislature, designed in the American state-capital style with an immense wooden dome. By the end of the decade, Adachi was making even large Western-style faux-masonry wooden buildings (such as the Sapporo Hōheikan of 1880) aided only by American carpenter's pattern books, of which the Kaitakushi had a large collection. In the late 1870s and 1880s, as Kaitakushi *daiku* began migrating back to their home prefectures, Hokkaido-like *wayō-setchū* buildings began to be erected all over Japan, especially in Tohoku (on the northern part of the main island of Honshu). Thus did *daiku* become among the earliest carriers of foreign knowledge to areas where foreigners themselves had yet to be seen.[91]

Centers of compromise like Yokohama and Sapporo and the compromise neighborhoods ("concessions") housing foreigners in Tokyo, Osaka, and other existing cities, were produced for the most part by *daiku* working with foreign amateurs, such as merchants and missionaries (even the Americans in Sapporo, though experts in civil engineering and agriculture, were amateurs in architectural design and construction). We know from surviving drawings in both Yokohama and Hokkaido that sketches drawn by foreigners were often redrawn by *daiku*, sometimes even as Western-style architectural plans, their mensuration being in Japanese units (*shaku* rather than feet). Graphical methods were thus traded and used along with materials, ornamental schemes, and forms.[92]

As Japanese scholars have themselves pointed out, the visibility of *wayō setchū* within (recent) architectural history has been part of the process of reproducing *daiku* as architect-ancestors. In art-historical texts, *wayō setchū* buildings are not only displayed as naive precursors of *yōfū* (*zōkagaku-shi* designed) buildings, but are severed, by this very act of display, from a large corpus of shrines, stores, and houses that continued to be made, often by the same people in the same period, with little or no *yō* (Western) character. The later are not only undisplayed but in most cases undisplayable, given that they were rarely drawn or photographed.[93]

Even when *daiku*-made buildings were as self-consciously Western in appearance as those made by *zōkagaku-shi*, they do not necessarily crystallize the same intentions. They cannot be said to evidence a westernization project within artisan culture, which Conder's *zōkagaku-shi* would subsequently bring to completion and perfection. Although we have little idea of what *wayō* meant to the *daiku* who created "it" (the term itself was created and inscribed onto this project only as it neared completion), many who designed "compromise" buildings did so without compromise in other contexts. *Wayō setchū* did not produce separate classes of "Western-style" and "Japanese-style" *daiku*. Pidgins are languages that occur between languages, specifically for purposes of trade. Many *wayō* buildings of the 1850s through 1880s were made specifically for foreign residency, to house the intermingling of foreigners and Japanese, or to house Japanese who were behaving in manners still coded as "foreign." They were not necessarily prototypes for wholesale relandscaping in the manner of the Ginza or student exercises in the *zōkagaku* course.[94]

We can deepen our understanding of *daiku* "compromise" by turning to *daiku* literature. Architectural historian Nakatani Norihito has completed a detailed study of one type, *kiku-jutsu* books, mathematical treatises that explain the cutting (jointing) and arrangement of timbers in shrine and temple construction. Although *kiku-jutsu* books first appeared in the eighteenth century, they were written and published in greatest numbers after the Meiji Restoration. Meiji *kiku-jutsu* consciously continued the tradition of Edo-period texts, which were based indirectly on the Japanese mathematical system known as *wasan*. Nakatani also points out, however, that *kiku-jutsu*, one of a number of mathematical systems for laying out

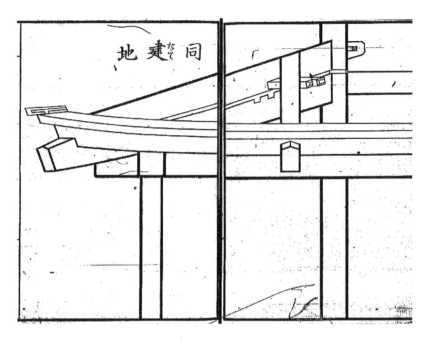

FIGURE 3

Images from two Meiji-period books of carpentry technique
(*kiku-jutsu-sho*). *Above (a):* A traditional rendering of a roof.
(From Saruta Chōji, *Daiku shoshin ʒukai,* 1883.) *Right (b):*
The author has experimented with perspective drawing using

carpentry in the Edo period, was the only one to survive the Meiji Restoration. The
reason, he argues, was the new value placed on flexibility. Being more geometrical
than other existing systems, *kiku* could be used to lay out even unusual forms, such
as Western-style (truss) roofs, as well as familiar Japanese ones. By the late 1880s
actual images of trusses began to appear in *kiku-jutsu* books, their layout and construction explained entirely in *kiku* graphics (i.e., in the same graphical form as the
explanation of temple roofs).[95]

Nakatani's research shows Meiji-period *daiku* turning to an existing technical di-
alect rather than a foreign technical language, but one that, within the range of existing choices, promised to best expand its speakers' abilities in the direction of new
forms and objects. *Kiku* itself changed as trusses, circular roofs, and other novel
forms passed into and through it. By the first decade of the twentieth century, it was
incorporating and explained the geometrical systems of imported Euro-American

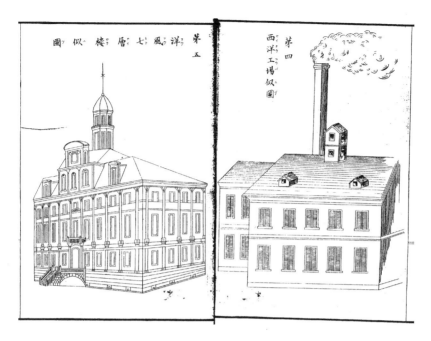

Western-style governmental and factory buildings. (From
Tanaka Kunishiro, ed., *Wayō kenchiku daisho haya wari hi den*,
1902.) Despite their differing emphases, the two books belong to
a continuous tradition of *daiku* technical literature with origins in
the Edo period.

carpenty books, capturing not only Western objects, but Western explanatory systems. Western geometry, once incorporated and explained within *kiku*, was no
longer readable however, as Western explanation. It is not even clear whether
kiku's explanations of Western geometry were readable by most Japanese architects, who were trained in systems of calculation identical to those practiced in
Britain and the United States.[96]

Kōbudaigakkō's *zōka* course was thus only one of a number of sites constructing
new archi-technical models for Meiji Japan. Compromise within *daiku* culture had
actually begun under the Tokugawa regime, and by the time *zōkagaku* arrived was
even taking on the characteristics of a creole—a pidgin that moves from being
strictly a language of trade between foreigners to one used in domestic communi-
cation. By the late 1870s *zōkagaku* came to define (indeed, was) "architecture." Yet
"architecture" (the site and its inhabitants) had as yet no monopoly on imagin-

ing/designing/making "Western" buildings, even within and for the Meiji state, and as yet nothing to do with "Japanese" ones.[97]

In order to understand how architecture as a state institution began to construct outward from its initial center, eventually incorporating other knowledge- and object-producing sites in a *kenchiku-kai* (architectural world), our discussion itself needs to expand from cultures of discipline, ritual, technique, and material to cultures of nature. Especially we need to bring in earthquakes.

TWO · Earthquakes

JAPAN'S EARTHQUAKE PROBLEM

From nearly its beginnings, the Japanese architectural profession was destined for a long and complex relationship with earthquakes. That Japan was an earthquake-prone nation does not sufficiently explain how and why that relationship became as strong and all-encompassing as it did. Before the Meiji Restoration, earthquakes had not been an obsession within any particular department of Japanese thought. In each generation of architects from the early Meiji to Taishō periods, however, few would stand fully outside of the project of an earthquake-proof Japan. The historic relevance of *taishin* (against earthquakes) both within the Japanese architectural establishment and outside it would extend beyond questions of prudence and safety to the construction of regimes of truth and meaning, to the mediation of relationships between foreigners and Japanese, foreigners and foreigners, and Japanese and Japanese.

The initial obsession with seismic activity in Meiji Japan occurred not among Japanese, who were accustomed to the shaking of the earth, but among foreign residents, most of whom were not.[1] Explaining or controlling earthquakes *(jishin)* was not among the many projects for which the Meiji government initially solicited Western advice. Before the Meiji period was over, however, the modern science of seismology would be largely founded in Tokyo, by foreigners in the employ of the Meiji state. The Seismological Society of Japan (Nihon Jishin Gakkai), organized in 1880 under the leadership of Kōbudaigakkō faculty members, would come to compete with the older and more generalist Asiatic Society as a focus of *yatoi* extracurricular energies. By the end of that decade earthquakes would find their way into the curriculum itself, becoming bound up with statements of fact about a constellation of seemingly unrelated things.

From the beginning, foreigners' discussions of earthquakes were inseparable from their discussions about *daiku*. In the writings of *yatoi* engineers and architects from the early 1870s into the 1890s, *daiku*-work was repeatedly cited as lacking even rudimentary seismic safeguards. The Scottish engineer R. H. Brunton, hired by the Tokugawa (and later Meiji) government to design its lighthouses, wrote in the *Transactions of the Asiatic Society of Japan* in 1875 that the Japanese house, "with its unnecessarily heavy roof and weak framework . . . is a structure of all others the worst adapted to withstand a heavy shock."[2] Architect Josiah Conder conceded, in an 1886 address to the Nihon Zōka-gakkai, that the historic development of a wooden rather than stone architecture in Japan may have been influenced by "the dread of earthquakes," as "the fear of such recurring phenomena no doubt made the old builders afraid to attempt the use of a heavy non-elastic material (i.e. stone)."[3] But beyond this simple choice of material, he claimed, Japanese carpenters had left the matter to nature. Said Conder before the Royal Institute of British Architects in 1887: "There is nothing in the construction of Japanese buildings which in any way makes them suited to earthquakes. They are, seismologically, exactly the opposite of what earthquake structures should be: they are extremely top-heavy to begin with; they have no diagonal ties or braces whatever. In the earthquake shocks with which in Japan we are familiar, these buildings sway about palpably in the most alarming manner."[4]

Similar statements were published by French architectural engineer M. J. Lescasse,[5] Kōbudaigakkō principal and civil engineer Henry Dyer, engineering professor George Cawley, civil engineer C. A. W. Pownall, and others. Even the wording of their verdicts took on, by the mid-1880s, the character of a formula: *daiku*-work was not just deficient, it was "of all structures the worst adapted" (Brunton, 1873);[6] "almost impossible to imagine a structure worse adapted" (Dyer, 1885);[7] "exactly the opposite" of what was required (Conder, 1887); "no form of architecture would appear, prima facie, to be less adapted" (Pownall, 1891).[8]

What an "earthquake structure" should be, according to these same Western-trained architects and engineers, was a masonry shell. To engineer Brunton, "the more solidity and weight in a building and the greater its inertia the less liable it is to derangement from a sudden movement of its foundations."[9] Kōbudaigakkō professor George Cawley agreed that "a structure to resist and palliate earthquake shocks should have cohesive strength and rigidity and not flexibility."[10] The words *rigid, strength, weight,* and *inertia* appear most frequently in these and other writings as "earthquake-resistant" characteristics. Japanese buildings, in the eyes of the same observers, were "flimsy" and "of an extremely fragile and temporary nature."[11] To Cawley they were "primitive and faulty in the principal of design, and lavishly wasteful in constructive methods."[12] The "waste" referred specifically to their complicated roof systems, which used far more timber than a European truss, yet did not allow for greater spans.

In most Japanese buildings, from temples to farmhouses, roofs were the major carriers of both technicity and appearance. Because Japanese structures were rarely taller than two stories (pagodas being a dramatic exception), much of their actual substance was contained in roofs, and roof construction *(koya-gumi)* was the age-old focus of *daiku* technique. Roof-making in Japan was not based on lining up a series of triangular frameworks (trusses) as it was in Europe, but building up and jointing together relatively large timbers in the form of a pyramidal crib. This roof structure was not supported by walls, but by a forest of posts rising from single stones set into the ground. Walls or foundations in the European sense did not exist. It was the openness of this intercolumnated space as much as its woodenness, an openness only accentuated by paper-covered screens that could be slid and even removed to create ever-changing floor plans, that encouraged Europeans to see Japanese buildings as less substantial than their own. The very substantial mass of timber above their heads either remained out of sight in most European accounts, or, once sensed, was treated as a matter for dread.

Japanese joints (the wooden connections between posts and beams) were unusually varied by European standards and of often puzzle-like complexity. In the twentieth century, the Modern movement in architecture would teach the lesson that Japanese buildings were "modular," stressing the existence of "standardized" components like the *tatami* mat. This neatly ignored the matter of Japanese joinery, however, a knowledge/practice involving a high level of skill and reserving great latitude of choice to the individual artisan. Partly because it is invisible once executed, joinery has enjoyed less status than *tatami* or *fusuma* (sliding doors) in an architectural economy based on photographic representation. Japanese joinery was much more visible to nineteenth-century European observers, but mainly as a matter for censure, just like the complex roof structures it made possible. If the roof structure was wasteful (and dangerous) on a macro scale, the intricate cutting of wood that was Japanese joinery was considered its micro manifestation.[13]

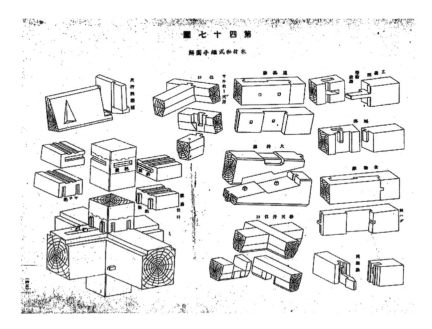

FIGURE 4

Typical Japanese carpentry joints. The illustration is from a book
promoting *wayō* (Japanese-Western) hybrid house construction.
In the matter of carpentry joints, the preference remains *wa*
(Japanese). (From Yoshihara Yonejirō, ed., *Wayō jūtaku kenchiku
ʒushū*, 1910.)

In European accounts, "wooden" was often used interchangeably with "Japanese," though it was the full range of Japanese decisions and actions that were
under critique, the choice of material being only one. British engineers believed
wooden structures might also be made earthquake-resistant through devices that
imparted rigidity and strength, such as diagonal braces and iron fittings. That diagonal bracing (a standard feature of European and American carpentry) was absent from the practice of *daiku*, was a consistent source of foreign wonder and concern. "The principle of the immovability of the triangle as propounded in Euclid's
7th Proposition," wrote Conder in 1891, "is rarely applied to Japanese buildings."[14]
Along with the principle of the arch, the structural stability of the triangle, particularly as embodied in the truss, was considered by Europeans to be among the
greatest technomathematical lessons they had to offer the Japanese. As the American biologist Edward Morse lampooned this attitude, foreign visitors were "seized

with an eager desire to go among these people as a missionary of trusses and braces."[15]

The metaphor of "technology transfer," evoking a box being packed and shipped at one point and opened and unpacked at a second, is unsatisfying as an explanation for the missionary zeal that Morse describes. Masonry in Britain—in the minds of civil engineers and masons, in treatises and textbooks, and in countless miles of walls, embankments, and breakwaters—was not designed as an earthquake-resistant technology. Neither were trusses, braces, or arches. Destructive earthquakes were not a phenomenon Englishmen had had much occasion to encounter, let alone resist.[16] Just as Kōbudaigakkō itself had no actual model in the West, so the earthquake-resistant masonry structures in which both Kōbudaigakkō and the new Japan were to be housed was not so much "transferred" as locally fashioned from heterogeneous elements. These had arguably less to do with Euclid or the technicalities of civil engineering than with European perceptions about the relationship of Japan (and many non-European places) to its own nature.

Many British engineers and architects held that the Japanese were a people nearly defenseless before destructive nature, that they were "of nature" and under its control in a way that Englishmen were not (and had perhaps never been). Brunton, Cawley, and others did not take *daiku* building practice to be simply in error. They suspected rather that Japanese culture had traditionally lacked an interest in guarding itself against earthquakes at all. The Japanese, in a developing European discourse, were categorized as intrinsically an artistic people, and even mystical and spiritual.[17] But not necessarily logical. They were deemed to be clever, however, and this quality allowed them to "imitate" more readily than other Asian peoples.[18] Accepting this premise, it was possible to believe that *daiku*, unable to cope with the complex and awful power of earthquakes ("the dread of earthquakes" as Conder had expressed it) had instead channeled their creative energies into aesthetics, into expressing rather than resisting the sublime. Ornamental *daiku* work was thus assigned to the (formative) knowledge-realm "art," and the nonornamental part of it was left to be explained in noninstrumental ways. British ambassador Sir Harry Parkes was "of the opinion that the light and elastic style of Japanese architecture had no reference to the necessities, or apprehensions occasioned by earthquakes." Japanese architecture was as fragile as it is, he told the Asiatic Society of Japan, because it derived from Chinese architecture, which had in turn evolved from tents.[19]

As early as 1873, in another paper to the Asiatic Society, Brunton had split carpentry into "higher" and "lower" branches inscribed with race and gender. The branch in which the Japanese excelled, he wrote, included "neatness" of workmanship, the cutting of joints "with the greatest nicety," making "delicate" window frames, and "beautifully" executing carved ornamentation. "But when it comes to the higher branches of carpentry, such as the arrangement of various beams so that they will be best adapted to bear the strains which are likely to come upon them, or a combination of timbers which will form a stiff, strong, and reliable structure, or the selection of the proper size of wood to stand the different strains which it will have to bear, then we find the Japanese very deficient."[20] Real (i.e., higher) carpentry was about "bearing strains" and being "stiff, strong, and reliable." The lower branch was mostly about using tools. The Japanese, said Brunton, were "very skilful in the use of their tools. They only require explicit and detailed directions."[21]

Conceding to Japanese superiority in the use of tools furthered the mapping of hand/mind and female/male dualities onto the East/West one, for by the 1870s, being good with tools was becoming a compliment reserved for nonwhite peoples. As Brunton's comment makes clear, the users of hand tools, even if skilful, left themselves open to direction by engineering minds.

THE JAPANESE CARPENTER
AS INTERNATIONAL EXHIBIT

In the very same years that foreigners were being enlisted to teach architecture and engineering in Japan, small groups of *daiku* were for the first time going abroad. Beginning with the international exhibitions at Vienna in 1873 and Philadelphia in 1876, the Japanese government sent advance parties of *daiku* to erect its pavilions. The *daiku* themselves were not sent as exhibits. From the Japanese perspective they were simply preparators. But wherever they appeared with their unusual uniforms, tools, and practices, they received as much attention from dignitaries and crowds as the porcelains, bronzes, and lacquer ware that their labor housed. In Vienna, the Empress herself is said to have plucked a thin shaving from a *daiku*'s plane, folded it like paper, and slipped it between her breasts.[22]

Part of the excitement was that, in the capitals and large cities of Europe and the United States, *daiku* were the first Japanese that many people had ever seen. The reputation of Japanese art preceded the exhibitions of the 1870s, at least among an educated elite, and Japanese paintings, ceramics, and bronzes were beginning to bring high prices in London and Paris. Those artisans who created vendible Japanese objects were never actually seen in Western cities, but *daiku* were. Thus did *daiku*-preparators come to represent "the Japanese artist" for exhibition-going connoisseurs.[23]

The elites who watched *daiku* perform carpentry in Western cities were just then increasingly dissatisfied with their own, native artisanal class, who were in the midst of organizing themselves into trade unions. Everywhere that *daiku* went, it seemed, middle-class people were eager to form exhibits in which Japanese artisans and native artisans might be brought into contrast. At the Philadelphia Centennial Exhibition, the *Scientific American Supplement* published regular reports on the progress of "the Japanese carpenters" and made separate, meticulous illustrations of each of their tools. In the journal's voluminous coverage of the exhibition, the tools of the Japanese were the only objects of a non-Western people singled out for illustration, and praise. These tool museums of the *Scientific American* were essentially exhibits within exhibits, entirely unplanned by the Japanese delegation. *Noko* (saws) and *kana* (planes) were favorably contrasted with the similar tools of American carpenters, and this at a fair meant to showcase the international ascendancy of American technology.[24]

American carpenters in the crowd that had gathered to watch the *daiku* were themselves pulled into the exhibit that the *Scientific American* conducted for its readers. Its reporter claimed to have overheard an American carpenter in the crowd say "either us or them fellers has got a great deal to learn in the way of carpenter's tools." But there was no question in the correspondent's mind as to whom should learn from whom: "We [Americans]," he wrote, dropping the vernacular, "have not succeeded in producing any better specimens of workmanship than our forefathers." Bigoted statements were assigned to the surrounding crowd: that the Japanese ways were "quaint" and that, compared to Americans, the Japanese carpenters were exceedingly slow. Another reporter, "Lavan," writing for the *Scientific American*, was moved to defend slow work, calling the Japanese pavilion "the finest piece of cabinet-work that has ever been produced in this country."[25]

The love of Lavan and his compatriots for The Japanese Carpenter/Artisan, one of the great interracial romances in the last quarter of the nineteenth century, has been taken as a pure one by generations of art historians, who have tended to ignore the set of social and cultural conditions that sealed this affection, that made it possible for white men of one class to hold white men of another to standards "set" by men of color. Constructing The Japanese Carpenter/Artisan as the Western tradesman's binary twin allowed each figure to be brought into contrast, although the lesson drawn from their "contest" would depend on who was speaking, and where. If the speaker were defending "art" at an exhibition site in a European or American city, the *daiku* would be a Jesus the carpenter come to kiss the Judas tradesmen, who had forsaken "craft" (a new, downward-directed keyword) for unionism and other modern lures. If it were a British engineer speaking in the name of "science" in Tokyo, the argumentative structure, if not the very same evidence, could be deployed to nearly opposite effect, the *daiku* becoming an impediment to Japan's modern progress. On one point both Western proponents of art and science were in agreement: building-carpentry, which in other circumstances might have been constructed as a shared trait of the forest-dwelling, wood-using cultures of northern Europe and Japan, was instead singled out as a primary marker of cultural difference.

In the journal *American Architect and Building News* in the months just prior to the arrival of *daiku* in Philadelphia, The Japanese Carpenter and The British Workman are the subjects in a series of separate yet intercolumnated articles. In January 1876, the journal notes that "the British workman has . . . been dragged before the public" by its English counterpart, *The Building News*. Tradesmen at the Westminster Aquarium stand accused of "soldiering" (conspiring to set an idle pace). The men have even "left their work in a body, and gone to the village green to enact Christy's Minstrels with blackened faces." Conditions in the United States have not reached this extreme, writes the editor, yet even there "all the concerted efforts of the trades tend directly to reduce the quality of the work done" and to poison class relations at the building site: "architects as a rule hold tradesmen in contempt and . . . workmen return the compliment." The same month there is a complimentary article on "Japanese Houses."[26]

On February 5 it is The British Workman again, now raising questions that "belong to all countries." "From all sides come the same story," laments the journal: "The workmen as a class are ceasing to respect their vocation. Politics, socialistic schemes, a hundred unreal questions and wild reforms, exercise active minds among them: their trades are to a great part of them only distasteful means of getting their necessary bread and butter and therefore all their effort is to make their labor as light and lucrative as possible." Carpenters and masons are "enslaved by the trades unions," which work not "to improve their mastery of their trades" but "to acquire social and political power." It is "the duty of architects," says the journal, to take "every means to interest the workman in his work."[27]

By February 12, "the Japanese have appeared in force at the Centennial grounds in Philadelphia with a freight of fifty car-loads." At the end of the same column it is "The Workman Again," no longer with a specific nationality or occupation; it is "the active-minded workman forgetting his uncongenial work to talk intelligent nonsense about social and political problems which he has no means of studying"; it is "the waste of mental force" and "two things which follow each other in a circle." Advises the journal: "To interest the workman in his work, improve the quality of it; to improve the quality of it, interest the workman in his work."[28] How to start this circular motion? "All sorts of ornament"; "the utmost variety of detail"; "work that must tax his brains to understand it"; "the battle of the styles, whatever opinion we may hold of it, has cleared the air, we must admit." Four pages later it is "Japanese Work at the Centennial Grounds."[29]

When this circle began its motion in the last quarter of the nineteenth century, The Japanese Carpenter and his Euro-American counterpart were both inside. As T. Jackson Lears has shown, The Craftsman of the late nineteenth century was a complex personality, sometimes The Japanese Carpenter, sometimes a colonial barrel-maker, and other times a suburban homeowner reading a journal by the same title. But always, The Craftsman was not the contemporary Euro-American Workman. The Craftsman was a spectral figure who proved again and again to the Western worker how alone he was in his modern condition, separated by a gulf called "skill" from the artisans of the past and of other nations.[30]

That European and Japanese carpenters were binary twins was demonstrated through actual performance at the Japan Society of London in 1892. Following a lecture by former Kōbudaigakkō professor Cawley, now in retirement, an audience of 236 watched as a *daiku* and an English joiner, arranged at opposite ends of a platform, manipulated their tools in concert. The secretary of the society was struck by the "entirely dissimilar" way the two men moved: "Both in sawing and planing their bodies had swayed in opposite directions, the Englishman pushing the tool away from his body, the Japanese drawing it towards himself. The British joiner held the wood on which he was working with his hands; the *Daiku* steadied his with his feet."[31] The only movement that the secretary detected that they shared, and which was just enough, he declared with relief, to "make all Mankind akin," was that they both spat into their hands.[32]

That the two carpenters would act out a dichotomy was anticipated by the audience. Sir Rutherford Alcock, the former British consul in Tokyo, had famously listed in 1863 a series of practices that Europeans and Japanese conducted in reverse fashion.[33] Carpentry, prominent on Alcock's list, was by the time of the Japan Society performance one of a stable set of metaphors for the more abstractly geographical "East vs. West." And in the lecture preparatory to the demonstration, former Kōbudaigakkō professor Cawley, echoing Brunton two decades earlier, extended and embellished the root antonym. There were, said Cawley, two types of carpentries, two types of carpenter, and two classes of tool: "The Japanese wood worker is a master of decorative rather than of constructive art. For the British wood worker I would generally claim the exact opposite."[34]

That the *daiku* showed "considerable skill" in the "purely manipulative part of his calling" was obvious, said Cawley, from the simplicity of his hand tools. "The more simple the tool employed," he ventured, "the more expert the skilled workman, and vis-versa." On the other hand, said Cawley, "The Japanese carpenter has . . . practically no knowledge of the higher branches of carpentry. . . . The principle involved in the construction of the most famous Japanese temples is no higher than that embodied in the fisherman's hut. The advantages of the framed structure specially designed to withstand certain known forces were apparently never known to the old Japanese carpenter. This is somewhat strange, I think, seeing that the Portuguese made a lengthened stay in Japan some three hundred years ago."[35]

Cawley's compliments to the Japanese as the more skillful tool-user of course set the London joiner on stage in a competition he could only lose. The Englishman's stage role was to help enact "East vs. West," but in doing so he could not help but demonstrate the residual nature of the tool-using British artisan. It was not the London joiner who was the real recipient of the compliments given British "constructive science," but Cawley's own profession of engineering.[36]

Mechanical engineers, said Cawley before the demonstration, "have completely inverted the relative values of the tool and the human worker" through the subdivision of labor and its mechanization.[37] The existence, offstage, of a world of mechanized "tools," gathered in immense factories, was part of what freed Cawley and the audience from any stake in the outcome of the competition between the hand tools on stage, and allowed them to even cheer the *daiku* on. The Japanese carpenter was made to win in all the areas that mattered in the new domain of art, while the British (or American) artisan, increasingly marked as dysfunctional within the knowledge-realm "technology," joined the Japanese carpenter as the Western representative of a tool-using, hand-spitting "mankind."

THE TWO BRITAINS

George Cawley concluded his Japan Society lecture with a salute not to Japan and Britain, but "the Britains of the West and of the East."[38] The formula was a common one among British *yatoi*, and was especially useful to Englishmen charged with maintaining the diplomatic, trading, and, eventually, military relationship with Japan.[39] It evoked a Eurasian land mass with island nations at either end, geoculturally closer to each other than to the continent over which each sought influence.

Yet there was another set of Britains operative at Cawley's lecture and demonstration, and at many forums where Englishmen and Americans discussed Japan:

the Britains of the Middle Ages and of the nineteenth century. In a famous passage, Sir Rutherford Alcock compared Japan to medieval Europe: "It is in order that the reader may more fully realize this Oriental phase of feudalism, such as our ancestors knew in the time of the Plantegenets, that I would pray him to keep the stereoscopic tube to his eye, and shut out all the preconceived views, and all surrounding objects, which speak of a late age and a distant race. We are going back to the twelfth century in Europe."[40]

The Japanese *daiku* on the stage in London evoked for Cawley the artisan of former times, whose "mind was not much disturbed by the exigence of social position . . . his ambition and the whole bent of his mind were centered on his work."[41] These were characteristics, the audience would have recognized, of the medieval craftsman of John Ruskin, William Morris, and Augustus Pugin. The skills of the Japanese *daiku* had grown up in a "feudal" Japan and would constitute a living demonstration to Western audiences of their own medieval past. To engineers like Cawley, the positive quality of feudal social order was that the worker "stuck to his bench." The negative quality was that "in Oriental countries such as Japan, in which the standard of material civilization has been stationary over a long period, the faculty of invention becomes deadened, and we therefore find the industrial methods of today practically corresponding to those in use a century ago."[42] It was Cawley and his colleagues at Kōbudaigakkō, the audience was made in various ways to understand, who had been instrumental in reviving this "deadened" Japan and in setting its "stationary" inhabitants in motion.

On the other hand, for those Englishmen (and Americans) who were suspicious of the faculty for invention of engineers like Cawley, and who took the feudal past as a positive model for the present and future, Japan was intensely attractive as a living exhibition of how beautiful and ordered that world had been, and could yet be. This class of reformer, which included an increasing number of Western architects and artists, were naturally dubious of the efforts of Cawley and his colleagues to convert "the Britain of the East" into the Britain of the nineteenth-century present.[43] Buried within the metaphor of a Far Eastern Britain was thus an inherent tension: with which period of British history, or which stage of British social and artistic development, would Japan converge? The Japanese Carpenter, as a figure uniquely vendible between art and architecture, artisanship and industry, the past and the present, and The East and The West, became in one sense the totem of this dilemma.

The two Britains were ultimately not moments in time, but reform projects occurring synchronically in different locations. It was location or geography, more than content or even intention, that most defines their difference, and that allows me even to speak of them as "projects." They were not practically or discursively unified except through place. On the one hand, there was the Euro-American project of making Japan "modern," centered in the late 1870s and 1880s in Tokyo's *yatoi* community, and particularly in institutions like Kōbudaigakkō. On the other was the project of reforming the West itself through medieval art and architecture, a project equally modern, for which a "feudal" Japan became a vital "place to think with." The spectacle of The Japanese Carpenter in a European or American setting could lend sustenance and meaning to both projects, serve and inform each constituency, and hold their tensions in check. When spokesmen for the two Britains encountered each other in Meiji Japan, however, the opposite sort of spectacle could result: tensions released, faults opened, and meanings pulled apart.

PAGODAS

Just such a rift occurred in the 1880s between a Japanophilic reformer of Britain and a British reformer of Japan, and produced, for awhile, two irreconcilable Japans. Christopher Dresser, Britain's first professional "designer," visited Japan in 1876–1877 and chronicled the journey five years later in *Japan: Its Architecture, Art, and Manufactures* (1882). One of a number of influential art critics to emerge around the time of the Crystal Palace Exhibition, and early under the influence of architect and Gothic Revivalist Augustus Pugin, Dresser had by the 1870s transferred any lingering medieval loyalties fully to The Orient. The hand-crafted objects of Asia, he hoped, might foster a revolution in British industrial design. Dresser differed from Ruskin, Pugin, and Morris, however, in being an enthusiast for mechanization. He traveled to Japan on the retainer of British manufacturers, intent on collecting Japanese "art" objects as prototypes for British industrial production.[44]

Dresser went to Tokyo (via the Philadelphia Exhibition) at virtually the same time as the architect Josiah Conder. He bore with him a collection of British art objects from the South Kensington Museum, whose schools he and Conder had both attended as young men, although not together. The British objects were to be exhibited in Japan at the Ueno Museum (for which Conder would subsequently design a brick building, that would be shaken to pieces in the Great Kantō Earthquake of 1923). Although there is no record of the two men having actually met, their interests, backgrounds, and even physical trajectories in 1876 were remarkably similar.[45] On returning to England, however, Dresser became one of the earliest and strongest critics of the Anglo-Japanese architecture project Conder was then in the midst of directing: "The Europeans in Tokio are encouraging the Japanese to build European houses with stones and bricks; and the Government offices are of these materials, while it is proposed that the new Mikado's palace be also of European character. To me nothing could be more absurd than this departure from architectural custom which has the sanction of ages; and the result of this incongruous innovation will probably be a return to the native style of building after the occurrence of some dire calamity."[46]

Already Dresser was sensitive to the potential of earthquakes to define the success or failure of Japan's relandscaping. He was also aware of the architectural-engineering discourse on *daiku*, and determined to upset it. Masonry in Dresser's account is potentially unstable, while Japanese houses are described as seismically indestructible. He compares them to tables, which remain sturdy despite the bouncing of floors beneath their legs, and attributes Japanese earthquake damage entirely to the falling of heavy roof tiles, a defect he suggests could be remedied simply by substituting wooden shingles treated with a fireproofing agent.[47]

Dresser concentrates his argument, however, on what he sees as Japanese carpentry's strongest suit: the survival of the pagoda. In the late nineteenth century there were still numerous five-story wooden pagodas in Japan, the oldest, at Hōryūji, dating perhaps as early as 670 A.D. A daring construction for an earthquake-prone country, the pagoda would always, after Dresser, be a phenomenon that anyone arguing about the effect of nature on Japanese architecture would feel compelled to explain. Visiting a pagoda with "my good friend Sakata," Dresser, assuming the attitude of a British engineer, purports to have been initially scandalized by the "absurdly excessive" waste of materials, especially a thick wooden mast that formed the pagoda's core. But Sakata then revealed that this mast was in fact a pendulum, suspended one inch off the floor, whose purpose was to swing freely during an earthquake, thereby keeping the center of gravity within the structure's base. Dresser concludes that "the employment of this scientific method of keeping the pagoda upright shows how carefully the Japanese have thought out the requirements to be met."[48]

Dresser's indestructible pagoda redrew the lines between "Japanese carpenters," "science," and "nature" in purposely disruptive ways. Scientific devices, he was arguing, were located within hand-crafted wooden objects. Masonry was at the same time destabilized as science (i.e., as a universally applicable object/knowledge/practice) and turned into a piece of British culture dangerously misapplied.

As architectural historian Suzuki Hiroyuki has chronicled, Dresser's claims for the Japanese pagoda were rebutted over a period of years in British architectural journals by Josiah Conder. Between 1882, when Dresser's argument first appeared in print, and 1887, when the matter came up in a question period at the Royal Institute of British Architects, Conder repeatedly denied that the structural system of pagodas was intended to be aseismic, arguing that their survival through centuries of earthquakes was in effect accidental. The central mast, he wrote, was designed to stiffen the tower in the face of wind and normal settling; it was not intended to be a pendulum, and did not function as one. One of his proofs was written descriptions of similar devices in the ancient wooden pagodas of China, a country where, he erroneously claimed, "earthquakes are almost unknown." Dresser defended himself in print at least once, but the contest was unequal from the beginning. Conder styled himself in one letter "Architect to the Government of Japan" and called in another instance on the testimony of "Prof. Kozima, M.A., Japanese Professor of Architecture at the Tokyo University," who had personally inspected the pagodas in question.[49]

Two decades after the publication of Dresser's book, a similar debate was initiated by the visit to Japan of the American architect and gothicist Ralph Adams Cram. Japanese architecture, Cram wrote in a subsequent article of 1898, was "as scientifically and elaborately developed as is any of the stone styles of Europe." Cram's bête noire was the common British position that buildings constructed of wood, including, by implication, most of those in Cram's own country, fell outside the definition of "architecture"; instead, he asserted that Japanese architecture "stands alone as the most perfect wooden style the world has known. As such it must be judged, and not from the narrow canons of the West, that presuppose masonry as the only building material."[50]

Cram's invocation of science, modest and limited though it was, brought him a scolding from Fellow of the Royal Institute of British Architects H. H. Stratham, who thought that Cram's "enthusiasm has rather run away with his grammar here." Conceding only that Japanese buildings might be "in some instances a little more scientific than is generally supposed," Stratham drew a classic distinction between the building art (and all else) East and West: "Western architecture appeals mainly to the intellect, Oriental architecture to the fancy . . . the farther we go east, the nearer we get to Oriental architecture uninfluenced by Western ideals, the more we find the architecture characterized by exuberant and fanciful forms and combinations. . . ."[51] Japanese carpentry, wrote Stratham, "rather gives the idea of something done from habit and as a traditional method, without any other reason for it." The work of *daiku* "certainly cannot be called scientific carpentry," he wrote, although "unscientific timber construction" of its type was still valuable for its "picturesque and pleasing" effect. Focusing on a woodblock print of an arched bridge, he concluded, "nothing could be more picturesque than this . . . and nothing more absolutely childish in regard to the principle of construction."[52]

Stratham's article included illustrations of two pagodas. One is a detailed cross-sectional drawing of the tower at Hōryūji (one of the oldest wooden buildings in the world), borrowed from Cram's own article, which carefully delineates the central mast and each surrounding member. Cram doubtlessly intended his cross-section to demonstrate to a Western audience the pagoda's structural logic, although one measure of the thoroughness with which Dresser's arguments had been vanquished by that time is that neither Cram nor Stratham seemed aware of the theory of the mast as pendulum. Stratham is impressed with the "logic" of the mast as a stiffener (a characterization originally given it by Conder), but his purpose in reproducing Cram's drawing, it seems, was to evidence the statement in the accompanying text that "in the typical Japanese structure there is a great deal of waste of materials." On the following page, as if to demonstrate that *daiku* work is "by nature" picturesque, he produced a watercolor by a British artist of a shadow-laden pagoda pitched at a steep angle against a cloudy sky.[53]

Stratham draws here on an orientalist tradition predating the Western encounter with Japan. But reports of the seismic defenselessness of Japanese buildings, which by the time of his comments had taken on the quality of fact not only in Europe but in certain quarters of Japan itself, added scientific authority to the reproduction of orientalist narratives and helps to explain why Cram's and Dresser's arguments remained, at least in the realms of art and architecture, dissenting opinions. Any defense of the ability of the Japanese *daiku* to think and create systematically seemed rhetorical beside reports from Conder, Brunton, Cawley, and others resident in Japan for years or decades, and entrusted by the government of that nation with educating its architects and engineers that, on the occasion of earthquakes, Japanese buildings simply collapsed.

As Stratham's map of Eurasia suggests, Japan's defenselessness before nature was a necessary corollary to its picturesqueness and mysticality, a characterization that grew rather than diminished as Japan became increasingly "known," especially within and through the knowledge-realm of art, in the late nineteenth and early twentieth centuries. Even Stratham's criticism of Cram, that his "enthusiasm has run away with his grammar," was logically defensible, given that Cram's larger discussion of Japanese architecture was organized around similar dyads. Wrote Cram in 1905: "[Japanese architecture] is the architecture of Buddhism, and it must be read in the light of this mystic and wonderful system. Finally, it is the art of the

Orient, taking form and nature from Eastern civilization, vitalized by the 'Soul of the East,' the artistic manifestation of the religion of meditation, of spiritual enlightenment, of release from illusion. It is separated from the art of the Western religion of action, of elaborate ethical systems, of practicality, by the diameter of being."[54] Stratham was thus extracting "science" from an argumentative and linguistic structure to which it was, increasingly, loosely connected.

The complex of metaphors, inscriptions, and binarisms that constructed "Japanese architecture" intermingled with those constructing "Japanese religion" and "Japanese art" and ultimately "Japan" in ways too complex to fully sort out here. But one illustration of how fact-construction in one knowledge-realm could influence adjacent ones is the statement by British book designer Walter Crane that his Japanese counterparts possessed "decorative sense" and "finesse . . . taste, in short," but not "real constructive power of design." Crane was writing here about books. But as evidence that "the Japanese artists are not safe guides as designers," he specifically cites the "absence" in Japan "of any really noble architecture or substantial constructive sense."[55]

Similarly, lessons drawn from Japanese painting aided fact-construction about Japanese architecture and vice versa. Stratham himself had drawn such a parallel: "Japanese artists are masterly in the drawing of fish and birds; when they come to the larger form of vertebrate animals, they seem to loose their feeling for realism, and paint creatures in Japanesque style. . . . The higher mammals . . . are treated in an exaggerated and semi-grotesque fashion."[56] There are of course few larger mammals indigenous to Japan besides horses and cows, and the bear on the remote northern island of Hokkaido. It came to be almost a rule in such writings, however, that, as Edward Strange put it, "in the making of little things" such as "furniture, writing cabinets, medicine boxes, and the like," Japanese artisans were "simply marvelous," but that "large" things were best handled by Europeans. Strange's comment was actually part of a defense of Japanese skillfulness, which he thought suffered abroad because of the poor reputation of Japanese architecture. Because Japanese were skilful on a small scale, he wrote, "we therefore cannot ascribe the constructive faults of their architecture to a want either of intelligence or capability."[57]

JAPANESE SKEPTICISM

Clearly Japanese did not see *daiku* as they were seen by foreigners, although neither can we underestimate the earnestness with which Meiji intellectuals, at least, sought to grasp the sight of themselves through foreign eyes. Dresser did not have to discover the aseismic qualities of pagodas. He was taken to one by a Japanese colleague, who also suggested its pendulum-like nature. In rebutting Dresser's characterization, however, architect Conder had deployed the written testimony of another Japanese colleague, Kozima, whom he had sent to investigate the same pagoda. In the midst of presenting his evidence, Kozima denigrates "the common assertion among Japanese carpenters and other people supposed to be versed in such matters, that the central post in these 'five-story' towers in our country is always suspended from the top and is meant to swing from side to side."[58] This passage tells us that Dresser, and even his Japanese tour guide, were thus repeating positions held by other groups of Japanese.

Confidence in the aseismic quality of *daiku*-work was not limited to *daiku* themselves nor restricted to the rare pagoda. As engineer M. J. Lescasse admitted in 1887, more than a decade into the *zōkagaku* project, "In Japan it is generally believed that timber constructions resist earthquakes better than buildings in masonry." Not only regular people believed this, he wrote, but "even trustworthy [Japanese] men." Lescasse noted that the cost of brick in Japan had recently decreased with more widespread manufacture, while *daiku*-work was becoming more expensive. "The most serious obstacle against the adaptation of brick buildings," he concluded, "is therefore now only the belief that they do not offer sufficient protection against earthquakes."[59]

The limits of Japanese trust became apparent with the planning of the new Imperial Palace, a project that began in 1879. As "Architect to the Government of Japan," Conder was initially invited to design a masonry building in the European style. But Kōbusho engineer Tachikawa Tomokata, who had entered Bakumatsu employment as a sixth-generation *daiku*, argued that the Emperor's life would be safer, in the event of an earthquake, within a wooden frame. In a *shoshin* (written opinion) submitted privately to his superiors, and only published by architectural historians in the 1930s, Tachikawa noted that certain Japanese temples had withstood earthquakes for over a thousand years. "It is wrong," he concluded, "to think that wooden buildings can't survive disasters." Referring to the Ansei earthquake of 1855, the last destructive seismic event to occur in Tokyo, he noted that "only the low-degree houses" had fallen, while those "above the middling level" sustained only the slightest damage.[60]

Tachikawa's memorandum not only defended *daiku* knowledge, but cast doubt on the earthquake-resistant properties of European masonry. He had heard that "in America and Europe, although there are no large earthquakes," masonry buildings still sustained damage in minor shocks. If Japan were rebuilt in stone, "all the country may become an empty field" in the event of an earthquake as strong as that of 1855. Tachikawa suggested that the Europeans themselves knew masonry to be weak, because they sometimes reinforced it with iron and lead, a procedure he had witnessed during the construction of the Yokosuka Iron Works and the Osaka Mint. Stone, he wrote, is "really ornament," the metal reinforcement being the true earthquake-resisting element. He contrasts this apparent trickery to the intrinsic virtue and appropriateness of Japanese timber. "This country has a lot of good woods, like hinoki [cypress], of which the western countries are envious."[61]

Tachikawa's position was strengthened when, during the construction of a temporary palace to Conder's designs, a minor earthquake caused some of the masonry arches to crack.[62] The half-completed walls had to be removed, providing space in which to rethink the entire project. A compromise was eventually worked out by which the portion of the palace housing the Emperor's residence was to be constructed in wood under the direction of Kigo Kiyoyoshi, the *daiku* to the Imperial court, while the part housing the Imperial Ministry (essentially offices) was to be built of brick to Conder's designs. The Palace project continued to be a site of struggle, however, between the *daiku* of the Imperial Household and *zōkagaku-shi*, one that we revisit in a subsequent chapter.[63]

In the wake of the Imperial Palace compromise, it became the convention among the Meiji elite to build mansions with the same split form: *daiku*-designed wooden residence quarters with attached architect-designed "Western-style" masonry pavilions for the reception of foreign guests.[64] This decision to retain *daiku*-designed residence quarters was certainly influenced by comfort and custom as much as by safety. Yet the Meiji elite, to whom all options were available, slept each night within a framework of wooden posts and beams rather than between walls of brick or stone. Thus was architecture, in the form of the leadership's own residence quarters, forced into a form of *wayō setchū* (Japanese-Western compromise).

The most widespread demonstration of Japanese doubt, however, was the existence of an even more compromising version of *wayō-setchū*, a novel building system that architectural historian Fujimori Terunobu has called "wood-framed masonry."[65] For clients determined to have a "masonry" building, certain urban *daiku* learned how to construct a wooden frame faced with stone or brick, essentially reducing European masonry to a thin, nonstructural veneer. In this particular form of *wayō*, masonry was made to serve the ornamental function that Tachikawa believed to be its true nature, while the guts of the building remained the *daiku*-built wooden frame. Wood-framed masonry was "supposed by some persons to be the best construction to resist earthquakes," wrote engineer Brunton in 1875, "on account of the wooden frame work preventing the outside lining of stones or other covering from being precipitated inward during a shock." Even very large masonry buildings were being constructed in this way by the mid-1870s, including certain of the buildings of Kōbudaigakkō itself.[66]

The hybridity of this method was despised by *yatoi* engineers such as Brunton, Henry Dyer, and George Cawley, the latter calling it a "mongrel system."[67] Its ubiquity likely contributed, however, to their repeated calls for purity in the application of European models. Hybridity extended beyond its unorthodox arrangement of materials and systems into the social network that deployed and sustained it. According to Fujimori, wood-framed masonry first appeared under the Tokugawa regime, but became particularly common in the compromise city of Yokohama in the early 1870s. Some of the largest examples emerged from a relationship between an American engineer, R. P. Bridgens, and a group of Yokohama *daiku*, including Shimizu Kisuke, Takashima Kaemon, and Kajima Iwakichi. Bridgens took responsibility for designing stone shells in conformance with the display expectations of architecture, while *daiku* were free to exercise their own knowledge in constructing the wooden frame behind. This demarcation of "ornamental" and "structural" zones of authority neatly reversed the characterization of *daiku* skills as "decorative" (exterior/superficial) and those of Western engineers as "structural" (interior/fundamental) and the gender inscriptions that the dyad carried and sustained.[68]

Unlike buildings designed by architects, wood-framed masonry buildings preserved age-old artisanal hierarchies that had been threatened by the coming of brick. Historian Hatsuda Tōru has described how the role of brick-mason was first filled in Japan by *sakan* (plasterers), the only one of the three main artisanal groups *(daiku, sakan,* and *tatami-ya)* who owned trowels and dealt familiarly with wet materials. Like Euro-American plasterers, however, *sakan* were captive to *daiku*, their normal work environment being the wooden frame that *daiku* had first to construct on the building site. In the new masonry building process, at least as conceived by foreign architects and *zōkagaku-shi*, the status relationship between *daiku* and *sakan*-turned-masons was to be reversed. Being a *sakan*-mason was now potentially more lucrative and important than being a *daiku*, as confirmed by a steady increase in the former's wage rate from early to late Meiji. Wood-framed masonry temporarily forestalled this reversal of status roles and extended traditional relationships between the trades. Stone or brick simply became the substitute, in this system, for the soil-based plaster traditionally applied over the *daiku*-designed frame. Whether this new object, the brick, would create a class of brickmasons captive to *zōkagaku-shi* rather than to *daiku*, or whether *daiku* would be able to incorporate bricks and the *sakan*-turned-bricklayers in the new conservative system of wood-framed masonry remained unresolved into the late 1880s.[69]

As for "pure" brick buildings of the type promoted by architects and engineers, Tokyo and other Japanese cities had few examples, by the late 1880s, that had not been commissioned either by the government, banks, or the largest industrial concerns. The technology had not made the transition to the vernacular. The most prominent attempt to rehouse Tokyo in brick, the shop-house district of the Ginza, had turned out to be a financial failure. Kōbudaigakkō architecture student Funakoshi Kinya gives us this picture of the Ginza in 1883: "The greater proportion of these buildings, which are away from the main street, are left unoccupied. They stand barren in a wretched and lonely appearance with grasses forming on their broken roofs, with green mosses on their walls."[70] Tokyo's first exercise in masonry had ironically become its first ruin. It is not exactly clear why the project failed to attract tenants, but its most obvious advantage—resistance to fire—was apparently not as crucial to shopkeepers as to the officials who had commissioned its construction. Funakoshi wrings his hands: "At present, most of the people of Tokio fully recognize the fireproof nature of brick buildings. And yet the richest men in Tokio today still look away from them. How stupid!"[71]

Expense, inconvenience, and unfamiliarity of layout and appearance may all have contributed to the Ginza's semiabandonment. Neither can we discount the possibility, however, that mistrust in the stability of masonry played a supporting role. In the case of a fire, one often has time to run away. Or so people may have reasoned. In the case of a sudden destructive earthquake, however, one's fate depends on the material above one's head.

It was natural and hardly surprising that Western learning should be subject to doubt in the world of *daiku*. More intriguing are instances of Japanese doubt emerging from the very institution tasked with the performance of Western architecture: the *zōka* course at Kōbudaigakkō. In the previous chapter, we heard intermingled among the voices of foreign professors and ministerial experts those of their Japanese graduate students—soon to become the first generation of Japanese architects—as they underlined and even extended points made by their teachers about Japan and "the Japanese." While many of these graduation essays straightforwardly report what appear to be classroom lessons, others take the form of a dialogue between Japanese student and foreign teacher, in which the student's use of "we" suggests he is speaking for Japan before a foreign audience (if only an audience of one—his grader). In writing for and about "the Japanese," the graduate students are often apologetic and reform-minded. But they sometimes attempt to explain a position they think has been misrepresented in foreign discourse. Other times their arguments in support of a *zōka* project will, by adopting different premises, serve in some sense to undermine it.

"A Thesis on [the] Future Domestic Architecture of Japan," written by *zōka* student Sone Tatsuzō in 1879, illustrates the essayist's struggle to reconcile the task he had been trained to perform—transforming Japanese architecture from carpentry to masonry—with his own doubts over Western claims of superior control over Japanese nature. Although Sone begins his essay with a long historical discussion of Japanese (*daiku*-built) architecture, he is not, like Tachikawa, writing as a partisan of *daiku* knowledge. "Japanese Carpenters," he tells us, significantly placing them in the past tense, "were both generally ignorant of science as well as literary knowledge and . . . all the buildings built by them were copying of the pre-existing ones, over and over again." This is consistent with the discourse, explicitly engaged elsewhere in the same essay, that *daiku* belonged to a "feudal" Japan that was entirely habitual. Sone is particularly contemptuous of the hybrid wood-framed stone buildings of contemporary *daiku*, which he calls "very degrading," although he does not explain how the "habitual" has so suddenly turned into the experimental. He also accepts—and extends—a premise common among his foreign teachers, that Japanese in feudal Edo were not particularly concerned with protecting themselves from natural disaster. Knowing that foreigners were inclined to attribute this to Japanese passivity or fatalism, however, Sone argues instead that fire was in some sense invited: "Its [fire's] frequency not only made the inhabitants of Edo fearless, but let them [be] boastful of the prosperity of the metropolis by the proverb that 'Kaji wa Yedo no Hana'—fire is the flower of metropolitan prosperity. They presumed a fire once in three years in the rich streets and once in five years in the poor. So why build expensive buildings?" Flammability (and its popular acceptance) is, for Sone, the major Japanese architectural problem, and its solution, he agrees, is in substituting European masonry for Japanese carpentry.[72]

Yet over the next few pages of Sone's essay, it becomes clear that the reason he has made so much of fire is that he accepts, like *daiku* Tachikawa, that Japanese buildings are inherently more earthquake-resistant than their Western counterparts. Wooden buildings "have advantages in earthquakes," he writes, as their collapse "will not afford as many injuries as brick or stone buildings." Using language nearly as apocalyptic as Tachikawa's, and whose drama is in some sense aided by its grammatical looseness, Sone writes, "where [masonry buildings] be overturned by earthquakes, how ! much vital may it be! [*sic*] for the inmates, contrasted to the former kind [wooden ones] and at the same time the loss of treasure will be great." In the face of seismic waves, brick buildings may become "merely a heap of blocks." Sone's fears are not based on theory or prejudice, he asserts, but on the evidence of his own eyes. Already in 1879, "the majority of the city buildings at Tokio have cracks and even the Museum, the Dormitory, and The College, the best building of the Metropolis, could not get rid of them." While he ascribes their weakness to poor workmanship, rather than poor design, he is "not positive for their no harm [sic] even carefully constructed with well-selected materials, inasmuch as I am told that some injury is often perceived in Italy where the earthquake as in our country frequently occurs." Tachikawa had also drawn on the evidence of earthquake damage "in Europe," but Sone, as an architecture student, can pinpoint failure with more geographic precision: not only Italy, but the walls of his own college, and even of his own dormitory.[73]

While Sone's essay shows wide reading—he even quotes from Charles Lyell's *Principles of Geology*—it returns again and again to experiences close to home, things he has obviously seen, heard, or discussed outside the classroom, though often still inside the college. Kōbudaigakkō students were in fact required to stay within the college grounds six days a week, and could only leave on Sunday with special permission. Besides the appearance of cracks in his own dormitory, Sone reports a lesson learned from the burning down the year before of the college kitchen, whose brick-masonry following the fire "was rendered so brittle that it could be no more used." Thus, he concludes, in another digression from classroom lessons, "we must not trust the brick building thoroughly as fireproof." He has heard that someone in America is experimenting with a fireproof coating for wood, and if this could be perfected, "I shall incline with Ernest desire to adapt that method for the Japanese habitually and materially wish to live in the wooden building." Just when Sone's essay seems almost to the point of abandoning European architecture altogether, he pulls back and makes a calculation that salvages the *zōka* project: fires are more common than earthquakes. "Which is better to build houses to resist the frequent or the rare evil?" Brick, being more fireproof than wood, must be the stopgap solution.[74]

Sone's classmate Tatsuno Kingo, who was destined to occupy Japan's first chair of architecture at the future Imperial University, also shows a healthy suspicion of received wisdom in his own graduation thesis of 1879. He objects, for example, to the European genealogy that traces Egyptian architecture to caverns, European architecture to huts, and Chinese architecture to tents. Japanese architecture descends from all three, he claims, and Japanese cave-dwellers were quick to build huts as well as tents. Besides, the common European impression that Japanese architecture was perishable was "not universally true," given the survival of wooden buildings from ancient times. He even draws parallels between Japanese "architectural rules" (the design systems of premodern *daiku*) and those of Roman and Renaissance architects.[75]

When it comes to masonry, "I strongly insist that the future city buildings [of Japan] should be built of stone or brick," writes Tatsuno, a position seemingly universal among Conder's students. But his thesis shows particularly deep respect for the power of earthquakes, providing two full pages of lateral stress calculations, and additional mathematical formulas for earthquake proofing foundations. Masonry must be fortified with iron bands, buttresses used wherever possible, and buildings kept to three (or preferably two) stories in height, he advises. The habits of seismic waves need also be considered. Earthquakes always strike Tokyo from a fixed direction, claims Tatsuno (from the west southwest or west northwest), citing as evidence recent seismic cracks in the arches of the Imperial Reception Hall—the same cracking that had elicited Tachikawa's memorandum. Thus buildings should be placed with their longer walls parallel to the anticipated direction of shock. Where Sone's text had registered angst and hesitation, Tatsuno's searches for specific strategies.[76]

Conder's penciled comments at the end of Tatsuno's thesis compliment his star student for considering earthquakes mathematically "with great care and skill."[77] Yet nowhere in Conder's own early writings does the earthquake danger loom so large or precaution against it require such novel approaches. It is unlikely that architecture graduate Funakoshi Kinya was repeating a Kōbudaigakkō lecture line when he wrote in 1883 that "our great enemy—*Earthquake*—is glaring at us incessantly, with its fiery keen eyes, to dash upon our houses, suddenly and unexpectantly."[78] It is difficult to escape the conclusion that Japanese students were more anxious about confronting seismicity than many of their foreign teachers. It was their own designs, after all, that would have to stand, and their attitude toward the new technology seems guarded even as they remain committed to its aim: a fire-proof, earthquake-proof Japan.

From the perspective of the architecture and engineering faculty at Kōbudaigakkō, the persistence of Japanese belief in the seismic resistance of *daiku*-work constituted an obstacle to the spread of European architectural and engineering knowledge. The logjam was earthquakes; it was there that the forces of knowledge gathered with their pikes. Christopher Dresser, as a teller of traveler's tales, was easily dismissed. As a *daiku* representing the old order, Tachikawa's influence hardly extended beyond the Imperial Palace project. The Kōbudaigakkō graduate students, despite the doubts expressed in their essays, would go on to make careers designing dozens of masonry buildings for the Meiji state. Yet beginning in the same period, deeper veins of doubt, if not resistance, to claims of Western understanding and control of Japanese nature began to open elsewhere in the Japanese academy, and in at least one corner of the Kōbudaigakkō faculty itself. In the decade of the 1880s these dissenting voices, British and scientifically credentialed, began to constitute a more formidable force for the proponents of Japan's Western relandscaping to overcome.

THREE · The Seismologists

NAPLES VERSUS YOKOHAMA:
THE PROBLEM OF INSCRIPTION

Kōbudaigakkō's faculty, although small in number and similar in age (mid-twenties) and nationality (British), did not constitute a solid phalanx of foreign knowledge, practice, and opinion. Its members had migrated to Japan from myriad disciplinary cultures and had diverse institutional affiliations, work methods, interests, and ambitions. Despite their inclination to form a small society among themselves, mediated by common objects, their various constructions of "Japan" did not invariably mesh. In the 1880s, the issue of seismic resistance became one of the more striking and controversial disjunctions in *yatoi* perceptions. At the center of the rupture was the new Anglo-Japanese science of seismology.

The Englishman John Milne came to Kōbudaigakkō in 1876 to teach geology and mining, the same year that Conder and Dresser arrived in Tokyo and *daiku* performed at the international exhibition in Philadelphia. After a moderately severe earthquake in Yokohama on February 22, 1880, Milne began to dedicate his non-teaching time to the study of earth movement, or, more precisely, to elevating "seismology" from a geological pastime into a modern (instrument-based) science. Founding, with other Kōbudaigakkō faculty, the Seismological Society of Japan that same year, Milne would successfully enlist members of the *yatoi* community, residents of Yokohama, Kōbudaigakkō students, and elements of the Japanese government into the construction of two machines: a physical one called a "seismograph" for inscribing earthquake shocks, and a human one of literally hundreds of people, all over Japan, who would monitor seismographs and other devices, send their inscriptions to Tokyo, and allow Milne to understand and report (initially to a European audience) what earthquakes were.[1]

At the first meeting of the Seismological Society in 1880, however, seismology was still neither machine nor science.[2] The standard European method of investigating earthquakes was to survey building damage, called "observational seismology" by its leading practitioner, Robert Mallet. Devices to record earth movements had long existed in Europe and China, but earthquakes often eluded inscription by overturning delicate instrumentation, moving in complex ways, or occurring in areas remote from any inscripting device. Only by mapping damage to buildings over a large area, and seeing how and in what direction walls and chimneys fell, had Europeans constructed maps of an earthquake's relative strength and direction of movement. These had been the methods by which Mallet famously "recorded" the Great Neapolitan Earthquake of 1857. The standard Rossi-Forel scale of earthquake intensity was mainly a measure of the intensity of damage to masonry buildings. Only by following the ruins could one locate and map an earthquake's presumed "epicenter" and surround it with concentric "isoseismal" lines.[3]

The trouble for Milne, eager to record the 1880 Tokyo-Yokohama earthquake in a way that would allow it to be compared with Mallet's data from Naples, was that Japanese buildings lacked the necessary display of damage. "Everywhere the houses are built of wood and generally speaking are so flexible that although at the time of a shock they swing violently from side to side in a manner which would result in utter destruction to a house of brick or stone, when the shock is over, by the stiffness of their joints, they return to their original position, and leave no trace which gives us any definite information about the nature of the movement which has taken place."[4] Mallet, whose views on earthquake movement Milne had resolved to dispute, had been able to gather data like an archeologist amid extensive Italian ruins. As he described the "meizoseismal area" (the epicentral zone) of an Italian earthquake, "The eye is bewildered by 'a city become a heap.' [The seismologist] wanders over masses of dislocated stone and mortar. . . . Houses seem to have been precipitated to the ground in every direction of azimuth."[5] Earthquakes were to be "seen" by sorting all this wreckage into patterns, and the location and depths of epicenters were to be mathematically calculated from the angles of wall-cracks. For Milne, it was exceedingly difficult to measure, trace, map, "see" the

Tokyo-Yokohama earthquake of February 1880. It had not sufficiently inscribed itself into the Japanese landscape.

There was, however, "one great seismometer," wrote Milne, in the form of the treaty port of Yokohama, full of European-style buildings of wood and brick, only "one or two" of which by his count had escaped any damage. Nearly all of Yokohama's brick chimneys had toppled, and a few of its Western-style houses had completely collapsed. Milne sent questionnaires to the foreign residents asking them to survey and describe their damage, such as whether their windows had broken and when, and in what direction their chimneys had fallen. It was by analyzing the responses that he formed his first picture of the direction and intensity of the seismic waves. "What consolation the residents in Yokohama may have received for the losses they have sustained, I am unable to say, but certainly if the houses in which they dwell had not been built our information about this earthquake would have been so small to be almost valueless."[6]

It was not a matter of the earthquake being stronger in Yokohama than other places, for Milne found "it was very noticeable that the Japanese houses [in Yokohama], with the exception of a few godowns [warehouses] which lost a little plaster, seemed hardly to have sustained any damage." The reason the earthquake was even referred to as having occurred "in Tokyo and Yokohama" was that, "on account of their containing many European buildings, they were the best marked [places]." In areas of Japan where the shaking might have been stronger, "owing to the flexibility of the houses, little or no permanent damage was experienced." Milne thus found it impossible to locate the earthquake's epicenter or map its outer limits. It was only through examining the toppled gravestones in the countryside around Tokyo—the only bits of stone-masonry general to the Japanese landscape—that Milne would eventually construct, for this and subsequent earthquakes, large-scale maps of the movement of seismic waves.[7]

The same search for traces eventually led Milne to the Ginza, the district of European-style brick shops erected in 1872 under the direction of English architect Thomas Waters. The Ginza was in 1880 still the most prominent example of European architecture in Tokyo, and, most importantly for Milne, consisted of 330 masonry buildings of nearly identical design and construction arranged along all points of the compass. Wrote Milne: "A number of similarly constructed buildings in a district may be regarded as a number of seismographs."[8]

Milne inspected the Ginza in the company of architect Josiah Conder, who was also one of the Seismological Society's original members. Together they discovered literally hundreds of cracks. In a later paper analyzing the crack patterns, which Milne considered important evidence of the directional movement of the seismic waves, he was forced in one section to rebut arguments that the Ginza cracks had been caused not by the earthquake, but by normal settling. Milne avoids naming the author of this countertheory, but given subsequent remarks, it is likely that it was his survey companion Conder, who was among very few with the information and authority to deploy a counterclaim.[9]

The Japanese landscape that Milne paints in scientific papers following the 1880 earthquake was of course nearly the reverse image of that of Conder and other *yatoi* architects and engineers. In Milne's Japan, earthquakes leave no trace of their presence on purely Japanese buildings, while the architect-designed Ginza, full of directional cracks, acts as a seismometer. Yet Anglo-Japanese seismology had no quarrel at first—or appeared not to have one—with Anglo-Japanese architecture and Anglo-Japanese engineering. Milne's observation that brick buildings cracked was not fashioned as criticism, but by way of drawing attention to a crucial source of inscription.

TERRESTRIAL PHYSICS

Or was it only that? The account I give over these few pages follows rather faithfully Milne's own description of how he came to investigate Yokohama and the Ginza, one in which evidence of whatever kind is pursued and analyzed wherever it happens to lay. Yet by the time Milne and others founded the Seismological Society in 1880, the relandscaping of Japan was already an issue that was beginning to divide the *yatoi* community, and, moreover, earthquakes had already been formulated as its Achilles' heel. Even the Ginza was already a subject of controversy well before Milne discovered cracks there.

In 1875, during the question-and-answer period following a paper by Brunton at the Asiatic Society, Kōbudaigakkō professor of natural philosophy and telegraphy W. E. Ayrton expressed doubt as to "whether Europe's ancient Gothic architects would approve of the new mongrel red-brick buildings" of Tokyo. Here the charge of inappropriate hybridity was being turned against architects who mixed brickwork into the Japanese landscape. Ayrton thought that Japan needed a European architect who had "studied the ingenious development of wooden structures in the United States" and would "with similar industry study Japanese buildings and their extreme suitability, in many respects, to the climate of the country and the tastes of the people." This type of architect was of course not Brunton, and neither was it Conder, who came the following year.[10]

Ayrton's architectural criticism is significant because it was he, in company with fellow physicist John Perry, who, the year after these remarks (1876), the year that Conder, Dresser, and Milne all arrived, initiated the scientific discussion of earthquakes, seismometry, and even aseismic construction methods among the Kōbudaigakkō faculty, a discussion Milne would eventually join and come to direct as the chief resident seismologist. As early as 1877, Perry and Ayrton had published a paper in the *Transactions of the Asiatic Society of Japan* describing a "recording seismograph" and how it might be connected to clocks and telegraphs at various stations around Tokyo, a plan that Milne would eventually accomplish with the help of the Kōbushō. Being physicists and not geologists, Perry and Ayrton did not call what they were doing "seismology," but rather "terrestrial physics."[11]

In 1878, two years before the Tokyo-Yokohama earthquake, Perry and Ayrton published and circulated locally a pamphlet, "On Structures in Earthquake Countries." The physicists were harshly critical of the practices of local architects, such as the design and construction of tall chimneys and heavy trussed roofs. The even heavier roofs of Japanese temples and houses, however, they declared to be seismically stable: "It was due to the viscous resistance opposed by the numerous joints and to the lavish employment of timber that the slowly vibrating Japanese house owed its comparative security."[12]

Thus even before Milne's survey of Yokohama and the Ginza, there was criticism of the Anglo-Japanese architecture project (and dissent from its characterization of Japanese buildings) from within the *yatoi* community itself. Voices that had initially spoken in the name of European art (even the Gothic Revival) returned to the same topic a few years later speaking the language of the physical sciences, and crediting Japanese roofs with "viscous resistance." Ayrton and Perry left Japan in 1878 and 1879 respectively, but not before Perry had developed a close relationship with Milne. Both physicists became overseas member of the Seismological Society on its founding in 1880, and Perry would subsequently do much to promote Milne's career in Britain.[13]

We cannot know if Christopher Dresser had contact with Tokyo's terrestrial physicists during his trip of 1876–77, but it is noteworthy that the term "pendulum," which he and like-minded authors used to describe the central mast of pagodas, also described the most basic component of nineteenth-century seismometers. Seismometers were essentially pendulums, and the most popular type were called "pendulum seismometers" and "inverse pendulum seismometers." According to the testimony of Conder's colleague Kozima, *daiku* already believed these masts to

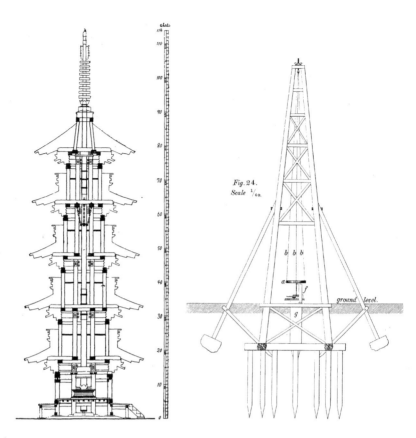

Fig. 24.
Scale 1/40.

b b b

a f

ground level.

g

FIGURE 5

Comparison of *(a)* the five-story pagoda at Nikko (from Ōmori
Fusakichi, *Bulletin of the Imperial Earthquake Investigation Committee* 9, 1918) with *(b)* an early pendulum seismograph of a type
invented and used in Tokyo (from James Ewing, "Earthquake
Measurement," *Memoirs of the Science Department, Tokio
Daigaku* 9, 1883). The *shinbashira,* or central mast, of the pagoda,
hanging from chains, can clearly be seen in Ōmori's cross-
section. Its resemblance to the pendulum used in seismographs
led seismologists to claim affinity between the two objects.

contribute to pagodas' earthquake stability. But comparing the central mast of a
pagoda specifically to a pendulum was, metaphorically speaking, moving the object
from the realm of architecture into the company of stable and instructive seismological instruments. It was through a similar linguistic transference that the roofs of
Japanese houses, shrines, and temples became proper objects of comment by physi-

cists (i.e., by their having demonstrated "viscous resistance" during periods of vibration).

Milne himself had contested the boundary between science and architecture before. His biographers tell the following story about a trip of his to Paris as a young geologist: "Beke [Sir Charles Beke, explorer and biblical scholar] suggested that his companion [Milne] should visit the Tuilleries which was then in the ruined state to which it had been reduced in the terrible days of the Commune. A sight, he said, well worth seeing. . . . He [Milne] came back laden with fossils he had found in the stones of the palace which seemed to interest him more than the building itself." And, quoting Beke: "[Milne's] first thought is the mineralogical character of each object that presents itself to his sight. As in the case of the Tuilleries, it is not the form, or age, or historical character of the buildings, so much as that stone of which it is built. It is the same with him all along; it is not landscape in which he is interested but the character of rocks."[14]

Milne is made to represent, both by his biographers and Beke, a new type of nineteenth-century man who drew his entire identity and language from one half of what was increasingly portrayed as a rigid divide between science and art. His reputation (including his self-representation) as a "specialist" would indeed become one source of Milne's power, just as the Seismological Society he founded seemed all the more focused and productive alongside the more generalist Asiatic Society, where Brunton and Cawley had read their papers.[15]

But at critical moments in his scientific writings, Milne paints landscape pictures. In his 1898 textbook, *Seismology*, for example, he introduces a discussion of factory chimneys with the comment that "in certain towns in Japan, like Osaka, [chimneys] are already covering the temples with a canopy of smoke and giving the city a Sheffield-like appearance." Whereas an author like Dresser or Cram (especially Cram) would linger over this scene and extract a fuller measure of dreadfulness, Milne uses a different, more powerful device, telling us in nearly the same breath that "whatever their [the chimneys'] form may be, when well shaken, after wavering back and forth through a distance of several feet, they nearly all fracture to a great extent vertically, and then collapse at about two-thirds of their height. To be on an eminence at the time of a strong earthquake, as many of my friends have been, and see tall chimneys swinging back and forth to join the ruins of the smaller chimneys from dwelling houses, is a sight which I have never witnessed. . . ."[16]

Yet a sight, to recall what Beke said of the Tuilleries, "well worth seeing." I am not suggesting here that Milne, or even Ayrton and Perry, are masking aesthetic concerns with scientific language. This is not a case of "masking" (i.e., deception), but of a certain convergence whose complexity still needs to be worked out. Standing on an eminence above a soot-blackened Japanese landscape, watching the tall chimneys sway and fall, Milne and his readers are not Brunton, Cawley, or Conder, laying up masonry down on the plain. It is uncertain in this and other passages whether, surveying this landscape in its entirety, Milne wants to help, or in some sense hinder.

If Milne was blind to the pleasures of European landscape, it might have been due to the less than gentle landscape from which he came—that of Lancashire in northern England. Milne would remember late in his career that, on first arriving in Japan, he "was struck by the wonderful clearness of the atmosphere at certain times of the year. I had been brought up in a town that received smoke from two counties (Lancashire and Yorkshire) . . . thus it was always smoking, except perhaps once or twice a year when we could see for about 7 miles. In Japan, however, I could see Fuji rising up 12,406 feet, at about a distance of 70 miles!"[17] Milne was so struck by Mount Fuji that he eventually photographed it from twenty-six different viewpoints and would continually refer to the mountain in scientific articles and addresses, even putting it on the cover of his seismological journal.[18] Milne was hardly alone, among European scientists in Japan, in finding this new landscape more to their liking—more invigorating, transforming, and evocative—than any they'd known.

"The factory chimney" and "the cottage" were, by the last quarter of the nineteenth century, classic literary tropes for the new industrial British world under construction and the pastoral world that was seen to be lost. Anglo-Japanese seismology would come to share with English literature of the same period a working landscape of solid thatched-roofed cottages and threatening red-brick chimneys. The very term "red-brick" evoked for sensitive Victorians the unstoppable mechanism of modern industry, the opposite color of green. Adding the element of earthquakes to the familiar troubled landscape of cottages and red-brick chimneys increased (and in a sense scientifically demonstrated) the cottage's virtue and the chimney's vice. More importantly, it reversed the fragilities, or relation of power, between the two objects and the regimes they stood for. No longer was the chimney stronger than the cottage, but far weaker. Nature had just possibly built into the "medieval" landscape of Japan a mechanism for keeping (or setting) things right.[19]

The power of seismology (or any other successful emergent science) lay in its ability to sense and construct convergence across a host of other already powerful domains. Tall red-brick chimneys were simultaneously inverted pendulums and symbols of controversial change. They were also "columns," as were pendulum seismographs and the overturned gravestones Milne used to draw his isoseismal lines. In the hierarchy of seismological usefulness, the column was more informative than the crack, which explains in another way why Milne, and later his student Ōmori Fusakichi, would always be intent on watching chimneys sway and fall. By noting the direction in which a column fell and, even better, measuring how it rotated before it fell, certain earth movements could not only be mapped, but quantified. Thus did "the column" bring seismology into closer convergence with physics through mathematics, as "the red-brick chimney" brought it into convergence with British literary tropes, and "the pendulum" made it converge with pagodas, *daiku*, and the landscape of Japan. Each of these convergences would inevitably bring Milne into contest with his colleagues in architecture and engineering.

THE SEISMOGRAPH

Milne the British scientist had this in common with British architects and engineers: he too felt the insubstantiality of Japan as he vainly tried to "see" the 1880 earthquake roll through its wooden townscapes. The houses swayed about, then snapped back again to their original positions, leaving few readable inscriptions.[20] The brick walls and chimneys of the Europeans were inscribed with cracks, but these were confined to Tokyo, Yokohama, and a handful of large cities, widely dispersed. And except for the Ginza, they were not sufficiently uniform in design and construction to be reliable seismometers. Wrote Milne by way of apology after presenting his data for the 1880 disturbance: "If this earthquake had taken place in other countries where instead of a single town like Yokohama acting as one great seismograph there had been many cities to act in that capacity the results which would have obtained would no doubt have been more accurate and more numerous."[21]

It was this very problem of insubstantiality, however, that helped propel seismology in the direction of instrumentation and Milne toward membership in the Royal Society. The lack of traces in the postearthquake landscape of Japan meant that Milne and the other Anglo-Japanese seismologists devoted inordinate attention, by European standards, to inventing and using inscripting devices. "At this time," wrote Milne, "Tokyo was in reality a city of many [seismological] inventions . . . their name was legion."[22] In addition to the British physicists Ayrton and Perry, we know that *yatoi* such as the Dutch linguist G. F. Verbeck, German meteorologist Erwin Knipping, British civil engineer W. S. Chaplin, and German chemist Gottfried Wagener had all constructed seismometers of novel design by the end of the 1870s, each attempting in his own way to measure, quantify, or record the earth tremors regularly felt in Tokyo.[23] Seismometry (the instrumental study of earthquakes) seems to have been one of the few *yatoi* interests that transcended discipline and nationality—an interdisciplinary research project that, having as yet no home in the Meiji academy, found one in a private society composed largely of scientists and other teachers in state employment.

Thus did Milne open the first meeting of the Seismological Society of Japan in 1880 by remarking, "We shall see around us a mighty forest of pendulums, springs, and delicately balanced columns."[24] As with California's Home Brew Computer Club (the nursery of the personal computer) nearly a hundred years later, everyone appears to have shown up with their own device, intent on displaying it to like-minded inventors and gauging each other's strengths and weaknesses. Most of these instruments would never advance beyond the stage of prototype, but one stood out. At the same meeting James Ewing, Kōbudaigakkō professor of mechanical engineering and physics, unveiled his relatively sophisticated pendulum seismograph—essentially a seismometer attached to a disc of smoked glass (and later a continuous roll of smoked paper) on which various features of seismic waves could be permanently recorded. Subsequently modified, using ideas from a similar device by Kōbudaigakkō professor of telegraphy Thomas Gray (exhibited at the same gathering) and further tinkered with by Milne himself, the resulting "Ewing-Gray-Milne" seismograph became the instrumental kernel around which the "new" science of seismology was subsequently built, yielding as it did a product (a "seismogram") that was not only highly readable, but, like a telegram, vendible (between Tokyo and Europe) and reproducible in scientific reports and papers.[25]

The Ewing-Gray-Milne seismograph (sometimes shortened to the Gray-Milne seismograph, although Ewing had likely made the greatest personal investment) soon reordered the relationships between the disciplines and practices (or disciplinary practices) that had constituted seismology in its preinstrumental stage. Robert Mallet, the founder of observational seismology, was a civil engineer, and hence well trained in observing buildings and the way they failed. The new seismograph freed Milne and his fellow seismologists from a complete reliance on such objects and skills, from needing to search out and catalog architectural and engineering failures in order to do their science. It also meant that a seismologist was now more appropriately a physicist, like Ewing or Gray, or a geologist, like Milne, who was willing to learn from physicists how to use and even construct sensitive instruments. Physics was the epistemologically dominant British science, not only in Britain but at Kōbudaigakkō, where many of the faculty were connected in one way or another to William Thomson, soon to be Sir William, then Lord Kelvin, and later president of the Royal Society.[26]

Milne, in joining Ewing, Gray, Ayrton, Perry, and others in a new arena called "seismometry," initiated the reconstruction of seismology as a geophysical science, a new set of practices and instruments between two disciplines whose relations were elsewhere strained. Geology had been a rising science in the middle of the nineteenth century under Charles Lyell, but by the 1870s its status as the site from which new and controversial questions came had largely shifted to biology. Geology nonetheless remained close to the biological sciences, and thus on the wrong side of issues between Thomson and Charles Darwin over the age of the Earth (issues that, with the eventual triumph of Darwinism, it came to be on the right side of). Milne, as a geologist among physicists—physicists with personal links to the powerful Thomson, very much interested in earth phenomenon, and willing to invent new instruments to inscribe them—was in a position not only to wrest earthquakes away from civil engineers, but to reinvent, through earthquakes, "the geologist" himself as a user of sophisticated inscripting devices.[27]

With the deployment of the seismograph, Anglo-Japanese seismology did not, however, retreat from a world of bricks and mortar into one of finely calibrated instruments and inscriptions on paper. Seismology had been born in masonry, and Milne would never entirely abandon this birthright. Once he was able to produce reliable methods of inscription outside architecture and civil engineering— inscriptions no architect or engineer could dispute as the result of settling cracks or some other normative phenomenon—he made increasingly authoritative excursions back inside.

At the point of seismology's transition from masonry to machines was the main building of Kōbudaigakkō itself. Shortly after the 1880 earthquake, Milne had discovered "a considerable number of cracks in the north-east end of the museum buildings." Over the next few years Kōbudaigakkō's main building, designed in 1877 by the French-Scottish architect Alfred Chastel de Boinville, would become Milne's largest single seismometer. His unique access to the site allowed him to not only tag, date, and measure existing cracks in the building's foundations, but monitor a series of seismograph-like devices attached directly to its walls. The performance of European masonry during Japanese earthquakes was now to be recorded on etchings in smoked glass, using the very building that George Cawley listed (in 1878) as among the "few examples of brick and stone structures in Tokyo by foreign architects which might be copied by native builders with advantage"—a building that was "proof of the confidence [its] architect has in brick and stone for an earthquake country, and of his professional courage and ability."[28] By the mid-1880s Milne's seismographs were recording during moderate earthquakes the walls of Kōbudaigakkō swaying back and forth like an inverted pendulum.[29]

As late as 1884, in an article published in the *Kagaku ʒasshi* (Science Magazine), Milne would still tell a Japanese audience: "According to experience, architectural materials in an earthquake country should be first of all bricks, and secondarily stone."[30] Yet in his report that very same year to his English patrons, the British Association for the Advancement of Science, Milne wrote: "I have previously called your attention to the great differences in effects which moderately strong earthquakes have produced upon European and Japanese types of buildings, the former being more or less shattered whilst the latter escape without any apparent damage. In one case we have a building of brick and mortar firmly attached by its foundation to the shaking earth, whilst on the other we have a light wooden structure resting loosely on boulders."[31]

Milne revealed in the same report that, acting on this difference in the performance of European and Japanese buildings, he had erected in 1883 an experimental "earthquake-proof" structure on the Kōbudaigakkō campus. It was constructed not of masonry but of timber, and rested not on a foundation, but "on four cast-iron balls." This building subsequently proved too flexible: it was sent moving back and forth by strong winds. Continuing experiments through 1884 eventually yielded a true aseismic structure—one that remained relatively stable through both earthquakes and typhoons. Milne's methodology had been to bed the piles forming the structure's foundation on smaller and smaller balls, eventually settling on shot (round bullets).[32]

It was becoming clear by this time that Milne intended seismology to overlap with, and perhaps even include, "constructive science," that the authority of his science would not, he believed, end at the surface of the Earth ("nature"), but extend up into the design and substance of structures clinging to that surface ("culture"). That Milne was increasingly confident in his ability to develop alternatives to standard European building methods came from his observation of Japanese ones. His ability to recreate an aseismic building with European materials (including linguistic ones), along with the results of his instrumental readings from Kōbudaigakkō, emboldened him to send a paper, "On Construction in Earthquake Countries," to London's Institution of Civil Engineers in 1885.

Prior to this, Milne's word pictures of European architecture "shattered" by Japanese earthquakes had appeared only in scientific publications. Now he brought the same imagery into the headquarters of British engineering itself. If Milne was right, then *yatoi* architects and engineers hadn't ought to continue designing brick and stone structures in strict accord with European models. They should rather investigate new structural systems, and even new principles of structural dynamics, which had originally been suggested to Milne by observing the work of *daiku*.

In a book written even prior to his London paper, but published the following year, Milne offered models of two ideal types of earthquake-resistant structures: a "steel box," which "even were it to roll down a high mountain would suffer but little damage," and a "wicker basket," which would survive the same test by virtue of its flexibility. "Wicker basket" was a code word for Japanese roofs, and followed from Ayrton and Perry's theory that such roofs offered "viscous resistance" to seismic motion. As Milne would later put the matter in his textbook, *Seismology* (1898): "In Japan we find that temples and other large buildings with heavy roofs have beneath the supporting timbers and the superstructure a multiplicity of timber joints forming corbel-work, which at the time of an earthquake yields, and therefore does not communicate the whole of the motion from the parts below to those above."[33]

Although more impressed by Japanese success with "wicker baskets" than European attempts to make masonry structures "steel boxes," Milne's dual metaphors invested the Japanese actuality and the European ideal with equal cogency, providing the architecture/engineering project with a way out of the dilemma Milne was himself leading it into.[34] He allowed that masonry buildings could become "steel boxes," however, only at an increased price. If they wanted to continue to use masonry in earthquake countries, Milne told the engineers in London, they would have to abandon the arch (which had been designed to resist gravity, not horizontal motion), align windows along diagonal rather than vertical and horizontal axes, break the connections between roofs and walls (or else eliminate roofs altogether by making them flat), dig much deeper foundations, and lay up much thicker walls (tied together with steel or iron rods).[35] Following Milne's suggestions would not only have made masonry buildings prohibitive for all but the largest and most important projects, but would change forms and appearances sanctioned by countless generations of European practice—forms and practices not just "used" by architecture and engineering, but virtually constitutive of each discipline.

An alternative option Milne held out for European buildings was to make them, as much as possible, "of light materials." Bricks might be made hollow and thinner, plaster be replaced by papier-mâché, and chimneys be made of sheet iron instead of brick. In other words, European buildings could become aseismic by either exaggerating their characteristics in the direction of the steel box, or by becoming altogether less solid, more flexible, and ultimately less substantial (i.e., tending toward "the Japanese").[36]

Subtextually, Milne was also arguing for a new, practical, and epistemological relationship between architecture and engineering on the one hand, and his own science on the other. His experimental gifts to the engineering community were delivered as "general principles." He left "all details of construction" to the architect and engineer. There was one very important detail, however, that he reserved for seismology: the necessity of conducting seismic surveys of building sites, to determine their geology and thus predict the likely character of their movement. Seismology spoke to the other constructive disciplines in the name of a newly unstable and dangerous earth. It would either map the terrain to show architects and engineers where they could safely build, or consult for the same purpose at the beginning of individual building projects. Milne, Conder, and other Kōbudaigakkō professors supplemented their incomes with consulting contracts with the various Japanese ministries, some of which equaled or surpassed their teaching salaries. The seismic survey could thus also be seen as the refashioning of the geological survey—the bread and butter of mining consulting—into a new instrument of geological consultantship within the domain of civil engineering and architecture.[37]

As a result of Milne's paper, tensions that had long been building in the close world of *yatoi* Tokyo began to be released in the professional societies in London. Henry Dyer, former Kōbudaigakkō principal and Milne's former superior, appended comments to Milne's paper (in the *Proceedings of the Institution of Civil Engineers*) intended to demolish every one of its claims. There was no necessity to improve or innovate building methods in Japan, he wrote, because if only the "elementary principles" of European buildings were followed, "little or no damage would have been done [to masonry buildings] by ordinary earthquakes." As for "extraordinary shocks by which the earth was rent asunder," he continued, "it did not seem possible to take any precautions." Milne's experiments were not only unnecessary and futile, suggested Dyer, but subversive to other Kōbudaigakkō projects. "The supposed necessity of making special designs for buildings in earthquake countries," he warned, "had a very bad effect on the development of architecture in those countries." By undermining Japanese faith in the stability of masonry, Milne was fostering instability across a wider front of foreign knowledge.[38]

Dyer was particularly sensitive to Milne's use of Kōbudaigakkō as a seismograph, and to the suggestion of foundational problems in the institution Dyer had built. In an echo of the earlier argument over cracks in the Ginza, Dyer wrote that Kōbudaigakkō's cracks "were not caused by the earthquakes but by the foundations not being sufficient" due to the Japanese government's desire to economize. The resulting settling had even been reluctantly "anticipated" by the architect. Earthquakes may have caused the cracks to lengthen, he conceded, "but not to any serious extent." In a sign of uncertainty, however, Dyer went so far as to relieve architect de Boinville of responsibility even for future earthquake damage. He argued that the Kōbushō's design program had called for a fire-proof building, and not an earthquake-proof one. The architect had thus taken "very few special precautions" against earthquakes. The Kōbudaigakkō building, suggested Dyer, was not to be used as a test case of the applicability of constructive science to Japan.[39]

Dyer's argumentative strategy would become a pattern in the years ahead. On the one hand, he was claiming that "elementary principles" of European civil engineering were sufficient to protect the new European infrastructure from Japanese earthquakes. On the other, the failure of any particular "example" would constitute evidence that the same elementary principles had not been followed, generally due to the intervention of a third party—the economizing client in the case of Kōbudaigakkō, or the unskilled worker, or their venal combination, the economizing worker or "jerry builder." The third party was in every instance Japanese, so that the failure of elementary principles to be given "a fair hearing" in Japan—that is, the failure of foreign knowledge to find its embodiment in buildings designed by actual foreigners—would generally be the fault of the Japanese themselves.

If Milne was right about Japanese carpentry, however, then a principal justification for the masonry project—protecting Japan from a previously unmanageable nature (a nature whose worldwide management was increasingly considered to be a Euro-American specialty)—was seriously flawed. Dyer thus turned attention to Japan's fragility, repeated the verdict of Brunton that "it [is] almost impossible to imagine a structure worse adapted for resisting earthquake shocks" than a Japanese house. The invariable fate of such buildings was "total collapse with a comparatively slight shock." Cognizant of how *daiku* impressed audiences at international exhibitions with their skillful use of tools, Dyer took care once again to separate the craftsman's hand from his mind: "Although the Japanese carpenters were very expert in the use of their tools, and the joints of their buildings were very neatly made, they had little or no idea of the proper disposition of material to ensure approximate uniformity of stress, and it was often found that the joints were snapped asunder on a sudden shock. . . ."[40] There seemed, moreover, no possibility of reform as long as *daiku* remained in charge of construction. *Daiku* experimentation with "Western-style" building systems was, to Dyer, "unthinking copying." These "so-called foreign houses," by which he meant *wayō setchū* buildings, and particularly those of wood-framed masonry, were critically "deficient both in strength and stability" when set beside the unadulterated masonry structures of the Europeans.[41]

The argument generated by Milne's paper in London reverberated in Tokyo. Conder, speaking before the newly formed Association of Japanese Architects that same year (1885), cited Milne's comments before saying: "The statements that, besides the general precaution of building in wood, there were, in connection with the modes of [Japanese] construction, inventions and arrangements specially fitted to cope with seismic disturbances, I regard as groundless fantasies. . . . I have failed to find any methods of construction in old Japanese buildings which recommend themselves as having seismic advantages, even accepting the seismologists' definition of what are seismic advantages." The typical features of Japanese wooden buildings, which Conder lists, were in his opinion "all in exact antagonism to the principles pointed out by the seismologists themselves." "The flexibility of the material [wood]," he went on, "is the one and only advantage, and this applies to all wooden structures whatever."[42]

There are two differences to note between constructive science as defended by Conder, and the same science as defended by Dyer, which measure small but important shifts in masonry's earthquake-resistance since Dyer left Japan in the early 1880s. For one thing, Conder no longer cites the flexibility of wood as a weakness, but, like Milne, as a potential advantage. When Dyer left Japan, flexibility ("Japanese-ness") was weakness, and rigidity ("European-ness") was strength. Conder is no longer certain that flexibility might not also equal strength. Yet in conceding the strength of flexibility, the latter property ceases to be "Japanese" in his account, and is pointedly extended "to all wooden structures whatever."

In conceding that wood may be both flexible and aseismic, however, Conder was not conceding that it should continue to be used, in Japan or anywhere else. Faced with resistance from the seismologists, Conder and Dyer each switch the force of nature that constructive science has been shielding Japan against. It is because of fire, Conder tells his former students in the same paper, that they must "discard, as much as possible, materials destructive to the security and subversive of the prosperity of the people."[43]

Dyer left Japan when seismology as an institution (i.e., a society and a journal) was only two years old and still lacked important patronage. To him and the other members of the civil engineering institute that published dismissive criticism of Milne's paper (a list that included R. H. Brunton and other former "Japan hands"), seismology was a weak and venturesome science seeking to undermine stronger ones before a Japanese audience. Their counterarguments thus ignored Milne's seismographs and seismograms, which in the largely noninstrumental culture of civil engineering did not yet constitute evidence. To Conder, on the other hand, who was still in Japan, surrounded by seismographs and witness to seismology's growing influence there, it became second nature to argue with Milne on the latter's grounds (i.e., accepting the seismologists' definition of what are seismological advantages). Indeed, one of Conder's own students, Taki Daikichi, had cribbed Milne's formulas describing the movement of masonry walls for his 1883 graduation exercise, and even expressed interest in the seismologist's unorthodox design recommendations.[44] A guarded interest in Milne among Japanese architecture students would only grow in the years ahead.

Milne published the first textbook of his new science, *Earthquakes and Other Earth Movements*, in the same year (1886) as the controversy raged over his paper "On Construction in Earthquake Countries." In two chapters on constructive science, he rather explicitly took on for the first time the role of challenger to architectural and engineering authority. Milne's textbook repeatedly praises the seismic resistance of Japanese wooden construction, while denigrating European construction for its absence. It also, for the first time, names opponents and allies.

> The ordinary European house, however solidly and strongly it may be built, is not sufficient to meet the conditions imposed upon it. What is required is something that will give way—an approximation to the timber frame of a Japanese house, so strongly condemned by Mr. Brunton and others.
>
> So far as my own experience has gone, I must say that I have never seen any signs in the Japanese timber buildings which could be attributed to the effects of earthquakes, and His Excellency Yamao Yōzō, Vice Minister of Public Works, who has made the study of the buildings of Japan a specialty, told me none of the old temples or palaces, although many of them are several centuries old, and although they have been shaken by small earthquakes and also by many severe ones, show any signs of having suffered.[45]

Yamao had not only been Dyer's direct superior within the Kōbushō, but the two had studied engineering in the same Scottish classroom. Yamao's observations about the seismic resistance of Japanese architecture were beyond publishable refutation, at least by members of the Kōbudaigakkō faculty. Milne had also been cultivating a patronage relationship with Yamao since at least 1880, when Yamao had been offered, but declined, the presidency of the Japanese Seismological Society. Dyer had argued with Milne in London over what should or should not be taught by Englishmen to Japanese. Milne's enlistment of Yamao not only adds "Japanese testimony," but relocates the argument itself outside the bounds of the faculty club. Yamao, who in 1885 retained an authority over Milne that Dyer no longer exercised, was being invited into Milne's text as reader and judge as well as witness.[46]

It was rare of Milne, or Conder for that matter, to name opponents. The two never, for example, name each other. Conder argues always with "the seismologists" and Milne is generally vaguer still. Although we cannot be certain why Milne chose to immortalize Brunton in seismology's first textbook, he was likely seeking to distance himself not just from Brunton's argument, but from the man. Brunton, who was among the first *yatoi* to arrive when Japan was still under the Bakufu, and the first to return to Britain, was by that time something of a legend among *yatoi* and their Japanese handlers for his inability to "get along" with Japanese, for his nearly open racism. Milne was obviously not looking to curry favor with the Institution of Civil Engineering by naming Brunton, a respected member. The naming is another small sign that he was now writing at least partly for a local audience, one that, as more and more *yatoi* went home, was increasingly Japanese.[47]

SEISMOLOGY AS ETHNOGRAPHY

The debate traced in the last section should not be taken as a neutral ("objective") science critiquing hubris and racism uniquely embodied in British architects and engineers. A disjunction had occurred, for various and intricate reasons, between two colonial projects. Partly it was a disjunction in their frames of reference, and partly in their different practices, ambitions, and even patronage strategies. British seismologists had made an alliance of sorts with Japanese *daiku,* one that was subversive to British architectural and engineering interests. But Anglo-Japanese seismologists were not *daiku,* nor were they Japanese. At least not yet.

Among the many ambitions Milne had for seismology was that it inform "the student of national character."[48] Subtextual to his science was the "problem" of why the Japanese were as they were to British eyes, for example, "timid" and "fatalistic," a people who cultivated "the temporary" and not "the permanent." A working hypothesis for Milne and certain other members of the Seismological Society was earthquakes and volcanoes. The idea that much of what appeared odd and unusual about Japan could be explained by reference to its natural phenomena helps to account for the breadth and depth of *yatoi* interest in seismology, an interest that extended well beyond issues of how and why the earth moved. It equally helps account for the interest taken in seismology by a large and influential group of Japanese.

In a paper entitled "Earthquake Effects[,] Emotional and Moral," which Milne delivered before the Seismological Society in 1887, he wrote: "Nations which have been subjected to influences like these [earthquakes] may possibly acquire some slight peculiarities, characterizing them from nations which have been free from such influences. . . . Certainly it may be said that the successful or serious nations of the present day, characterized by their enterprise and commerce, are not those whose misfortune it has been to fight against unintelligible terrorisms of nature."[49] The modifier "unintelligible" allows the dike-building Dutch to remain with the "successful" nations, while the terms "present day" and "serious"—markers for the Scientific Revolution—modify the obvious successes of Greece, Rome, Byzantium, and Spain. Although these Mediterranean civilizations "have led nations," Milne admitted, they were also artistic and superstitious, with "a passion for games of chance" and "the cultivation of arts conducive to pleasure" (i.e., like the Japanese). Asked Milne: "Is it not likely that a continuation of these conditions might result in a disregard for the serious affairs of life, and unfit a nation for competition with those living in more favored regions?" "Where," he rhetorically asked, "can [we] find a light-hearted carelessness, pleasant geniality, and a happy disposition better developed than is met with in this country [Japan]?" His answer was Naples. Thus did Milne hope to build a common ethnography of what he referred to in this and other writings as "earthquake countries."[50]

The mechanism in Milne's scheme by which earthquakes had made nations "unfit" for "competition" resembles Darwinian selection, which informs its language throughout: "Not only may seismic forces have stimulated the imagination to the detriment of reason, but amongst the weaker members of a community, by the creation of feelings of timidity resulting perhaps in mental aberrations like madness and imbecility, the seeds have been sown for a process of selection, by which the weaker members in the ordinary course of racial competition must succumb."[51] The "community" that Milne describes seems at once Japan itself and the "community of nations" with which Japan is in "racial competition." He was simultaneously providing an explanation for "Japan" to an audience of Europeans, and attempting to isolate for an audience of westernizing Japanese the most fundamental barrier to their identity as successful Darwinian competitors.

Darwinian schema and language were then rampant among the younger, intellectual species of the Japanese archipelago. Milne could have been confident of sharing basic assumptions with those in his Japanese audience who had grown used to examining their "national character" through the eyes of foreign teachers and analyzing their "national condition" using a toolbox of foreign texts.[52] Among the original patrons of the Seismological Society was Imperial University President Katō Hiroyuki, one of the most famous Japanese proponents of Spencerian (social) Darwinism.[53] Katō would soon be the first president of the Imperial Earthquake Investigation Committee.[54]

Milne's own mix of Darwinism and geological determinism was informed in particular by Henry Thomas Buckle, whose *History of Civilization in England* was "a great favorite" among Imperial University students (according to the memoir of then–Prime Minister Itō Hirobumi) and had already inspired the first Meiji-period Japanese cultural history, Taguchi Ukichi's *Short History of Civilization in Japan* (published serially from 1877 to 1883).[55] It was on reading Buckle that Imperial University President Katō had famously converted, in 1879, from the doctrine of "natural rights" to that of "natural laws."[56] "Buckle," said Milne in his 1887 Seismological Society address, "shows how the wonder of a people may be excited with all great natural phenomenon."[57] Buckle presented England as the normative state of both society and nature, realms he explicitly linked. Britain owed its multiple successes, according to Buckle, to a lack of "destructive perturbations" that elsewhere had shaken societies off a natural evolutionary path toward liberal democracy.[58]

The gist of Milne's claim was that a major determinant of Japanese evolution was identical with the object of seismology, a science increasingly confident in its ability to mitigate these same factors through new types of construction, and eventually prediction. The seismograph, for all of its usefulness in recording earthquakes, was clearly imagined by its inventor and others to be evolving into a predictive machine. Controlling the "terrorisms" of destructive nature through fortification and prediction, Japanese would for the first time control their national/"racial" destiny.

The most novel aspect of Milne's ethnography, which may have further convinced him of its palatability to a Japanese audience, was its vitiation of the binarism "East and West." Japan was now to be classified with nations that were wellsprings of European civilization. Moreover, notions about inferiority and superiority so vaguely (and hence insidiously) contained in the broad "East and West"—a geographic determinism so general and multifaceted as to be beyond isolation and refutation—were shifted in the direction of natural, mechanical causes, which might be overcome in equally mechanical ways.

It testifies to the strength of the "East and West" polarity that at least one important member of Milne's audience attempted to preserve that mapping using Milne's own evidence. In the discussion following Milne's lecture, Basil Hall Chamberlain, Imperial University professor of philology and Japanese, claimed to have surveyed Japanese literature and poetry for references to earthquakes and found only a single one. Rather than concluding that Japanese culture had been relatively uninfluenced by the shaking of the earth, Chamberlain, seeking to bolster a part of Milne's case, cited the very absence of references to earthquakes as an indication of their profound effect, of their having produced a "lesser range of imaginative facility" in the Japanese mind. Certain as he and other Europeans were that earthquakes were the penultimate Japanese natural phenomenon, their absence from the national literature could be explained only by a gradual dulling of the collective imagination brought on by the phenomenon itself. Ignoring entirely Milne's category "earthquake countries," Chamberlain concluded that this lack of "imaginative facility" was what "distinguishes the Japanese, and Eastern Asiatics in general, from the nations of the European race." In Greece and Rome the same natural phenomenon had had the opposite cultural effect.[59]

Chamberlain's response was too much for Sekiya Seikei, appointed the year before to the first chair of seismology at the Imperial University. Sekiya pointed out that after the Ansei earthquake, which destroyed Edo in 1855, eighty works on earthquakes had been produced by Japanese authors, ranging from the scientific to the literary. In answer to Chamberlain's suggestion of Japanese passivity, Sekiya noted that the disaster generated great excitement and even spontaneous acts of charity. As for Milne's paper, Sekiya was more circumspect, saying only that Milne "threatens to exhaust all that there is for workers in seismology to investigate," a statement that could be read a number of ways.[60]

Sekiya's response to Chamberlain underestimated, if anything, the presence of earthquakes in Japanese historical and literary works. Andrew Markus has suggested that "in sheer volume, the Ansei earthquake ranks among the most extensively 'reported' events of early modern history." Most of the literature (and related objects such as board games) inspired by this event was anonymous in authorship, produced by Edo's *gesaku* (native prose) industry, and thus likely not "literature" in Chamberlain's eyes.[61] Neither, perhaps, were the drier, official accounts of earthquakes, which also had a long history of Japanese authorship. Sekiya and Milne's student Ōmori Fusakichi would subsequently collect excerpts from nearly five hundred books, diaries, and other written materials relating to over two thousand earthquakes between 416 A.D. and 1867, which were published in 1904 as "The Materials for the Earthquake History of Japan from the Earliest Times Down to 1866."[62] Access to this historical database of earthquakes, culled from written sources, would greatly aid the practice of Japanese seismology in the late Meiji period.

In replying to both Chamberlain and Sekiya, Milne sided with Chamberlain, however, despite Chamberlain's mangling of Milne's argument. "All great calamities produce mental effects," stated Milne, "and with savage nations these were more permanent than with civilized nations." Chamberlain's evidence described for Milne a permanent effect from the period of Japan's primitiveness, while Sekiya's was drawn from the late Tokugawa period, when Japan was more civilized. How the intense interest in the Ansei earthquake could have arisen in spite of a "permanent" dulling effect on the Japanese imagination was a question that went unasked.[63]

It also escaped comment that much of Milne's evidence of "timid" feelings and mental strain was drawn not from the community of Japanese, but the community of foreigners in Japan. His paper actually begins with the effects of an earthquake on "a visitor in an earthquake country." The foreigner develops a "feeling of timidity" over time through repeated seismic events, one advanced rather than mitigated by his contact with the local (foreign) community. "The reason that the mental condition of the new comer becomes changed is possibly the influence of those with whom he is associated, who have gradually impressed him with what might be the result of the gentle motion he feels, or perhaps it is an increasing nervousness and fear as he gradually recognizes his utter inability to avert these disturbances or predict their consequence. In this way a whole community by repetitions of small earthquakes may be gradually worked into a state of mental nervousness."[64] Milne gives the concrete example, obviously from a personal experience, of a dinner party interrupted by an earthquake, where "the chandeliers commenced to oscillate": "Some [guests] rise from their seats, others perhaps for example's sake, perhaps from stupification, keep their places, but each fixes his gaze upon his neighbor."[65] Thus was "gradually develop[ed] an increasing terrorism" that according to Milne had even been responsible, "in the case of persons of delicate health," for death.[66]

Milne was not alone in depicting Japan's foreign residents as suffering from permanent feelings of anxiety. Dyer wrote of "the numerous nervous disorders so common among the foreign residents in Japan"[67] and Cawley of "the shock to the nervous system induced by an ordinary earthquake." Cawley credited his own nervousness "more to the creaking and rocking motion of a flexible house than the vibrations of the ground." It was partly "to palliate this nervous shock," he wrote, that he preferred "rigid to flexible buildings."[68] Conder too had spoken in London of how Japanese houses "sway about in the most alarming manner."[69] It was the seismograph of the foreign body that, in the accounts of foreigners themselves, was most consistently recording shock and alarm. Japanese were generally described, in the same accounts, as being relatively impervious to the same effects. Hence the importance of the foreign body (specifically the foreign nervous system) as an earthquake "witness" in Milne's account. "Foreign" feelings—terror and dread—became in these accounts normative reactions. Their absence among Japanese was at the root of the phenomenon to be scientifically explained, yet through evidence provided, in large part, by the foreign body itself.

Milne's paper and the follow-up discussion demonstrate that seismology was not just subterranean science. Like so many nineteenth-century science projects, it was also bedrock for new constructions of race, even if the category "earthquake countries" (and its less visible twin, "nonearthquake countries") threatened to disrupt the controlling binarism "East and West," and even if "earthquake countries" and other biogeologic mappings suggested that Japan's "problems" might be not simply "racial" but environmental, and even mechanical—that they might be "fixed" by controlling nature.

Seismology and architecture had this in common: both sought to explain national character with reference to geology. In the case of architecture, it was who used stones and how, and who didn't use them and why. Seismology and architecture had a common origin in mines and quarries. They both plumbed the "permanent" and eschewed the "temporary." Yet Milne's "earthquake countries" constituted a remapping impossible for either architecture or engineering, whose own origin stories were set in Milne's "unsuccessful" Mediterranean basin. Architecture could never have accepted an ethnogeography in which imagination was pathologized, and the "art countries" Italy and Japan were separated from Britain by a line of "reason." In civil engineering's map of Eurasia, on the other hand, Japan was simply a lone wooded isle at the outer periphery of a stone-using continent.

ARCHITECTURE AS BIOLOGY

Biology not only informed Milne's ethnogeologic geography but also undergirded his and other foreign scientists' conviction that Japanese buildings must have "adapted" over time to earthquakes and destructive nature. To Englishmen trained in the natural sciences, it would have seemed "natural" by the 1870s that there was a close fit between indigenous buildings and nature, that "native" building systems would have "evolved" survival mechanisms suited to their local environments. This assumption was so basic to seismology (geology sharing an important border with the biological sciences) that it was rarely articulated. It was clearly among the factors, however, that prevented Tokyo's British and American *yatoi* from teaching their Japanese students, and communicating among themselves, in a single foreign language.

The debates occurring within and around the biological sciences in the last quarter of the nineteenth century were as yet distant from architecture and engineering, at least as they were taught and practiced in Japan. To these disciplines, Newtonian mechanics was much closer and more "real" than Darwinian or Lamarckian biology. Concerned above all with gravitational force, the image- and language-world of civil engineering was dominated by "resistance." Even when a word was shared between biology and constructive science, it did not necessarily share a common sense or meaning. When Brunton wrote in 1873 that Japanese buildings were "of all structures, the worst adapted" to (earthquake-prone) Japan, he was constructing a sentence that would have made little sense to students of biology. Yet it was not unreasonable when spoken to other civil engineers, who conceived nature as a force to be "adapted," rather than one that primarily adapts.[70]

Unquestioningly, engineers knew more than seismologists, geologists, and biologists about the difficulty of adapting (or, to use the term they really preferred, "overcoming") natural (i.e., mechanical) forces. They knew how difficult it was a build a bridge and have it stand. Mistrusting the abilities of Japanese to resist phenomenon as sublime as earthquakes without masonry and iron, Newtonian physics, and large amounts of capital and disciplined labor, was not only a racist position. British civil engineers, who knew that they needed all of those things and more simply to resist gravity, and even then sometimes failed, could not believe that Japanese had solved the problem of saddling much more ferocious and mysterious forces while lacking these and other advantages.

Architects also knew more about certain things than seismologists, geologists, biologists, and civil engineers. They knew, for example, that the category "buildings" was divisible not just by geography and materials, but also by class. The raison d'être of their profession was the material, spatial, and ornamental expression of the brutal but magnificent fact of social and political difference. They believed (so foundationally that, again, it was never stated) that buildings were "adapted" not primarily to nature but to power. It would have been their sense that, if pagodas stood, it was because the Buddhist priesthood was powerful enough to command them to do so, by commanding *daiku* talent. Architects could not have believed, constitutionally, that Japanese unable to afford "architecture" could nonetheless protect themselves from the calamities of nature or power, or nature and power working together.

The biological reading of Japanese architecture was manifest as early as Christopher Dresser, who, besides being a professional designer, was a well-known botanist and had actually taught that subject at South Kensington.[71] It is even more manifest in Edward S. Morse, the Imperial University professor of zoology who was the first to teach Darwinian theory in Japan. A scholar and collector of brachiopods, Morse's cataloging of Japanese sea shells soon expanded in the direction of human habitations. He eventually produced a three-hundred-page treatise on ordinary Japanese houses, profusely illustrated with his own sketches, published in 1886 as *Japanese Homes and Their Surroundings*. Recently republished in paperback, the book is still the standard English-language text on Meiji-period domestic architecture.[72]

When Morse moved to cataloging Japanese houses, however, they were not clearly marked as belonging to the domain of architecture. Just as pagodas were first examined by a botanist, and the roofs of Japanese temples came to be examined and explained by physicists, Japanese houses were first picked up as scholarly objects by a zoologist. Science so easily extended its inquiries in each case from the natural to the cultural in Japan, because "nature" and "culture" there were not neatly demarcated. Architecture, which helped guard that border in Europe, was uncertain about its jurisdiction in this new wooden place; architects, engineers, and scientists were all equally unclear about which side of the great divide to put the work of *daiku* on.[73]

On the other hand, Morse's work constructs its own divide, cutting across nature and culture, between European and American ways of knowing. The myth of a unified Western knowledge was undergirded by that of a unified Western geography. The exchange between Cram and Stratham demonstrates how English and American attitudes toward Japan could differ over differing knowledge about wood. Although many Americans absorbed the British sense of wood as a "temporary" material and one less "architectural" than stone, they also, like the Japanese, lived in wooden houses. Morse, a skilled classifier of similarity and difference in brachiopod architectures, made the difference in American and English comfortability with Japanese "fragility" explicit: "An Englishman particularly . . . recognizes but little merit in the apparently frail and perishable nature of these structures [Japanese houses]. He naturally dislikes the anomaly of a house of the lightest description oftentimes sustaining a roof of the most ponderous character, and fairly loathes a structure that has no king-post, or at least a queen-post truss; while the glaring absurdity of a house that persists in remaining upright without a foundation, or at least without his kind of foundation, makes him furious."[74] This is also the voice of an Anglophobe or, more accurately, someone who came to admire Japan more than Europe, mapping them as poles that America stood between.

Morse was also unusual among English-speaking writers in dismissing concern with Japan's flammability. In doing so he shows an American's comfortability not only with wood but with fire. Conflagrations were another shared trait of the United States and Japan that differentiated them from modern Europe.[75]

> A fireproof building is certainly beyond the means of a majority of this people, as, indeed, it is with us; and not being able to build such a dwelling, they have from necessity gone to the other extreme, and built a house whose very structure enables it to be rapidly demolished in the path of a conflagration. Mats, screen-partitions, and even the board ceilings can be quickly packed up and carried away. The roof is rapidly denuded of its tiles and boards, and the skeleton framework left makes but slow fuel for the flames. The efforts of the firemen in checking the progress of a conflagration consist mainly in tearing down these adjustable structures.[76]

Firemen (tobi) in Edo and early Meiji Japan were closely allied with daiku, who were not only numerous, widespread, and used to organizing other artisans or workers, but had the skills and tools to quickly dismantle wooden structures.[77] That Meiji Tokyo was a city of renters helps explain why the householders in Morse's sketch are more concerned with rescuing furnishings than entire house-frames. As Jordan Sand has pointed out, rented houses typically came without tatami mats or fusuma (interior sliding screens), which were leased to tenants by specialized businesses.[78]

Morse's is one of very few foreign accounts that show Japanese proactively resisting fire. Compare his passage, for example, to one by former British consul Sir Rutherford Alcock, in which Japanese are said to "take the burning down of a whole quarter periodically, much as they do the advent of an earthquake or a typhoon—calamities beyond the power of man to avert. They build their houses accordingly with the least possible expense, as foredoomed sooner or later to be food for the flames."[79] Alcock's account of Japanese passivity ignores not only the existence of firemen but a centuries-long history of fire-safety laws, such as the 1661 regulation mandating the replacement of thatch with tile in urban areas.[80]

While Alcock's unfamiliarity with Japanese building regulations is understandable, less so is his failure to mention the fireproof dozo or kura (private warehouses) that peppered the wealthier urban neighborhoods. Daiku had indeed developed a relatively fire-proof structural system, but one whose expense restricted it, at least in the Edo period, to specialized buildings for the storage of valuables. Due to the application of successive layers of earthen plaster over an unusually sturdy wooden framework *(dozō-zukuri)*, fire and earthquakes could, within limits, be jointly controlled. As wealth increased with commerce in late Meiji, it was *dozō-zukuri*, more than brick-masonry, particularly for buildings such as stores and banks, that became the most reasonable fire-proofing solution.[81]

The system of "wood-framed masonry," which I previously described as an architectural pidgin—a compromise between masonry and carpentry, architecture and indigenous building—might also have been understood by clients and builders as a new form of *dozō-zukuri*. Applying masonry facades over wooden frameworks accomplished one of the tasks of applying mud—it kept the fire away. Wood-framed masonry was in this sense not only a "compromise" between the foreign and the indigenous, but a new expression, using foreign material, of an existing indigenous principle: a dual resistance to both earthquakes and fires, and, moreover, a resistance that, in the form of the *dozō*, had been given material expression by *daiku* long before.[82]

With a wit and irony rare among the parties to the earthquake debate, Morse questioned the credentials of any Englishman to advise Japanese on how to resist destructive nature. "The observation of a Japanese has shown him that from generation to generation the houses of his people have managed to sustain themselves; and if in his travels abroad he has chanced to visit England, he will probably recall the fact that he saw more dilapidated tenements, tumble-down shanties, broken-backed farm-houses, cracked walls, and toppling fences in a single day in that virtuous country where there are no typhoons or earthquakes, than he would see in a year's travel in his own country."[83]

Yet irony was as far as Morse would go in contesting the seismic inadequacy of Japanese architecture. He does not mention earthquakes a second time in over three hundred pages of almost encyclopedic detail, including a section on carpentry. Morse turned "the problem of Japanese carpentry" into "the problem of Englishman unused to carpentry." Yet he did so in a witty prose form not meant to be taken for "science." His very investment in scientific rituals of testing and proof likely advised him to mark such criticisms as ironic and "literary."

Nonetheless, with Milne's *Earthquakes and Other Earth Movements* and Morse's *Japanese Homes and Their Surroundings* published the same year (1886), the project of a masonry Japan—which had from the beginning been promoted on the basis of science as much as art—found itself undermined from within the community of "scientific men" in which *yatoi* architects and engineers also counted themselves members. Conder showed his sensitivity to insider criticism by characterizing such arguments as "romantic and fallacious prejudices" that "sound like a mockery when coming from the lips of those who at the same time advocate advance in other kindred sciences."[84]

FOUR · The National Essence

THE NATIVIST TURN

So far we have been tracing a debate within a relatively closed circle of foreign academics attempting to make sense of a place that was not their home. Japanese—students, young professors, and bureaucrats—occasionally contributed to this foreign-directed discourse, but without critically altering its dynamic. Amid massive social and political changes from the late 1860s to the mid-1880s, a period of relative seismic quietude in Japan, Japanese journals and newspapers were far more interested in domestic politics, foreign policy, and new habits of dress, diet, and religion than in intractable forces of nature. The Meiji government patronized architecture primarily as a branch of diplomacy, geology as an aid to mining, and engineering as the means to industrialization. Within the economy of early-Meiji public discourse, little space was reserved by the Japanese for catastrophe, which would not have accorded well with the period's surface optimism and drive toward "civilization and enlightenment."

This began to change in the later 1880s, as debates among foreigners were met, if not imbricated, by a more widespread Japanese critique of the westernizing project itself. Under the slogan "preservation of the national essence" *(kokusui hozon)*, things "Japanese" were positively reexamined, and "foreigner worship" named and problematized by young intellectuals of the Seikyōsha (Society for Politics and Education), led by Shiga Shigetaka and Miyake Setsurei.[1] Educated by Western teachers and texts, this generation was able to "speak back" in the language of science, art, and nation, while constructing a Japan based largely on indigenous aesthetics and landscape. *Kokusui* (national essence) was inscribed onto "the land itself," according to Julia Thomas, particularly after Shiga's publication of the best-selling *Nihon fūkeiron* (Japanese Landscape) in 1894.[2] Coincidentally or not, the actual landscape of Japan became more seismically active in the late 1880s, starting with an earthquake that shook Tokyo in 1887 and the explosion of the Bandai-san volcano the following year, events that would begin to increase the popular audience for seismological teaching. Thus would the Japanese politics of landscape and the Japanese science of earthquakes—which contained within itself a theory of landscape—develop with a certain synchronicity.

The Seikyōsha, and its journal *Nihonjin* (which began publication in 1888), was only one articulate channel, however, for an emergent multifarious nationalism. While the promulgation of the constitution in 1889 helped the Imperial state galvanize patriotic feeling, emergent public opinion focused on the government's continuing inability to revise the hated "unequal treaties." The state made a major concession to conservatives in 1890 with the Imperial Rescript on Education, with its invocation of "teaching bequeathed by Our Imperial Ancestors." The new nativism had subterranean chambers as well. In 1889 the *Japan Weekly Mail*, calling *kokusui hozon* "the guiding principle, the first duty, of the present generation," dated the advent of this "mood" to 1886, "when the adaptation of foreign female costume became an article of official faith. . . . It was just when an undercurrent of discontent had been set flowing by this bold innovation that the capital witnessed something like a carnival of social entertainments in foreign style."[3] Historians have discussed the nativist turn of the later 1880s as releasing tensions between generations, between "Western" and "Japanese" identities, and between national aspirations and continuing fears of colonization.[4] The editor of the Yokohama newspaper detects something else: "Western learning" by Japanese women as a trigger to essence preservation, a moment of instability in the gender of foreignness itself.

One symbolic center of the new criticism was the Rokumeikan, a Euro-Saracenic brick building designed by Josiah Conder in 1882 and 1883 for the Ministry of Foreign Affairs. In the later 1880s it was the site of lavish government masquerades where Japanese politicians were known to dance with their wives and foreign guests. From Euro-Saracenic ornament, to Japanese men dancing, to Japanese women in European clothes, to foreigners wearing kimono at costume balls, the Rokumeikan was a temple to cross-dressing of every kind. Even English translations of its name reproduce gender ambiguity, some historians preferring

"Deer Cry Pavilion" and others "Hall of the Baying Stag." The Rokumeikan was also the very archetype of the "unduly luxurious buildings" Shiga and the Seikyosha were wont to censure, along with, incidentally, "civil engineering work which has not been urgently needed."[5] The fall of Prime Minister Itō Hirobumi in 1889 has been called "the end of the *Rokumeikan* era," so closely were he and his government ("the dancing cabinet") associated with the building in the minds of conservative opponents.[6]

The Rokumeikan era was likewise a period of transition in the Japanese academy. In 1886 the Kōbushō expired in bankruptcy and the government began to privatize state-run industries. Kōbudaigakkō became the engineering faculty of the new Imperial University (the present-day University of Tokyo), whose other branches had been established some years before by the rival Ministry of Education (Monbushō). This change coincided with the expiration of the contracts of many of the foreign professors. That conflicting views were suddenly and frankly expressed in the mid-1880s may have been due to the recognition that the Japanese use of *yatoi* was coming to an end. The faculty of the new university was composed mostly of young Japanese selected from the first generation of graduate students trained by foreigners.[7] Conder had already surrendered his position to one of his students, Tatsuno Kingo, in 1884; although he would lecture at the new university as late as 1888, he did so as an architect in private practice.[8] Conder would continue to be patronized by the powerful, however, such as the Iwasaki family of the Mitsubishi *zaibatsu*, who engaged him in the planning of the all-brick Marunouchi quarter adjacent to Tokyo Station, the capital's first modern office district.[9] He also remained an active participant in Japanese cultural politics through his leadership of the Association of Japanese Architects (Nihon Zōka-gakkai).

Architectural historian Cherie Wendelken has noted the political emergence in these same years, however, of Kigo Kiyoyoshi, *daiku* to the Imperial court. The project of building a new Imperial Palace, a site of conflict between architects and *daiku* since the 1870s, was suddenly given over to Kigo in 1887.[10] One factor may have been the relatively strong earthquake that shook Tokyo that January with "a frisky energy which frightened even those hardened folks into something very like a panic," in the words of *yatoi* engineer and journalist H. S. Palmer.[11] While Japan's bureaucrats and capitalists were willing to take the risk of building in masonry, the safety of the Imperial body was beyond experiment. Now the entire palace was to be wooden, Japanese, and *daiku*-designed and -built. Two years later (in 1889), Kigo was placed on the *zōkagaku* faculty at the Imperial University itself, now under the control of Tatsuno, and began teaching *daiku* work to architecture students. Kigo's instruction—

particularly field-work he conducted at shrines and temples—would eventually help invigorate the project, which Conder had found intractable but his students never abandoned, of discovering a "Japanese style" of modern architecture.[12]

As Western-style architecture became vulnerable to (if not generative of) cultural recoding, nature-resisting pagodas and chisel-wielding *daiku* appeared in Japanese literature of the same period as symbols of masculine virtue. *Gojūnotō* (Five-Story Pagoda) was the title of Kōda Rohan's influential novel of 1891. Rohan, one of the novelists most associated with a contemporary turn to Edo-period themes (another manifestation of *kokusui hozon*) tells a story of rivalry between a master *daiku* and a young journeyman over the building of a pagoda. The ambitious younger *daiku* seeks to convince a temple priest to allow him, rather than the master *daiku*, to undertake the project. After various intrigues the master concedes the pagoda to his rival, but on the condition that the resulting structure withstand the strongest earthquakes and typhoons. After the completion, and on the night just before the dedication, a huge storm comes up. The young *daiku* climbs to the top of the tower with a chisel, intending to ride out the storm, or use the chisel to kill himself if the tower falls. The typhoon lays waste to surrounding temples, but when it passes, the pagoda stands.[13]

Rohan's novel uses the five-story pagoda as a metaphor for the new Japan and the *daiku* as exemplar of virtue in its youthful builders. The exchanges between Conder and Dresser had ended only a few years before, and the argument between Conder and Milne was then fully engaged. Rohan (and his readers) not only takes for granted that *daiku* are resisting destructive forces, but his novel makes the act of resistance the very definition of manhood and Japanese-ness—and the inability to resist, a mandate for self-destruction.

There is one more related fault line to be mapped onto this shifting landscape: a rift between Japanese architecture and Japanese art, which, like every other manifestation of essence preservation involved foreign and Japanese personnel on both sides of the divide. As art historian Lawrence Chisholm points out, "Western approval was important, particularly for anti-Western opinion."[14] The American Ernest Fenollosa worked tirelessly in this period with Okakura Kakuzō, circles of Japanese painters, and elements of the Education Ministry, to delimit European painting and drawing (including European instruments and materials) in order to make space for a formative domain of "Japanese-style painting" *(nihonga)*. Their faction scored one success after another throughout the 1880s. Western-style paintings were excluded from government art shows in 1882, the conservative Kanga-kai (Painting Appreciation Society) was founded in 1884, its members sent abroad as a state-credentialed art commission by the Education Ministry in 1886, and a new government art school opened in 1889 that institutionalized instruction in "traditional" art as a function of the Imperial state.[15]

Fenollosa, who joined Milne's Seismological Society on arriving in Tokyo, had been hired to teach philosophy at the Imperial University on the recommendation of zoologist-turned-architectural historian Edward Morse. As Morse had lectured on Charles Darwin, Fenollosa lectured on Herbert Spencer, and both Americans ended up working at cross-purposes to Conder and Anglo-Japanese architecture. Each success of Fenollosa and Okakura at promoting *nihonga* further isolated and rendered more difficult Conder's attempt to keep Japanese architecture closely allied with European art. As a British gentleman, Conder never mentions Fenollosa or Okakura by name, just as he refrained from openly attacking Milne, but they are clearly the "official tyros" and "so-called connoisseurs" he refers to in an 1886 address before the Association of Japanese Architects. In 1885 the Fenollosa-Okakura faction had succeeded in banning the use of pencils from elementary-school art classes, substituting the brush. Pencils, which were seen as subversive to Japanese painting, were the principal tools of Japanese architecture and engineering.[16]

The retirement of Conder and the ascension of court *daiku* Kigo, the growing success of Fenollosa and Okakura in promoting traditional art, and the new intellectual and literary concern with preserving the national essence provided a context in which seismology's lessons about Japan's traditional architecture seemed increasingly to fit. The new science may even have contributed to the broader cultural turn by opening additional space for the positive reexamination of pre-Meiji knowledge and practice. The discipline of architecture, on the other hand, despite much concern with developing a Japanese national style, necessarily remained open to accusations of Eurocentrism. Kigo's appointment at Imperial University, for example, though unprecedented, signaled no sea change in the general attitude toward masonry in a department run by Conder's former students. Tatsuno Kingo, who held the university's chair in architecture into the Taishō period, would never design a wooden, *daiku*-like building, but carry a brick-with-stone-trim Queen Anne style (reinforced with significant amounts of imported steel) through over two hundred consecutive design projects.[17]

CONDER'S DILEMMA

More than any other figure in foreign Japan, Josiah Conder was caught in the interstices of its unstable binarisms. It is time to free him, to some extent, from the company of engineers like Brunton, Cawley, and Dyer, for his situation was altogether more complex. Although prone to speak for "science" and against "romantic and fallacious prejudices," his principal allegiance was to a culture of "art," which, at the time he lived, was reconstructing itself as a romance in which science played increasingly little part. Resident in what, to the European art world, was the most romantic of places, Conder's mission and that of his students was to relandscape it in accord with the westernizing inclinations of its native elite. This project increasingly distanced him from those streams of Western art and architecture then internalizing "Japan," even as it began to dissolve his authority to speak, within Japan, in the name of Western science.

Conder's situation is the more striking in that, like Christopher Dresser, and unlike his colleagues on the engineering faculty, he arrived with a disciplinary respect for Japanese abilities and with his mind on synthesis. He had apprenticed to William Burges, the great English gothicist and Japanophile, for whom "feudal Japan" and feudal England were indeed stereoscopic images, to return to Alcock's metaphor. Conder worked in Burges's office alongside E. W. Godwin, one of the founders of the Aesthetic movement, which sought to rework European art and architecture after Japanese design.[18] At a particularly difficult moment during his argument with the seismologists, in 1891, Conder wrote: "My desire and intentions on first arriving in this country were to follow, in new buildings, as far as possible, the character of the old architecture, and avoid losing the national type and style which already existed. . . . Why is it then, that these first ideas and resolutions have all disappeared, and that modern architects are engaged in erecting edifices almost completely in foreign style? It is because such theories as the above have proven impossible of practical realization."[19]

The dilemma that Conder could not (and could not have) overcome was that Japanese architecture was wooden framing, and the European Gothic tradition in which he trained and practiced was entirely masonry. "A translation of the native wooden style into more permanent materials," he wrote in 1893, proved "an impossible problem."[20] Stone and brick coursing would not reconcile with the open framework of wooden posts—the utter lack of solid walls—that was a central fact of Japanese building practice. One "solution" he latched upon was to selectively apply the decorative motifs of wooden buildings to stone ones, but its obvious artificiality left him unsatisfied. By the early 1880s he had turned, for his larger commissions, to a synthesis that was British colonial and completely detached from Japanese precedent: he used European forms decorated with Saracenic (Indian) elements. Drawing on the tradition of a distant but stone-using Asian country, he wrote shortly before his death, was the only way to maintain a "systematic method" when building in masonry, yet still convey an "oriental character." As Suzuki Hiroyuki has further pointed out, Conder placed Japan on a map of Buddhist Asia, a map convergent with the Indian-Chinese-Japanese order of lectures in the history and art section of the _zōka_ course.[21]

Suzuki has also suggested that Conder was discouraged in his early efforts to use Japanese design motifs by his Japanese patrons. As an architect, he was expected by the Meiji government and private clients to provide them with accurate Western-style ministerial buildings and country houses. His Japanese patrons were a revolutionary and westward-looking elite for whom art patronage was initially bound with up with foreign relations. State architecture in the Tokyo of the 1870s and 1880s was essentially crystallized diplomacy, a series of arguments in masonry for Japan's acceptance by and integration into a Europe-centered world order. Conder was Architect to the Government of Japan, a foreigner expected to lend and exercise foreign talents.[22]

Neither could a real (i.e., unconventional) synthesis have satisfied Conder's other patrons, the Royal Institute of British Architects, who had sent him to Japan as the Soane medalist and elected him a Fellow in 1884. The institute was his major connection to Burges and other former teachers and colleagues, to whom he also sent Japanese pupils, beginning with Tatsuno Kingo. The consumption by British architects of "Japanese design" did nothing to destabilize the importance of solidity, mass, and weight in their own design work. As late as 1893 Conder was still prefacing his remarks about "Japanese architecture," in papers sent abroad, by defending his combination of the two words.[23]

Pushed toward an abstract orientalism by European architecture's imbeddedness in stone, and his Japanese patrons' disinterest in expressing uniqueness or locality, Conder had to look outside his profession to satisfy a real desire for intimacy with Japanese art. He wrote books, not on architecture, but on flower arranging and landscape gardening. He wore kimono, and learned Japanese dance and Kabuki performance. While Dyer sent for and married his Scottish fiancée in Japan, Conder had a child with a geisha. Eventually he married another Japanese, Maenami Kume, and together they adopted his illegitimate child.[24] He even apprenticed to an elderly Japanese painter, Kawanabe Kyōsai, who gave him the name Kyōei (a combination of Kyōsai and the Japanese word for England). It was into painting that Conder poured the yearning for synthesis that he had ruled out of his architectural design work. Standing before a pagoda with Kawanabe, Conder taught him how to calculate perspective. In a long obituary he wrote at his master's death in

1889, Conder would describe Kawanabe as the man he had never become, one who respected "the scientific knowledge of anatomical form, perspective and sciography revealed to him in foreign works" yet was "a reverential copyist of all that was worthy in the works of the [Japanese] past."[25]

In the case of "Japanese architecture," on which he wrote authoritative articles for the Royal Institute, Conder reconciled love and displacement with the idea of a ligneous past and a lithic future. "Japanese architecture" became a site for archeological investigation and recording. Despite the great age of the pagoda at Hōryūji and other Japanese temples and shrines—unusual even by European standards—Conder stressed their imminent disappearance.[26] Archeology became the mechanism for their preservation as European-style inscription (i.e., architectural drawings). In Europe, archeology and modern design were coproductive, but Conder wrote of "an almost impossible gulf between the ancient and the modern [Japanese] architect," turning autobiography into historical process.[27] "To adopt the ancient methods of construction" to contemporary purposes, he wrote elsewhere, was "like trying to make modern cruisers and yachts in the materials and after the semblance of the picturesque old sea junks and fishing boats."[28] Stone and brick had become, in Japan, materials as modern as steel.

It was not only East and West that Conder could not reconcile in his professional work, but art and science, and here it was Milne and the seismologists who appeared to him as active agents pulling that fragile combination apart. Conder wanted an architecture "such as is consistent with the progress that is being made in the other arts and sciences" but also "an art culture that is fitted to go hand in hand with other branches of modern training."[29] This protomodernist formula would eventually find fulfillment, and Japanese designers would, ironically, be in the forefront of that synthesis. But it was not to happen in Conder's lifetime. Too many forces beyond his control had set themselves against it.

SEISMOLOGY AND THE MEIJI STATE

While Anglo-Japanese architecture was increasingly challenged by the new political mood of the 1880s, Anglo-Japanese seismology only grew in influence. Milne managed to remain at the Imperial University (as professor of geology and mining) longer than most of his foreign colleagues, and successfully cultivated patronage from an expanded array of governmental agencies and actors. The most tangible sign of his success was the establishment in 1886 of a chair in seismology at the Imperial University, the first of its kind anywhere in the world. The position went to Sekiya Seikei, originally the student of James Ewing; Sekiya became a protégé of Milne after Ewing's return to England. With Sekiya's premature death in 1897 (he had contracted tuberculosis while abroad), the chair would go to another of Milne's students, Ōmori Fusakichi.[30] These and other young Japanese research scientists filled the gap left by the steady departure, through the end of the decade, of most foreign members of the Seismological Society of Japan.

Milne remained after the others had gone because of a talent, evidenced from an early date, in cultivating patronage at home and abroad. After the original Ewing-Gray-Milne seismograph was built in 1881, he had taken the device to Britain and had a second one made by a Glasgow scientific instrument company, a project paid for by his patrons at the British Association for the Advancement of Science. The "new" device was taken back to Japan as a gift from the British Association to the Meiji Emperor in 1883. The Emperor had it set, on Milne's advice, inside the Imperial Meteorological Observatory, as the instrumental kernel of a new earthquake bureau. Thus began a formal relationship with the well-organized meteorologists that would greatly advance seismology's goals. The machine's seismograms were to be regularly sent to the British Association as well as consumed by domestic scientists.[31]

A device originally constructed in the Emperor's own workshops under the auspices of one of his employees, had been taken to Britain, constructed again, and returned to Japan as a gift from British science. The Emperor used it to provide valuable local data to those same English scientists. In the complex exchange relationship constructed around the Ewing-Gray-Milne seismograph, Milne was the agent mediating everyone's relationship to the device, which was, as its name makes clear, also his.

Milne was also allowed to organize an elaborate seismic exhibition at the palace itself. A miniature Japanese landscape complete with towns and villages was set up with an explosive charge buried in its center. By pushing a button at Milne's direction, the Emperor caused an "earthquake" to lay this miniature Japan to ruin. "That[,] sire," Milne later recorded himself as saying, "is exactly the way an earthquake does its work."[32] This story, as told by Milne and transmitted by his biographers, places English scientist and Japanese Emperor in the classic roles of foreign teacher and native pupil. Yet in order for Milne to speak with authority about earthquakes, he had increasingly to cultivate the patronage of the Imperial state outside Kōbudaigakkō and the Imperial University. His demonstration at the palace was a ceremonial version of experiments he had been conducting for some time at the pleasure of the Navy and War ministries: manufacturing seismic waves with relatively large amounts of dynamite and creating controllable "earthquakes" that were more readily studied than the unpredictable and uncontrollable kind.[33]

Milne had to bring various organs of the state into seismology in order to make his science grow in productivity and certainty. As early as 1880 he arranged fifteen pendulum seismographs over the Musashi Plain (west of Tokyo) "through the keen interest taken in science by Yamao Yōzō," the Public Works minister.[34] The seismographs were initially placed in telegraph offices, which contained both accurate clocks and disciplined operators. The Ewing-Gray-Milne seismograph itself had been partly built in Kōbudaigakkō's telegraph laboratories, and early versions had used pieces from a Morse telegraph to move the paper on which the seismic wave patterns were inscribed. Thus did seismology become more definite and real by borrowing resources from other better-established practices and institutions— meteorology, telegraphy, military science, and the more general apparatus of state bureaucracy.

In 1882, Milne began mapping earthquake frequency on a national scale by enlisting civil servants as actual seismographs. Beginning with Tokyo, he sent bundles of postcards to local government offices (often post offices and schools), with instructions that each week one card should be returned to him, inscribed with the number of shocks the bureaucrat had felt. "The barricade of postcards," wrote Milne, was then extended northward in increments "systematically pursuing earthquakes." When the inscriptions of the bureaucrat-seismographs had been mapped, Milne was able to plan and chart out the placement of instruments (in this case special clocks) along the lines where earthquakes were most frequently reported. The clocks were designed to shut down on the occasion of a disturbance, making time-readings that could be correlated over long distances.[35]

But moving from postcards to clocks did not free up civil servants; the clocks were to be placed in field stations of the Imperial Meteorological Observatory. In 1883 the Seismological Society established the Committee on a System of Earthquake Observations, which drew up painstaking instructions on how the time records were to be kept and transmitted. "Observation books" were provided to the station operators, in which they were to enter, in duplicate, "all the regular daily comparisons of clocks with the noon signal [an accurate telegraphic transmission of Tokyo time]. One of these sets should be weekly torn out and sent by mail to the Seismological Society. By this method the Society can keep a close watch on the performance of the clocks."

What was being monitored here was not earthquakes, but the daily reliability of the clocks and operators. Milne was essentially conducting a daily inspection of distant and dispersed instrumentation. The operators were also to enter, in separate books, and again in duplicate, "the records whenever any clock is stopped by any cause whatever." These pages were also to be ripped out and sent to Tokyo. By 1885, according to Baron Kikuchi, systematic earthquake observation of this sort had been established throughout the empire.[36] Milne had successfully piggy-backed seismic monitoring onto the existing tasks of a host of government functionaries.[37]

The John Milne we have been following was not an isolated foreigner merely thinking about earthquakes or monitoring a few laboratory devices in Tokyo. By 1885 he was, metaphorically speaking, the commander of an Imperial army, with a general staff at the university, an officer corps at the Seismological Society, battalions of meteorological station tenders and their time-pieces, and even soldiers setting off explosions: a technoscientific network that, after the manner of Bruno Latour, we might more honestly call "John Milne."[38] Many of the Emperor's own servants and instruments helped demonstrate to Milne "the way an earthquake does its work" before he in turn demonstrated this knowledge back to the Emperor. Anglo-Japanese seismology was a large and complex apparatus that only grew successively larger. Following the Nōbi earthquake of 1891, Milne would drew up a fifty-question circular, of which ten thousand were sent and processed at state expense.[39] By the time he had left Japan in 1895, nearly one thousand seismographic stations (most attached to metrological observatories) were feeding information to Tokyo for correlation by a small army of students and ministerial employees.[40]

At the founding of the Seismological Society in 1880, Milne had been unable to interest Yamao Yōzō in serving as its first president. Intent on having a Japanese patron, he had eventually chosen not a government official but Hattori Ichizō, a professor at the Kaisei Gakkō (the predecessor to the Imperial University), who had written an early article on Japanese folkloric descriptions of earthquakes in English.[41] By 1883, however, the president of the Seismological Society of Japan was the Minister of the Interior, General Yamada, and its journal, formerly printed by a newspaper office, was produced at the government printing office. In 1888, Milne's relations with the state grew even closer when he was appointed to a committee, chaired by Education Minister Mori Arinori—whose portfolio included the new Imperial University—to "discuss the system of building best suited to withstand earthquakes." In conjunction with the appointment, Milne was given *chokunin* status by the Emperor and decorated with the Order of Merit with the Cordon of the Sacred Treasure.[42]

In early 1889, Milne prepared for the committee a large volume, *Construction in Earthquake Countries*, that brought together scholarly papers, building codes, and other regulations from various "earthquake countries" where he had cultivated correspondence. It also included detailed summaries of his own research. The title of this semiofficial report was nearly identical to that of Milne's controversial paper presented a few years earlier to the Institution of Civil Engineers in London. Milne clearly intended to steer the committee toward adopting national building regulations based upon seismology's program for the reform of architecture and engineering.[43]

Over the course of the 1880s, the Meiji state had thus been brought into seismology, and seismology into the Meiji state. It becomes clearer why Milne so forcefully contested "constructive science" with architects and engineers, and even, perhaps, why he had taken his "Japanese" case before an obviously hostile audience of engineers in London. The question of the strength or fragility of the new European infrastructure was of little interest to Milne's patrons at the British Association for the Advancement of Science, who expected his seismograms to contribute answers to fundamental questions in geophysics. But it was of intense interest to Milne's ever more powerful patrons in Japan, who cared relatively little about the structure of the Earth. The two patronage relationships were equally vital, and complementary. Without the Japanese government, Milne could not have maintained the resources necessary to produce "science" for the British Association. Without the authority provided by the British Association, it would have been more difficult for Milne to overcome the arguments of his opponents in Japan. Thus did seismology have to expand in two directions at once in order to expand at all.[44]

The state's willingness to make seismology its own should not be interpreted as that science proving itself more "true" than architecture or engineering. Or, more precisely, the question is not one of truth in the abstract, but how the proofs of Milne's science came to be valuable to elements of the Meiji state. Milne's growing foreign reputation (dependent on a continually growing access to the state's own technical apparatus) was one factor. "Foreign knowledge" (made in Japan) about what earthquakes did and did not do was becoming more solid and powerful through foreign publishing and foreign reading. A report in the American journal *Science* in 1884 claimed that "seismologists the world over must look for enlightenment to young Japan," whose earthquake researchers "far outstripped European seismologists" in the development and use of instruments. An 1886 article in the London *Times* claimed that "Japan, as the world knows, is and has been for many years the chief seat of learning of the science of seismology," and gave primary credit for that development to Milne. No other area of Japanese science in the mid-

Meiji period could have invited such foreign publicity and praise. It helped, of course that the writer of the *Science* article was a former *yatoi* (H. M. Paul, a professor of astronomy), and even the London *Times* article was written in Yokohama by H. S. Palmer, a British journalist and engineer.[45]

But other, more exclusively domestic factors also contributed to the growth of seismological authority. We know from statements by the foreign observers M. J. Lescasse and Edward Morse, and by Milne himself that educated Japanese were predisposed, in the 1880s, to believe in the stability of *daiku*-work and suspect the performance of masonry. Milne was nearly singular in the *yatoi* community in repeating something very close to common Japanese belief, yet in the language of Western science. A shift was being engineered in the very definition of "Japan's earthquake problem." As Milne told his English patrons in 1889, the subject of earthquakes had become of "vital importance" to the Japanese government because they "are continually erecting European structures."[46] In other words, the problem had moved from one of how to replace fragile wooden (Japanese) structures with strong masonry (European) ones, to one of how to protect a fragile new masonry infrastructure from the strength of Japanese nature. Seismology had helped the Meiji government problematize a controversial piece of foreign knowledge using Western tools. Milne in effect told Japanese, using the apparatus of instrumental science, that in the matter of resisting earthquakes, they had been close to right all along.

A GROWING TREMBLING

Following the 1880 Yokohama earthquake, which gave birth to the Seismological Society, central Japan remained relatively free of destructive geological events for seven years. Awareness of seismicity increased in this period, however, as the proliferation of Ewing-Gray-Milne seismographs with constantly finer sensitivities inscribed far many more earthquakes than Japanese had ever realized they had. In 1884, one of Milne's devices recorded an earthquake that he did not himself feel, and thus, he concluded "must have reached his station from a great distance."[47] The enlistment of a nationwide network of seismic observers also meant that local tremors that had previously passed with little or no comment were now the subject of studied surveillance and record-keeping. Milne would eventually publish a catalog of 8,331 Japanese earthquakes (many of them unfelt except by instruments) that occurred between 1885 and 1892. Thus did a growing number of Japanese academics and bureaucrats become earthquake-conscious, and Japan develop a reputation at home and abroad as a nation of earthquakes, even in the absence of cata-strophic events.[48]

Beginning around 1887, however, Japanese seismicity began to telegraph its presence to an audience larger than the compilers and readers of scientific reports. It began with the relatively strong earthquake that shook Tokyo and Yokohama in January of that year, and likely decided the matter of the Imperial Palace project in favor of time-tested carpentry. Though these seismic waves were the strongest to hit the capital since the Great Ansei Earthquake of 1855, they were not very de-structive, throwing down a handful of brick chimneys and cracking some walls, but mostly damaging the homes of peasants in hamlets on the city's outskirts.[49] As nearly always with earthquakes that hit Tokyo from the sea, the shaking in Yoko-hama and the resulting damage there were more severe than in the capital. Thus did earthquakes traditionally raise more excitement in the Yokohama-based foreign-language press than the Tokyo-based Japanese tabloids. In the decade after 1887, however, during a period of particularly strong and regular seismic events, Japa-nese newspapers began reporting even nondestructive earthquakes, relying for part of their copy on the pronouncements of seismologists about causes and origin points. By 1900, the geologist Kotō Bunjirō could note that "nowadays in Japan, even daily newspapers speak of dislocation earthquakes whenever a shaking is no-ticed."[50] The reading public was becoming earthquake-conscious, in other words, as previously "local" earthquakes became national news.

Even more dramatic than the 1887 earthquake was the eruption of the volcano Bandai-san, located to the north-northwest of Tokyo, on July 15, 1888. Half of the mountain was blown away in a sudden, thunderous avalanche (similar to the one that destroyed Mount St. Helens in 1980), and close to five hundred people in surrounding villages were buried alive. The Tokyo press corps, accompanied by seismologist Sekiya Seikei and other young Japanese scientists, rushed to the dis-aster site (a two-day journey from the capital via railroad and *jinrikisha*) and set about documenting the catastrophe to international standards. Ever since the erup-tion of Krakatoa in 1883, exploding volcanoes were certified global news-makers. Thus did an image of Bandai-san in ruins become the first photograph ever pub-lished in a Japanese newspaper (the *Yomiuri Shimbun*), and similar attention was given the event by the world press.[51] Although over fifty potentially active volca-noes existed in Japan, there had not been so elaborate or deadly an eruption in the country since the late eighteenth century, or before the living memories of most Japanese. Bandai-san had itself been quiet, or relatively so, for nearly a thousand years.[52]

Volcanology, in the late nineteenth century, was not clearly separate from the study of earthquakes, although Japan's nascent seismological community was beginning to debate whether the two phenomena were closely related. They had already noted, for example, that most earthquakes in the area around Tokyo originated to the east (the sea) rather than in the volcanic mountain ranges to the north and west, suggesting that regular seismicity had a separate and more elusive origin. Nonetheless, because volcanic eruptions and earthquakes were both perceived to involve the release of steam (this in a particularly steam-conscious age) and because eruptions were often preceded by earthquakes, Japanese seismology early claimed the study of volcanoes within its own jurisdiction. Volcanoes had one clear advantage, as scientific objects, which earthquakes lacked: they could be easily pinpointed on a map and repeatedly visited, often in advance of their eruptions.[53]

The 1887 Tokyo earthquake, the Bandai-san eruption of 1888, and (to a lesser extent) the destructive Kumamoto earthquake in Kyushu in 1889 were also moments of public (i.e., journalistic) emergence for Sekiya Seikei, Japan's first credentialed seismologist. It was Sekiya more than Milne who provided scientific information to the press and, six weeks after the Tokyo earthquake, delivered the definitive report on the event to the Seismological Society of Japan. Likewise it was Sekiya who was dispatched by the Imperial University to Bandai-san and co-authored with a young geologist (Kikuchi Y.) a report considered even today a "classic of vulcanology."[54] The clear, engaging, and occasionally dramatic style of Sekiya's prose made it a good source for journalistic quotation both in Japan and abroad. Even the London *Times* gave his theories prominence, calling Sekiya at the time of the Bandai-san eruption "a young seismologist already known to the world," which likely referred to prior writings in the *Transactions of the Seismological Society of Japan*.[55] Like Milne himself, Sekiya (and even more his successor Ōmori Fusakichi, for Sekiya was destined to die young) would henceforth work to satisfy both a scientific and journalistic market for explanations of natural spectacles, which would become increasingly regular as both young scientists came of age.

As with other Japanese of his generation, Sekiya would often take the opportunity afforded by a foreign audience to correct foreign impressions of Japanese fragility. Thus does one of his early articles for the Seismological Society journal, in describing damage to rural hamlets in the path of the 1887 Tokyo earthquake, complicate the formerly stable category "collapsed": "Although there are thousands of wrecked houses in the district of origin, on the verge of falling down, and looking as if a strong breeze would be enough to blow them over, buildings of this class nevertheless withstood the violence of the earth movements so far as to escape actual demolition. The writer saw only two small rotten hovels which had been thrown down. This circumstance shows the tenacity of wooden framed structures."[56] Although he elsewhere repeats the orthodoxy that Japan will eventually be reconstructed in brick or stone, Sekiya assigns this necessity to the need to resist fires, not earthquakes, reminding his (mostly foreign) readers that "in sites little liable to danger from fire, one may find, in this country, wooden houses built three and even four centuries ago."[57]

Sekiya's scientific voice was not identical to that of his foreign teachers, even if he shared many of their concerns. He devotes four pages of his Bandai-san report, for example, to the examination of old chronicles, including documents discovered in Buddhist temples around the mountain's base, which Milne could not have deciphered. He also reports extensive conversations with area residents regarding the time, intensity, and nature of the explosion, comments that he gathers into an appendix. While Milne had instituted a formal system of engagement with earthquake witnesses through standardized postcards, which Sekiya continues to rely on as well, his report displays an almost ethnographic intimacy with the landscape, history, and inhabitants of the disaster site that no European scientist could have managed.[58]

The Bandai-san explosion and subsequent eruptions likely contributed to a growing "volcano consciousness" in late Meiji Japan that would most famously culminate, six years later in 1894, in the publication of Shiga Shigetaka's *Nihon fūkeiron*. Shiga would claim aesthetic priority for Japan's landscape, as compared to that of England, partly of the basis of his country's volcanic cones. "There is not even one volcanic mountain in the United Kingdom. Japan has all the beautiful scenery that Lubbock [a British writer] had expressed, and above all, it has volcanic mountains—kings of scenery between heaven and earth—everywhere in Japan. . . . Much superior."[59] In celebrating not only the beauty but the latent strength *(sensei ryoku)* in Japanese nature, Shiga was rejecting Thomas Buckle's theory that nations with gentler landscapes (those which had escaped "destructive perturbations") were inclined to greater progress. We know Shiga was also a reader of Milne because he introduces his own discussion of volcanoes by approvingly quoting him on the beauty of Mount Fuji.[60]

THE TWO ITALYS

Shiga notes at one point in *Nihon fūkeiron* that the origins of Western civilization lay in the volcanic peninsula of Italy, which remained a crucial comparative site for discussions about Japan through the Meiji period and beyond.[61] A few years prior to the publication of Shiga's book, in fact, the running debate between Japan's architects and seismologists had temporarily migrated to a small island off the west coast of Italy, near Naples, very near the site where Robert Mallet had invented the science of "observational seismology" in 1857.

The island of Ischia in the Bay of Naples had experienced two major earthquakes, in 1881 and 1883, the second killing over a thousand people. The Italian government used the opportunity of the rebuilding to devise guidelines for earthquake-resistant construction, which it intended might serve as an experiment for the nation at large. Three new construction systems were prescribed, two combining masonry with an internal wooden skeleton, and the third, masonry and belt iron.[62] Milne included these Italian guidelines, along with others from the Philippines, South America, and other earthquake countries in the thick report he prepared for the government's new earthquake commission in 1889. He did not single out the Italian code as a model for Japan, but only, it seemed, as an example of what other governments were doing in the way of establishing codes and regulations.

Josiah Conder, however, saw in the inclusion of the Italian regulations something pernicious. In June of 1889 he wrote a letter to the *Japan Weekly Mail* that shifted the ground of his argument from Japan to Italy. Milne's report had yet to be released, but already, wrote Conder, a flawed reading of the Italian regulations had "pertinaciously forced itself into high quarters." According to that reading,

> The Italian government, owing to the prevalence of earthquakes, had forbidden the construction of solid buildings and decided in favor of wooden structures. The original statement had no doubt been more qualified, but the bare impression which remained, whether so intended or not, was that a civilized European country possessing some of the most solid architectural monuments of antiquity had at length in this nineteenth century determined to resort to a ligneous [wooden] one only. Absurd as such an impression appeared, and detrimental to engineering enterprises in this country if true, a denial upon presumption alone was hardly calculated to have weight against the representation of apparently disinterested reporters fresh from the spot.[63]

The "reporters fresh from the spot" were members of a recent Japanese art commission to Italy headed by Okakura and Fenollosa, both of whom Conder believed were in league with Milne, and had likely informed him about the Italian regulations.[64] The forces of "Japanese art" and "Japanese science," it seemed, were closing in on "architecture" and "Europe." It was in order to look into these incredible reports, Conder claimed, that he had recently obtained a copy of the Ischia regulations himself. His reading revealed that "there is not contained in them even the narrow foundation which I presumed for the erroneous statements to which I have referred. Suffice it to say that even for the Island of Ischia, the Commission do not hesitate to sanction brick and masonry structures. . . ." Conder declines to say more, as "I have no right to forestall the Society by the publication of extracts."[65]

But forestalling the seismologists was clearly the intention. Conder was right in singling out Ischia as potentially damaging to his own case. Although it was true that the Italians had not rejected masonry, it was only because, to quote the report, it "cannot be prohibited" given that it was "customary, and almost imposed by natural conditions." Constructions in iron or wood, the report went on, were "much safer." The Italians called buildings of timber "safe even in the most dangerous districts."[66]

The Ischia regulations had even more to attract Milne, for not only did they parallel his own thinking about the need to create a new architecture in Japan, and to enforce it through regulations and laws, but the effort came from Naples, the seismic laboratory of his predecessor and rival Robert Mallet. Mallet had written, after the Great Neapolitan Earthquake of 1857, that "where the masonry [in Naples] was of the best class, and such as would be so recognized in England, the buildings thus constructed stood uninjured in the midst of chaotic ruin. . . . Thus the frightful loss of life and limb were as much attributable to the ignorance and imperfection displayed in the domestic architecture of the people, as to the unhappy natural condition of their country as regards earthquakes."[67]

Milne's own work had aggressively disputed this statement, both its confidence in the earthquake resistance of "the best class" of good English-style masonry, and its easy declaration of indigenous ignorance. Significantly too, Mallet had been quoted at length by Brunton and others of Milne's opponents, who thrust forward classical examples of stone architecture in the Mediterranean with the frequency that Dresser had pagodas.[68] That the Italian government, led by its own seismologists, had prescribed new and experimental systems of masonry reinforcement seemed an answer to Mallet and Brunton, and a vindication of Milne's own agnosticism toward European architecture as precedent.

But even if Italy were an earthquake country—an important site in the formative history and ethno-geography of seismology—it was ancient and sacred ground to architecture, and impossible for Conder to concede. As an "earthquake country," Italy's proper Japanese spokesmen were seismologists; as a "nation of art and architecture," its natural spokesmen were architects (although Conder's letter signals that spokesmen for Japanese art were then also speaking for Italy in Japan). Conder's intervention shows an eagerness to take the argument to classical soil. But it also confirms Ischia's potential, as one of the epicentral zones of European civilization, to persuade the Meiji government in Milne's favor, in a way that regulations from South America, the Philippines, and other non-European places perhaps lacked the power to do. In other words, it was Italy's very status as a nation of art and architecture that made it more valuable to Milne as an earthquake country. In turn, it was its status as an earthquake country that made it valuable to Conder as a nation of art and architecture, and model for Japan.

The *Japan Weekly Mail*, where Conder's letter appeared, amplified and broadened his carefully circumscribed remarks with an editorial in the same issue. Conder's letter, it wrote, "re-opens an often discussed question—solid structures versus wooden edifices in earthquake countries. We say 'often discussed' but we should also add 'still undecided' so far as Japan is concerned."[69] The editor, who was a former Kōbudaigakkō professor of mathematics and close friend of Henry Dyer, now determined, however, to decide the question.[70] Until Conder's letter, he wrote, "it was generally supposed" in informed circles that the Italians were preparing to abandon masonry. Now that Conder had shown that assumption to be erroneous, he wrote, attention should shift to the purveyors of that misconception, "the folks who cling to wood just because it is Japanese." Their position, the editor went on, now merits "no more consideration than would be accorded to one who should preach the perpetuation of *hara-kiri* or *kataki-uchi* [revenge killing] for the sake of the fine old-fashioned flavor possessed by those sanguinary customs."[71]

Such a strong analogy was justified, in the editor's view, by the earthquake debate having diverted Japan's attention from its true natural enemy—fire. "It is thirty-four years since Tokyo was visited by an earthquake sufficiently severe to knock down any buildings, and this event had been preceded by a far longer period of complete immunity. On the other hand, during the past fifteen years the average number of houses destroyed annually in the capital by fire has been 5,514, and their total minimum value twenty-five millions of dollars. . . . Is it not the acme of absurdity, then, to set earthquakes against fires? . . . It is against fires that people have to guard, not against earthquakes."[72] As earthquakes receded in importance, the paper's firestorm burned in the direction of the seismologists themselves: "What name are we to apply to persons who encourage the citizens of such an unhappy town to go on building their houses and shops of flammable materials, lest, forsooth, they may be visited by a calamity that is as likely as not never to make itself felt fatally at all?"[73]

The Ischia debate was not confined to the foreign-language press. It would be joined by Conder's protégé Tatsuno Kingo, now the head of the architectural department at what had become the Imperial University. As the most prominent Japanese architect, Tatsuno would soon be enlisted into the Ministry of Education's earthquake-resistance project and would for the rest of his career serve, alongside seismologists, on official committees and bureaus charged with guiding state-sponsored seismic research and policy. Tatsuno was not only Conder's student but had virtually replicated his teacher's career path, having been sent to work in London for the same architects, William Burges and Roger Smith, who had trained Conder as a young man. Tatsuno was deeply committed to architecture, masonry, and an English design vocabulary.

As the first Japanese professor of architecture, Tatsuno was responsible for institutionalizing that discipline—among the most conspicuously foreign of the new technical callings—within a newly nativized academy at a time of essence preservation. He could not afford Conder's position of aggressive skepticism toward a rising, state-sanctioned science, but neither was he inclined to reject the teachings of his discipline. In 1890, the year after Conder's letter to the *Japan Weekly Mail*, Tatsuno gave his first public lecture on earthquake construction before the Nihon Zōka-gakkai.[74] The position he chose to take in this difficult atmosphere might be called "accommodation to plan but resistance to details." There was no resisting seismology's new control over the agenda of constructive science. But Milne himself had stated that seismology was to teach "general principles" and leave architecture the "details." Milne's *Construction in Earthquake Countries* was nonetheless full of details, in the form of all those building codes and regulations. It was the regulations from Italy that Tatsuno chose as the exclusive topic of his talk.

The Italian question was sufficiently important that Tatsuno had actually visited Ischia on the way back from his apprentice training in England. He mentions that Milne had exhibited in Japan an actual model based on the Ischia regulations. Tatsuno accompanied his own lecture with another model, based on detail drawings he had brought from Ischia, but constructed in the form of a Buddhist temple. He justified the continuing attention to Ischia with the statement that, although Milne's long report of various countries' earthquake regulations was "not so useful for us scholars," the report from Ischia was perhaps "the most useful" of those Milne had presented.[75] Yet reading Tatsuno's lecture, Ischia seems "useful" only in casting doubt on seismology's claims. Tatsuno was unimpressed by what he had seen in Italy. "If we compare this structure [one of the reinforcement systems called for by the regulations] to our own building," he wrote, "it can't even come up to the standard of our warehouse construction." The climate of regulation he encountered on Ischia was "excessive," yet with no guarantee that the structures so regulated would actually withstand earthquakes. "I believe the [different] vibration rates of wood and stone will cause rather more and unpredictable damage," he wrote, drawing his language and concepts from seismology. "I don't understand," he concluded, "why the Italian government adopted these regulations." He found the whole situation "very sad," and clearly no model for Japan: "[Ischia] is a small island with a population of only 20,000, so the use of these regulations as a model for our own capital is problematic. It would prevent the development of architecture in our country."

Dismissing the regulations themselves, Tatsuno excavated from the ruins a lesson very similar to the one drawn decades earlier by Mallet in nearby Naples: "The reason people died there [in Ischia] was not because of architecture, but because they were too poor to strengthen their buildings. I don't know why the Italian government did not pay attention [in the rebuilding] to conventional, sturdy, architectural methods, rather than instituting new regulations."[76] When Tatsuno writes that the Ischians had not been killed by architecture, he means by the European masonry tradition upon which his own training and disciplinary acculturation had been strictly based. It is clear that for both Conder and Tatsuno, it was architecture itself—its history, materials, practices, and very identity—that Milne had seemingly placed on trial.

Tatsuno's Italy was not, however, Conder's. Conder had dismissed the radical reading of the Italian regulations as mistaken; the Italians were still, he argued, set on stone. Tatsuno fully conceded that the Italian regulations abandoned "conventional, sturdy, architectural methods," and instead built his case on their misplaced attempt at innovation. Tatsuno also avoids presenting himself as in reaction against seismology's claims. He speaks rather as a fellow researcher (he had after all gone all the way to Ischia) as keenly interested in understanding earthquake construction as the seismologists themselves.

In the dynamic political situation of mid-Meiji, seismology's ascendancy within the Japanese bureaucracy was in no sense assured. Milne's new patron, Education Minister Mori Arinori, was assassinated in 1889 for a perceived insult to Shinto (he was a Christian). In the same year, treaty negotiations with Britain were broken off by a new, more conservative government. Milne complains in the introduction to *Construction in Earthquake Countries* that certain crucial experiments he had recommended to the committee had not been carried out. In the same introduction, incidentally, Milne thanks Conder for assistance in correcting the proofs and for "many valuable suggestions." But papers by Conder or other architects are conspicuously absent. There is only one article by an engineer, M. J. Lescasse, who as a Frenchman among English *yatoi* was something of a dissenter.[77] Milne was still taking risks, running ahead of (and sometimes over the top of) better-established disciplines, as Tatsuno's reply makes clear. His science of catastrophe needed, above all, a greater sense of looming catastrophe. It needed nature to "speak" more forcefully, which, from the early 1890s onward, Japanese nature began to do.

FIVE · A Great Earthquake

THE NŌBI PLAIN, OCTOBER 1891

On the morning of October 28, 1891, an unusually powerful earthquake centered in the Nōbi Plain near Nagoya rocked central Japan from Osaka to Tokyo. Shock waves were felt over virtually the entire nation, from Tohoku (northern Honshu) to Kyushu in the far south. Contemporary seismologists, estimating on the basis of the yet-to-be-invented Richter scale, place the earthquake's magnitude as 8.4, making it the strongest seismic event in modern Japanese history. The Great Kantō (or Tokyo) Earthquake of 1923, by comparison, measured 7.9. Approximately 7,300 people were killed in four prefectures, tens of thousands injured, and over a hundred thousand made homeless, mostly in the towns and agricultural hamlets scattered in Nagoya's hinterland. Death and damage on this scale had not been seen in Japan since the 1855 Ansei earthquake destroyed Edo.[1]

The alluvial Nōbi Plain, "the garden of Japan," was among the most productive and densely populated rural districts in the country, and lay astride the highways, railroads, telegraph lines, and other infrastructure linking Tokyo with points south. Originating in the Neo Valley to its north, the earthquake rolled across the sandy plain like so many ocean waves. The provincial capital of Gifu and the castle town of Ōgaki, both near the epicenter, were almost entirely destroyed, mostly in the resulting fires. Osaka and Nagoya were also badly shaken, and fires broke out in the latter city. This was primarily a rural rather than an urban disaster, however, as only

30 people were killed in Osaka and only 190 in Nagoya (out of a population of 165,000).

Given the power and extent of what would be named "the Great Nōbi Earthquake," it was natural that all parties to the seismic question would flock to the ruins and draw lessons.[2] The range and diversity of the destruction between Nagoya and Osaka indeed provided the evidence for many types of argument. On the one hand, there were tens of thousands of collapsed and/or burned Japanese wooden farmhouses. On the other hand, a number of very large European-style buildings and engineering structures had also dramatically failed. One of the latter was a long steel-truss bridge of the Tōkaidō Railroad whose supports gave way, sending the central sections crashing into the Nagara River.[3] Two large brick textile mills collapsed in Nagoya and Osaka, killing scores of workers and seriously injuring scores more.

In Tokyo the images of the earthquake arrived in a particular order, and formed themselves into patterns that later reportage would only partially reweave. The quake was strongly felt in the capital, stopping clocks, knocking crockery off shelves, and rocking the city slowly back and forth for an unprecedented twelve minutes. The seismic waves were too depleted to do much damage, however. One embarrassing exception was the new building of the Home Ministry, which lost some of its chimneys. In Yokohama, the tall brick chimney of a power plant also fell, damaging machinery and stopping the city's electricity. This may be why, on the day following the earthquake, the Tokyo newspaper *Asahi shimbun* centered it in Yokohama, which had been "shaken quite a lot." In spite of the rain, not a few people there went out of their houses into the street. This was especially true, reported the paper, in the foreign sections. "The foreigner's astonishment was extraordinary . . . but damage was not especially great." Thus was the Nōbi earthquake registered initially by the *Asahi shimbun* as a seismogram of foreign anxiety.[4]

The next day (two days following the quake), the same paper reported that in Osaka, "many houses" had been destroyed, "many *dōzō*" (warehouses) damaged, and even brick buildings, including a large mill, had collapsed. A detailed accounting of houses "totally destroyed" and "partially destroyed" began to be published for various areas. It was now realized that the earthquake was unusually widespread. Only one ruined factory building, the Naniwa cotton textile mill, was singled out by name. But the impression now conveyed by the paper was of serious general damage.[5]

In Yokohama's English-language press, the initial reports came exclusively from Osaka and Kobe, so the earthquake was thought to have been centered there. News of the destruction to rural towns and hamlets arrived more slowly, because there were no reporters in the countryside to send correspondence. The *Japan Weekly Mail* reported on October 31 that, although Osaka had been given a strong shaking, nearly all of its Japanese houses had survived. Well-informed by the seismic debate, the editor unhesitatingly attributed this to their material: "Nothing seemed to prevent the complete collapse of some houses but the fact that they were built of wood, and so stood the strain far better than brick would have done, as proved by the terrible disaster at the mills in Osaka." The "terrible disaster" was the complete collapse of the Naniwa cotton textile mill, "a three-story red brick building in the usual English factory style," which had "only been standing for a few months." Twenty-one people were killed immediately as the walls fell in, the same number seriously injured, and over fifty more sustained lesser injuries. In the common experience with Japanese earthquakes, this was an unusually large number of people to be killed and injured in a single building. Even more damning, early reports anticipated what the later official tally would confirm: that the only building in Osaka that had been completely destroyed, and the one in which most people had been killed, was the new brick mill. According to the same reports, "all other foreign-built factories were more or less damaged," as were "the houses in the Osaka Concession" (the foreign residents' district). The visiting Bishop of Exeter narrowly escaped being crushed by a falling chimney in the home of a local missionary.[6]

On November 3 the *Asahi shimbun* again reported the collapse of houses and other Japanese buildings, including 1,052 in the city of Nagoya. It now singled out, however, the destruction of "those magnificent brick buildings" such as the Nagoya Post Office, the divisional headquarters of the army, and a large spinning mill, that, together with the Tōkaidō Railroad (also damaged and stopped) constituted the very infrastructure of the Meiji state. "More than 200" women workers in one mill were dead or injured. The victims were pictured being excavated from beneath piles of brick.[7]

It was the collapse of the "foreign" structures that began to bring the "natural" disaster into technocultural focus. The full list of damaged or collapsed brick buildings in Nagoya would grow to include the governor's residence, city council chambers, high court, police office, military headquarters, prison, electricity company, a hospital, and certain schools.[8] Red bricks, which for the last twenty years had been among the most visible symbols of progressive Japanese change, were depicted in postdisaster accounts as particularly nefarious, "flying around" and "attacking people" in one case and "raining down like snow and hail" in another. Masonry was singled out as producing particularly ugly (and new) types of wounds: "Japanese-style buildings hurt people [when they collapse] by breaking bones or arms. But brick buildings give the body harsher damage because bricks fall and cut people, and mortar gets deep into their cuts. The mortar can't be gotten out, so the cut festers. People can't be saved."[9]

In addition to the dead and injured young women of the highly mechanized Owari Spinning Mill in Nagoya, pilgrims on their way to a temple were described as being trapped under the collapsing brick wall of the Nagoya Post Office.[10] Indeed, some of the disaster-related books rushed into print in the following weeks chose as their cover illustrations a simple drawing of a half-collapsed brick wall, sometimes with unstrung telegraph wire laying about its base.[11] This emphasized the point that electronic communications had been cut by the earthquake as effectively as masonry had been shaken down.

Within days of the disaster, papers like the *Mainichi shimbun* and the *Choya shimbun* began condemning "the negligence of the architects and engineers who planned and superintended the erection of buildings which have been found faulty in their design." The government was also blamed for having let these foreign disciplines operate without controls.[12] Imperial University seismologist Sekiya Seikei issued a circular in Japanese (which was also translated and printed in the English-language papers) encouraging civil engineers and other building professionals to examine and record evidence provided by the ruins, at the same time faulting them for not heeding the lessons of seismology: "This kind of investigation had hitherto been left, for the most part, to scientific men, practical workers giving themselves little concern about it, which is to be regretted."[13] Even those Westerners still confident about masonry, such as "A.C.S.," writing from the earthquake zone to the *Japan Weekly Mail*, acknowledged that "a great, and I think unjust feeling against the use of brick [that] has undoubtedly been caused by the failure of so many brick buildings and the great loss of life their fall had caused."[14]

The critique of Western technology in the aftermath of Nōbi did not stop at brick buildings and railroad bridges. Even small-scale Western technologies introduced for the sake of convenience and modernity over the previous twenty years began to be singled out as maladapted to the earthquake zone. New pumps provided to towns like Gifu and designed to be lowered into wells in the event of fire, proved ineffective when seismic action suddenly lowered water tables or dirtied water with fine sand or silt, which clogged hoses.[15] Western-style oil lamps, increasingly in fashion at the time of the earthquake, proved so prone to overturning that they were temporarily banned from postdisaster Nagoya, people preferring to substitute Japanese-style candles. In the aftermath of the Nōbi disaster, seismologist Sekiya would invent an "earthquake-proof lamp" that would not burn one's house down if suddenly overturned, a device subsequently displayed by the government at overseas exhibitions.[16]

Only in the first week of November did detailed reports of the damage to rural areas begin to appear in the press. The *Jiji shinpō* reported, for example, that out of 4,439 houses in the town of Gifu, only 118 had escaped "without injury." The same paper reported that in many towns the majority of temples had also been destroyed, in some cases killing as many as were killed in the mills.[17] To the initial shock of the collapse of European mills was added the aftershock of large numbers of collapsed Japanese buildings. Or had the latter actually collapsed? Perhaps they had mostly burned. First reports were unclear.

CONDER AND MILNE
ON THE NŌBI PLAIN

Conder and Milne rushed separately to the earthquake district within a few days of the disaster.[18] Conder was actually dispatched there, along with his former student Sone Tatsuzō, by his patron Iwasaki Yanosuke, the president of Mitsubishi. In a letter to an associate suggesting that Conder be asked to go, Iwasaki wrote that "until we have some concrete information, I do not feel safe to sleep in a wooden house." Given Mitsubishi's extensive, engineered infrastructure, it is notable that it was Iwasaki's faith in *daiku*-work, rather than masonry, that was most immediately shaken.[19]

After separately arriving in Nagoya, Conder and Milne began reporting what they saw in regular articles to the Yokohama English-language newspaper, *The Japan Weekly Mail*. Both chose to publish their observations anonymously, Conder signing his articles "X," and Milne, "P.Q." Others also sent descriptions to the papers, but few of them chose to use aliases. While the names "Conder" and "Milne" were associated with public positions on earthquake construction, "X" and "P.Q." could navigate the ruins as seemingly unprejudiced observers.

X and P.Q. initially traveled along the same route (from Nagoya to Gifu) and filed descriptions of similar scenes. Arriving in Nagoya, P.Q. found "the thing most notable was the Post Office, a large brick building, little more than a heap of ruins."[20] X, standing before the same ruins, wrote: "The Post and Telegraph Office, concerning the collapse of which so much has been said, seems to have been very poorly constructed. Indeed I doubt whether it would have passed an ordinary Building Act inspection in a non-earthquake country. . . ."[21] P.Q. notes that a

European-style building had collapsed, and moves on. X lingers and explains. X would have known, although he does not tell his readers, that the Post and Telegraph building had been designed by Satachi Shichijirō, one of the initial four graduates of the *zōka* course.

The collapse of the Post and Telegraph building was particularly embarrassing given that it was a principal local emblem of the Imperial government, and the one most associated with the new technology. More than that, however, it stood next to the city's best *ryokan* (Japanese-style inn), a two-story wooden building, which would have escaped undamaged except that the collapsing upper story of the post office crushed one of its wings. A distant member of the Imperial family who was staying at the inn was slightly injured. A photographer who happened on the site in the days following the disaster was careful to place both buildings in his viewframe, thus memorializing the contrast in their condition.[22]

X's and P.Q.'s attentions to detail reverse when it comes to Nagoya's wooden houses. From X's vantage, "common Japanese houses, where isolated, have in many cases fallen in like a pack of cards."[23] P.Q. is more precise, noting that "at one place a house had fallen absolutely flat," and later, "In a row of houses one here and there is completely wrecked, whilst those on both sides, apparently of similar construction, stand unharmed."[24]

X and P.Q. are neither ignoring nor altering "evidence." Each has arrived in Nagoya anxiously curious, carrying the baggage of years of statements about what earthquakes do. For each, attention is focused, initially at least, not on the evidence that most obviously aids his own case, but that which threatens to contradict or complicate it. Standing before the post office, X is compelled to explain its collapse both to his readers and to himself. P.Q. is not—he had explained it long ago, was perhaps even anticipating it. P.Q.'s gaze lingers instead on the collapsed Japanese houses, a scene he had not previously envisioned. The same sight does not, apparently, surprise or much interest X.

But as both men grow used to the devastation around them, and become increasingly confident in their ability to explain unexpected phenomena, they begin also to repeat, from the ruins, things they had been saying and writing for some time. Writes P.Q.: "In spite of their massive roofs, temples have come off almost unscathed."[25] In Ōgaki, X notes that "7/10ths of the killed were burnt, and it is supposed that more than half were burnt alive."[26] P.Q.'s caveat: "From the appearance of such houses [in Ōgaki] that have not been burned, some of which are still standing, little, if at all damaged, and many not completely ruined, I doubt if the actual earthquake here has been much more severe than in Nagoya or Gifu."[27]

At a certain point after viewing the town of Gifu, their inquiries take X and P.Q. along different routes. X even notes that Milne and his party have decided to follow the railroad line, "as was probably necessary owing to his connection with the Railroad Department."[28] X goes straight to Osaka, the site of the collapsed Naniwa mill, which P.Q. never reaches, continuing to explore the remains of villages. During only a portion of their journeys did the two correspondents see the ruins of the same "Great Nōbi Earthquake," and even then, the manner in which things were seen and not seen differed.

The composite picture becomes no clearer if we add the testimony of others wandering through their own small portions of the ruins at the same time as X and P.Q. Observation and analysis sometimes fail to align even within the same account. The engineer W. Silver Hall, for example, wrote that "the damage [to houses] was confined almost entirely to houses so rotten and rickety that it is a wonder they survived the last strong gale of wind." And a little later: "As regards wooden framed buildings, it is scarcely an exaggeration to say that every well built house in good condition is still standing, the damage being confined almost entirely to the plastering and the tile roofs." But following this seemingly unqualified praise for the abilities of *daiku* (which conflicts with reports by both Conder and Milne), Hall expresses the opinion that "the Japanese is an admirable cabinet maker, but a miserable carpenter . . . he cannot separate the two arts." He means that *daiku* cut overly complicated joints. "The wonder," continues Hall, "is not that Japanese houses come down, but that they stand as long as they do, especially as the vital necessity for diagonal struts and braces is entirely ignored."[29]

As the correspondents define "the Great Nōbi Earthquake," they simultaneously read, and respond to, each other's published newspaper accounts. Conder was compelled to stop and explain the collapse of the Nagoya Post Office because "much ha[d] been written" about it in previous press accounts. Yokohama architect John Smedly was apparently responding to W. Silver Hall's denigration of *daiku* when he wrote, in the next issue of the same paper (locating himself before a temple): "I have heard it averred that the Japanese are bad carpenters. Let anyone visit this temple, for, however differently it may be constructed from our Western ideas, one must acknowledge it had wonderfully carried out the purposes for which it was erected, and is a triumph of the carpenters' skill."[30]

One thing that almost all of the foreigners agreed upon was that the temples stood. Not so the Japanese correspondent of the *Jiji shinpō*, who reported that the Kaijiyen temple in Ōgaki "fell with a crash," killing more than 150 persons congregated inside. "Two men only escaped and they were seriously injured. Before any effective steps could be taken to discover whether any of the unfortunate worshipers survived, the fire came and settled the question."[31] The same report said that out of 700 temples in Gifu prefecture, more than a third had been totally destroyed, and that of 25 temples in Ōgaki, near the epicenter, only three escaped injury. A later article in the same paper reported that "out of 50 [temples] in the districts of Nakajima and Tokai, the whole, with the exception of Fukusen-ji, were destroyed, and out of 20 in the Nishi-Aichi district, only three remained standing."[32]

Japanese correspondents were altogether more active in reporting the destruction of temples than their foreign counterparts. It could be that, as Japanese, they were able to listen to stories about collapsed and burned temples, while foreigners saw only piles of ash and lumber, oblivious to what type of building it had been or how many had been killed inside. Or it might be that reporters at the *Jiji shinpō*, the organ of westernizer Fukuzawa Yukichi (who had famously urged Japan to "escape from Asia"), were more inclined to report catastrophe as it affected rural Buddhism, which was widely seen as constituting a center of conservative reaction.[33] In the weeks following the earthquake the *Jiji shinpō* severely criticized the inaction of "degenerate" Buddhist priests, and the slow response to relief by the Eastern Hongangi of Kyoto, whose income was largely derived from its numerous followers in the earthquake zone. This the paper contrasted to the immediate and generous monetary relief offered by the foreign community.[34] Given the Westerners' own obsession with the fallen mills, fastidiousness about reporting the fall of temples may have been viewed by some Japanese reporters as symbolizing the futility of rejecting foreign knowledge.

THE EARTHQUAKE
IN WOODBLOCK PRINTS

The most vivid and perhaps widely consumed "descriptions" of the earthquake were not newspapers articles, however, but the multicolored woodblock prints that began appearing for sale within days of the disaster, probably vended on the street much like the newspapers themselves. A collection of such prints preserved at the Nagoya City Museum mostly bear the signatures of Tokyo artists, who probably relied for their information on newspaper reports or early rumors from the disaster zone. The prints generally present the earthquake as a spacious landscape either still in the full throes of catastrophe or coping with its immediate aftermath, in scenes that artists in the capital could not have directly accessed given the temporary breakdown in transportation. The apocalyptic scenes they conjure are more allegorical than real, crowding into a single canvas what were actually widely scattered places and incidents obviously culled from discrete news reports.[35]

Even more so than in the newspapers, the favorite subject of the illustrators is the collapse or destruction of Western-style icons—brick buildings, railroad bridges, telegraph wires, and even railroad trains. Tall chimney stacks are depicted in midfall or belching fire; bricks rain from the air off Western-style cornices, and quoined masonry walls lie in toppled heaps; trains in full throttle plunge into ravines, or, on the cover of one book of earthquake lithographs, a still-steaming locomotive lies entirely upside down with dead bodies scattered about its carriages. In some cases the artists have clearly borrowed from news reports, such as those describing the fall of the Nagoya Post Office and the Nagara River railroad bridge. In others they have taken dramatic license. Although the earthquake destroyed over ten miles of rail line, for instance, no trains were actually derailed, and no railroad passengers were among the dead or injured.[36]

The broken, largely Western-style townscapes in the foreground of these post-disaster prints are commonly set against a tight backdrop of comparatively serene Japanese landscape features. Mountains form a remote and solid backdrop to the broken flotsam of the plain. Sometimes the mountains are local—and even named—although in the case of the overturned locomotive mentioned above, the backdrop is Mount Fuji, much too far from Nōbi's epicentral zone to have been visible to its victims. Next to Fuji-san in the same illustration is a generic castle, which like the mountain (but unlike the locomotive) has survived seemingly unharmed.

Seventeenth-century Nagoya Castle, its keep towering solidly and undamaged between columns of smoke from burning ruins, emerged in both graphic and prose accounts as one of the major icons of the catastrophe. Indeed, the castle is made to look almost mountainlike in certain prints, looming against the sky in a visual counterpoint to nearby peaks. Most artists placed the intact castle keep in the background of their canvases (or to one side) while arranging collapsing brick factories, fallen steel-truss railroad bridges, and/or derailed trains in the foreground or center. The castle's survival was celebrated in prose accounts as well, one writer describing how the gold whale-shaped crests atop its roofs were "still shining in the sky." In contrast to modern Nagoya, "not even a single piece of *kawara* [roof tile] or a single piece of gold filigree" from the castle was displaced, according to the same account.[37] Architects who subsequently inspected the castle would differ, finding numerous dislocations large and small, but by that time the earthquake-resistant reputation of Nagoya Castle was essentially unshakable.[38]

Nagoya Castle was constructed between 1610 and 1612 by Tokugawa Ieyasu as a residence for his ninth son, Yoshinao. The Owari branch of the Tokugawa family, which subsequently used the castle as its residence, was among the most important collateral branches of the Shogunal dynasty, and the area around Nagoya and Gifu was particularly rich with early Edo-period associations. Indeed another famous castle, in Ōgaki, much closer to the epicenter, also remained undamaged and came to be featured in postdisaster illustrations. That the contrast in survivability between architectural features was also one between political regimes may have added to its ironic potential, although no commentaries make this explicit.[39]

Each of the woodblock prints includes a text box with a running commentary on the disaster, mixing hyperbolic description of the earthquake's power with stories about survival and escape. At least two of the artists tell the story of passengers from the fictional train trapped within its carriages, who subsequently wander through the postcatastrophic landscape searching for food. They are reduced, in other words, from the most modern of Japanese to the most pitiful and primitive. For the most part, however, the commentaries are eclectic and almost breathless, evoking a lost or orphaned child in one line and a falling inn or post office in the next. At least one artist claims that the disaster is an extraordinary natural occurrence *(tenpenchii)* without historical precedent, either forgetting the destructive earthquakes of the 1850s or convinced by the early news accounts that Nagoya indeed lay completely in ruin with the better part of its citizenry dead.[40]

An unmistakable impression left by these woodblock prints, extending the lesson of certain news reports, was of the fragility and danger of the new Western-style landscape. More graphically and dramatically than prose accounts, the prints neatly reversed the colonizing tropes so common in Meiji discourse over the previous two decades, which had located fragility exclusively in the "feudal" landscape and volatility in Japanese nature. While ostensibly illustrating the disaster with a new realism (born partly out of the artists' exposure to Western methods of illustration), such depictions are not only polemical, but edit much information out. The collapse of Japanese dwellings, temples, and shrines, for example, while not neglected by woodblock artists, appear in their canvases mainly as "filler." Traditional storehouses *(kura)* are caught up in the maelstrom in many illustrations, but the number of brick walls and casement windows in the process of disintegration certainly exceeded the actual percentage of such features in Nagoya. Even the choice of illustrating the catastrophe as urban, when most of the death and destruction actually took place in towns and villages on the plain, was likely conditioned by the greater illustrative quality of Nagoya's architectural icons.

The depiction of Japanese mountains as silent witnesses to the social disaster also diverges from the many prose accounts in which the opening of chasms, creation of new lakes, cutting of roads, and even the partial collapse of mountains (in the form of landslides) were well discussed. For observers on the ground, including many residents of the earthquake zone, changes to the natural landscape such as ground cracking "was a very big, weird change—very dramatic," according to one report, especially when "new lakes were found where water had come up from the ground." Even some of the woodblock artists, in the commentaries accompanying their prints, mention mountains falling and ground-cracks opening although they choose not to draw them. Such changes to the landscape were more difficult to illustrate, of course, nor would they likely have captured the attention of urban audiences as much as the spectacle of a railroad train careening into a chasm.[41]

Yet there seems more at stake here than simply spectacle, or even the contrast between foreign and Japanese fragilities. That the physical infrastructure of the state or other elites (such as the new industrial concerns) should be particularly susceptible to damage from natural disaster was arguably unusual in the Japanese experience, and a reversal of an age-old order in which suffering had been more clearly demarcated along lines of wealth and power. Woodblock artists seem to have chosen to emphasize this element of the drama. As long as Japan had enjoyed a sophisticated building-carpentry tradition, its traditional elites of aristocrats, upper samurai, the shogunate, and the priests of wealthy temples had often been able to afford limited protection in the form of the best materials pieced together by the most skilled craftsmen. In other words, they had been able to buy talent, making it more likely that their own buildings would ride out the seismic waves that shook down flimsier and less expensive structures.

In the last great seismic disaster before Nōbi, the 1855 Ansei earthquake, the damage to Edo had indeed been disproportionately concentrated in the residential districts of the lower town. The great temples and shrines, and the residences of the Shogun, daimyo, and samurai had been comparatively less affected than those of the artisan and merchant classes. Thus did a popular woodblock print made in 1855 illustrate a *gojūnotō* (five-story pagoda) in Asakusa that had famously withstand the waves despite its great height, with only the bent metal mast atop its roof providing evidence that the pagoda had been violently snapped about. Tokugawa elites had also commandeered relatively high, rocky ground for themselves away from the alluvial plains where the effects of earthquakes were most severe, but where common people often had no choice but to cluster and build.[42] Here is one explanation for the survival in 1891 of Nagoya Castle, and certain large Nagoya temples,

FIGURE 6

Woodblock print of the Great Nōbi Earthquake in Nagoya (*Meiji 24 nen 10 gatsu 28 nichi daijishin-goẓu,* by Toyohara Kunitaru, 1891). A derailed train and fallen railroad bridge are visible in the center and center-left of the full canvas *(opposite)*. Telegraph wires lie in the foreground, and collapsed brick buildings to the far right. Victims are being aided by men in uniform. An undamaged Nagoya Castle *(upper right, opposite, and detail above)* and a local mountain tower over the disaster site. (Courtesy of the Nagoya City Museum.)

FIGURE 7, *opposite*
Detail from the woodblock print *Gifu shigai daijishin no ʒu* (1891)
depicting the Great Nōbi Earthquake. Nagoya's post office sheds
bricks in the foreground while, at top, a train plunges into a
ravine and telegraph wires snap. Only a local mountain peak in
the background provides a stable reference point. (Courtesy of
the Nagoya City Museum.)

FIGURE 8, *above*
In this detail from *Meiji 24 nen 10 gatsu 24 nichi daijishin ʒu*
(1891), a brick building, telegraph poles, and a train are engulfed
in the maelstrom of the Nōbi Earthquake. (Courtesy of the
Nagoya City Museum.)

while the residential city around them—despite being built of similar materials—
was largely shaken down. The survival of these iconic structures when confronted
with seismic activity was not so much "the old vs. the new" or the "East vs. West,"
but a simple physical expression of the privilege of class and state.

It was precisely that privilege that foreign architects and engineers had seemingly failed to re-create for the new Meiji state, and this is the story line the woodblock artists seize upon. The contrast was not entirely a fair one, of course, for railroad and telegraph lines had to be thinly arranged over very long distances and
were thus unable to avoid faults of the type that bisect the Nōbi Plain. Moreover,
the alluvial plains at the mouths of rivers were necessarily developed into new

ports, not only at Nagoya but also Yokohama, that would always shake more violently in large earthquakes than would nearby cities like Tokyo. The brick chimneys integral to steam-powered mills were much simpler structures than five-story pagodas, and hence more susceptible to seismic damage. They inevitably fell before (and on) surrounding structures, even in comparatively light earthquakes, while nearby pagodas remained standing despite the severest shocks.[43] Moreover, the wooden structures that housed the businesses and residences of common people remained, in 1891, as vulnerable as they always had been. The vast majority of those killed by the Nōbi earthquake had actually been crushed or burned to death in wooden houses. In Gifu, nearly the whole city was destroyed in a massive postearthquake fire, a common and age-old fate of Japanese towns and cities too close to earthquake epicenters. A similar fate befell Ōgaki. Even so, it was "shocking" in both an aesthetic and political sense for the 1891 earthquake to have shattered the state as easily as it shattered the lives of peasants and townsmen, a spectacle over which symbols of the old order, most notably Nagoya Castle, seem in the woodblocks to be bearing mute and judgmental witness.

AFTERSHOCKS: ADMINISTERING
THE "RETURN TO NORMAL"

By embodying itself in railroads, telegraphs, brick buildings, and other Western-derived infrastructure, the Meiji government may have actually expanded the potential destructiveness of "natural" disaster. In the immediate aftermath of the Nōbi earthquake, modernity had seemingly made the new regime not stronger than its predecessors, but weaker against a powerful force of nature. European knowledge of how nature might be "overcome" or "tamed" had proven too Eurocentric, or rather too narrowly focused on how nature (and engineering) worked in northern Europe. At least this seemed to be the common narrative of seismologists, many newspaper reporters, and woodblock artists alike. Architects would arrive at different explanations.

Among destructive events of nature, earthquakes are arguably subject to the least control by states and their credentialed experts. No one, in 1891 or indeed today, could or can accurately predict their exact timing, location, or intensity. Unlike in floods or typhoons, populations cannot be publicly marshaled to resist or fortify themselves against the coming disaster. And unlike in an epidemic, new behavioral regimes and medico-political ceremonies cannot simultaneously preserve public health while expanding state power. Following a destructive earthquake, even the ceremony of rescue is morally and politically ambiguous, as rescuers fight not against nature but against the twisted ruins of their own design failures.

States can, however, and in the case of Japan always did, seek new control over epicentral zones, as places where natural and social disruption potentially merge. To put it another way, the Japanese state long sought, and was often able to achieve, some control over the phenomenon of aftershocks.[44] Corresponding to an old pattern, there were riots in Gifu following the Nōbi earthquake, and troops were deployed in the winter of 1891. People who had lost everything had little left to fear.[45] The "return to normal" is also aggravated following earthquakes—as it is not after fires, floods, and storms—by continuing aftershocks of the natural (and not just metaphorical) kind. No one could tell how long they might continue, how strong they would become, or even if they presaged another severe earthquake. For people huddled within hastily built or partially collapsed structures, aftershocks make the experience of an earthquake into a nearly continuous traumatic experience for a period of days, weeks, or even months, and contribute to spontaneous population movements that authorities may seek to stem or channel.[46] A notice from the government office in Gifu, published in the local newspaper in the days following the disaster, warned that "some of our people . . . say that at X time on X day, we'll have a big earthquake again" and ordered that such rumormongers be reported to the police.[47]

A government circular widely posted in the epicentral zone around the same time—and bearing the name of Prof. Sekiya Seikei—told people that aftershocks tend to lessen over time, and do not usually result in a second destructive earthquake. "Tranquility of mind may now be restored," wrote Sekiya, calling on the evidence of "the history of earthquakes from the earliest times."[48] Sekiya was performing a service that Japanese intellectuals had long provided the state following disastrous earthquakes: the "calming of people's nerves" and the fostering of the "return to normal" by declaring the event to be over. According to historian Hashimoto Manpei, an almost identical message had been posted in Edo following the Great Ansei Earthquake of 1855, telling people that there would not be a second one, and they should return to their homes and sleep lest they become sick. Still the rumors spread (in both 1855 and 1891) that an even bigger earthquake would occur the next day, or even that night. People naturally questioned how the government could predict the future when it had failed to anticipate the present.[49]

That earthquakes were singular events, and that their aftershocks decreased in intensity and frequency (the formula for a return to normal), was not necessarily the common Japanese experience, nor an experience that could be readily verified by the record of history. The last "great" earthquakes had come in a tight series, beginning with two in western Japan on consecutive days in 1854 and climaxing a year later with the devastation of Edo. Even this last earthquake (the 1855 Ansei disaster) had occurred in two discrete shocks. The coming of the Westerners—Perry's ships having arrived in Tokyo Bay in 1853—thus came to be seen as an omen of these seismic events, just as the fall of the Shogunate in the following decade could be retrospectively seen as their conclusion.[50] "People are gossiping that possibly the government will fall," said one account written after the destruction of Edo in 1855 (and republished in the aftermath of the Nōbi disaster); "this [the earthquake] is a sign of that."[51] Whether such linkages were explicitly made in the aftermath of the Nōbi earthquake—and we have no clear evidence that they were—the government had every interest in controlling aftershocks.[52]

The return to normal, however crucial, is at bottom fiction. Earthquakes can indeed remap social, political, and economic landscapes, something well understood by the inhabitants of Edo in 1855. Woodblock prints called *namazu-e* (catfish pictures) produced just after the Ansei earthquake destabilize even our modern reading of earthquakes as "unmitigated disasters." According to the common Japanese sense, earthquakes were caused by the movements of a large catfish who carried the archipelago on his back. In the *namazu-e*, this catfish is neither ferocious nor sublime, but an animal who redistributes good and ill fortune. In one example, people on shore welcome the arrival from the sea of a whalelike catfish who spouts gold coins from its blowhole. In another, more politically precise blockprint, members of the landlord class attack and attempt to punish two large catfish, while artisans, who have come to love the catfish, attempt to restrain them. The comparatively less prosperous artisan class—the "common people" of Edo—particularly *daiku* and other building artisans—were the major beneficiaries of the redistribution of wealth following Ansei and other destructive earthquakes or fires. According to one modern account, the catfish after Ansei even came to be depicted as a god "who would equally distribute all wealth and create an ideal society."[53] Edo-period earthquakes thus became agents in the popular utopian dream of world rectification (*yonaoshi*), or the setting right of unjust social, political, and economic orders.[54]

In graphic and prose accounts of the Nōbi earthquake, catfish rarely appear.[55] Yet the Edo-period sense of earthquakes as agents of *yonaoshi* arguably found new expression as the sudden reversal of "Japanese" and "Western" fragilities and knowledges. A discourse formerly about class and state-subject relations becomes one about civilizations. With the survival of a core "Japan" in the form of ancient architectural and landscape features, the destruction on the Nōbi Plain is not un-mitigated, but in some sense revelatory, sorting the "foreign" from the "Japanese." Social relations between Japanese, however, are far flatter in accounts of 1891 than in the often richly ironic ones of 1855.[56] The Nōbi disaster creates, graphically and textually, largely undifferentiated "victims" in the disaster zone itself, and those (unaffected) Japanese outside it who are tasked with delivering relief. In other words, there is something resembling a nation.

The farmers on the Nōbi Plain were not urban artisans, and could scarcely have hoped to catch gold coins. Most of those who survived in the epicentral zone collected only further misery. Yet even there the earthquake created at least two new classes—those who have houses and still-cultivatable rice fields, and those who are without one or the other (or both). Among the latter, the state saw the opportunity to find subjects for, among other things, its faltering colonization project in distant Hokkaido.[57]

Much has been written of the Sino-Japanese war of 1894–95 as a landmark "na-tionalizing" event and a crucial moment in the popular representation of the Im-perial institution. The 1891 Nōbi earthquake was in some sense a dress rehearsal for 1894; it was one of the first nonpolitical spectacles to receive sustained nation-wide news coverage, and the impetus for a national mobilization to aid the disaster victims. There was some precedent for these moves in the Bandai-san eruption of 1888, but this time the tragedy was so much greater and the possible story lines more prolific. The government sought to exploit this coverage by constructing the Imperial family as actively involved in the relief of victims. This campaign was not entirely successful, as Imperially directed relief efforts competed with the newspa-pers' own substantial—and unprecedented—collection of relief funds. But the tone of much news coverage and other popular writing in the aftermath of the dis-aster portrayed government officials, especially the Emperor, as moved by the plight of victims to the point of tears. Here was a much different Japanese govern-ment than the one that had lived in mysterious seclusion in Kyoto or Edo, or the one that would soon turn the Emperor into a taciturn military hero. Here was also a dif-ferent moral universe than the one that surrounded the Ansei quake of 1855. In the Nōbi earthquake, the previously sharp Japanese sense that disaster critiqued the order of things and redistributed good and ill fortune was buried behind a façade of a collective "human emotion" and concerted "national" action.

In the days following the disaster the Imperial family was among the first to do-nate relief money, initially 3,000 yen. "When telegrams came in and he realized how extensive the damage was," according to one contemporary source, the Emperor supplemented his original contribution by an additional 10,000.[58] This substantial increase in largesse may have been spurred by the virtual flood of fundraising efforts, coordinated by Japan's newspapers and nascent professional organizations, that accompanied early reports of the disaster. But for those who made much of the Imperial response to the disaster, such as two Nagoya City officials who authored a popular postdisaster book, the escalating donations by the Emperor were part of a narrative of ever-greater empathy and involvement, one that would eventually affect even Imperial body-functions. "Every time the Emperor and Empress hear more [of the suffering of victims]," wrote the Nagoya officials, "they deeply grieve and nearly forget to have a meal or sleep." Those immediately around the Emperor were portrayed as constantly in tears with each new expression of his largesse, or in the words of one writer, "subjects were moved to cry as if his benevolence were free-floating." When the Emperor called his forester and told him to cut down trees on lands belonging to the Imperial family in order to supply lumber to victims, the man had to "squeeze out his sleeves because they were full of tears." When the governors of the affected prefectures met with the Emperor and showed him photographs of the damage, "after a while the Emperor's eyes leaked, he could not talk, and the governors couldn't help crying, so they had to leave."[59] Prime Minister Matsukata was portrayed in a separate account as shedding tears on visiting victims of the disaster, not because of their misery, but on seeing their own emotional reaction to the news he bore of the Emperor's charity. Minister of Communications Count Gotō was depicted in another, intentionally less flattering portrayal, as literally running around his garden on receiving news of the disaster, pale-faced and overwhelmed by his new responsibilities.[60]

There is no question that the Imperial family was active in performing new ceremonies of consolation in and around the disaster zone. In the days following the event the Emperor sent his chamberlain, Mori, and later Baron Takesaki and other members of the nobility to the two affected prefectures "not the make the usual trip and just meet high officials [but] to console victims." On instructions from the Emperor, his representatives "walked the streets" of the disaster zone, rather than take a carriage, and even "camped out" so that busy prefectoral bureaucrats would not be distracted by their presence. Baron Takesaki capped his tour with a visit to a village of Burakumin, to which "normal people were reluctant to go."[61] According to one description: "Despite his precious and holy body, the Emperor's representative did not mind going to this village. How gracious. His action enshrined the village. The injured were moved to tears because of their treatment. Who can stop crying if they hear about this benevolence."[62]

Female members of the Imperial family were even more active in relief work. The Empress herself briefly visited the disaster zone, and organized a charity ball at the Rokumeikan, while Princess Toko organized a relief fund, Baroness Takashima collected rolls of cotton, and the Aristocratic Ladies' School sent train-loads of rice.[63] The Japanese Red Cross, of which of the Empress was patron, portrayed itself as having been personally dispatched by her to the disaster site, along with certain physicians associated with the Imperial household.[64] The Empress also sent her own consoling message to victims within days of the disaster, which was widely reprinted in Japanese newspapers. This again foreshadows the very active role the Empress and her circle would perform in providing relief to soldiers in the Meiji period's two Imperial wars.

The Meiji press was brought to task, however, in the same popular book published by Nagoya city officials, for not giving more prominent coverage to role of the Imperial family. "We are so lucky in being born in the time when this Emperor and Empress are reigning. However, what makes me feel regrettable is that although subjects get affectionate treatment, this can't be heard by people because of newspapers' constant annoying reporting. All of you and your relatives and friends should widely talk about their benevolent behavior."[65] In fact the press was rather consistent in presenting the Imperial family as actively engaged with—even actively commiserating with—the Nōbi victims. The "annoying reporting" might refer to prominence given the press's own parallel relief efforts, which eventually brought in the staggering sum of 141,393 yen. Independent donations were also made by many Chinese associations and even the Yokohama Jinriksha Drivers. An additional 61,875 yen was donated by people taking advantage of the offer by Mitsui Bank and Japan Usen Company to transmit money orders without charge to officials in the disaster zone. These amounts dwarfed the donations by the Imperial family, though the aristocrats' donations may have helped set the pattern for the Japanese public to follow.[66]

One likely spur to all this gift-giving was the new press language of dramatic and emotional description, quite different in tone from the allegorical and often ironic reportage that had accompanied the Ansei earthquake. Just as the Emperor, and nearly everyone around him, were portrayed in the uncharacteristic posture of shedding real tears, so descriptions of the victims in newspapers and books seemed to compete with one another to tweak the popular emotions with images of unmitigated suffering. The rumble of the earthquake was "like a voice from hell."[67] The devastation was so total one "couldn't even see the shadows of trees" (not even trees were left standing). The postdisaster landscape was "like a world full of

勅
使
を
羅
害
者
を
御
慰
問
を
人
民
の
感
泣
の
図

FIGURE 9

Officials representing the Imperial family visit a shattered village
on the Nōbi Plain (from Kizawa Noritoshi and Yamawa Yoshihiko, *Meiji shinsai shūroku*, 1891). Note the exaggerated difference
in appearance between the mustachioed visitors and the mice-like
villagers. Written by two Nagoya city officials, the book is largely
a homily on the Imperial family's involvement in disaster relief.

demons," and "the living wished that they had died." There were also recordings
of the loss of faith. People said openly (according to one reporter) that "Buddhism
has no power."[68]

If people were to be unified in emotion, however, they were also to be unified in
knowledge. Readers of newspapers and popular books were invited to shed tears
on one page and consider scientific explanations for the cause of the disaster on the
next, a rhythm now normative in the reporting and consumption of disasters, but
one still in the process of formation in mid-Meiji Japan. Even more so than after the
Bandai-san eruption of 1888, the Great Nōbi Earthquake made "science" an essential chapter of even its cheapest and most popular published accounts. The hastily
assembled *Aichi Gifu daijishin no sanjyō* (Aichi Gifu Great Earthquake's Miserable
Spectacle) exactly located the epicenter, provided data on the subsidence of after-

shocks, and described the seismic waves as having "four seconds between the vertical" and "six seconds between the horizontal" components of their motion. "What is the cause?" became an obligatory question in newspapers and the many popular books rushed into print by newspaper editors. The *Nichi nichi shimbun* declared it to be the explosion of a nearby mountain, but most writers at least dipped into seismology for more elaborate or sophisticated theories, even if their plurality left the reader in doubt. The condition of doubt itself (in the form of conflicting scientific hypotheses) reflected a sense of modernity for some authors. "In the past we said catfish," wrote the editor of one account, "but now we have many explanations in our heads."[69]

The figure of the *jishingakusha* (seismologist) was introduced by the Nagoya-published *Daijishin no jikkyō* (The Actual Condition of the Great Earthquake) as a new type of scientist whom readers were not assumed to be familiar with. He was not a mere collector of field data, the author was at pains to point out, but a man who "begins with academic theories," which it went on to detail. This fastidiousness about job descriptions may suggest that field workers—those legions of local government functionaries who had been sending seismic data to Tokyo via postcard for the better part of a decade—were becoming familiar enough to be potentially mistaken for *jishingakusha* of the professional kind. In other words, "amateur" seismology may have been rife in the land, practiced by schoolteachers, postal workers, telegraph operators, weather observers, and others enlisted in Milne's network. Indeed one popular book published by a Nagoya newspaper with the assistance of the deans of two local schools shows one or both of the schoolmasters to be unusually well informed about earthquakes. Over twenty pages are dedicated to global earthquake folklore, classical European and Chinese explanations, and a summary of contemporary theories, which the authors conclude in the end are "not at the trustful stage yet" because "different disciplines are arguing against one another."[70] Their arguments would not soon cease.

THE EARTHQUAKE AS PHOTOGRAPHS

Immediately on returning to Tokyo, John Milne prepared a book of large-plate photographs taken by his travel companion, Kōbudaigakkō professor W. K. Burton, and captioned mostly with passages from his newspaper articles, entitled *The Great Earthquake in Japan, 1891*. Wandering through the wreckage of Nōbi, an earthquake that equaled "any movements recorded in the annals of seismology," was an event of great personal and professional consequence to Milne, and his desire to broadcast it in the form of photographs (rather than the inscriptions of seismographs) was not without purpose.[71] When Milne's controversial paper of 1886 had been presented before the Institution of Civil Engineers in London, the society's president began the question period with the blunt comment that "The paper was one of an unusual character, which fortunately did not interest Englishmen very much."[72] By showcasing both the destructive power and the human pathos of a major earthquake, Milne's book of photographs could not help but focus attention on seismology as a socially relevant science, perhaps more relevant than astronomy, whose status and funding he openly covets in his introduction.[73]

Milne's theme is the utterness of the destruction, and he accordingly divides his plates between collapsed Japanese farmhouses and collapsed examples of Western-style engineering, including the Owari (Nagoya) Spinning Mill and the Nagara River railway bridge. Yet this "symmetry" was itself polemical. The latter photos are the more dramatic, as they document the failure of large Western-style structures supposed to be earthquake-proof. The two plates of the Owari Spinning Mill show not only toppled brick walls and chimneys but, prominently, fallen or dangling trusses, the icons of the new architecture's mathematicality. Milne's caption suggests that it was the trusses themselves that, on account of their heaviness, and thus their inability to move synchronically with the brick, brought down the walls. "It is notable," he writes with a final twist of the knife, "that the earthquake was not particularly severe at the Spinning Mill, Japanese houses near it not having been much damaged."[74]

Milne is noticeably kinder to railroad engineers, even attempting to edit the reading of his most dramatic photograph: "When looking at illustrations of the railway bridges," he writes, opposite a plate of the collapsed steel-truss span at Nagara, "it must be remembered that, for five years, not only have they withstood all ordinary traffic, but they have been subjected without injury to unusually heavy floods, which have devastated the surrounding country, and have withstood the force of typhoons which have overturned locomotives and caused the collapse of many brick buildings and chimneys."[75] It might be that for Milne, bridge designers were, in contrast to architects, men of science, or that the prior strength of the bridge revealed earthquakes to be the strongest of the destructive forces of nature, or that the collapsed bridges were more useful to seismology than the ruined mill: "A bridge which has been partially destroyed by an earthquake . . . becomes a seismometer, and leads to the determination of the rate at which the motion was applied. . . ."[76]

Or it might be that those concerned with railroads in Japan and Britain's colonial possessions were one of the principal audiences Milne's book was intended to

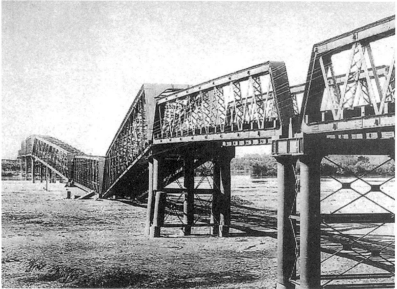

FIGURE 10

The ruins of the Owari Spinning Mill *(a)* and the collapsed Nagara River railroad bridge *(b)*, Nagoya, 1891. These were two of the most often reproduced photographs from John Milne and W. K. Burton's *The Great Earthquake in Japan, 1891*. They eventually became part of the Imperial University's College of Science display at the World's Columbian Exposition in Chicago (1893).

reach. X had pointed out, in one of his articles from the Nōbi Plain, that Milne was "connected" to the Railway Department of the Imperial government, as was the bridge's designer, C. A. W. Pownall, a member of the Institution of Civil Engineers.[77] Although he might never interest most Englishmen in seismology, Milne could well interest those constructing railroads and other engineering structures in what he would refer to in later years as "our earthquake-shaken colonies."[78] Milne would even spend a portion of his career adopting the seismograph into an instrument that measured the vibration of trains in motion, a device useful to railroads but with little significance to science.[79]

Clearly a great many wooden farmhouses fell down on the Nōbi Plain, a fact that Milne makes no attempt to mask. But the photos of earthquake survivors walking and huddling among wrecked houses are not architectonic, the structures having been reduced to mere piles of lumber. Milne's focus here is on the people, and his captions describe death and suffering and occasionally Milne's own emotions. In his later *Seismology* (1898) Milne would reuse many of the photos of failed bridges and other engineering structures, but the photos of human suffering and collapsed farmhouses would not reappear. The word pictures of Nōbi that Milne scattered in other places, such as in the journal *Nature* in December 1891, also tilt away from the fragile balance of his photo-book: "In many places the so-called 'foreign' buildings of brick and stone—undoubtedly put up in the flimsiest manner—lie as heaps of ruins between Japanese buildings still standing."[80]

Yet the collapse of so many Japanese houses on the Nōbi Plain did noticeably affect Milne's subsequent writing. He was more cautious about praising Japanese carpentry, and even created distance between his own experiments with aseismic buildings and the methods of *daiku*. In his mid-1880s report to the British Association for the Advancement of Science, Milne's discussion of Japanese buildings had immediately preceded that of his own experiments, making their linkage explicit.[81] Yet in his 1898 textbook, their order of presentation is reversed. Milne first describes his own experiments, distances them from other, prior European experiments of similar character, and lastly distances them even from the work of *daiku:* "An unintentional form of aseismic arrangement is found in ordinary Japanese frame buildings, the sills of which rest loosely upon the upper surfaces of stones or boulders planted in the soil. From experience we know that houses of this description suffer less destruction than common masonry structures, but to what extent this is due to the free foundation cutting off the motion imparted by the moving ground is not known."[82]

The Japanese system is now "unintentional," in contrast with Milne's own very intentional experiments, and the caveat in the second sentence casts doubt even on its effectiveness. Exactly how the Japanese foundation works is "not known" (at least by Milne). The similarity between his own aseismic joint and the common foundations of Japanese buildings begins descending toward the status of footnote.

CONDER ON THE EARTHQUAKE:
THE DISCOVERY OF JAPANESE WEIGHT

Milne and Conder each delivered two public lectures on Nōbi in the months following the earthquake. In one sense their public talks continued their postearthquake correspondence in the Yokohama papers, the lectures being printed in the same papers, often with follow-up editorials. The difference was that the authors now signed their pieces; they were now expressing views as credentialed experts rather than reporting facts as anonymous journalists.

What had begun as a mere dissonance between scholarly papers in the early 1880s, and had become an erudite argument within scientific societies in the middle of that decade, was now, in the early 1890s, the issue of the moment in both the Japanese and foreign-language press. At the beginning, scientific papers had been published in diverse settings at unpredictable times, by people who might or might not choose to engage one another's arguments. Now lectures and articles were being published with regularity by two small and stable groups intensely interested and aware of what the other was saying. Careers if not professions were now at stake. Scientific paper, public lecture, and newspaper article merged, as did previously distinct audiences of architects, seismologists, "men of science," Japanese, Westerners, and so forth.

Conder spoke twice on the subject that winter, once to the Tokyo Elocutionary Society in December 1891 and once before the Association of Japanese Architects (Nihon Zōka-gakkai) in January 1892. He began his first lecture by acknowledging "the general distrust of brick and stone buildings," which he ascribed, however, to a mood of "panic."[83] The defensive tone that had characterized his response to Milne since the mid-1880s was now replaced by one more confident, and analytic. The very future of the Anglo-Japanese architecture project meant salvaging Japanese trust in masonry, and to do this Conder needed to construct a cogent explanation for the full range of phenomena in Milne's photographs, newspaper articles, and other public records.

There were many ways he might have navigated through the new accumulation of evidence. He might, for example, have dwelt on the destruction of tens of thousands of houses as further proof of the now decades-old claim of Japan's fragility.

He might also have used the reports from Japanese newspapers about the fall of temples, which in some cases killed many more people than had died at the mills. Although he would later deploy just such evidence in a foreign setting, Conder's Tokyo lectures of 1891–92 barely touch on these matters. He acknowledges rather that "purely Japanese buildings, such as the castle *tenshu* [keep] and the *hondō* [main hall] of the largest temples, have shown by far the best record in the late convulsion, some of them remaining entirely uninjured"[84] and turns to analyzing why. Moreover, he acknowledges for the first time that certain features of Japanese construction might be seismically superior to European ones of the same type. For example, although the European truss was "scientific," he wrote, "the [European] roof as a whole is often a very unscientific structure indeed" because the connections between the trusses are left to carpenters, who rely on "rule of thumb" methods to join them together.[85] He contrasts this with Japanese roofs: "Though the ancient Japanese roof is a heavy, wasteful, and unscientific structure, it appears to me to possess certain advantages not generally present in the ordinary European roof; it is equally stiff in every direction, and is in fact a continuous, united framework and not, like the modern roof, a series of detached frameworks."[86] This was, on its surface, a remarkable concession from a man who had long denied, repeatedly and in the strongest terms, the aseismic properties of Japanese buildings.

But read more carefully, Conder's statements were no reversal. Most obviously, there was his continued insistence on the dyads scientific/unscientific, efficient/wasteful, and ancient/modern. *Daiku*-work, despite "possess[ing] certain advantages," remained somehow fixed on the wrong side of each divide. Conder's concession of the vulnerability of European roofs was also carefully circumscribed. The zone of "science" was now tightly redrawn around the truss as object, while the rest of the European roof became an artifact of carpenters and their "rule of thumb" methods. It was in this newly opened artisanal (nonscientific) space between the individual roof trusses that the failure at the Owari Spinning Mill was presumably to be located. Conder concludes his analysis not by calling for the adaptation of the Japanese roof, but the improvement of the European one, by making it too "a continuous united framework" and "equally stiff in every direction."[87]

Conder's ostensible retreat was in actuality a new way of advancing old and strongly held positions. The Japanese roof he now found admirable was a different "Japanese roof" from that of the seismologists. To the latter, *daiku*-work was above all a network of flexible joints that performed a "basket-like yielding."[88] To Conder, it was now "equally stiff in every direction." Stiffness was of course a characteristic associated with masonry, and being "stiff, strong, and reliable" was the very set of qualities R. H. Brunton had assigned, two decades earlier, to "higher" (European) carpentry, in contrast to the "lower," decorative carpentry of the Japanese. Japanese roofs were now to provide a model because, in resisting the earthquake, they had proven their conformance to "fixed principles" of European constructive science. It was this set of fixed principles that Conder was actually intent on salvaging, even to the extent of locating them, for the first time, in the structure of Japanese roofs.

This newly discovered convergence of Western scientific principle with Japanese carpentry practice was still, for Conder, more accident than design. This emerges most clearly in his explanation for the survival of castles and large temples. Here the seismologists' description of Japanese structural properties is also neatly reversed. It was not, as the seismologists had long claimed, isolated foundations and flexible joints that had kept these buildings intact, argued Conder, but "the enormous mass and weight of [their] material," which "neutralized to a great extent their inherent defects."[89] This was consistent with his earlier position on pagodas: that the only force their builders were consciously resisting was that of gravity. Moreover, assigning the survival of these buildings to their "enormous mass and weight of materials" made castles and temples analogous to "the massive stone keeps and cathedrals of the west." Again, Conder was explaining the superior performance of certain Japanese buildings by inscribing them with the characteristics of European ones, and thus salvaging existing principles of constructive science. Japan's wooden castles and temples were being redesigned in such a way as to bolster European masonry's case.

By the same token, the failure of the mills and other brick buildings in Nagoya and Osaka were explained by their having taken on Japanese characteristics. The masons had made the walls too thin, imparting to them the "lightness" characteristic of Japanese carpentry. They had made the window openings too large, again due to a local insistence on closely uniting inside and outside. Neither had they constructed enough interior walls, given the Japanese preference for uninterrupted interior space. It was the sum of these and other declensions from European practice (if not cultural sensibilities), Conder seems to argue, that explained the mills' failure.[90]

The fallen mills, described in the newspaper reports as "European," became, in Conder's account, Japanese, while Nagoya Castle and the surviving temples graduated into the small circle of Japanese buildings that illustrated European structural principles. "Solid," "substantial," "well-executed" European masonry remained intact as an earthquake-resistant material. Conder listed, in fact, a half dozen large masonry buildings or complexes in Osaka, "properly built under the direction of experts," that had survived unscathed. These included an even larger cotton mill than the one that collapsed. Conder acknowledged that it was "open to speculation" how these buildings would have fared in Nagoya or Gifu, closer to the center of the shock. But for now at least, architecture remained above and unaffected by Japanese nature and its calamities. Western architectural and engineering knowledge had been shaken but not brought down.[91]

Having designed a coherent explanation for the phenomenon on the Nōbi Plain—one that required no displacement of the lessons taught at Kōbudaigakkō, Conder moved architecture into the offensive. The solution to the disasters in Osaka and Nagoya was a more rigorous application of European knowledge through increased supervision.

> A drawing is not all that is required from an expert. . . . There are hundreds of points in the actual construction of brick and stone buildings which require the constant attention of trained and experienced men. The Japanese carpenter is himself a kind of architect, acquainted, as far as his lights go, with the properties of the material he works with; the brick layer, on the other hand, is an ignorant drudge whose one idea is to work against time and shirk where possible the directions of his overseers . . . it is necessary, therefore, not only that the designs of all important structures should be subject to the approval of certified inspectors; but that the work itself should be executed by men carrying undeniable proofs of knowledge and competence in such matters.[92]

In calling for "a proper system of building control,"[93] Conder was repositioning the architectural profession as a police force as much as a design force. *Daiku*, rehabilitated by public opinion, are no longer the principal object of reform. The problem was a new class of hybrids: Japanese masons.

It was partly this heightened sensitivity toward the need for constructive control that led Conder, at the end of both papers, to reframe Anglo-Japanese architecture itself as fundamentally a science project. "The architect of the modern day must be a scientist first and an artist afterward," he told the gathering of his former students; "he must at any rate be content to be so in a country subjected to earthquake convulsions." The word "science" had long been contested by Conder and Milne, but with the authority of "art" rapidly receding, Conder now transferred the full weight of his identity into the more powerful term. "Scientific men," he said to the Elocutionary Society, "may be divided into two classes." The first, clearly meant to include himself and other architects, engaged in "wisely and consciously applying . . . fully established theories." The other, just as clearly the seismologists, were "occupied with searching, probing, and speculating upon the hidden and unknown mysteries of unrevealed science."[94] A compliment, perhaps, but one whose every adjective is a synonym for not knowing. "The fully established theories" architects were to apply as science were clearly those conceived in Europe and not Japan.

Conder ended by offering the Meiji state an alternative to Milne's collection of foreign building regulations, an alternative way of constructing "constructive science." He and other architect-scientists had returned from the Nōbi Plain with numerous drawings of successful and unsuccessful details. He suggested that the Nihon Zōka-gakkai take the initiative in "drawing up certain principles with regard to buildings erected in Japan" that the government might then codify. Nōbi had, for the first time, provided architects the opportunity to create earthquake knowledge in their own medium—the sketch or drawing—which might complicate the information in seismograms, photographs, and other instrumental records.[95]

By reinvesting architecture's identity in "science," Conder was in one sense attempting to steer the nascent Japanese architectural profession into a position of greater local authority and respect. Conversely, and perhaps unwittingly, he was setting his students on a road that would distance them even further from their European and American counterparts, who increasingly aspired to an art without science. "It is a very regrettable fact," he wrote, that the art of architecture in Japan "can never aspire to that freedom of perfection" it had attained in nonearthquake countries: "Architecture may hope to make advances as a science which will compensate to some extent for lack of artistic development. The architect will always be cramped and confined in his creations by fear of this dreadful enemy of stability."[96] Wrapped within this "concession" of Japan's inability to match Europe in architectural "artistry" was Conder's own long inability to synthesize British and Japanese design. In a certain sense seismology had provided him a "scientific" way out of this intractable "artistic" dilemma.

MILNE ON THE EARTHQUAKE: THE LESSON OF MOUNT FUJI

Milne organized public lectures even prior to Conder's, before the Geographical Society in November, and at a special meeting of the Seismological Society at the Imperial Hotel in early December. Now named the father of seismic science by the same newspaper editor who had recently called earthquakes chimeras, Milne spoke in the first instance in a hall "crowded to the doors," and in the second before a standing-room-only crowd of nearly five hundred. Japanese were "very numerous" among the Imperial Hotel audience, and Milne's talk there was partially translated. He was also given two introductions, the first in Japanese by mathematics professor Kikuchi Dairoku, and the second by fellow member of the Royal Society Dr. Divers, who exclaimed, according to the papers, that "this society was not only the Seismological Society of Japan, but was also the Seismological Society of the whole civilized world."[97]

Most of Milne's lecture time was devoted to explaining what caused the earth to move. The theory of seismic origins that he presented as most likely held that, during the slow upward thrust of mountain ranges, there were occasional moments when tensions were suddenly released, causing the surface of the earth to "snap." These could be initiated, he supposed, by any number of triggers, including meteorological and/or astronomical events. Even electricity. "I see electrical theories are very popular," said Milne; "we generally resort to them when we cannot explain anything (laughter)."[98] The *Japan Weekly Mail* frequently wrote "(laughter)" or even "(Great laughter)" after one of Milne's remarks.[99]

But it wasn't just humor that eased the transmission of seismological messages that winter, for it was a changed audience that Milne had to be good before: one increasingly less European and more Japanese. While sharing laughter at the expense of electrical theories (and, subtextually, physicists), Milne used a different approach in introducing the theory, which he took more seriously, of the relation between earthquakes and subterranean steam.[100] He began with the Confucian view that "within the earth there are certain vapors which shake the ground in endeavoring to escape." Actually, Confucian explanations were, as Milne and educated members of his audience would have known, more varied and complex, involving sudden imbalances among ethers, or the four elements (soil, water, fire, and air), or positive and negative poles above and below the surface. Milne probably simplified to make Chinese philosophy resonate more closely with his current hypothesis (and, incidentally, with Shakespeare, whose passage on "the imprisoning of unruly wind" he also briefly quotes as "the same idea" as that of the Confucians). "Now we have exactly the same idea," he continued, "only the vapor we think about is the vapor of water; we think about steam. . . . We think that steam may have something to do with the earthquakes felt every day."[101]

Milne's interest in Confucian explanations, especially those ascribing earthquakes to an imbalance among the fundamental elements of soil, water, fire, and air, was not only rhetorical (although I mean to foreground its power as rhetoric). That he was able to build a bridge between *yōgaku* (Western studies) and *kangaku* (Chinese studies) had partly to do with their convergence. Historian of seismology Hashimoto Manpei paraphrases the *Taikyoku Jishinki* of 1662, the earliest of the Japanese Confucian texts to explain earthquakes, as follows: "It compares the earth to a three-legged pan over an oven. If you add wind, the fire is more active, the water boils, and the lid moves, and that is an earthquake. The world is large, so in various areas the proportions of these elements varies. Also, in the time of an earthquake, very often the sky is cloudy and it rains. The reason is that from the soil steam comes up, and that becomes clouds and rain."[102]

Milne's seismology had still not discounted, as an explanation for why seismic tensions were suddenly released, an "imbalance" among soil, water, fire, and air. According to an 1889 *Nature* article, Milne hoped to experimentally verify that tremors are "closely connected with wind" and with "the escape of underground gases." Statistical evidence suggested some correlation between seismology and meteorology—the subterranean and the atmospheric—which was another reason Japan's seismographs were located at meteorological stations.[103]

Milne still had the choice of constructing similarity or difference between seismological and Confucian texts. That he chose to build continuity, and find further parallels between Chinese views and those of Shakespeare, was consistent with his pattern of trying to weave the two halves of Anglo-Japanese seismology into an ever stronger whole. *Yōgaku*, he was suggesting, would seamlessly succeed *kangaku*. He denied an epistemological break.

Milne's vitiation of "East and West" and "ancient and modern" continued, more brilliantly, when he changed the topic to earthquake construction. He began by placing himself outside a debate he had started, and exclaiming ignorance of a subject he was determined to teach. As he was paraphrased by a newspaper columnist: "No doubt there were many people who said brick buildings fell because they were put up badly. Others would probably say they fell because brick buildings were not able to withstand such motions. He would leave that to the architects. He had very little experience with brickwork—very slight indeed—but that had told him that brickwork varied greatly."[104]

Milne would have known from the reports of X that Conder had many explanations for why particular buildings failed; Milne was being careful not to let himself be cornered in the ruins. "Of the recent earthquake he would not speak much in detail," continued the newspaper account, "because the audience would gain their information from the views to be exhibited by Messrs. Burton and Kajima." These were sixty magic lantern slides made from the dramatic photographs in Milne's book (and supplemented by slides from Manila and Ischia) scheduled to close out the lecture.[105]

Leaving the earthquake "itself" to be reported by the photographs, Milne moved his audience from the Nōbi Plain into his own laboratory, describing experiments he had conducted using shaking tables and brick columns, "a lot of experiments in which Mr. Tatsuno and other gentlemen assisted." Conder's star pupil was here rhetorically stolen away as Milne's lab assistant, suggesting young Japanese architects might still shed the prejudices of their teachers. The result of these shaking table experiments, said Milne, was that he was "able to calculate how it [a column] should be built. It ought to follow a certain curve, which was quite calculable." Rules for earthquake construction were now to come out of lab experiments and calculations, and be embodied in curves. Constructive science had now fully abandoned observational seismology and the business of sifting through ruins.[106]

At this point Milne deployed a skilful metaphor. The curve that had been calculated from shaking table experiments, he said, already existed in the Japanese landscape itself. Turning to the castles at Nagoya and Ōgaki, which Conder had also used to effect, Milne noted that "they follow a particular shape which gives stability." That is, they had broad bases and a superstructure composed of successively smaller units. "As a matter of fact," said Milne, "they follow the Fuji-san curve." He was referring to the gradually curving lines that famously trace the two slopes of Mount Fuji. These were very similar, he claimed, to the lines traced out by his shaking table. Again, as paraphrased by the newspaper:

> The contours of Mt. Fuji excited the admiration of poets and painters; but it also should demand the attention of every engineer, for it conveyed numerous lessons of practical and applied science. He would not ask them to build exactly the same as Fuji, but Fuji was theoretically correct. They would find that Fuji had a base sufficient to support its height and if they wanted to build Fuji bigger—he did not care who the engineer was—with the same material, they must increase its base. And every time the engineers passed Fuji it seemed to him the mountain must convey a lesson better than any Molesworth's Pocket Book—(Applause). They could not do better than take the lesson conveyed in that beautiful curvature.[107]

He re-created the scene in his second lecture:

Painters had stopped before Fuji, poets had written about it; but every engineer who passed it ought to lift up his hands and thank nature for that beautiful monument of mathematics crystallized before him. It was perfect in its curves; it was one of those figures that could be discussed by x's and y's.[108]

Why did the first audience burst into applause? Perhaps it was the low esteem in which engineers and architects were held just after Nōbi, and the audience's delight at having the voice of "pure science" put them in their places. But also contributing to the applause was the brilliance of Milne's landscape picture. While architects and engineers had been reading their British engineering pocket books, the "lesson" of how to counteract Japanese earthquakes was visible all the time, in the most omnipresent of Japanese natural features. In Fuji-san Milne found an object more powerful than pagodas—although their discursive similarities are noteworthy—one that brought together the curve of laboratory-based experiment with a curve deeply meaningful to Japanese (and many foreigners). Fuji-san also symbolized the new relationship Milne sought to force between seismology and architecture, for Mount Fuji, the source of this wisdom, was a seismic feature. If engineers had read the earth, rather than their Molesworth, and had noticed that the curve of Mount Fuji was replicated in the curve of the Japanese castles, their structures might have survived as well as the castles and not come crashing down. The new lessons of seismology now merged with lessons learned by *daiku* long ago.

Milne and Conder were in one sense making the same case. No longer speaking primarily to an audience of Europeans, each was enlarging the circle of Japanese objects that their scientific arguments enclosed. In Conder's case the enlargement was the more striking, as he had started with incommensurable circles of European stability and Japanese fragility. The circle of stability had now been enlarged to include Japanese castles, temples, and even common roofs. But Milne had drawn his already generous boundaries wider still, capturing the landscape—Japan—itself.

Having made important places in their schemes for castles and temples, neither Conder nor Milne chose to use the evidence of Japanese newspaper correspondents that temples had also fallen.[109] Milne "again called attention to the fact that many of the temples had remained standing" during his second lecture.[110] The "fragility" of Japanese houses also ceased to be an issue between them, as the new discussion turned around Japanese strength.

By this time (1891–92) it seems more accurate to refer to Conder and Milne not as "British," but, like the disciplines they founded, "Anglo-Japanese." Not only had

VOL. III. 1894.

FIGURE 11

Cover illustration of the *Transactions of the Seismological Society of Japan*, 1894, showing Fuji-san. The volcanic mountain became a seismological lesson in the wake of the Great Nōbi Earthquake, "one of those figures," as Milne put it, "that could be discussed by x's and y's."

both men been in Japan for nearly two decades, but Milne had already married the daughter of a Buddhist priest, and Conder would marry Maenami Kume the following year. Milne's biographers believe that by this time he was "content to remain [in Japan] the rest of his life" although he was fated to leave forever in 1895, when his house and all its contents were burned, in what may have been an act of arson fueled by growing nativism. Conder, after returning from a long trip to Britain and Europe in the mid-1880s, seems to have concluded there was no place for him there; he would stay in Japan for the rest of his life. The energy with which both men tied their projects more closely to Japan in the winter of 1891–92 may mirror their recognition of mixed nationality or hyphenated identity. Their British families and patrons were increasingly far away, and their Japanese ones more importantly present.[111]

THE EARTHQUAKE IN THE WEST

The Nōbi earthquake increased the seismic resistance of "Japan" in Japan. But it did nothing to decrease the fragility of "Japan" in the West. Milne's book of photographs, for example, despite the prominence it gave to collapsed examples of Western architecture and engineering, was read in English architectural and engineering circles as a further condemnation of Japanese abilities. Edward F. Strange wrote in *The Architectural Review* in 1897 that "the researches of Messrs. Burton and Milne have proven that the Japanese have been somewhat mistaken" in choosing to construct their country of wood. "In most cases the supports [of wooden buildings] collapsed, as Prof. Milne puts it, 'much like the houses children build with playing cards,' and the great roofs crashed through with most terrible results." Strange acknowledges that brick and stone buildings also fell down, "but careful inquiries showed that every case of exceptional damage could be traced to defective workmanship or materials, the conclusion being that thoroughly well built brick or stone work is always the best in the long run, even in a country subject, like Japan, to the most violent earthquakes. . . ."[112] Recaptioning Milne's photographs with Conder's judgments, Strange placed the burden for disasters like the Owari Spinning Mill squarely on the Japanese: "Unfortunately there are signs that the most fatal vice of jerry-building is among them."[113]

The same lesson was drawn by George Cawley before the Japan Society of London in 1892, in the lecture preceding the performance of the joiner and the *daiku*. To Cawley, who as early as 1878 had advocated an entirely masonry Japan, Nōbi had finally cured "the delusion" of "any supposed advantages of the ordinary Japanese house in respect to earthquakes." After describing the death and destruction attendant on the Japanese attachment to their own domestic architecture, Cawley turned to the Owari Spinning Mill, not as an illustration of failure, but as a model: "In the midst of all this ruin a tall brick factory chimney at a cotton mill in Nagoya stood without suffering a crack for the greater part of its height. Where then, is the advantage of wood over brick in reducing danger from earthquakes?"[114] Cawley was likely referring to one of Milne's photographs, showing a half-collapsed chimney beside a thoroughly ruined mill where scores of workers had been killed. Milne's caption had particularly noted the survival of nearby Japanese houses.

Milne's Fuji-san lesson, like Dresser's lesson of pagoda as pendulum, never informed British architect H. H. Stratham, who wrote in 1912 that Japanese architecture was not "logical," because "it runs all into curved lines, and it is not the natural structure of lumber to treat it in curves." The Japanese "passion" for curved lines, he pointed out, was even manifest in their castles, which should be the very archetypes of utilitarian principle. "That kind of beauty which is called the beauty of 'fitness' [for purpose]," he concluded, "does not recommend itself to the Oriental mind."[115]

Conder discussed Nōbi at least once before a wholly Western audience, and the lesson he drew was different still. In a lecture on Japanese architecture he prepared for the 1893 World's Columbian Exposition in Chicago, he begun by defending the necessity to remake Japan in brick and stone before what he assumed would be a hostile audience of American Japanophiles under the influence of Fenollosa and Morse. "That such modern advance should to some extent conflict with the preservation of ancient forms of art is unavoidable. . . . Nor is it surprising that said achievements in the path of progress should be decried as imitations, and the servants of her [Japan's] growing necessities reproached as heartless vandals by those enthusiasts who are concerned only with aesthetic externals."[116]

After a long discussion of Japanese castles, Conder ended his comments with the great earthquake itself. He first located the notoriously collapsed mills outside the bounds of constructive science by noting "a growing tendency on the part of commercial companies" to erect "flimsy brick constructions." While "certain buildings of this class" had been damaged in the earthquake, "solid structures of more substantial and scientific construction presented a very good record." Like Cawley, Conder saw the disaster as having "totally upset the theories as to the resistance which the native wooden structures might be expected to present." Excepting a few temples and shrines, "the Japanese buildings invariably collapsed, and to the catastrophe of earthquake was added the calamity of fire. Thousands of wounded people imprisoned in the fallen wooden structures far outnumbering those killed and injured by the earthquake were estimated to have been burnt alive."[117]

FORESHOCKS:
PORTENTS AND PREDICTION

In the immediate aftermath of the Nōbi earthquake, seismology commanded state patronage as a science of aftershock, the successor to Confucian scholarship in the same role. Yet given the newly revealed fragility of imported infrastructure, its potential value was even greater in the long term as a science of foreshocks, a machine for prediction, which both its practitioners and patrons in 1891 indeed believed it would become. This goal eludes seismology still, and seismologists have consistently suffered, institutionally and sometimes personally, for their failure to live up to the model of scientific prediction set by astronomers or even meteorologists. As a fledgling geophysical science in mid-Meiji, however, and one whose warnings about Western architecture seemed to have been proven true in the immediate aftermath of Nōbi, the Japanese state had every reason to invest resources in seismology on the promise that the mysteries surrounding earthquakes would eventually be explained. The Imperial Earthquake Investigation Committee (Shinsai Yobō Chōsakai), the first interdisciplinary scientific research body established by the Meiji state, was a direct result of the Nōbi earthquake, and would oversee one of the most high-profile Japanese science projects of the Meiji and Taishō eras. Thus was the Nōbi disaster converted into a scientific opportunity dedicated, in the last analysis, to protecting the state from future risk.

Meiji seismologists had to wrestle not only with the legacies of the physicist Sir Isaac Newton and the naturalist Alexander von Humboldt, but also with the presumption that, because they lived in a place where earthquakes were already considered, by many, to be subject to prediction, nature offered no true mysteries to the careful observer. That is, Confucian scholars had always claimed, in the centuries before seismology, that earthquakes were preceded by signs or portents. According to historian Hashimoto Manpei, books issued immediately after major earthquakes (from the *Kokinchobunshū* of 1254 to the *Ansei kenbushi* of 1855) generally reported anticipatory phenomenon, such as the appearance of lights in the sky, the sudden appearance of water in dry wells, the strange behavior of catfish (small ones) and pheasants, rainbows, strangely shaped clouds, and dreams.[1] This provided a sense of security—and authority for the scholarly classes who turned local oral reports into written ones and circulated them throughout the whole country—that earthquakes were as predictable, in some sense, as storms, if one could only read the signs. The problem from this perspective was not the lack of observations, but the lack of some way to gather and communicate their message beforehand.

Thus did journalists and other writers who traversed the Nōbi Plain in the aftermath of the earthquake report, in late 1891, that the usual signs had indeed been noticed. "It was warm a couple of days before the quake," wrote a Tokyo journalist in a book published a few weeks later, "despite the fact that it was autumn, so some people thought a quake was coming."[2] Read another retrospective account: "The weather was very gloomy. Steamy [unseasonable] hotness. The weather gave the impression to people that they may have an earthquake. People felt really weird. People welcomed the night [before the earthquake] with this weird feeling."[3]

Even newspapers reporting that portents had not been seen, like Gifu's *Nichi nichi shimbun*, did so with the understanding that such phenomena were normative: "Usually people say before a big earthquake that we can see signs. But this time we didn't see any. There was small shaking a couple days before, but no one paid attention to it. Wells in the city sometimes dry out before an earthquake. But this time the climate was not stable—rain, then dryness—so people really couldn't tell if the wells were drying. Before an earthquake, usually the days are hotter. But this time, there was a short rain, and the sky was clouded. Until the big earthquake came, no one noticed signs."[4] Clearly Japanese did not wait in total ignorance and fear for the coming of earthquakes. They sought knowledge of immanent disaster by a close reading of the sky and landscape, much as they would for a storm or flood.

In fact it was only with the coming of seismology that Japanese people received the claim that earthquakes were not, at least not yet, subject to prediction. Expatriate scientists like Milne were inclined to denigrate commonly accepted forms of prediction in order to prepare the way for the instrumental kind, based on the perfection of seismographs and other devices.[5] Japanese seismologists like Ōmori Fusakichi and Sekiya Seikei, however, carried the burden of convincing a population already attuned to predictive signs that a more convincing and prescient reading of the Japanese landscape could be organized. In other words, seismologists were tasked with making their own instruments and theories as reliable as the portents that even many educated people—even many Japanese seismologists themselves—believed were somehow relevant indicators of imminent catastrophe. Ōmori and Sekiya were the first in a long line of Japanese researchers to study catfish, eels, pheasants, and other animals believed to be so attuned to seismicity as to exhibit behavioral changes. Neither did they discount folk wisdom about "earthquake weather," believing as they did—as many geophysicists at the time both inside and outside Japan still believed—that there may be an essential relationship between seismicity and meteorology through changes in barometric pressure. These were problems and relationships that Japanese (and later, Chinese) scientists would pursue—and still in some instances continue to pursue—more assiduously than their western colleagues.[6]

Another area of geophysical research in which Japanese came to specialize in the aftermath of 1891 was the relationship between seismicity and magnetism, which was initially suggested not by European theories, but by a famous incident in the late Tokugawa period when a large magnetized stone in an Edo (Tokyo) glass shop dropped dozens of keys and needles attached to its surface just prior to the Ansei earthquake. As the story was recounted in a popular book published after the Nōbi disaster, the stone drew back the needles and keys in the aftermath of the earthquake. This spurred the owner to construct a primitive "seismograph" combining a magnet, a candle stand, a bell, and a "clock-work mechanism" perhaps inspired by illustrations in Dutch books. One post-Nōbi book even reconstructs a drawing of the instrument, claiming that "we used to have an [original] picture of this device, but it is now lost." The story of this magnetic seismograph was frequently cited in mid- and late Meiji however, and helped to justify the considerable resources the Japanese government expended on the relationship between seismicity and shifts in magnetic fields, a research program that remains active but controversial to the present day.[7]

The Tokugawa-period "earthquake stone" was considered by its post-Nōbi chronicler to be a *kojie* (small knowledge) of "old times" that could be "re-considered with scientific theory applied."[8] In fact much of the corpus of pre-Meiji earthquake portents fell into the category "small knowledge" that Japanese researchers would seriously take up and attempt to scientifically prove (that is, render logical before the bar of international science) in the years and decades after Nōbi. In this sense the Western dichotomy between instrumental science and superstition was relatively less rigid in Japan than it was, for example, in northern Europe, where there was no folk wisdom about earthquakes for geologists to concern themselves with. But it also conforms to the "lesson" of the survival of Nagoya Castle and five-story pagodas. If premodern carpenters had come to an understanding of seismicity effective enough to keep castles and pagodas standing, might not folk knowledge of earthquake portents also have some basis in reality?

WESTERN LINES AND JAPANESE MAPS: THE ŌMORI SCALE

Sekiya Seikei and Ōmori Fusakichi, as the first generation of Japanese seismologists—the first professional seismologists in the world—would have a different relationship than their mentors to the Europe-centered professions. Although acculturated into "Western science," their own particular science was more famous and better institutionalized in Japan than anywhere in the West itself. Thanks largely to Milne, it also began life with a critical attitude toward foreign knowledge, one that would be greatly burnished as it became an entirely Japanese discipline.

Ōmori's scholarship in particular evidenced a strong desire to define "Japan" in the course of defining nature. Ever since Mallet's report on the Great Neapolitan Earthquake, seismologists had mapped earthquakes as a series of isometric (or, isoseismal) lines, indicating degrees of intensity (or, acceleration) at various distances from the epicenter. The isoseismal map was the geographic expression of an earthquake as the seismograph was its geophysical one. In 1883, Swiss and Italian seismologists had developed the Rossi-Forel scale of earthquake intensity in the first effort to standardize the placement of these lines, the standard being the human and physical geography of Europe. For example, 8 marked the area where chimneys fell and walls cracked. The zone just beyond, where the walls did not crack but plaster fell, was marked 7. Each gradation was also defined by nonphysical markers. Within a magnitude 7 zone, for example, the population experienced "general panic" and church bells rang. In the zone marked 6, even further from the epicenter, there was a "general awakening of those asleep, general ringing of bells, oscillation of chandeliers, stopping of clocks," and other traces, but no falling plaster or panic. And so on.[9]

Needing to draw isoseismal lines on the Nōbi Plain, Milne's student Ōmori found the Rossi-Forel scale useless, given Japan's paucity of church bells, chandeliers, chimneys, etc. Ōmori also calculated that the scale's maximum level of intensity (expressed as the innermost line, marked 10) represented an acceleration rate of 2,500 millimeters per second per second. At that degree of ground movement, it was presumed, devastation of the built environment would be total; there would be no further markers of seismic acceleration for a seismologist to read as he approached the epicenter. But the built landscape of Japan, according to Ōmori, continued to survive and sustain measurable degrees of damage after this presumed point of maximum acceleration had been reached. Japanese seismology thus had to come up with additional categories, and key all of them to a new series of "Japanese" markers. Tracing out the geography of Japanese earthquakes had been Milne's problem and concern from the beginning, but the unprecedented degree of devastation on the Nōbi Plain provided Ōmori with a new wealth of landscape inscriptions. He sorted them out and drew his isoseismal lines using what came to be known as the Ōmori scale.[10]

Because European scales were and would remain normative, Ōmori took the additional step of keying each zonal or magnitude number on his own scale to a particular acceleration rate, so his map could be compared to those drawn by Europeans. European maps, however, had yet to include acceleration readings; if Europeans wanted to compare their own maps to Ōmori's, they would first have to do what he did—assign rates of acceleration (measured in millimeters per second per second) to all the lines. In seeking to make Japanese maps "comparable" to European ones, Ōmori actually made Europeans change or refine their own maps in order to make them comparable to his.[11]

But there were other messages in the Ōmori scale that had nothing to do with numbers. Writing in 1898, Milne quoted Ōmori as to the following definition of a 2,000 millimeters per second per second (or magnitude 4) earthquake: "In districts where the acceleration exceeded 2,000 mm per second per second, a few temples had collapsed, and although all European brick buildings—which it must be admitted were not types of good construction—were entirely destroyed or much shattered, some 10 per cent of the Japanese buildings were entirely overthrown."[12] When Ōmori published this scale himself two years later, the caveat on the quality of workmanship was omitted. It now read simply that "the majority of the ordinary brick houses are partially or totally destroyed" when an earthquake reaches 2,000 millimeters per second per second. "Japanese buildings," on the other hand, had become even more earthquake-resistant than in the version published by Milne.

Some of the wooden houses were destroyed at that intensity, Ōmori wrote, clearly intending his qualifier "some" to represent a very low figure. At the even higher rate of 2,500 millimeters per second per second, only "about 3 per cent of the wooden houses are totally destroyed." As the acceleration reaches 4,000 millimeters, "great iron bridges are destroyed," but 20 to 50 percent of the Japanese houses remain standing. At the maximum acceleration—above 4,000 millimeters—all buildings are completely destroyed "except for a few wooden houses." Perhaps to answer the potential skepticism of European scientists, who would have expecting the scale to end with complete devastation, Ōmori explained at the end that "a few wooden houses could not be totally destroyed by an earthquake, however violent."[13]

In rewriting the Rossi-Forel scale to Japanese specifications, Ōmori had written the survivability of "Japanese" buildings and the fragility of "foreign" ones directly into the content of seismology. Their unequal relationship was now fixed, at least in Japanese practice, as scientific fact. A 2,500 millimeters per second per second earthquake was, by definition, one in which about 3 percent of the Japanese houses are destroyed. The ratio (in some cases the percentage) of destroyed "Japanese" and "foreign" structures was now to be the normative sign of a particular acceleration of seismic waves.

It is interesting to compare Ōmori's scale to another Italian earthquake scale, the Mercalli, developed around the same time as a replacement for the Rossi-Forel, and adopted by most Western governments in the first two decades of the twentieth century. While Ōmori's scale assumes a seismologist reading architectural and landscape inscriptions, Mercalli's places equal stress on oral interviews. In the Mercalli scale, an area is to be marked 2 if the earthquake is "observed only by persons in a state of perfect quiet, especially on the upper floors of houses, or by very nervous people." In the zone marked 3, "people say 'it was scarcely felt' without any apprehension and generally without having noticed that it was an earthquake." And so on. Even after the intensity increases to the point where physical damage becomes visible, Mercalli does not abandon human seismometers. In the area of magnitude 8 (categorized as "ruinous"), the earthquake not only "collapse[s] some houses" but is "observed with great terror."[14]

In Ōmori's scale, not only are there no human reactions to be collected, but there are no dead bodies to be counted. Mercalli's scale, after a certain point, is full of victims. Relying on physical markers, Ōmori's scale has a greater number of categories in the range of "serious" quakes, while Mercalli's, relying on human perception, makes its finest divisions among lesser quakes, before any physical damage occurs. Yet the two scales have this much in common: each provides the seismologist with not one but a pair of everyday seismometers. In Mercalli's case it is Italian people and Italian buildings, both of which are presented as ubiquitous and unproblematic (normative) devices for the collection of data about nature. In Ōmori's, the equivalents are wooden houses and the iron and masonry infrastructure recently introduced from abroad. The difference in the choice of seismometers highlights the way in which Ōmori and other Japanese seismologists had come to read their own landscape: as above all a collection of "native" and "foreign" elements. In Japan, fundamental knowledge about natural phenomenon would come not from the resonance between two local seismometers, as in Italy, but the dissonance between seismometers local and foreign.

It may have been the very importance of foreign seismometers that made oral interviews seem as problematic to Ōmori as they seemed natural to Mercalli. Would Euro-Americans resident in Japan record the same reactions as the Japanese? If they did not, what would that mean? Would the reactions of Japanese, gathered through interviews, be accepted in the West as normative or a proper data set from which to draw isoseismal lines? Milne himself had always favored the foreign over the Japanese body as an accurate seismometer; he had not always found what ordinary Japanese said (through translators) to be useful as data. As he wrote from the Nōbi Plain: "Attempts to find out what sensations were experienced by the people at the time of the shock are unsatisfactory. People questioned will tell trivial circumstances—how they tumbled from the top to the bottom of the stairs whilst hurrying to get out of doors—girls tell how they began to cry, etc."[15]

Japanese had obviously experienced sensations, but had not experienced seismology. Excepting the government employees in seismology's larger network, few Japanese had yet to be trained to notice and record those specific sensations seismologists found useful as data. On the occasion of a rare British earthquake (in Hereford) in 1896, the seismologist Charles Davison expressed surprise that "one in every five" of those interviewed in the affected zone "gave unasked his impression of the direction of the shock." What had surprised Davison was that so many Englishmen had learned the seismological lesson that earthquakes were waves, and knowing they were waves, had expected them to move directionally. With little "common" knowledge about earthquakes to interfere with their "scientific" knowledge about wave theory, and without having to worry that their roofs were about to fall in, inhabitants of Hereford had unreflectingly made themselves into seismographs. The Mercalli scale and others like it were in one sense sets of instructions to the populations of earthquake countries as to what should be felt, said, and remembered.[16]

The one group of Japanese Milne had relied upon as seismographs were civil servants, but always secondarily, as when he sent out barrages of postcards to pinpoint the best locations for instruments. In the case of the meteorological stations, Milne had created a monitoring system that made human reaction all but superfluous. Ōmori was thus acculturated into a discipline that from the beginning eschewed Japanese bodies as reliable or necessary recording devices. Anglo-Japanese seismology was mostly about instruments.

Previously I suggested that seismometry (the making of earthquake-related instruments) found its locus in Japan's foreign community, rather than in Europe, because the Japanese landscape lacked European-style inscription. It was not just the buildings, however, but the people of Japan who were not inscribed by earthquakes in ways European scientists found easy to read. This distrust in Japanese witnessing carried over from Anglo-Japanese into Japanese seismology because the "correct" witnessing procedures had been embodied in instruments and practices even before the first students were trained.

The result was that Japanese seismology relied far less on human seismometers than the same science practiced in Italy, Britain, or the United States. In his 1907 textbook on "seismic geology," the American geologist William H. Hobbs describes the postearthquake investigation this way: "Notebook and map in hand, the student traverses the wrecked district, and while memory is still fresh, gathers, sifts, and correlates the observations made by an army of non-scientific observers."[17] These field interviews were to be followed up by barrages of questionnaires, on which would depend the final placement of the isoseismal lines. Japanese seismologists also depended on local information in order to locate traces, but their mapping techniques relied not on "an army of non-scientific [yet still white] observers" but on displays of overturned gravestones, quantities of collapsed houses, and other information literally objective to a foreign scientific audience.

Object-based or instrumental seismology was thus simultaneously a set of colonizing practices and a potentially powerful commentary on the colonial project itself. As long as Ōmori relied solely on physical markers, questions about the reliability of Japanese witnessing would never be raised. On the other hand, his particular arrangement of physical markers raised a host of questions about the reliabilities of European engineering knowledge. The Ōmori scale of earthquake intensity managed to isolate a fragile foreign infrastructure within a landscape of indigenous tenacity.

The cultural politics of Ōmori's science is more evident when one compares it to British seismology in India, which drew different cultural and political conclusions from similar circumstances. Following the Great Indian, or Assam, earthquake of 1897, the Indian Geological Survey experienced the same problems of isoseismal mapping. The lines it eventually drew over the 160,000 square miles affected by the earthquake were, according to seismologist Charles Davison, "purely diagrammatic," revealing only where the lines would "probably" be "if we might suppose that local conditions were uniform." Explained Davison in his reading of the survey's report: "It must be remembered that one third of the area over which the shock was sensible was one from which no observations could be obtained, while another third was inhabited by ignorant or illiterate tribes"; tribes whose houses had not fallen in, however.[18] In the 30,000 square miles surrounding the epicenter (a third of the area of Great Britain), only 1,542 people died, 600 of these in a single landslide. Within the same area, according to the survey, "all brick and stone buildings" (the buildings of the British tribe) "were practically destroyed." It was only by locating and charting these scattered examples of shattered brickwork—essentially cataloging the damage to the colonial infrastructure—that seismic mapping was able to take place at all, that "the 30,000 square miles surrounding the epicenter" became a geographical and geophysical entity, that the earthquake was describable as affecting 160,000 square miles (the area within which "nearly all brick buildings were damaged"). When Davis writes that the maps "suppose that local conditions were uniform," he means they suppose that India were not India, but Britain. They map, quite literally, where general damage and destruction would have occurred had India been constructed of European material.[19]

To Davison, areas where no observations could be obtained map land inhabited by ignorant or illiterate tribes. Ōmori maps them, in the Japanese context, as areas of indigenous skill and stability. To Davison, the work of the Indian Geological Survey is a triumph of European science amid difficult local conditions. To Ōmori, isoseismal lines trace out the failure of European science to come to terms with unexpected local difficulties.

JAPANESE SEISMOLOGY
AS INTERNATIONAL SCIENCE

Japanese seismology, more than most Japanese sciences, would have many foreign readers in the late nineteenth and early twentieth centuries. Seismology in the decade after Nōbi became a dominant research project in Japan: well funded, increasingly institutionalized, and capable of attracting patronage at the highest levels. Part of it was Japanese interest in strengthening what was now openly described as a vulnerable foreign infrastructure, yet one that was also identical with the state and the new industrial concerns. But another factor was the high visibility Japanese seismology was capable of maintaining in the international scientific community because of Milne's growing influence abroad, and because Japan was now universally recognized to be an earthquake country.[20] Given the paucity of well-funded seismology projects in Europe and the United States, the production of knowledge about earthquakes was a scientific niche Japan could fill, at least into the early 1900s, with only limited competition. Just after the Nōbi earthquake the *Japan Weekly Mail* had editorialized that "Japan's prospects of establishing a scientific reputation" were mostly contained in seismology.[21] Or, as Kikuchi Dairoku put it in 1904, "organized scientific investigation connected with seismology [is] a duty that Japan owes to the scientific world."[22]

The Imperial Earthquake Investigation Committee (IEIC), formed the year after the Nōbi earthquake under the authority of the Minister of Education, would monopolize Japanese earthquake knowledge production until the Great Kantō (Tokyo) Earthquake of 1923. Sekiya served as its secretary until his untimely death in 1896; Ōmori succeeded him the following year. The committee's presidency was initially too valuable to be given to a practitioner. Its first two chairmen were also the presidents of the Imperial University (soon to be Tokyo Imperial University), and the second of these, Baron Kikuchi, would eventually became Minister of Education. The IEIC was both figuratively and literally the successor to the Japan Seismological Society, having been founded the same year the Seismological Society expired. Committee members Kikuchi, Ōmori, and Sekiya had all been active in the Seismological Society from the beginning.[23] Milne was the IEIC's only foreign member, virtually all other founding members of the Seismological Society having by this time left Japan.

The IEIC's research commenced in a period of unusually strong seismicity that afflicted Japan for at least six years following the Nōbi earthquake. Other destructive earthquakes occurred in Noto (1892), Kagoshima (1893), eastern Hokkaido (1894), Tokyo (1894), Shōnai (1894), Ugo and Rikuchū (1896), Nagano (1897), and Sendai (1897). All paled, however, beside the Great Sanriku Tsunami (a tsunami is a seismically induced sea wave), which killed over twenty-two thousand people along the extreme northeast coast of Honshu on June 15, 1896. This was the most deadly tsunami in Japanese history, and might have been a greater cultural event than the Nōbi catastrophe but for its distance from Tokyo and the public's acceptance, by 1897, of the regularity of natural disaster. There were also several dramatic volcanic eruptions in the same period. In other words, the decade in which

Japan won its war against China and began its own imperial expansion was also a time of unusual violence in domestic nature. Readers of Shiga's *Nihon fūkeiron*, the decade's best seller, could hardly doubt his observation that the Japanese landscape held latent power.

Given this atmosphere, many scientific disciplines other than seismology, from geology and physics to meteorology, oceanography, engineering, and of course architecture, were compelled to jump on the research bandwagon that the Imperial Earthquake Investigation Committee offered. Among the strongest jumpers were physicists, who could claim priority in studying earthquakes from the time of W. E. Ayrton, John Perry, and James Ewing. The first generation of Japanese physicists, led by Tanakadate Aikitsu, would not let this legacy lapse. Although attracted more by the study of magnetism than seismicity, Tanakadate led his own expedition to the Nōbi earthquake site in early 1892, and discovered that the isomagnetic lines mapped over the plain in an earlier survey had now shifted. Based partly on this discovery, and with the legacy of the Ansei-period earthquake stone supporting an historic link between seismicity and magnetism, Tanakadate convinced the IEIC to sponsor a new magnetic survey of the entire country. Conducted from 1893 to 1896, this project enlisted nearly all of the Japan's physicists, and two of its three seismologists (Ōmori and Imamura Akitsune). Tanakadate would remain involved in earthquake research for the rest of his career, even inventing his own seismographs in the tradition of James Ewing.[24]

Japanese geology likewise moved in this period from the study of inert rock strata to recording a landscape in dramatic motion. Geologist Kotō Bunjirō made an international reputation by physically tracing the fault line bisecting the Nōbi Plain after the great earthquake, and thus proving that the seismic waves had been caused by faulting action rather than the other way round.[25] Encouraged by the IEIC, Kotō would next conduct a volcanological survey of Japan, which in the spirit of his faulting research would aggressively challenge European theories (as well as seismology's claim to priority in volcanology). At several points in his report on volcanoes Kotō uses his location, if not his birthright, to add weight to his findings, as when declaring that in Japan "grand physical phenomena and Nature's scourges are being displayed in a full degree unparalleled in any other spot on earth." In criticizing the conclusions of a German geologist who had argued for a link between volcanism and seismicity, Kotō wrote that, "born in a volcanic and earth-shaking country, I cannot from my own convictions and daily experience, agree with him on many points."[26] There is more than an echo of Shiga Shigetaka in much of Kotō's prose.

The writings of Kotō, like those of Ōmori and Sekiya, demonstrate that the first generation of Japanese scientists, though trained by foreigners, hardly considered themselves passive collectors of data for European interpretation. In a nationalist and imperialist age, Japanese scientists were little different than their European counterparts in wanting to compete for territory, stake claims, and receive priority. The violence of Japanese nature was in this sense a font of capital for those scientific disciplines able to link it to their research. Japan "is a land of typhoons, volcanoes, and earthquakes," wrote Kotō, an observation that would henceforth register more as opportunity than vulnerability across a range of scientific disciplines.[27]

The meaning of "Japanese architecture" (or "the Japanese house" or "wooden houses") also continued to change as seismology made the transition from an Anglo-Japanese to a fully Japanese science. Milne's invocation of *daiku*-work had always been by way of casting doubt on European building knowledge in earthquake countries. His immediate agenda had been to enlarge seismology's domain—its general principles—to include constructive science. For Milne, "the Japanese house" was an object located in the space between his own science and its rival disciplines of architecture and engineering.

Japanese seismologists may not have abandoned imperial ambitions vis-à-vis architecture and engineering, but phrases like "the aseismic qualities of Japanese building" held for them certain meanings that they had not had for Milne. Sensitive to the anomaly of Japanese scientists producing knowledge for a Western audience, the IEIC was particularly desirous of refuting the orthodoxy of Japan's long defenselessness before nature. The nationalistic character of Japanese seismology—the fact that it was intended by the state to be highly visible to an influential foreign audience—gave the aseismic quality of Japanese architecture (that is, traditional or *daiku*-built Japanese architecture) a currency in science that it never attained, or needed to maintain, in Japanese architecture or engineering, which performed primarily before local audiences. To Japanese seismology, "Japanese architecture" was located not between two disciplines, but between Japan and the West.

The shift in the definition of "Japan's earthquake problem" from one of Japan's defenselessness before nature to one of "foreign" buildings' defenseless against Japanese nature, a change Milne had initiated, was thus accelerated under Japanese auspices. As Baron Kikuchi wrote for a foreign audience in 1904: "On the practical side [of seismology] were considerations of houses built in foreign styles, arches, bridges, chimneys, etc., new to Japan; these were constructed without proper attention to the probable effects of the earthquake shocks peculiar to this country."[28]

In the speech he prepared for Chicago's 1893 Columbian Exposition, Conder had portrayed Japanese bodies burnt alive beneath fallen structural timbers. But in the exhibit sent to Chicago by the Education Ministry (whose jurisdiction included both the Imperial University and the IEIC), the emphasis was quite different. The university's College of Engineering represented itself through six objects. One was a model of a pumping station, and another was an "automatic electric recorder" of Japanese invention. The other four, however, were not pieces of contemporary technology but scale models of early *daiku*-designed buildings, including, most dramatically, a one-twentieth-scale copy of the five-story pagoda at Nikkō. The model was built, according to the guidebook, by Sentaro Kurasaki, "a native carpenter." But the project was "superintended by Ishii Keikichi, Assistant Professor, Engineering College, Imperial University, under the direction of Kingo Tatsuno, Professor." The model was constructed as a vertical section, so that observers could clearly see the central mast hanging from chains, in the manner of a pendulum. "Great constructive ingenuity is revealed in the use of the centre shaft," read the official guidebook, giving the pagoda "the power to resist violent winds, as well as great earthquake shocks, which are well known to be frequent in Japan." The description of the pagoda, including a detailed explanation of how the central mast maintained "the center of gravity" took up most of the space in the Engineering College's section of the official catalog. The "automatic electrical recorder," by contrast, received not a single descriptive word.[29]

In choosing to display the pagoda at Nikkō, among all those available, the exhibit planners were perhaps exploiting Nikkō's name recognition as a major Japanese tourist site. Yet the Nikkō pagoda was also particularly well suited to the exhibit text. Unlike most such towers, its *shinbashira* (central mast) hung from chains, making its portrayal as a pendulum particularly clear and graphic. Then too, the pagoda at Nikkō was only ambiguously "historic," having been built in 1820, within the lifetimes of many contemporary Japanese. Like the automatic electrical recorder, the Nikkō pagoda was a nineteenth-century object, yet one that preceded the arrival of Westerners. This last point was not clearly conveyed to fairgoers, yet may still have been meaningful to the exhibit planners, who could just as well have displayed the pagoda at Hōryūji, part of the oldest wooden building complex in the world. In any case, a model developed under the supervision of Conder's student Tatsuno was now teaching Dresser's lesson to the world.[30]

Turning from the pagoda, visitors next encountered the College of Science exhibit, which was given over entirely to seismology. Seven Japanese-made seismographs and one earthquake clock steadily recorded the steadiness of the ground in northern Illinois. The Japanese-ness of the seismograph was made explicit in the catalog: "Many special forms [of seismographs] have been designed in Japan, with the result that rather than Japan borrowing from Europe and America, these countries are using inventions which had their origins in Japan." An accompanying photograph of an early Chinese seismometer helped establish an Asian ancestry for the machines and further erase European fingerprints. There was also a "Model of an Earthquake" (a wire bent by Sekiya to show the complex movement of a single particle of earth) and an earthquake-proof lamp, also of Sekiya's invention. At the end of the display were a series of photographs of the destruction on the Nōbi Plain, probably (judging from their captions) selected from among those taken by Milne and Burton. Of the fifteen photos, three or four (again based on the captions) would have shown collapsed or semicollapsed Japanese buildings, although one of these (labeled "Sunken houses in the Neo Valley") more vividly recorded the phenomenon of sinkholes. By contrast, there were two photographs of a collapsed Nagoya spinning mill, three of the collapsed Nagara River railroad bridge, another of a "twisted railroad line," and two additional photographs of failed bridges. The balance of the images were of natural features, most prominently Mount Fuji.[31]

The main Japanese pavilion (the Hō-ō-den or Phoenix Hall) at the Chicago exposition, an architect-designed interpretation of an eleventh-century temple, is justly famous among art historians as the building that defined Japanese architecture for a new generation of Americans, including Frank Lloyd Wright, who were beginning to be conditioned by the Colonial Revival to see art and beauty in ligneous construction. The contrast between this small *daiku*-built (but for the first time architect-designed) temple-pavilion on the Wooded Isle in the middle of Grant Park, and the elephantine Beaux Arts buildings surrounding it, is often pointed to by the fair's historians as reflecting Japan's understanding of its place in the world order, and its willing self-portrayal as a nation of art and nature.[32] Yet there was this additional portrayal of Japan as a scientific nation, a nation with some degree of control over a uniquely destructive nature, a portrayal that enlisted "cultural" objects such as pagodas and made "scientific" devices such as seismographs important carriers of culture. To the Japanese exhibit planners, there was perhaps no discontinuity of narrative between the Hō-ō-den and the seismographs, especially if one considers the cross-sectional model of the pagoda as their bridge. The Chicago fairgoer was being taught that, in Japan, earthquakes, scientific instruments, and indigenous architecture maintained some kind of vital balance in a loop closed to foreign knowledge.

A similar message is conveyed through prose, drawings, and, above all, photographs in Baron Kikuchi's *Recent Seismological Investigations in Japan* (1904), written in English specifically for a foreign scientific audience. The book's purpose was to support Japanese claims for influence in the nascent International Seismological Association, then being organized by German scientists in Strasbourg. Once again Kikuchi sorts, rearranges, and reframes Milne's photographs of the Nōbi earthquake. The Nagoya spinning mill and the collapsed Nagara railroad bridge are two of the initial three images. The third is a photo that had not appeared in Milne or at Chicago: of seventeenth-century Nagoya Castle, whose stone foundation and wooden superstructure had withstood the shock, according to the caption, with "slight effects." While the theme of Milne's photo-essay had been the utterness of Nōbi's destruction, Kikuchi's was more its selectivity—the peculiar vulnerability of the new "foreign" infrastructure. In place of the equally devastated rural landscape (which Milne had also showcased), Kikuchi presented photos of sophisticated wooden models of "earthquake-proof" farmhouses and schools, newly developed under the auspices of the IEIC. We examine these models in more detail in the following chapter.[33]

The year after Kikuchi's book was published, Japan would defeat a European nation (Russia) in war and Japanese seismology would begin to mount overseas expeditions in the manner of the European sciences, even producing knowledge within and about Anglo-Saxon domains. In 1905 Ōmori led a group of scientists and architects to India to record the aftershocks of the earthquake in Assam, and in 1906 he and others went to San Francisco following the destructive earthquake there. As the IEIC's knowledge-producing ambitions become pan-Asian and pan-Pacific, it gained increasing attention in Europe, and Ōmori's reputation began to equal or even surpass Milne's.[34]

It was partly a matter of resources. By 1907, Milne was coordinating forty-one seismographic stations scattered throughout the British Empire from his house and laboratory on the Isle of Wight, supported by the British Association for the Advancement of Science. Milne's jurisdiction was theoretically the world itself (or at least the world as ruled by Britain), yet he was underfunded and somewhat remote, both physically and epistemologically, from the centers of British science. Ōmori's seismographs were concentrated in a much smaller empire, but he had almost twice as many (seventy-one stations in 1907), and because seismology was a major organ in the anatomy of Japanese science, the IEIC was able to support Ōmori more thoroughly and consistently than the British Association did Milne. It not only translated large numbers of Ōmori's articles into foreign languages and sent him overseas for months at a time, but also funded the production of dense and beautiful maps and other graphics of earthquake-country-Japan irresistible to the authors of European textbooks.[35]

Japanese seismology also benefited from its early monopoly on knowledge production around the Pacific rim, where seismic activity was unusually great at the turn of the century, most famously at San Francisco in 1906. At the time of the San Francisco earthquake there was not yet an American seismology. It was, rather, a child of that event. Milne had written in 1895 that "at present, Siberia and America are regions of seismic darkness."[36] San Francisco was thus recognized by Europeans as well as Japanese as belonging in Ōmori's research sphere. This seems to have been accepted as well by California's community of geologists, who invited Ōmori and the architect Nakamura Tetsutarō to sit on the scientific subcommittee of California's hastily established State Earthquake Investigation Commission in the aftermath of the 1906 disaster. Ōmori's report from San Francisco, written in English and accompanied by beautifully drafted multicolored drawings of the San Andreas fault and other features, was likely the first detailed record of the earthquake to reach a European scientific audience. The IEIC even used the paper on San Francisco as a catalyst for launching an English-language journal *(Bulletin of the Imperial Earthquake Investigation Committee)* that was thereafter published concurrently with its existing English-language *Report* series.[37]

Ōmori and his Japanese colleagues had been stoned and slightly injured by American children as they walked through the ruins of San Francisco in 1906. The incident resulted in an apology from California's governor, but it illustrates the precariousness of the role "Japanese scientist" in an age of open racism. One can't know how many slights Japanese scientists experienced as they entered the unfamiliar territory of foreign knowledge-making, despite all the seeming international goodwill. The stoning incident is the most graphic that comes down to us, and then only as a secondhand remembrance, written in an obscure little book—Ōmori's only biography—produced fifty years after his death by the parent/teachers' association of his home town.[38]

By the time he returned from San Francisco, however, Ōmori was more accurately "Ōmori," the individual human face that an increasingly large and well-organized Japanese seismological community presented to Western science. Ōmori authored over three quarters of the foreign-language *Reports* (a total of ninety-eight papers), and his name would appear in over 98 percent of the articles in the English-language *Bulletin*. In the IEIC's Japanese-language *Report* series, by contrast, Ōmori shared space with eighty-two other authors. Still, his total publications run into the hundreds. In a sense "Ōmori" was the successor to "Milne," shorthand for the dozens of active members of the Japan Seismological Society, Kōbu-daigakkō students, and the countless and far-flung civil servants who formed his knowledge-producing network. "Milne," since leaving Japan, had actually reverted to Milne, a man who, despite his location at the center of a worldwide web of seismological stations, was now working out of his home, far from universities, graduate student assistants, and even other British seismologists.[39] And besides that, the Germans were closing in.

SPEAKING FOR PLANET EARTH: GERMANY AND BRITAIN AS EARTHQUAKE COUNTRIES

Despite Japan's reputation as an earthquake country, the financial resources of the IEIC, the Imperial University chair in seismology (with its access to graduate students and lab equipment), the translators and chart-makers, the seventy-one seismograph-equipped observatories and fourteen hundred additional recording stations, and the well-managed reputation of Ōmori, Japan still did not become, in the first decade of the twentieth century, the undisputed center of world seismology. The reason was that certain astronomical instruments owned by the German physicist Ernst von Rebeur-Paschwitz, but based on the principle of James Ewing's original seismograph, had become so sensitive by the late 1880s that waves from the relatively strong Kumamoto (Japan) earthquake of 1889 were faintly registered at his laboratory in Potsdam. This event, confirmed by Milne before leaving Japan, had led Lord Kelvin himself to implore the Japanese government to support seismology even more rigorously than it had been. Although physicists had been present in seismology from the beginning, heretofore seismology had been as a sideline to their real interests, one of which was the structure and age of the Earth. Now that seismic waves were seen "to travel round the earth," as Milne put it, they began to be treated as enormous x-rays that, through the timing of their speeds and trajectories, might reveal the inner structure of the planet, an astrophysical entity. Seismographs, seismograms, seismometry, and seismology itself would be increasingly pulled into the orbit of the gathering scientific constellation soon to be known as geophysics.[40]

Ironically, the interest taken in seismology by Lord Kelvin and, even more importantly, German physicists, in the decade after 1889 diminished Japan's ability to control the course of earthquake investigation even as it increased the currency of

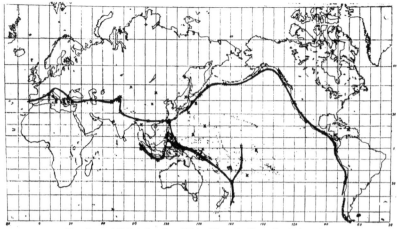

The small crosses (×) indicate the positions of Origins of the prominent large earthquakes in recent years.

FIGURE 12

Japanese scientific ambitions in the early twentieth century extended beyond the collection of local data. Ōmori was among the first to map fault lines as a globe-spanning system *(a, above)*, recognized only later as the boundaries between tectonic plates. He also created historical earthquake maps for specific areas, such as southern Italy *(b, opposite)*, with the intention of predicting the locations of future disasters. (From Ōmori Fusakichi, "Earthquake Zones in and around the Pacific," *Bulletin of the Imperial Earthquake Investigation Committee* 11, no. 1 [March 1923]: 30; Ōmori Fusakichi, "Preliminary Report on the Messina-Reggio Earthquake of Dec. 28, 1908," *Bulletin of the Imperial Earthquake Investigation Committee* 3, no. 1 [1909].)

this most Japanese of sciences in the scientific West. To the extent that seismology was more about planet Earth (whose spokesmen would for the immediate future be Europeans), it was less about Japan or even earthquake countries. In fact the ownership of sensitive instrumentation could now make any nation a potential earthquake country, not only because seismic waves could be detected and telegraphed from distant points, but because formerly stable ground in places like England and Prussia was revealed to be seismically active below the threshold of human perception. As the different European powers began founding seismological organizations in the first decade of the twentieth century, Japan took on new importance

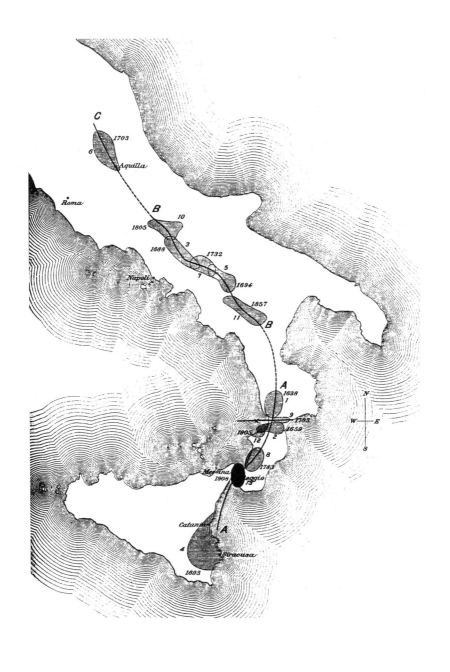

as the remote point of origin for seismic signals detected by a battery of sophisticated instrumentation on the other side of planet Earth.[41]

Japanese seismology escaped outright colonization in the same manner as had the Meiji state: it traded seismograms with each foreign power, let each contribute instrumentation and advice, sent students to all of the important overseas centers, and continually built up its own resource base. Alliances were made with the Germans in order to avoid domination by the British (i.e., Milne himself), and knowledge was produced for the foreign geologist-seismologists—those who spoke for "the crust" of planet Earth—as well as the physicist-seismologists—the spokesmen for "the core." This former group (the geologist-seismologists) included large numbers of Americans, who formed an important counterweight to the largely European-based practitioners of geophysics when the United States entered seismology following the San Francisco earthquake.[42]

Japan supported the move by German physicists to order global seismological observation through the International Seismological Association founded in Strasbourg in 1904. The alternative was to accept coordination by Milne and the British Association for the Advancement of Science, which even to the British-trained scientists like Ōmori Fusakichi and Kikuchi Dairoku seemed retrogressive. Wrote Kikuchi in 1904, "The British Association for the Advancement of Science [BAAS] has done well in inviting the cooperation of different countries in seismological work, but something more than a private enterprise, and international organization with nations contributing, is necessary for work of this kind."[43] Milne should now treat Japanese seismologists as members of a national research team, Kikuchi seemed to be suggesting, and not as former pupils, naturally and forever a part of his own network. One issue involved instrumentation. "The BAAS has laid much stress on making observations with similar instruments," wrote Kikuchi, "but this seems to me to be by no means essential."[44] The Ewing-Gray-Milne seismograph, which had revolutionized global earthquake observation from Tokyo, was now a fixture of British (and British colonial) seismology. But even as Kikuchi wrote, it was being replaced in the land of its birth by a more Japanese device.

The Bosch-Ōmori seismograph was the Japanese answer to Milne's insistence on instrumental coordination. The prototypes were first built by Ōmori around 1899, and by 1909 examples were being vended internationally by the J. A. Bosch firm of Strasbourg. Entering into a close relationship with a Strasbourg instrument-maker may have helped cement a relationship between Japanese seismologists and their German counterparts, who were headquartered in the same city. And giving the name "Bosch" priority likely helped ease the novelty of European or

American scientists using a laboratory instrument invented by a Japanese. By 1910 Bosch-Ōmori seismographs were monitoring earthquakes in the Panama Canal Zone and at the MIT observatory on Mount Kilauea in Hawaii. In the following decade they were recording earthquakes at the University of California (Berkeley), Boston College, Georgetown, and stations in Shanghai, Manila, and Havana.[45] To Ōmori's reputation as a researcher was added the charisma of invention, precisely the path followed by Milne.

THE LESSONS OF SAN FRANCISCO
AND MESSINA

Even as the possibility that Japan might control a global scientific agenda slipped away, Ōmori's importance to the "new seismologists" (as those in the geophysical branch of the science called themselves) allowed more measured, yet no less ambitious, Japanese agendas to be globally pursued. Among all the seismograms, isoseismal maps, graphs of foreshocks and aftershocks—the tracings constituting the everyday currency of international seismological trade—Ōmori tucked into the several journals published by the IEIC numerous demonstrations of the Japanese ability to control destructive nature. Just as the Nōbi earthquake had been highly productive of lessons about Japan and the Japanese, so Ōmori's chronicles of major earthquakes continued this teaching mission.

In his report on San Francisco, for example, Ōmori pointed out that the burned area (4.1 square miles) was six times the size of the Great Fire of London of 1666. The postearthquake fire broke out in numerous places, burned for three days, and was stopped only by dynamiting rows of masonry buildings to form firebreaks. The following year, as he sat down to write a seemingly unrelated article about the statistical links between earthquakes and meteorological phenomenon, Ōmori's mind was still on conflagrations. After the Great Ansei Earthquake of 1855, he wrote, fires had broken out at thirty-two places in Tokyo. But all of them had been put out before daybreak, and the aggregate of the burned area was only about one square mile (the same as the London fire). Ōmori credits the success of the Japanese firefighters with the "stillness of the air" on the night of the disaster. Yet a major point of his article was that earthquakes almost never occur during stormy or windy weather, a claim he had proven statistically, and for which he assumed there was a physical explanation. As was previously pointed out, seismology in this period had yet to divorce itself from meteorology; atmospheric and seismic conditions were believed to be in some sort of synchronous relation. The danger from conflagration following an earthquake, Ōmori concluded, was comparatively slight "provided means be properly taken for subduing the flames."[46]

In divorcing earthquakes from the well-known "fact" of Japan's flammability as a wooden nation, and locating the Ansei conflagration within the range of Europe's own experience with urban fires, Ōmori marked San Francisco's postearthquake conflagration as uniquely ferocious. This was all done so subtly, however, that it likely had little impact on European and American images of Japan as particularly vulnerable to urban disaster. Other lessons were imparted more forcefully, however, and show clear evidence of overseas absorption.

On December 28, 1908, the most destructive earthquake in European history occurred in Calabria and northern Sicily, centered near the city of Messina. Within 35 seconds, about 120,000 people died or were mortally wounded, 55,000 in Messina itself and 9,000 to 10,000 in nearby Reggio. Both cities were essentially laid flat, about 98 percent of their houses collapsing, killing, in the case of Messina, over 50 percent of the urban population. Virtually all of the buildings in Messina and Reggio were of masonry construction.[47]

Ōmori seems to have had excellent contacts among Italian scientists. He immediately led a research team to the earthquake zone, collaborated with Italian seismologists, and filed a preliminary report on Messina in the IEIC bulletin a few months later, in early 1909. As in the case of San Francisco, Ōmori's was the first and most complete record of the earthquake published by an English-speaking scientist, the Italian seismologists preferring to write and publish in their own language. Thus did Ōmori find himself, sixty years after Robert Mallet had named seismology in nearby Naples, reporting the greatest of great European earthquakes to the English-speaking scientific world.[48]

"The enormity of the destruction in Messina," wrote Ōmori, "is really beyond one's imagination." It was not rare, he stated, "that 15 or more dead bodies were found buried one upon the other in the space of a single small room at the ground floor." Because the apartment houses in Messina were four to six stories tall and the streets narrow, "it was certainly impossible for the majority of the people to save themselves, even if they had succeeded in escaping out of doors."[49] Ōmori compared the horrors of Messina to the situation in Nagoya following the Nōbi earthquake. The rates of acceleration (intensity) in Messina and Nagoya were roughly comparable, he wrote, the Nōbi quake being, if anything, slightly stronger.

The population of Nagoya in 1891 was 165,339, which was nearly equal to that of Messina and the vicinity, and of which only 190 were killed in the earthquake.

Thus, even supposing the intensity of seismic motion in Messina (1908) to be equal to that in Nagoya (1891), the number of the persons killed in the former city was about 430 times greater than that in the latter. That is to say, about 998 out of 1,000 of the number of the killed in Messina must be regarded, when spoken in comparison to a Japanese city, as having fallen victims to seismologically bad construction of houses.[50]

Ōmori had actually made this observation about lethality rates at least nine years earlier, and using data that had been available not only to him, but to everybody, since 1891. Even in those areas most devastated by the Nōbi earthquake, he noted in an article of 1900, only 4 to 5 percent of the population had died. Within the eighty thousand destroyed houses in the earthquake zone, about seven thousand people were killed, or one for every eleven houses collapsed. "The comparatively small number of the killed" on the Nōbi Plain, he wrote in 1900, "was doubtless due to the fact that common Japanese houses are built of wood."[51] This meshed with Sekiya's observation, made as early as 1887, that when Japanese houses collapsed they usually did so only partially, often allowing their inhabitants to walk from the ruins.[52]

It is noteworthy that mortality statistics were cited neither by Conder nor Milne in their post-Nōbi lectures, given that accurate figures for each Japanese town were published within weeks of the disaster. Milne in particular would have known that in the Great Neapolitan Earthquake of 1857, the death rates in Saponara and Montemurro, the towns closest to the epicenter, were 50 percent and 71 percent, respectively. The Ischian earthquake of 1883 had killed 41 percent of the inhabitants of the main town, Casamicciola. Such high death rates had been consistently reported for destructive earthquakes in Europe from at least the seventeenth century.[53]

Why were comparative lethality rates never part of Milne's seismology, especially when they would have supported certain of his longstanding claims against European architecture? One explanation is that, by late 1891, they no longer served any argumentative purpose. In the wake of Nōbi, Conder had chosen to abandon the traditional portrayal of Japan as fragile, while Milne was embarrassed to discover Japan was more fragile than he had supposed. The collapse of the brick mills and iron bridges now drove their discussion, one that Milne increasingly sought to move from the field into the laboratory. The disparity in lethality rates simply found no place for citation, at least in the texts of Western scientists.

Only in Ōmori's science would comparative lethality become a category of seismological fact-creation, predicated as Japanese seismology was on the comparison of the native and the foreign. And this Nōbi lesson would indeed be learned in other parts of the world. In his book *Building Structures in Earthquake Countries*, published soon after the Messina earthquake, Italian seismologist Alfredo Montel discussed the devastation and sought to draw lessons from the ruins. Much of what he claimed to have learned about earthquakes and earthquake structures he credited to the published research of Ōmori. Indeed, large sections of Montel's book merely report Ōmori's findings as the best available science. There is, one suspects in reading Montel, a felt solidarity with Japan, another earthquake country, politically unified in the same decade as Italy, and whose native seismologists had only recently taken control of their own landscape from the scientists of Britain.[54]

Noting Ōmori's comparison of Japanese and European death rates, Montel echoes his conclusion: "This shows that the death of so many people in Messina, Reggio, etc., was primarily due, from the seismological point of view, to the completely unsuitable construction of the buildings in those cities."[55] Montel does not go so far as to condemn masonry. He writes that "having taken root in Italy to such an extent," it is far better to "adapt" masonry "instead of declaring it unsuitable." But it is the new technology of reinforced concrete in which Montel invests his confidence in the future of "masonry."[56] He even concedes to wood the title "ideal material" for earthquake resistance, and devotes an entire chapter to designs for earthquake-resistant wooden construction recently developed by the IEIC (and which, as we see in the next chapter, were based largely upon European details).[57]

Like each of the previous Nōbi lessons, the one taught at Messina did not come self-evidently. Ōmori had fashioned it from statistics more than a decade earlier, but in order to achieve the status of fact, it had required a major European earthquake, a Japanese scientist traveling to Italy, the production of an article by the same scientist in English (and published earlier than anyone else's), and probably its repetition in print by a European scientist.

JAPANESE SEISMOLOGY AS COLONIAL PROJECT: THE LESSON OF FORMOSA

I have presented Japanese seismology in previous sections as both a critique of colonization and a set of self-colonizing practices. It was also, in certain circumstances, a colonizing project.[58]

In 1906, a few months before the disaster in San Francisco, a powerful earthquake hit the south-central portion of Formosa (Taiwan), a Japanese colony recently wrested from China through war. Ōmori led an expedition to the epicentral zone and published his findings in the second issue of the IEIC bulletin, just after his report on San Francisco. "The island of Formosa," he began, "is preeminently an earthquake country," having suffered eighteen severe shocks between the mid-seventeenth century and the present. Six of these had occurred since 1901. The quake of March 17, 1906, however, was, "as far as the loss of life is concerned [and] among the recent Japanese shocks, only second to the great Mino-Owari [Nōbi] catastrophe of 1891"—it killed 1,266 people and wounded twice that.[59]

In setting Formosa's 1906 earthquake into the chronology of "Japanese" shocks, Ōmori made the seismological and political maps of the island converge. But there the similarity of Formosan to Japanese earthquakes ends. "The heavy amount of the casualties," Ōmori reports, was "due to the weakness of the native dwelling houses, which mostly have no capacity of resisting earthquake shocks, being built of *dokaku*, or sun-dried mud blocks." In the town of Dabyo, he reported, the houses were leveled to the ground. Only the Japanese Sub-Prefectoral Office (of brick) remained standing amid the ruins.[60]

Ōmori also published two photographs from the town of Shinko, showing, at top, the town's Japanese Sub-Prefectoral Office (this time wood-framed), damaged but not destroyed, and, at bottom, "the native Maso Temple," a heap of ruins. "This building was completely destroyed," reads the caption beneath the fallen temple, "owing to bad masonry and weakness of wooden timbers on account of ravages of white ants." White ants, now infamous in the United States as Formosan termites, the scourge of New Orleans, are an unusually ferocious wood-eating insect. Although Ōmori's caption is quite honest about the ants, his juxtaposition of the ant-infested Chinese temple ruins and the apparently ant-free Japanese administration building leaves the question of ant responsibility unclear.[61]

Clear, however, is Ōmori's sense that the casualties on Formosa were "due to the bad construction of the native houses": "Had the same earthquake taken place in small towns of Japan proper the casualties would have been very slight. The intensity of motion in the most strongly shaken area was nearly half of that at Gifu or Ōgaki on the occasion of the [Nōbi] earthquake. . . ." Japanese buildings on Formosa, he tells us (those built in "ordinary Japanese style"), "received no particular damage, except cracking of plastered walls and the disturbance of roof tiles." This comparison of Japanese and Formosan buildings was also made statistically, using the same formula (persons killed per houses collapsed) later deployed in Messina.

The article includes a table generated after the earlier severe earthquake of 1904, listing numbers of casualties beside numbers of "totally destroyed," "greatly damaged," and "slightly damaged" houses. "According to the above table, 1 person was killed for every 3.4 houses totally destroyed. This ratio is much smaller than what takes place in Japan proper: thus, for instance, in the great [Nōbi] earthquake of 1891, there was 1 person killed for every 11 houses totally destroyed."[62]

Leaving aside questions of differing habitation densities in Japan and Formosa, Ōmori calculates the Formosan ratio (1 death per 3.4 houses) based on the number of houses in Kagi prefecture classed as "totally destroyed" (425). Yet some portion of the dead might well have inhabited the 1,021 houses classed on the same chart as "greatly damaged." "Greatly damaged" did not exist in Japanese disaster nomenclature at the time of the Nōbi quake, when houses were simply classed as "fully" or "partially" collapsed. The business of statistically comparing "fully/partially collapsed" wooden houses in Japan to "totally/greatly/slightly destroyed/damaged" mud-brick ones in Formosa deserved, at least, a fuller evaluation. If one were to include the 1,021 "greatly damaged" houses among the potential killers, then the lethality rate per house on Formosa would be roughly equivalent to what it was on the Nōbi Plain.[63]

Ōmori also points out that the epicentral zone contained "a large number of houses or cottages built of bamboo, with very light roofs," which generally escaped damage. But the article's major pole of contrast remains "Japanese buildings" and "Formosan buildings." The former (mostly the structures of the colonial administration) emerge as well-suited to earthquake country Formosa, while the later are revealed to be inexplicably fragile and out of sorts with their own natural environment. Formosan earthquakes, like Japanese ones, are revealed through the comparison of "Japanese" and "foreign" seismometers. But Japanese stability is now embodied not in architecture indigenous to Japan, but in a Japanese colonial infrastructure that, in some cases at least, is "Western-style" and built of brick.[64]

Ōmori's report from Formosa was primarily written not for Japanese or Formosans, but European readers. At stake was not so much the character and reputation of Formosan buildings, but of Japanese ones, and particularly in this case the performance of Japanese buildings in comparison to those of another Asian people. Such a comparative framework had already been constructed in the Education Ministry's catalog for Chicago's Columbian Exposition of 1893, where it was explained that although the pendulum device in Japanese pagodas originated in China, "in China this excellent mode of construction has been lost." Setting the tenacity of the Japanese buildings in a landscape of Formosan fragility extended the critique of Europe's colonial project while justifying the Japanese one on similar scientific grounds.[65]

LESSONS FROM OLD JAPAN

Later in life, Ōmori would chip away at the concept of a unchanging, "habitual," "traditional" Japanese architecture, one that did not accumulate knowledge in historical time. On the occasion of a severe earthquake near Nagano in 1918, he reported an instance from the Edo period in which building practice had been reformed in the wake of a major disaster. In 1847, after Nagano had been virtually destroyed by an unusually powerful earthquake, the city had prohibited the construction of two-story houses (then the regional norm) and had fixed the maximum height of one-story houses at eleven *shaku* (just short of eleven feet). Ōmori credited the 1847 reforms, along with the employment of "thick, strong, wooden posts" (both of which he calls "seismic precautions"), with saving the Nagano district from a similar disaster in 1918.[66]

In the same article, Ōmori defines a small destructive earthquake as one "sufficiently strong to damage ordinary brick chimneys, stone structures [and] badly built brick houses." A great earthquake he defines as "one capable of completely destroying a wooden Japanese dwelling house." A small destructive earthquake, however, "may prove very disastrous in some other places such as Southern Italy, where houses are made of very bad building materials."[67]

Japanese had also figured out, according to Ōmori, and long before the Europeans arrived, how to make masonry itself resist earthquakes. In an article prepared in early 1918 entitled "Note on the Form of Japanese Castle Walls," he wrote, "The curved form of a large stone *ishigaki*, or dry masonry retaining wall, is a feature peculiar to the Japanese castle building not to be found in the architecture of China, Chosen, and other countries. Its origin was probably in the idea of making the stone wall earthquake-proof." He goes on to render such a wall in the form of a mathematical equation.[68]

The ultimate deployment of proof in this line of argument came in an article of March 1921, entitled "Measurement of Vibration of Gojūnotōs, or 5-Story Buddhist Stupas (Pagodas)." Nearly half a century after Dresser had associated pagodas with seismological instruments, Ōmori actually hooked up seismographs to a number of pagodas, bringing the ancient and the modern devices into communion. The vibration of six towers was recorded using a portable tremor recorder (a form of seismograph). Ōmori had measured the Hōryūji pagoda as early as 1910, but the others were subjected to testing in a burst of energy during 1919 and 1920. In this unusually long (fifty-one-page) article, instrumental readings are presented in sixteen tables, along with detailed reports of experiments in which the oscillations of the central masts were measured after deliberate shakings. Their movements were translated into mathematical formulae, and even the acceleration rate required to overturn them was precisely figured. "The gojūnotōs, though tall and apparently unstable, are in reality very stable and can resist over-turning by earthquake shocks, however violent," Ōmori concludes, finally "proving" instrumentally what Dresser had earlier claimed. Seismograms for each pagoda were also included in eight foldout sections.[69]

As important, Ōmori found considerable variation in construction technique over time. The six pagodas were not simply "examples" of a single prototype, but embodied inventive change. Thus he reconciled Conder's and Dresser's seemingly contradictory observations about the character of the central mast. The *shinbashira* in three of the towers indeed rose from a stone base, as Conder had said they did. Yet they were still "pendulums," as Dresser had believed them to be, simply inverted ones (that is, they were secured at the bottom, but minimally and loosely connected to the superstructure for the rest of their length). There were further differences. The *shinbashira* at Hommonji rose from the second story, while those at Asakusa (1692) and Nikkō (1820), built later than the other four, were "true" pendulums (that is, suspended). The earthquake-resistant mechanism of the later two towers, according to Ōmori, was even more complicated than previously thought, a combination of the "ordinary pendulum" of the *shinbashira* interacting with an inverted pendulum in the form of the tower body. So great was the variation in construction techniques, dimensions of parts as well as wholes, base/height ratios, and other factors, that the physical mechanisms by which the different classes of tower "resisted" earth motion were also theoretically distinct, and had to be explained by Ōmori using different series of calculations.

The point he seems to have been making was that the *daiku* in charge of each project had had to think the matter through. The builders had not simply relied on the amorphous concept of "tradition" to "guide their hands." Pagodas were no more the same object than were the various cathedrals of Europe or the great steel bridges built by Euro-American engineers. All of the pagodas he tested worked to resist earthquakes, but they did so in slightly different ways.

Ōmori's turn to architectural history in the early Taishō period helped solidify the global reputation of Japanese seismology as having deep cultural roots, even as it remained within the scope of investigation set by British expatriate scientists from early and mid-Meiji. Within Japan, however, Ōmori could not settle the question even of pagodas, which remained a source of controversy between himself and Japanese architects. As we see in the next chapter, architects would also turn to historical themes in the years and decades following the Nōbi disaster, but with somewhat different intentions and results than their scientist-colleagues.

SEVEN

· Japanese Architecture
after Nōbi

SAVING THE ARCHITECTURE PROJECT

The collapse of masonry buildings in Nagoya and Osaka in 1891 was, despite Conder's cogent explanations, a crisis for the Japanese architectural profession. Although *zōkagaku-shi* had designed relatively few of the failed buildings, they were inescapably identified with the new technology. The Association of Japanese Architects held no less than fifteen meetings on Nōbi in an effort to reach agreement on what it meant, and what to do. Most of the practicing Japanese architects and at least fifty *zōkagaku* students were dispatched to the ruins to observe and draw details.[1] One of Tatsuno's students, Itō Chūta, helped compile the official report. Itō concluded, not surprisingly, that the reason for the damage to the brick and stone buildings was bad construction. "I want to be fair," he wrote; "my opinion is not that brick is superior to wood, but I can't stand to hear those people who speak ill of brick too much." The architecture component of "Western learning" stood helpless before public opinion. "The masses," revealed Itō, "clamor against brick."[2]

The first response of Japanese architects was to attempt to make European brick-masonry more earthquake resistant. The pre-Nōbi position of Conder, Dyer, and others—that it was sufficient to follow the "elementary principles" of European constructive science—was quietly forgotten as the standard brick wall was subjected to an orgy of reinvention. The pages of the architectural journal *Ken-*

chiku zasshi were full of experiments and suggestions for saving the masonry project, including the reshaping of bricks themselves so that they could be locked together, even with the aid of pins—a solution that crept slightly but unmistakably in the direction of carpentry.

Tatsuno himself designed and had built at Tokyo University around 1893 an earthquake-proof house with brick walls of parabolic section.[3] The discovery of the aseismic properties of the parabola was Milne's Fuji-san lesson, determined from the shaking-table experiments in which Tatsuno assisted. Parabolic masonry walls had historical as well as "natural" sanction in the familiar retaining walls of Japanese castles, including the one at Nagoya. Tatsuno's design experiment, like Milne's laboratory experiments, thus presented Western science as recovering lessons learned by Japanese long ago. Yet Tatsuno accomplished a further reconciliation in his earthquake-proof house: science, Japanese nature, and Japanese building tradition all came to the aid of salvaging European masonry.

Creating parabolic walls in brick was, however, difficult, expensive, and ultimately wasteful of floor space. It was justified in this case by the building's small size and function (it was used as a seismological observatory).[4] Milne cited Tatsuno's experiment in his 1898 seismology textbook, calling it "an excellent object-lesson" but one "not to be recommended as a type of structure for an ordinary dwelling" on account of its "excessive use of materials." This last criticism was one architects and engineers had long made against the practices of *daiku*.[5]

But the meaning of Tatsuno's experiment transcended utility or science. The community of Conder's students needed, in the years following Nōbi, to make bricks resist earthquakes at whatever immediate cost. Like their European teachers, they had yet no firm identity apart from masonry. On the other hand, Tatsuno's parabolic building embodied the search for a solution somewhere between Conder and Milne, and between art and science as the Europeans conceived them. It was a solution to the problem of resistance, but also to the problem of conflicting knowledge, and perhaps conflicting loyalties. That Tatsuno's building was used as a seismological observatory—architecture as an extension of seismological instrumentation—made both its monumental and healing functions all the more clear. The earthquake-proof house was the artifactual expression of a new but tenuous alliance between architecture and seismology forced by the creation of the Imperial Earthquake Investigation Committee (IEIC).

Tatsuno's model laboratory seemed to demonstrate that individual brick or stone buildings might be strengthened against earthquakes of any magnitude given sufficient time and money. But the ambitious project of a entirely masonry Japan

now lay in ruins. An interim solution seemed necessary if architecture was to continue to speak authoritatively about the future of the Japanese built landscape as a whole, and the only other material readily at hand was wood.[6] The serious reexamination of wooden structural systems by Japanese architects presented a host of technocultural difficulties, however. Wood was a material and knowledge-realm then inseparable from *daiku*, against whom the first generation of Japanese architects had constructed their own knowledge and identity. Conder's students were taught relatively little about wood or building-carpentry (as opposed to truss calculation), but a great deal about the status of that material and practice in (European) architectural discourse. The problem in the wake of Nōbi, then, was how to know wood and carpentry in a different (and yet more complete) way than *daiku*, while remaining true to the heritage of Western architecture.

The production of Japanese architectural knowledge about the wooden world proceeded along two avenues in the years after Nōbi. One was the appropriation of the *daiku*-work of the past through the medium of architectural history *(kenchikushi)*. The second was through the cultivation, if not the invention, of "Western carpentry" *(yōfū daiku shigoto)* as a Japanese academic specialty.

ARCHITECTURAL HISTORY AND
THE SEARCH FOR A JAPANESE STYLE

As discussed in previous chapters, Imperial *daiku* Kigo Kiyoyoshi had been brought to the Imperial University even prior to the Nōbi earthquake to teach courses in Japanese carpentry. The generation of architecture students studying at the time of Nōbi would attempt to reconcile Kigo and Conder in much the same way that Tatsuno reconciled Conder and Milne. The young architect most associated with Kigo's teaching was Itō Chūta, the graduate student who, sent to the Nōbi ruins in 1891, could not stand to hear "those who speak ill of brick too much." Itō was in no sense alienated from the masonry project; his graduate thesis of 1892 had involved the design of a Gothic cathedral. That same year, however, he began to make measured drawings of old shrines and temples as part of a government-sponsored inventory project, and in 1893 he published a study of the Hōryūji temple as his doctoral dissertation. This was the first detailed analysis by a Japanese architectural student of a *daiku*-designed building, albeit one that was coming to have the status of a national treasure. Itō's movement from European masonry to Japanese carpentry can also be seen, less radically, as a move from European to Japanese religious architecture or from European to Japanese architectural history.[7]

Itō and other second-generation architecture graduates were continuing Conder's interest in archeology, yet eagerly leaping the wall he had erected between archeology and design. In the early 1890s the students of Kigo would create a "shrine and temple style," based on archaeologically derived details but applicable to banks and exhibition halls. Thus began the long and ultimately compelling search for a "Japanese" architecture that would break more radically from European forms and details. In one sense, however, this generation would adhere more closely than Conder himself to the contemporary European performance of architecture, in which archeology deeply informed design, and architects appropriated the identity "master-builder" through "continuing the tradition" of building in stone. Here the appropriation would be of *daiku*-work—the tradition of building in wood. Itō and the other *zōkagaku-shi* were not becoming *daiku*, but transforming the *daiku*-work of the past into architecture through the acts of measuring and drawing historic buildings. The best *daiku*-work of the past became the seemingly natural inheritance of their own profession, a touchstone for the conception of a national architecture.[8]

Itō emerged in the same period as the main proponent of architecture as art, as opposed to the position, embedded in the *zōkagaku* course and only reinforced by Conder's statements after Nōbi, that architecture in earthquake-prone Japan must become science and technology. It was Itō who, in an 1894 article, advocated that *zōkagaku* be replaced by *kenchiku*, as the original term could not convey the fine-art sensibilities embodied in the Japanese term for "architecture." Itō objected to *gaku* (learning) as too evocative of science. In seeking to make Japanese architecture a fine art (though one informed by the science of archeology and the technoscience of photography), Itō was simultaneously aligning his discipline with European practices and meanings while distancing it from overtly European forms, at least contemporary ones. As Cherie Wendelken has pointed out, another goal of Itō's project was establishing "a trans-Asian connection between the temples of Japan and those of ancient Greece." Itō even undertook an extensive study tour of Asia, particularly the Indian subcontinent, making notes and sketches in the manner of a British architect in Italy, Greece, or "the Orient."[9]

In appropriating the *daiku* of the past, however, Japanese architecture was simultaneously isolating and bastardizing the *daiku* of the present. Before Nōbi, "architecture" was quite clearly and self-consciously foreign knowledge. Itō gave it a Japanese lineage: the *daiku* of Hōryūji and the Ise shrine now become ancestral figures to the new architectural professional. This new genealogy called into question the relatedness of the *daiku* of the past, however, to *daiku* still living. Contemporary *daiku* would come to be seen in many writings not as descendants of the builders of Hōryūji, but as a lesser species or strain partly invented by westernization itself: the bastard children of an epistemic break in *daiku* culture fostered by capitalism, contracting, and modern change generally. Passage into what was now a distant *daiku* homeland would require following maps drafted by the architectural profession itself—the path of architectural history.

There was nothing peculiarly Japanese about this knowledge-producing strategy, even its application to carpenters. In the United States, "Colonial architecture" and The Colonial Carpenter were simultaneously under design and production by design professionals, while "the half-timbered house" and The Medieval Carpenter were being recrafted by their counterparts in Britain. All of these objects/figures were distantly related to "Japanese architecture" and The Japanese Carpenter, as both had been exhibited overseas since the 1870s. The physical and chronological similarities between them (their woodenness, nativeness, and historicity) signal a common architectural instinct by the turn of the century to create a new center of critical knowledge outside the increasingly powerful culture of engineering, which was coming to own the emblems of metal, empire, and futurity. Yet architectural history also ordered the relationship between the cosmopolitan professional and the (much larger) group of indigenous tradesmen with whom he daily interacted. The contemporary artisan-turned-tradesman was not only rendered ancestorless by architectural history, but made the monstrous offspring of modernity. The Architect, having "inherited" (through archeology) the knowledge of artisan ancestors (i.e., craft), now knew more about wood than carpenters, and more about stone than masons. Or so many architects came to believe. Architects could now assume the pedagogical mission of teaching contemporary tradesmen their craft (the practices and rituals of the dead ancestors). In the new formulation, being an artisan was no longer a living, inherited way of knowing and being, but a body of knowledge to be excavated from historic buildings and refashioned as an object of academic instruction.

In the Japanese case, however, bringing the most ancient temples and shrines into the fold of architecture did not mean legitimizing the contemporary Japanese practice of carpentry. The passing of a Temple Preservation Act in 1897, for example, which brought larger numbers of architects into intimate relations with historic buildings, initially meant the further extension of foreign knowledge into the old object-world. Architects preserved famous temples using truss calculation and metal reinforcement. Euclid's seventh proposition and prefabricated iron sections from Scottish rolling mills began to be applied to protecting large statues of the Buddha.[10]

On the other hand, some architects used their new archeologically informed knowledge about ancient *daiku*-work to counter Japanese seismologists' claims of *daiku* scienticity. Itō Chūta's explanation of pagodas, for example, moved them decisively away from the world of science, seismological instruments, and conscious invention. According to Itō:

> Really, gojūnotō is the tomb to enshroud Sarira [an earth goddess in Shinto cosmology]. The central post is placed as a tomb-mark, so as to conceal Sarira; then the many-storied frame was constructed around the central post to support it, and the present style of gojūnotō was developed. In former times, the central post was erected upon the base stone. The frame around the central post settled gradually and the joint of the central post and the top roof yielded an opening. As this is not good against rainfall, the central posts of some gojūnotō were suspended from the upper story, in the last half of the Tokugawa era. From these points of view, it is clear that the central post is not a mechanism intended to resist earthquakes.[11]

Itō's argument closely followed that of Conder, adding only the elements of Buddhist belief and ritual—which Itō would have learned about through involvement in temple archeology and preservation—and weatherization. To Conder, *daiku* suspended the central mast to counter shrinkage, while to Itō, they were countering rain damage. In both cases the force of nature *daiku* were resisting was the relatively mundane one of water. To Itō, resistance to the sublime and infinitely complex power of earthquakes, a force of nature mysterious and threatening even to modern architects, was not encompassed by *daiku* knowledge, even of the ancient kind.

If architects could not concede aseismic knowledge to the *daiku* of the past, then the basis for a contemporary aseismic Japanese carpentry would have to be located elsewhere. An alternative way of knowing about wood was thus crafted by Japanese architects in the same period, one that has received less attention from foreign scholars because it seems less "Japanese" than the excavation of traditional architecture (although it is arguably more so). Beginning in the year of Nōbi (1891) and extending into the first decade of the twentieth century, Japanese architects began synthesizing diverse elements of American, European, and even Japanese carpentry practice into what came to be called "Western carpentry." Like Western masonry before it, Western carpentry was expected above all to resist earthquakes, something that few of its European and American models claimed to know how to do. The architect most associated with this new knowledge-realm, at least in the immediate aftermath of the Nōbi earthquake, was also named Itō—Itō Tamekichi.

"AMERICAN ARCHITECT
AND CARPENTER" ITŌ TAMEKICHI

Itō Tamekichi benefited from being the first Japanese architect, in the weeks and months following the Nōbi disaster, to publish a coherent and well-thought-out solution to "the problem of the Japanese house." Problem, solution, and Itō's identity as an "architect" were in fact all coemergent. Unlike Itō Chūta, Itō Tamekichi's claim to the title *zōkagaku-shi*—his claim to legitimacy as a producer of new knowledge—would always be fragile. Itō had briefly attended Kōbudaigakkō as a free student, yet never received a degree. Perhaps because his father had been a draftsman on the Imperial Palace project, he managed to become the assistant to the Italian architect and former *zōkagaku* professor Giovanni Cappelletti, and accompanied Cappelletti to San Francisco in 1885, where he worked for three years as a draftsman in the latter's architectural studio. On returning to Japan in 1888 he established a private design office, which he later claimed was the first in the country. His resorting to private practice mainly demonstrates, however, his outsider status in these early years.[12]

Two years after his return, in 1890, Itō constructed an experimental wooden house for himself in the Kanda ward of Tokyo, the first of three he would build on adjacent lots. He called this project the "Safe from Three Damages House" *(Sangai anzen kaoku)*, the "damages" being earthquakes, floods, and typhoons. Ironically, the house was eventually destroyed by the one force of nature Itō had not guarded against—fire—following the Tokyo earthquake of 1923. It had survived the earthquake itself.[13]

Although Itō was on the periphery of the formative architectural world, his Safe from Three Damages House well demonstrates the rejection, in that then-small world, of the idea of the traditional Japanese house as a nature-resisting object. Itō entirely eschewed *daiku* systems in favor of one based on American carpentry. His house frame was a series of large trusses, designed to be assembled on the ground as "bents" (identical, flat, cross-sectional frameworks) and then raised into place in the manner of traditional Anglo-American houses and barns. Each bent was stiffened by long pieces of lumber thin enough to be fastened with nails. But unlike squarish American house frames, Itō's was triangular in cross section, similar to the frame of typical American roof. His other name for the house was in fact *sankaku nagaya*, or Triangular House.[14]

The triangle and its material expression, the truss, were talismanic in Meiji Japan. Because triangles in Europe and America successfully overcame gravity and wind pressure, they came to Japan inscribed with an almost abstract resistance to natural forces in general. Earthquakes and floods, however, were forces of nature that Western trusses had little record of resisting. The logic of Itō's claim to safety was his having used the truss to eliminate Japanese roof framing, long condemned by *yatoi* architects and engineers as dangerously heavy and complex. The center of gravity in Itō's frame was approximately in the middle rather than the top, a change in the physics of the Japanese house as well as its form and techniques. Itō's design was lightness and simplicity itself.

Assembling trusses, raising bents, and nailing things together were all outside the practice of *daiku*. Itō's house was avant-garde in both technology and form and made no concession to Japanese construction knowledge or skills.[15] In a further display of Americanness, he patented its design. Patenting, a procedure unusual even within Western architect culture, was in keeping with Itō's other self-identity as an inventor (and perhaps as an American). The house itself consecrated Itō as an architect; he was accepted as a secondary member of the Association of Japanese Architects the year of its completion.[16]

The Safe from Three Damages House might have remained an anomaly, like Milne's own aseismic house or a dozen other experiments, were it not for the Nōbi earthquake. In 1890, Itō had sent a descriptive letter and photographs of the house to the governors of each prefecture (who were then major patrons of Western architecture in the form of *daiku*-designed *wayō setchū* schoolhouses, assembly halls, police stations, etc.) yet got only a single response. But the great earthquake of following year, in the words of Itō's biographer Muramatsu Teijirō, "decided his whole life." Itō joined the procession then touring the ruins of Nagoya, Gifu, and Ōgaki in the late fall of 1891, and although he left no detailed account of what he saw there, his preexisting ideas about earthquake resistance seem to have emerged from the ruins buttressed rather than shaken. His summation could indeed serve as the collective verdict for the postearthquake investigators: "It was just as I had expected in Tokyo."[17]

On returning to the capital, Itō quickly compiled a book on earthquake-resistant house construction, published in December 1891 as *Nihon kenchiku kōzō kairyōhō*, which he translated himself as *Improved Architecture for Japanese Dwellings*. By dividing the cover and title page into English and Japanese sections, he was not only communicating with two audiences, but signaling the Westernness of his proposals to his predominantly Japanese readers. On the Japanese portion of the title page he styled himself, in Kanji (Chinese characters), "American Architect [Beikoku kenchiku-shi] Itō Tamekichi."[18]

In Itō's "improved architecture," the Three Damages House became one of a series of new systems, though not the most prominent. Its frame was now dressed as a thatch-roofed Japanese farmhouse, nativizing its avant-garde reality and better fitting it to the geography of the Nōbi epicentral zone. Metaphorically sending the Tokyo house to the Nōbi Plain also cleared urban space for new, less avant-garde solutions, for Itō had now decided to reform rather than supplant Japanese knowledge—to enter into a dialogue with *daiku*. Nōbi had created an expanded audience for earthquake resistance that might be captured by seemingly more pragmatic solutions. Abandoning the lightness, simplicity, and triangularity of his first experiment, he moved in the direction of the familiar. The bulk of his book took the urban Japanese house frame as its new reform object.[19]

Accepting the customary dimensions and arrangements of Japanese framing members, Itō redesigned all the connections, peppering the typical frame with sometimes intricate, location-specific iron fittings. His design instincts remained radical, but they had moved from form to detail. The work of holding the Japanese frame together, previously done by intricately cut wooden joints, was now to be done entirely by iron straps, dowels, and stirrups. More precisely it was to be done with the nails or bolts attaching these fixtures to the frame. Itō made nails and bolts—technologies foundational to American carpentry—the basis of his new Japanese carpentry as well. Yet he did so without radically changing the form of the Japanese house frame or those of its several parts.[20]

Itō's new plans even preserved joinery, one of the principal reservoirs of Japanese skill. The timbers in his system were still to be jointed—fit together by cuts—underneath the metal fixtures. Yet every wooden joint was redesigned, abandoning traditional mortises and tenons for surface-mounted lap joints shallow enough to be held by nails. Moving the wooden joints to the surface (something made possible by the strength of the new metal fixtures) also accomplished a change long

FIGURE 13
Itō Tamekichi's "Safe from Three Damages House." This structure was originally conceived as an urban dwelling, but Itō gave it a thatched roof following the Nōbi earthquake. Although it had the basic form of a Japanese farmhouse, the frame was radical in both design and construction, relying on American-style nailing and metal straps rather than Japanese joinery. (From Itō Tamekichi, "Anzen kenchiku tetsugu oyobi kairyō kōzōhō," *Kenchiku zasshi* 74 [1894]: 39–44.)

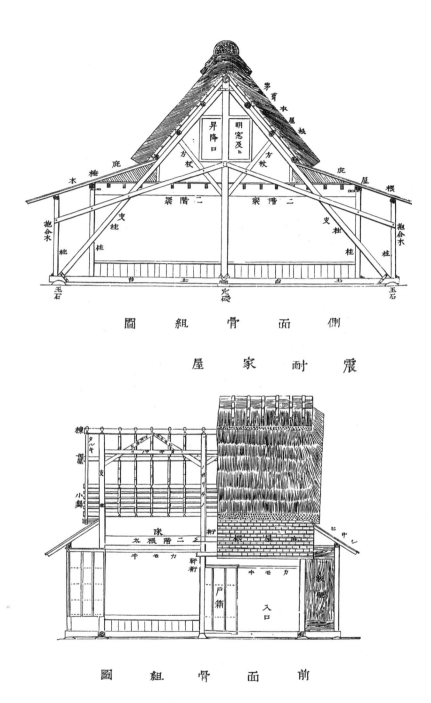

側面骨組圖

震耐家屋

前面骨組圖

recommended by *yatoi:* "preserving" the "full strength" of the posts and beams by "not cutting them full of holes."[21]

Itō's package of compromises was an ingenious technocultural solution, and his book went to press with the endorsements of Kikuchi Dairoku (Tokyo University mathematician and future chairman of the new IEIC), architect and Zōka-gakkai regular member Nakamura Tetsutarō (one of Conder's students), and John Milne. Itō must have made Milne's acquaintance in the fall or early winter of 1891, when the latter was lecturing in Tokyo and calling for reforms in the typical Japanese house frame, and convinced him that his own system was in line with Milne's policies. In the front of Itō's book was an endorsement, signed by Milne, but appearing under the heading "Seismological Society of Japan," which read: "It must be clear to any one who passed through the Aichi and Gifu prefectures after the last great earthquake, that much of the destruction might have been avoided by slight modifications in the system of building—lighter roofs, less weakening of timbers by the formation of joints, and greater rigidity by the insertion of diagonals, would undoubtedly give greater safety to the buildings. These and other things Mr. Itō proposes to do, and we trust his efforts will meet with every satisfaction."[22]

Conder gave his own indirect endorsement before Japan's architects in 1892: "There is lately a movement for improving common Japanese structures, which is worthy of all encouragement, amounting to nothing more or less, I imagine, than introducing European principles of jointing and stiffening into such constructions."[23]

To Milne, Itō was making "slight improvements" to *daiku*-work, while to Conder, he was doing "nothing more or less" than introducing European principles. The two statements illustrate the success of Itō's synthesis, Milne noticing his retention of Japanese forms, and Conder that he was "stiffening" that form with European jointing. Yet Itō's improvements were hardly "slight," nor were they merely the introduction of principles from abroad. As valuable as it proved to reconcile the positions of the two Englishmen, and even to marry his American knowledge with Japanese practice, Itō had many additional things to either reconcile or resist before his "improved architecture" became an unproblematic solution.

Given his self-naming as an "American architect," it is worth noting certain famous principles of American carpentry that Itō was not at all interested in. In the United States, iron had entered carpentry not only as a strengthening agent, but a "labor-saving device." Its use was accompanied in the early to mid-nineteenth century by a corresponding simplification and interchangeability in lumber types, a process most dramatically embodied in the American "balloon frame" (which was nothing but nails and dimensionally uniform—2 x 4—lumber). These developments did not necessarily constitute "deskilling," a twentieth-century term coined for the factory rather than the building site, because craft-conscious American tradesmen still owned and used a wide variety of tools. But these and other changes were clearly related to the desire for increased speed and ease of erection, and keeping the wages and availabilities of the same tradesmen relatively uniform over space and time.[24]

Despite his three years' residence in San Francisco, Itō was uninterested in saving labor or the interchangeability of parts. There were clearly no monetary savings in using nails in Japan, as the country was still dependent on expensive imported iron. Neither were speed or ease of assembly among his system's obvious qualities. Nailing diverse and complex metal fixtures to timbers whose diversity remained unchanged (and had still to be cut with relatively complex joints) would not have been a speedy activity, especially when performed by *daiku* wholly unfamiliar with nails, bolts, and straps. By retaining wooden joints under the new iron fixtures, Itō was not eliminating traditional *daiku* tasks but supplementing them. He was increasing, not reducing, house building's overall complexity, and both the time and knowledge required of the builders.

Itō's overriding concern was resisting earthquakes, a project that would increasingly come to dominate the Japanese architectural profession as a whole. Especially following Nōbi, this goal had such priority that it overshadowed interest in economy or the ease of technological diffusion. Architects were, after all, a community that had earlier been intent on reconstructing Japan in brick and stone, a similarly costly if not utopian project. Itō was developing a product salable not so much within the money economy as within the cultural economies of Japanese architecture, the new Imperial Earthquake Investigation Committee, and the Meiji state. A sudden, embarrassing void had opened in the knowledge of Itō's chosen discipline that his solutions conveniently filled.

THE SHOKKŌ GUNDAN

Itō's intentions were not only technical, just as Western technical solutions like masonry, trusses, and iron fittings were not only technical. His "improved architecture" was in fact the material component of a planned reorganization of the entire building act. Although he had made a step toward *daiku* practice, he went a step further by attempting to redesign *daiku* themselves. The social side of Itō's system surfaced in 1892, less than a year after the publication of his book, when he formed the Shokkō Gundan.

The new Meiji word *shokkō* was a combination of the first character of *shokunin* (artisan) with the character *kō*, which, as noted in an earlier chapter, was taking on the connotation "industrial" or "technological" (as in the names Kōbudaigakkō and Kōbushō). The closest English translations are "industrial worker" or perhaps "technician." The *shokkō* was a wage-earning employee trained in new techniques, rather than a member of the traditional artisan class. But to define *shokkō* (or even the English term "industrial worker") as simply economic actor-categories frames their meanings too narrowly. Itō's Shokkō Gundan was a worker army. The word *gundan* translates as "corps," in the military sense.

The purpose, organization, and character of the Shokkō Gundan were explained in Itō's subsequent book, *Mokkōjutsu kyōkasho* (1894), a title he translated as *Wooden Work Manual*. *Mokkō* (wooden work) was another new word that abstracted carpentry away from *daiku* (the existing Japanese term for carpentry being literally "*daiku*-matters"), in much the same way that *shokkō* moved workers away from artisanship. Itō's title page was again divided into English and Japanese sections, but this time he styled himself, in English, "Itō Tamekichi, Practical Carpenter, Architect, and Builder." In Japanese, he was still "American Architect Itō Tamekichi."[25]

Compound self-titles like "Architect and Practical Builder" or "Practical Builder and Carpenter" were common among the authors of antebellum American carpentry texts, which would still have been circulating during the years Itō was in San Francisco. An American would never have inverted the titles "architect and carpenter" (which constituted an inversion of status), but Itō was particularly insistent in this book on speaking above all as a "carpenter." In subsequent writing he would also call himself a *daiku*, although his *daiku* credentials were even more tenuous than his architect ones.[26]

Itō claims in his introduction that the book completes a project initiated by his mentor Cappelletti. The Italian *yatoi*, he writes, loved Japanese *daiku*-work and considered it the most sophisticated carpentry system in the world. It was Cappelletti, during their initial journey together to the United States, who first opened Itō's eyes to its uniqueness and value: "Cappelletti often told me those excellencies [of Japanese carpentry] can compete with the Japanese Imperial household's virtue, the mountain rivers' beauty, and Japan's pleasant climate. . . . It was then that I knew for the first time that Japanese woodworking was so excellent and skilled."[27] His revelation led to this question: "How could we maintain its value and develop it forever?" Itō presents his book as the result of that inquiry.[28]

Itō's project now had two foreign godfathers: Milne, who had entrusted him with "slight modifications" to Japanese carpentry in the aftermath of Nōbi, and now

Cappelletti, who placed Japanese carpentry in the same class as the Imperial family and mountain streams. But Itō's plans were no more colored by veneration than they were "slight." Like the Meiji political leadership, he was a revolutionary couching his project in restoration language.

"Artisan spirit has declined," wrote Ito, and Japanese *daiku* now "lack a moral sense." They had become "very cunning" and even unskilled: "As far as their occupation is concerned, they don't know their work well, and their knowledge is very inferior, and it is obvious they can't compete with civilized people *[bunmeikaku-jin]*."[29] The moral decline of *daiku* had been Itō's principal lesson of the Nōbi earthquake. On the Nōbi Plain, he writes, "houses big and small were remarkably [indiscriminately] destroyed." What separated the standing from the collapsed was not size or cost, but age. It was "the new architecture" that suffered most, while "the old architecture survived." The earthquake had thus been "a criterion of artisans' morality *[seiji]*. . . . Of course we cannot say that there weren't other reasons [for the destruction] but the most important cause was that today's artisans are not honest."[30]

The claim that newer houses in Nagoya and its hinterland suffered more than older ones contradicts the testimony of engineers like Smedly and Hall, who found the aged houses much more vulnerable. Even Conder, no partisan of *daiku*-work, had described older houses as collapsing more readily.[31] Yet Itō draws here on a standard trope of late-nineteenth-century Anglo-American architecture, which Conder himself had used to explain the collapse of the brick spinning mills: the decline of artisanship, or jerry-building. Conder had drawn a distinction, however, between skilful *daiku* and jerry-building brick-masons. As a British architect, he could not have overcome the irony of referring to *daiku*, the very model for the Western craftsman, as jerry-builders. Itō was under no such cultural restraints, and consequently made jerry-building a more general historical and moral condition. The sins of Conder's brick-masons were extended to all contemporary artisans, while the strength of Nagoya Castle represented their ancestors' skill and morality.

Itō's use of the jerry-building trope was consistent with the discourse on artisanal decline, spoken and written, in the United States and Britain. There architects were also broadly condemnative of contemporary artisanal practice, invoking "craft" as pertaining to a distant time or place, yet a time and place that often included Japan. To English and American architects of the late nineteenth century, a reliance on metal at the expense of wooden joints was the very mark of the jerry-builder, or proof that the carpenter did not know his craft. British architect H. H. Stratham, who would call Japanese carpentry "unscientific" and childish in 1912, made an exception for the Japanese method of cutting joints. "We respect it [Japanese carpentry]," he wrote, "for its absence of mere fastenings." Cram had admired the fact that Japanese structures were "mortised in such a way that neither pins nor nails are necessary," and Stratham agreed. "In a structural sense," he wrote, "that is the best point about it" because "such a method of putting timber together is analogous to the system of bonding in masonry." Japanese buildings were analogous to Gothic ones, thought Stratham, because they "stand by the balance of pressures," as opposed to structures "which can only be made safe by tie-rods." In other word, in Britain (and to a lesser extent the United States) actually cutting into wood with chisels was a sign of "honest craftsmanship," while attaching metal fittings to wood was mongrel-like and declensionary.[32]

Itō's condemnation of contemporary *daiku*-work as "jerry-building" *(yamashi)*, and his promotion of metal fixtures as the cure of that condition—as the very restoration of *daiku* honesty and skill—thus inverted Euro-American discourse even as it faithfully translated it. In Europe and the United States, "the jerry-builder" and "the Japanese carpenter" functioned in many respects as mirror-image twins. Itō was fashioning a "Western carpenter" for the East to match "the Japanese carpenter" of the West.

For Itō the wellspring of reform was the *shokunin* spirit, which he defined as "to not be too greedy" and "to be honest, unsophisticated, and good natured." Although "wildness and stubbornness" were also ingrained in the *shokunin* character, he believed those latter traits could be expelled through closer association or consciousness of the group. Itō did not include group consciousness in his description of pre-Meiji *shokunin*, despite the existence of Edo-period guilds. Within the guild network, *shokunin* had been organized as families, famous for their secretiveness and rivalry. Moreover, Japanese journeymen had always, like their American counterparts, been highly mobile, moving between a number of masters in the course of a typical career.[33]

Itō's reform model was not, in any case, the Edo-period guild but the Meiji-period professional or alumni association. Association attracted him as a device for enforcing virtue and good behavior through appeals to honor: "Students, once they graduate, make much of the honor of their school, and those members who belong to some association make much of it. So these people don't do bad things."[34]

Not being a graduate of any school, Itō's most intense experience with the group would likely have been his membership in the Association of Japanese Architects. His status as a "secondary member," however, left him forever outside the regular membership composed of Kōbudaigakkō and Tokyo University graduates. Itō, whose very identify as an "architect" was dependent on the most fragile of associations, contrasts in the starkest terms the morality of "the associated" with the degeneracy of the overly independent artisans: "Artisans, once they learn skills and escape from their masters, spread east and west. There is nothing to regulate them. No one commands or leads them. They don't have belongings. They are the most pitiful creatures in our society. They are incubators of sin *[tsumi]*. . . . So we have to teach them new knowledge and make them have *shokunin* virtue . . . make people know that they also have a lovable nature, which is naive."[35]

His solution for the artisans was not the loose association of the architects, however, but military organization and discipline. The Shokkō Gundan, according to regulations bound into his *Wooden Work Manual,* was to "conform to the army system."[36] He even designed Western military-style uniforms, wholly unlike the traditional artisan uniforms whose large Chinese characters identified workers with the house of their master. The corps's martial character was underlined by a system of ranks, from the superintendent general at its head to sergeant-majors and sergeants who controlled building sites and took the place of traditional masters. Those in the lowest ranks—the *shokkō* themselves—would, according to the regulations, "follow the orders of the upper-level members."[37]

Itō's worker corps was clearly aimed at replacing the artisanal structure of master-journeyman-apprentice. His was a wholly different strategy than that of new *daiku*-turned-contractors such as Shimizu Kisuke, who gathered artisan families into new, more extensive subcontracting networks without changing their internal structures. Even today the large Japanese construction companies, even more than their American counterparts, are largely umbrella organizations with relatively few regular employees but extensive subcontracting networks. The officers of the Shokkō Gundan, however, were to take on all the roles of mastership: finding jobs, purchasing materials, allocating and policing labor, preparing bills, and collecting fees. Clients desiring the corps's services were to apply to their local branch office (Itō envisioned offices in each Tokyo ward), which would "immediately send officers to explore the site, discuss the project, and start construction." Apprentices would be trained by the corps in special night schools. If members "were found to be lazy or unkind" at the construction site, the officers would "investigate" and mete out discipline. But while apprentices had traditionally been expected to show loyalty to their masters, Itō's carpenter-soldiers were above all to show loyalty to the public. They were to "respect and love the employer," the person commissioning the work.[38]

The corps aimed to remold not only artisan organization and culture, but the individual artisan's behavior and character, if not his soul. The regulations dealt at length with the personal, moral changes to be worked on the membership. *Shokkō* were to "avoid useless chattering," "not be drunken," be frugal, have "loyalty and courage," "practice justice," and even "love other people" and "lead other people to righteousness." Here the language of military or labor discipline shades into that of the Protestant mission, for Itō was a Christian convert and the Shokkō Gundan a salvation army, directly influenced by the British organization of that name. "About Meiji 24 [1891]," wrote Itō in a reminiscence about the founding, "when I read in the *Yomiuri shimbun* about General Booth's Salvation Army, I wondered how their social work could be assimilated in Japan."[39]

Although there was no insistence that Shokkō Gundan members be Christian, they were not to work on Sunday, and were to "study subjects decided by the Sunday school." The regulations repeatedly emphasize the sacredness of Sunday, as in "Sunday should be made the happiest, most pleasant day for family and self" and "Sunday should be spent developing the spirit." The corps aimed to merge the "*shokunin* spirit" of old Japan and the military spirit of the new Japan with the missionary spirit of Anglo-American Protestantism, both its moral and productive sides.[40]

The Shokkō Gundan was an actual organization between 1892 and about 1899, although we know little about the extent or character of its membership. According to Itō's biographer, the corps at its height might have contained a hundred members, not large for an "army," but far larger than the typical Meiji-period building-contracting organization.[41] It also published a newspaper, the *Shokkō shimbun*, and planned (but failed) to establish a night school for apprentice training. Perhaps for symbolic as well as practical reasons, Itō hoped to find apprentices among the orphans of the Nōbi earthquake. The Shokkō Gundan was not without powerful collaborators and backers. Although Itō was its superintendent general, the corps was founded and managed by a committee of five, and, according to Muramatsu, an early list of outside supporters ran to forty-four names, including some with ties to the nascent Japanese labor movement. When Itō sought to raise money for his apprentice school in 1899, his list of sponsors had increased to 124, including ex-prime minister Count Ōkuma Shigenobu, Education Minister Ozaki Yukio, and the future prime minister Inukai Tsuyoshi.[42]

Muramatsu notes that the Shokkō Giyūkai, the kernel of what became the influential Rōdō Kumiai (Laborer's Union), was founded at the same time as the Shokkō Gundan (1890 or 1891) by Japanese living in San Francisco. Itō had left San Francisco a few years earlier and is not known to have had any contact with its Japanese labor organizers. But clearly the Shokkō Gundan was not isolated from the contemporary Japanese interest in worker organization. Its goals of increasing the social status of *shokunin* and reducing the length of the work week were universal ones of the late-nineteenth-century trade union movement. Yet other important trade union characteristics, such as workers' management of their own affairs, fighting for increased wages, and acknowledgment of the differing interests of capital and labor, were nowhere manifest in Itō's worker army.[43]

In inventing first an earthquake-resistant architecture, and secondly a salvation army to construct it, Itō had designed a virtually complete if heterogeneous technosocial system, one that combined metal fixtures, Anglo-American evangelical Protestantism, the Imperial Army, brick foundations, "the *shokunin* spirit," nails, "Western knowledge," the Nōbi earthquake, John Milne, and vocational night schools. Itō's choice of technical elements like metal fittings was not incidental to his choice of moral elements like honesty, or social elements like discipline. The ability of a traditional Japanese building to resist earthquakes was largely dependent on the design and execution of its joints. Once completed, joints were forever hidden from view, unless rent asunder, and thus revealed to have been defective from the start. Itō's metal fittings not only removed from *daiku* any temptation to "cheat" on the workmanship of joinery, but moved the joint itself from its hidden chamber (in the junction of framing timbers) to the outside surface, where it was easily inspected. The metal straps, bolts, and stirrups thus made *daiku* technique transparent, in the same way that evangelical Protestantism made transparent the workman's character and intentions.

CONFLICTING WAYS
OF WESTERN KNOWING:
ITŌ AND THE IMPERIAL EARTHQUAKE
INVESTIGATION COMMITTEE

In the wake of the Nōbi earthquake, Itō had emerged as the first Japanese architect with an innovative or reformist solution to the problem—for those who considered it a problem—of how to rebuild in wood using "Western knowledge." The Japanese railroad administration (to which Milne was connected) used one of his systems to reconstruct its wooden stations in the earthquake zone. Over the next three years his designs were serialized in articles in *Kenchiku ẓasshi*, the journal of the Association of Japanese Architects, and he was invited to work as a researcher with the new IEIC (Imperial Earthquake Investigation Committee), an unusual honor for a man lacking a university degree or state-granted credentials.[44]

One of the charges of the IEIC was to separate the truly earthquake-resistant from the non–earthquake-resistant, based on the examination of models by architects and seismologists, and the collection of data from shaking-table experiments. If Itō's designs received state sanction, they might become a basis for instruction, or even be disseminated throughout the empire in the construction of schools and other public buildings. The IEIC's full range of powers was as yet unclear; Itō's decision to organize *shokunin* into a uniformed army, as opposed to a construction firm, might even have been made with an eye on potential state patronage. The state was simultaneously making similar attempts to reform *shokunin* practices through the development of trade schools.[45]

As it turned out, however, placing himself at the mercy of the state and its scholars proved to be Itō's undoing. In an unpublished narrative he wrote as an elderly man, Itō claims he was mistrusted by unnamed members of the commission, and even called an "imposter" *(yamashi)*. This was the same Japanese word that Conder had used interchangeably with "jerry-builder" to describe those who had constructed the fallen mills.[46] Itō's ongoing design work was systematically excluded, his narrative claims, from the IEIC's official publications. What he was specifically accused of doing, according to his own account, was "ignoring Western opinion." It was claimed there was no "research and persistent effort" behind his design work, but only "his own peculiar originality." His designs would be published only, he was told, "if some other books come to similar conclusions." Eventually he despaired: "I thought someone like me that studies new, novel things is not at all useful, so I resigned as a part-time member of that committee."[47]

We cannot know for certain who Itō's tormenters were, but Muramatsu suggests they were three architect-members, Sone, Nakamura, and Katayama, all Conder's students. The fourth architect-member was Tatsuno. The committee eventually published a series of earthquake-resistant framing plans "invented by the committee members," according to Itō, "using what is called applied Western knowledge." The architect-members, rather than the committee's seismologists and other scientists, would have been the logical designers, and an article describing models made from the plans indeed appears under their four names.[48] The models were subjected to shaking-table tests, according to Itō, but the results, which might have favored his own house frame, were never published. "But why on earth did they not publish the results? . . . I really regret it, and I can't forget it even now. I'd like to warn people that the four earthquake-resistant houses advertised in the committee's report are actually unfinished ideas. I myself was watching at the test place, so I know the results. But I don't have the freedom to tell you whether the result was good or not. . . . Among those [designs] considered useless, there might have been house-frames very good and effective against the earthquake of Taishō 12."[49] Those who won the argument with Itō left no account of it, but we do have their designs, which the committee published in 1895 following another destructive earthquake in Yamagata prefecture, north of Tokyo. Plans and actual models were rushed by the government to distant Yamagata, although it is not clear what, if anything, was done with them once they arrived. Nonetheless, the same IEIC designs were published in architectural and seismological books into the early twentieth century, becoming nearly official aseismic models within both disciplines.[50]

Comparing the IEIC plans to Itō's, we can begin to piece together what was at issue. The problem, as in the debate between Conder and Milne, was that elusive phenomenon "Western learning." Excepting perhaps Tatsuno, who had trained in England, the *zōkagaku-shi* lacked Itō's experience with actual Western carpentry. They might never have seen a nail being driven or a bent being raised, nor even have known very much about Japanese house construction, which was well outside the *zōkagaku* curriculum. They knew a great deal, however, about the virtues of triangles, and how to overcome certain natural forces through calculation. The most important component of all four official designs was the roof truss.

Itō's Safe from Three Damages House had also been based on the truss, and "Triangular" was its second name. But the Three Damages truss was not the truss as taught at Kōbudaigakkō. Itō had used trusses only to exploit their triangular shapes. Because the base or "chord" of Itō's trusses actually rested on the ground, they were hardly behaving as trusses at all. Kōbudaigakkō trusses hung above one's head in the orthodox way; as in America and Europe, they constituted roofs and not whole buildings. Because they were intended to resist gravity, they were great reservoirs of mathematical calculation. Itō's were just large triangles—light, simple, and practical, like American roofs. Kōbudaigakkō trusses were British: heavy and complex, the province of experts.

Itō's design interests had in any case turned away from his original emphasis on triangles to concentrate on metal fixtures, a different Western technology that actually obviated the need for triangularity. He had abandoned triangularity in an effort to enlist *daiku*, in the sense of both enlisting their interest (by creating a system that eschewed the unfamiliar truss), and enlisting their bodies and souls into the Shokkō Gundan. Dexterity in combining objects and people is one definition of invention. Before Itō was an architect, he was an inventor.

The architect-members of the IEIC were also inventing, but their particular combination of elements revealed different technosocial purposes. Above all they were looking to introduce to Japan a coherent, well-tested body of Western knowledge, centered in this case around the truss. They were not intent on enlisting *daiku*. Their goal was to enlist educated Japanese opinion behind the discipline of architecture as constructive science, a set of objects and practices whose reputation had been badly tarnished in the Nōbi quake. Itō could well have appeared from their perspective to be an imposter, because he exercised none of the physical and mathematical skills that formed the basis of their own training. The charge that Itō was exercising "his own peculiar originality" was a serious one to a community whose Western-derived orthodoxies had been called into public question, and thus required defending.

Architecture's reputation had suffered an additional shock in 1894, the very year that the IEIC plans and models were created, when a rather strong earthquake occurred in Tokyo itself, further damaging the city's masonry infrastructure. According to Kikuchi, "No house was absolutely destroyed, but in the lower part of Tokyo many brick buildings received severe damage, and large numbers of chimneys were thrown down."[51] The need of Conder's students to create objects that were earthquake-resistant, yet rooted in the *zōkagaku* curriculum, was thus acute. The nightmare of Nōbi seemed just then to be constantly recurring.

Itō's bad experience with his university-trained colleagues actually pushed him farther in the direction of *daiku* practice. One thing his designs shared with those of the IEIC members was the liberal use of metal fittings. In the British fashion, the committee's architects had connected their trusses and other framing elements with an almost baroque assortment of metal plates and bolts, stronger and more complex than Itō's and all the more beyond the ability of regular *daiku* to either purchase or comprehend.[52] Reluctant, perhaps, to mount an attack on trusses, Itō turned against ironwork in general, which also meant turning against his own system.

In a *Kenchiku zasshi* article of 1895, written shortly after his rivals' designs had been published by the IEIC, Itō claimed to have "run out of patience" with ironwork, which he now believed "it is better not to use." He consequently redesigned his own system to rely more heavily on wooden joints, although these were still greatly simplified compared to traditional ones and were still fully inspectable from the outside. He was also experiencing difficulty training members of the Shokkō Gundan in such an alien technique, complaining, for example, of their inability to correctly set bolts. It could also be that, because his "improved architecture" had heretofore existed only on paper, he was beginning to realize its technical limitations in practice.[53]

In the memoir he wrote as an elderly man, Itō ridiculed the architect-members of the IEIC as "using what is called applied western knowledge." But the contest to define Western knowledge was an unequal one from the start, and never, despite Itō's personal disappointment, reached the point of open rupture. Itō's status as an architect depended entirely on the indulgence of his university-trained fellows, who ruled the Zōka-gakkai. Around the same time he wrote, in his *Wooden Work Manual*, of the precipice between isolated and independent *shokunin* and those who command respect because "they belong to some association." Despite the bitter and aggressive tone of Itō's memoir, he and the Shokkō Gundan continued to associate with Conder's students in other ways.

One was by taking on the role of masons. Conder had blamed the collapse of masonry in 1891 on "glaring disobedience" by masons, and had called for "more stringent expert control."[54] To Japanese architects, Japanese masons were architecture's weak link. Thus they enlisted Itō's worker army to construct the brick Mitsubishi Building in the Marunouchi section of Tokyo in 1894, a project designed by Conder and superintended by Sone Tatsuzō, one of the architect-members of the IEIC. The new Marunouchi district would become the principal showcase of a new "earthquake-resistant" Tokyo in the years ahead, and the Mitsubishi *zaibatsu*, Conder's principal patron, would construct over twenty buildings there prior to the Great Kantō Earthquake of 1923. Given its investment, Mitsubishi would take inordinate interest in aseismic technology and the new types of labor organization it seemingly entailed. Although the Gundan was only the first of a series of contractors used by Sone (who subsequently headed the Mitsubishi construction department), the form of labor discipline that the Gundan brought to "Mitsubishi Building No. 1" would henceforth define the Mitsubishi approach and culminate in the actual importation of American structural engineers and site management methods in the huge and influential Marunouchi Building (Maru biru) Project of 1919–1922.[55]

Thus at the very time Itō's technical system was being marginalized, his social one, the Shokkō Gundan, was enlisted in the survival of conventional masonry, providing that technical system with the heretofore missing ingredients of obedience and control. Sone was so eager to have the Gundan play this role that he funded its payroll from his own resources, Itō not having the capital of a typical masonry contractor. The niche Itō thereafter occupied was providing highly disciplined labor on large and sensitive masonry projects, such as building the arches on the new Tokyo courthouse. The Shokkō Gundan became the ultimate instrument of earthquake resistance, yet in furtherance of a technology in which its founder had little personal interest or stake. Eventually Itō stopped playing the role of masonry contractor of his own accord, withdrawing the Gundan from working on any project that he himself did not design and supervise. But withdrawing from the patronage umbrella of Tatsuno, Sone, and other architects proved the beginning of the end of the worker army.[56]

In his textbook *Seismology* (1898), Milne would publish a photograph of one of Itō's house frames under construction, captioned "A New Type of Japanese Dwelling." It was the only earthquake-resistant frame Milne ever illustrated. "Several examples," he wrote, had been built or were building in Tokyo, and "in the writer's opinion [these houses] will stand shocks that will destroy ordinary buildings." This endorsement was even stronger than his earlier one, and would have been all the stronger, in Japanese eyes, for having been made in a foreign textbook. But Itō could have read it only with mixed emotions. Milne, writing from England, had forgotten his name. The system was developed and patented, he wrote, by "Mr. Inouye, a private architect."[57]

Itō had not been powerful enough to hold the various elements in his system together; they began to disaggregate almost as soon as they were deployed. The Shokkō Gundan was picked up and used by the regular architect-members of the Zōka-gakkai and the IEIC for their own purposes. Itō's system of metal fixtures, initially abandoned, was eventually adopted by the academy itself, becoming one element in the inventive tradition of Western carpentry examined in the next section. Although reworked in its details, Itō's system of supplementing hidden carpentry joints with inspectable, surface-mounted metal ones actually forms the basis of the present-day, officially sanctioned earthquake-resistant Japanese house frame, called *zairai-kōhō*, literally "the way we now build."

"WESTERN CARPENTRY"
AS ACADEMIC LANGUAGE

Experimental and even classificatory Western science had largely abandoned an interest in carpentry by the last quarter of the nineteenth century, because wood and its manipulation were seen to be culturally residual, and outside the story of progress. But in Japan, at least following the Nōbi earthquake, Euro-American carpentry was to be given a new life in science. "Western carpentry," whose beginnings are seen in the work of Itō and the architect-members of the IEIC, was the unique invention of a Japanese architectural profession newly suspicious of brick and stone, yet constitutionally wedded to the language, practice, and value of Western science.

Outside Japan, there was really no such thing as "Western carpentry," if one meant by that a body of written and teachable knowledge intended to travel across national and cultural borders. "Western science" was itself a chimera, but its numerous spokesmen nearly all stood witness to its universality. By the 1890s, however, no one in Europe or the United States spoke of carpentry—particularly house carpentry—as a practice that could be transnationally codified. Carpentry in the late nineteenth century in Europe and the United States tended rather to be constructed as an active site of national and cultural peculiarity and difference: native, botanical, ancient, artisanal, and ethnic.

This had not always been so. Carpentry had been regularly spoken of as "science" as late as the 1840s. Even in the 1870s and 1880s, British engineers invoked British carpentry as an element of constructive science in combination with masonry (e.g., in the form of roofs). But European and American carpentry was more commonly spoken of, at least by the 1890s, as a "craft," or a dependency of the new realm of art. In the course of the nineteenth century carpentry was gradually descientized in language and presentation. We can trace its transition from science to craft by comparing two English textbooks written almost fifty years apart— Thomas Tredgold's *Elementary Principles of Carpentry* of 1828 and the anonymously authored *Notes on Building Construction* (sometimes called "Rivington's Notes on Building Construction," after the name of its publisher) of 1875. I choose these particular texts not only because they were popular and influential in Britain, but because they were both used from the beginning in Conder's *zōkagaku* course, and were thus the two texts on Western carpentry most available to Japanese architectural students of the 1870s through 1890s as they struggled to learn and understand what that was, and how it might be adapted to Japan.[58]

Thomas Tredgold's *Elementary Principles of Carpentry* was the only textbook on Conder's original course list that dealt entirely with wood. Tredgold was not a carpenter, however, but a civil engineer, and his book was part of a series that included *The Steam Engine, A Practical Essay on the Strength of Cast Iron and Other Metals, A Practical Treatise on Rail-Roads and Carriages,* and *Principles of Warming and Ventilation.* Tredgold's stated intent was to apply science to the useful arts, "extending the views of the artist, substituting certainty for uncertainty, security for insecurity." Beginning with a definition of "the science and practice" of carpentry, in which he taught that "timber is wrought into various forms according to the principles of geometry," wooden framing was organized into rules of seemingly universal application, and wood itself typed, balanced, measured, subjected to complex equations, and arranged into tables.[59]

The existence of English carpentry as a dense body of inherited (or living) knowledge and practice goes unacknowledged by Tredgold; he is not reporting what contemporary carpenters actually did. His purpose in explicating elementary principles is rather to seize proprietorship over carpentry from this very artisanal class. While this purpose was in some sense well suited to that of Japanese architects, it would have been impossible for someone unfamiliar with an English building site to learn from Tredgold how elements like an English roof or roof truss were actually constructed. Tredgold's abstract diagrams and formulas for trusses were intended to teach students only how these elements might be calculated. Someone else (who was not the writer or, necessarily, the reader) presumably knew how to form them and put the pieces together.

This is probably why Conder supplemented Tredgold's text with *Notes on Building Construction*, an actual English architecture school textbook "arranged to meet the requirements of the syllabus of the Science and Art Department of the Committee of the Council on Education, South Kensington." The South Kensington Museum, now the Victoria and Albert, then conducted trade school classes that Conder had himself attended as a young man. *Notes*, which includes sections on brickwork, carpentry, iron, slate roofing, and the like, is organized as a series of small detail drawings with explanatory captions. This book, more than Tredgold's, would have been the principal window through which Japanese architectural students glimpsed the techniques of English building practices. The metaphor of the window is appropriate, however, because moving from Tredgold's *Elementary Principles* to the anonymously authored *Notes* did not mean moving from the "outside" to the "inside" of carpentry, but to another, different, exterior vantage.[60]

The difference between *Elementary Principles* and *Notes* is the difference between an English engineer's window view and that of an English architect. Tredgold abstracted carpentry using the mathematizing voice of early-nineteenth-century civil engineering. But by 1875, when *Notes* was produced, the project of "explaining" carpentry had passed largely to the architectural profession, engineers having become less interested in wood. In establishing "building" (including carpentry) as a subrealm of "art," however, nineteenth-century architects constructed its separateness to the point of being unwilling or incapable of speaking in a proprietary voice. Architects writing about what went on at the building site used the language of reportage, in the manner of ethnographers. As a craft rather than a science, carpentry was a land that could be visited, observed, and described, but neither reduced nor reconstituted. *Notes* was indeed nothing more or less than ethnographic description, a guidebook to the English building site for the architectural visitor, who might also find himself the "gentleman in charge."

From its very first page, *Notes* divides "building construction"—already one-half of a binarism—into a nearly endless series of additional, mutually reinforcing binarisms. The course will teach "the principles, as well as the practice" of construction. The reader will labor "with his head at the same time as with his hands." The text divides into "elementary" and "advanced" lessons, and all before the end of the Preface. The purpose of the constant bifurcation is it to establish a set of abstract redoubts into which the student can escape the reality of his subjects' craftness and materiality. The student is not to emerge an artisan, but someone who understands artisanry's "basic principles," who understands from a distance, and yet more fundamentally than the artisans whose work he is observing.[61]

Unlike Tredgold, *Notes* does not claim to own any of the details it illustrates either through invention or classification. Neither is any claim to authority made on the (anonymous) author's (or authors') ability to execute the work described. The book has the feel of a dictionary. "Cogging," it tells us, is also called "caulking" and "corking." A detail is described as having an advantage over another; a defect is pointed out. Yet the text does not actually construct a building or any of its major pieces. Readers who have never visited an English building site cannot be certain where any of the illustrated details belong, what are their orders and frequencies, why certain of them are chosen for use rather than others. The whole of which the illustrations form the parts—that is, the wooden frame itself—is strangely absent, as are the acts and actors, the actual action of putting it together.[62]

My point is that English architecture could only in a limited sense explain English carpentry to Japanese architectural students, because it had only very limited intentions in explaining carpentry—or masonry, or any other trade—to itself. The vocabulary of the English architect was expected to overlap to a certain degree with that of tradesmen, and it was the dimension of that overlap that *Notes* was intended to map. As Conder had himself pointed out, architects were expected not to "contaminate their fingers with contractors' details." Although *Notes* was as technical as English architecture could be, the carpentry that raised roofs in Britain every day and the carpentry in *Notes* were still too far apart to allow what is hopefully and unproblematically referred to as "technology transfer."

None of this was necessarily a handicap, however, to the Japanese project of adapting Western carpentry. Tredgold taught Japanese students that carpentry could be a science, while *Notes* provided them a wealth of disembodied details drawn from common (English) practice. The science of Western carpentry, as practiced in Japan, would combine the detail-images found in *Notes* and similar texts into new earthquake-resistant forms, through a practice that might be called "graphical experiment." Taki Daikichi's *Kenchiku kōgi roku* of 1896, for example, is largely a translation of *Notes*, and borrows most of its images from the English textbook without alteration. In the case of one roof drawing, however, Taki has not simply copied it, but inserted horizontal stiffeners and braces.[63] It was just this sort of roof that had fallen in at the notorious spinning mill in Nagoya, whose ruins had been photographically broadcast by Milne. This was also the type of roof Conder had suggested be stiffened in accord with Japanese carpentry practice. It was left to Taki to start the process of earthquake-proofing the British truss roof by altering the illustration in the textbook from which he and other *zōkagaku-shi* had been taught.

A second example involves *Die Hochbau-Constructionen: Des Handbuches der Architektur* of 1891, a German text that, like *Notes*, displayed hundreds of different carpentry details as small drawings. One set of drawings represents six different ways of constructing a brace (see figure 14a). No one drawing is privileged over another, nor is there much discussion of their frequencies, locations, or meanings. They are presented as words in a German carpenter's vocabulary (probably many carpenters' vocabularies) but one whose linguistic rules remain obscure.[64]

In a *Kenchiku zasshi* article of 1894, Taki also illustrates two bracing methods in the same abstract form (see figure 14b). One example he takes from Anglo-American carpentry practice, while a second figure closely resembles one in the German book, from which it may have been redrawn (the German textbook was available in the Imperial University library). Taki does not identify the two braces as being English or German. He argues, however, that one of his two examples is superior to the other, in an earthquake-prone country, because of the small space between the post (the vertical component) and the ends of the brace (the diagonal).

FIGURE 14

Top (a): Typical German framing configurations. (From Erwin Marx, *Die Hochbau-Constructionen*, 1891.) *Lower left (b):* Taki Daikichi compares two European frames and declares the one at bottom the more earthquake-resistant. (From *Kenchiku zasshi* 74 [1894]: 51.) *Lower right (c):* An elaborate earthquake-resistant frame using Western details in a uniquely Japanese configuration. (From Mihashi Shirō, *Dai kenchiku-gaku*, 1915.)

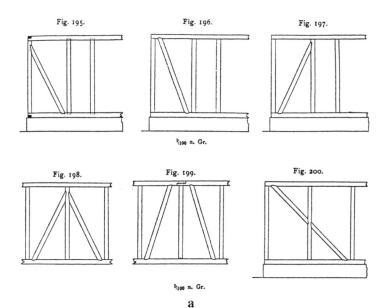

Fig. 195.　　　　Fig. 196.　　　　Fig. 197.

Fig. 198.　　　　Fig. 199.　　　　Fig. 200.

$^{1}/_{100}$ n. Gr.

$^{1}/_{100}$ n. Gr.

a

外へ押出す氣味があつて柱の柄を壞しますから、第十圖の樣に、柱面から少なくも二寸位離して組合せたならば宜からう、現今の議會の壁が斯う出來て居り升、此方ならば此柱の柄を潰して外へ押出す樣な事はあるまいと思ふ、夫で此取附け方は今迄の樣に柄で入れるのはいけない、何ぜかと云へば、組付が兎角理屈通り出來兼る故である、之は建前の出來た所で、柄あしにして橫から叩き込みたいので升、夫では橫に脱けはせぬかと云ふ御心配があるかも知れぬが、十分重みが掛つてから、

第九圖

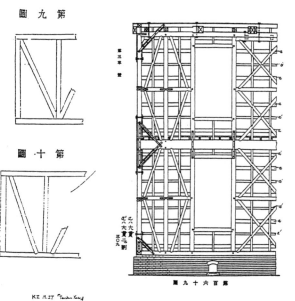

第十圖

KZ. 11.27 "Tanaka Kazu"

第三本壁

二六寸貫
乙一八寸丸大貫二重割
九〇八

第百六十九圖

b　　　　　　　　　　**c**

When an earthquake occurs, he reasons, the post might dislocate, knocking away the brace if the two features were touching. He thus recommends the German detail as the more earthquake-resistant.[65]

The difference between how the same image is used in the German book and in Taki's article is the difference between ethnographic description (with its consciousness of ethnicity) and scientific experiment (ethnicity's conscious erasure). An illustration of how German carpenters in a particular region arrange bracing is separated out from among countless such illustrations as the ideal solution for Japan. The German detail becomes earthquake resistant through an act of graphical comparison.

There is nothing peculiarly "Japanese" about this process. Arguably all artifacts have their meanings transformed as they are picked up, reillustrated, and redeployed in new places. But as Euro-American features were manipulated on paper in more complex ways, carpentry systems began to appear in Japan that bore little or no resemblance to those in Europe or the United States. Although still called "Western" by their inventors, they were Japanese by virtue of their singularity. The details of the earthquake-proof frames in a 1915 treatise by Mihashi Shirō, for example, are all similar to those in Western textbooks, but the overall forms are well outside any European or American carpentry tradition (see figure 14c). In fact frames of this complexity (and expense) were probably not constructible. Mihashi here demonstrates, however, his ability not only to manipulate diverse Western features (with some Japanese details mixed in) but arrange them into something entirely new: a Japanese-designed "Western" system tailored to resist Japanese destructive nature.[66]

With Taki's earthquake-proof frame (and similar examples), Japanese meanings cease being merely inscribed onto Euro-American artifacts. Euro-American details are now being reworked into uniquely Japanese objects, which nonetheless still carry Western inscription. Western carpentry becomes a truly domestic, inventive, productive design medium, separate both from Euro-American carpentry traditions and the traditional practices of *daiku*. Japanese architects now have a carpentry all their own.

Japanese "Western carpentry" evolved in an atmosphere of partial knowledge, rooted in the partial understandings of British architects and engineers. But it was this very partiality that made carpentry such a fertile site for Japanese invention. It would even be presumptuous to assume that Japanese practitioners desired a more complete understanding from Western sources. Japanese architects had come to understood, by the 1890s, that resisting earthquakes was no Western specialty—

that seismic stability was not to be received, like a package, in any particular Western book or drawing. An aseismic structure might be achieved, however, by carefully choosing and arranging details, as one makes a new type of machine out of common or standard parts. The Euro-American illustrations were received and used essentially as a kit, out of which not only new forms but new meanings were capable of construction in diverse ways.

There remains one additional stage to this process: the deployment of these Japanese-Western artifacts in a westward direction, a movement that sanctifies them as objects of a new Japan. The book on Japanese seismology that Baron Kikuchi prepared for the international scientific community in 1904, the book that sandwiched an undamaged Nagoya Castle between two of Milne's photos of collapsed "foreign" structures, also presented models of wooden earthquake-proof buildings recently developed by the architect-members of the IEIC. These were the same models whose performance in shaking-table experiments Itō Tamekichi would later question. Originally developed in 1894–95, and sent to earthquake-stricken Yamagata prefecture as the official solution to the problem of how to safely rebuild, the models and their accompanying details were pure examples of Japanese "Western carpentry," wholly unlike *daiku*-work and likely unbuildable in the rural area of Tōkaidō to which they were rushed. At least one of the IEIC-sanctioned details, a truss roof with lateral stiffeners, was identical to the image in Rivington's *Notes* that Taki had "corrected" in his translation of the English textbook. Other details were taken from German texts. In at least one instance, the design for a thatched-roofed Japanese farmhouse seems to have been influenced by the iron-intensive roof frames for large European exhibit halls. At the same moment that the Japanese government was having *daiku* erect traditional Japanese pavilions at Chicago and other overseas exhibitions, a different branch of the government was attempting to replace these very same small buildings at home with something like Euro-American exhibit architecture.[67]

Or were they? It is impossible to know the degree of earnestness with which such plans and models were sent to distant Yamagata. There is no mistaking, however, the seriousness with which these same systems were displayed before foreign audiences. Not only are they conspicuous in Kikuchi's book, but they were among the very few work products of Japanese architects to be published in the foreign-language report series of the IEIC, a series otherwise dedicated to Ōmori's seismological research. And like Ōmori's seismological lessons about Japan and the Japanese, these earthquake-proof carpentry details had a measurable impact overseas.[68] The IEIC report on earthquake-proof carpentry became an entire chapter ı Alfredo Montel's *Building Structures in Earthquake Countries* of 1912, where it was presented as "Japanese Rules for the Construction of Earthquake-Proof Houses." To a European unfamiliar with the various carpentry traditions of his own continent, and who had little or no familiarity with the traditions of *daiku*, the IEIC details could well have been read as a complex modernization of an indigenous system. The drawings arrived in Europe lacking a genealogy, temporal context, or human author, bearing only the inscription "earthquake-proof." Montel gave them the additional inscriptions "Japanese" and "rules." The circular journey of Western carpentry was now complete. It had arrived in Italy as a modern Japanese solution to an international problem.

Thus in the decades following the Great Nōbi Earthquake did the students of Conder and those of Milne continue to construct their sometimes differing, sometimes complementary narratives of Japan. To Ōmori and the seismologists, resisting destructive nature was a Japanese specialty demonstrated through the survival of *daiku*-work both ancient and contemporary, and the comparative fragility of imported foreign systems. Pagodas were fitted with aseismic pendulums, Japanese houses were in dialogue with the earth, and European masonry inadequately resisted disaster even at the centers of European civilization. It was not only the legacy of Milne that nurtured Japanese seismology's nativist caste, although the concerns, practices, and behaviors of the second generation form a continuum with those of the first. Japan's scientists carried the special burden of having to demonstrate rationality to a European scientific community that openly equated aptitude with race. Ōmori's reputation and authority within geophysics came in large part from his citizenship in an earthquake nation. His development and presentation of the history, constitution, and character of that nation was a project logically, practically, and politically related to his ability to do his science.

While architects such as Tatsuno Kingo and Itō Chūta subscribed to elements of the seismological discourse in the immediate aftermath of the Nōbi earthquake, the narrative of Japanese architecture as it continued to develop in late Meiji Japan complicated and even contradicted the seismological one in crucial ways. Architects could not concede to *daiku*—even those who lived in the distant past—an understanding of nature and its ways altogether superior to their own. It was not only that *daiku* were architects' living rivals. The principal audience for modern Japanese architecture, unlike the audience for Japanese science, was primarily domestic. Like Conder himself, his students' main currency was as "architects to the government of Japan." The turn toward archeology, the development of a Japanese architectural history, and even a Japanese architectural style in the later 1890s were all consistent with the growing sense of nation, even as they converged with the performance of architecture as internationally codified.

At the same time, Japanese architects after Nōbi accepted the need to alter European and American building technology to suit Japanese nature, turning what was formerly a self-conscious practice of inheritance into a mandate for invention. The re-creation of Japanese architecture as a site for invention offered enough convergence with the contemporary seismological discourse to allow both professions to not only coexist, but coproduce. The invention of "Western carpentry" is an example of how Japanese architects managed to reconcile their foreign and domestic loyalties, import foreign knowledge to correct foreign mistakes, and know about wood without becoming *daiku*. By building into "Western" systems resistances they did not formerly have, such technocultural artifacts became "Japanese," and Japanese architecture began to become something other than Western architecture in Japan. This process would be taken much farther in the succeeding Taishō period, as Japanese architects largely abandoned wood and masonry both and learned how to resist earthquakes with novel materials.

"Resistance," however, was to remain a relative concept. Despite all the lessons of the Nōbi earthquake, nothing would save modern Tokyo when the next great earthquake came.

EIGHT

· The Great Kantō Earthquake
and the Submergence of
the Earthquake Nation

THE RESIST-EARTHQUAKES REGIME

Although seismology had forced Japanese architecture into a more complex relationship with the Earth following the Nōbi earthquake, Japanese architects long retained other interests. Buildings were designed to serve purposes, be aesthetically
satisfying, express the power and status of patrons, define a new Japanese design
tradition, demonstrate mastery of a European design tradition, and so forth. In
their hearts, resisting earthquakes was not what the first generation of Japanese architects, such as Tatsuno Kingo, or the first generation of their students, such as Itō
Chūta, most wanted to do. They wanted to share the identity "architect" with Europeans, while developing their own national style (itself, of course, a European
concern, and one whose trajectory had been influenced by the Nōbi disaster).
Though driven by circumstances into opposing mysterious and intractable forces
of nature, it was a role they rarely celebrated.

For the generation educated after the crisis of Nōbi, however, earthquake resistance *(taishin)* cemented a different and more positive set of relationships. The
Japanese architectural academy rebuilt itself in the early twentieth century around
a new material—ferro-concrete—closely associated with Tokyo Imperial University professor of architecture Sano Toshikata, who had studied with Ōmori and
even accompanied him on an official tour of postdisaster San Francisco in 1906.
Sano's walkabout through San Francisco's ruins taught him that steel framing, then

the latest in American building technology, was comparatively weak against seismic waves. He was more impressed by the survival of buildings framed with ferroconcrete (concrete poured around a lattice of thin iron bars), a system then largely restricted to industrial structures. Thus he developed a theory, subsequently worked out mathematically and published in 1915 as *Kaoku taishin kōzō ron* (Anti-Earthquake Structural Theory for Buildings), that rigid frames (e.g., ferroconcrete ones) provide excellent resistance to earthquakes. Sano's discovery would have a major effect on the appearance of Taishō-period Tokyo, particularly in the Marunouchi office district where, following Conder's work there for Mitsubishi, Japanese architects would find some of their most sustained patronage. The built-up portions of Taishō and early Showa Tokyo would thus come to be characterized by comparatively low (though expensive) concrete-frame buildings rather than the soaring steel-framed skyscrapers of American downtowns.[1]

By the First World War, Sano and other students imbued with the lessons of seismology stood at the center of Japanese architecture, making decisions and setting priorities in an unprecedented way. Sano gained his authority, at least in part, because he bridged both disciplines, providing a measure of closure to their nineteenth-century polemics. Engineering seismology or applied seismology (as the nascent discipline of earthquake engineering was then called) was also compelling to architecture's patrons in government and industry, while aesthetics (based on European models) seemed a less vital national project in an era of increased Japanese diplomatic confidence. When Sano ascended to a chair in architecture at Tokyo Imperial University around the time that Tatsuno Kingo retired, it seemed that Milne's arguments had finally won the day. The architectural legacy of the Great Nōbi Earthquake became, by the time of the First World War, the vision of a concrete Japan.[2]

The concrete, earthquake-resisting nation was a complex imaginary, animated by many of the Meiji-period plots, tensions, and strategies, but with a dynamic all its own. On the one hand, the newness and technological sophistication of ferroconcrete made it seem, in Japan as in much of the world, a decisive break with the architecture and very life of the past. To Japanese architects of Sano's age, however, this break was not so much chronological as geopolitical, if not anticolonial; it was seen as an escape hatch from the art and cultural legacy of the West itself, one that, in the aftermath of the Nōbi and San Francisco earthquakes, had failed to fully graft itself among the new generation of Japanese practitioners. More earnestly than the European avant-garde, and even prior to the end of the First World War, Sano and his colleagues began discussing the rejection of "art" (i.e., the performance of European culture in Japan) and the complete merger of architecture with science (the "Japanese" science of seismology) through the medium of ferro-concrete. The new technology was fully sanctioned by the Japanese architectural academy at a time when, in Europe, its principal spokesmen were still primarily engineers and the avant-garde architects who took engineers as their models.[3]

Sano has been largely shunned by contemporary art-historical scholarship because he was so uninterested in the aesthetic or expressive aspects of design. He was the "bad king" whom a subsequent generation of young designers—such as Maekawa Kunio and the Bunriha, well chronicled by Jonathan Reynolds—were intent on overthrowing. One condition for the emergence of a 1920s avant-garde in Japanese architecture was Sano's 1915 reform to the Tokyo Imperial University architecture curriculum, which split "structure" from "design." In the short term, this delivered higher status and resources to Sano's *kozo* (structure) faction and eventually helped push more design-oriented young professionals into creative engagement with European modernism.[4] "I believed that whether a building was good looking or not or what color it was," Sano would write in his autobiography, "were only women's things and men should not talk about them."[5] One of Sano's graduate students, Noda Toshihiku, even published a "Technological Non-Art Theory" in 1915, in which he wrote, "Architecture is not art. . . . Architecture is okay if it is a daily necessity; it is unnecessary that it house the expression of beauty . . . it is wrong to try to decorate cities or nature using architecture."[6] Resisting sublime nature not only masculinized Japanese architects in Sano's eyes, but separated them irrevocably from their Euro-American colleagues, who remained "in the shell of art." "Japanese architects are essentially different from European and American architects," declared Sano, because in earthquake-country Japan, construction took precedent over design.[7]

While Sano's emergence seemed to mark the triumph of science over art in Japanese architecture, in other ways it completed the program of his nineteenth-century predecessors. In the post-Nōbi despair of 1891–1892, it was Josiah Conder himself who had told his Japanese students to turn more fully toward science, as Japan's seismicity precluded the production of real artworks. Sano and his colleagues took Conder's advice seriously, while adding the element of disdain for the European culture of art that Conder cherished. Yet Sano's attraction to rigid frame structures over flexible ones was closer to the preference of Conder than that of Milne. Even prior to the Nōbi earthquake, both Conder and Tatsuno had taken to strengthening masonry with iron, and eventually steel. Ferro-concrete, despite its nature as framing, could be seen as a continuation of this Meiji-period strategy of marrying masonry with metal. In ferro-concrete, Japanese architects had finally found the strong, weighty, solid, nature-resisting system that, until Nōbi, they thought they had in brickwork and stone. While the new material promised European avant-garde architects a longed-for break with the tradition of the nineteenth century, to Sano and other Japanese architects concrete was more the fulfillment of the nineteenth century's broken promise.

In embracing ferro-concrete, Japanese architecture also continued to shun the dynamical insights of *daiku*, for whom flexibility had been the favored path. Sano's rejection of more flexible (and potentially taller) steel frames would be challenged in the late 1920s and 1930s by certain structural engineers as rigid in the ideological sense, provoking rather bitter exchanges in scholarly papers.[8] The present consensus is that Sano's critics were right. Modern-day Tokyo is increasingly full of steel-framed skyscrapers designed to sway but not fall in the next major earthquake (like pagodas, as some architects point out). Sano's stubbornness was neither irrational nor naïve, however; the relatively low ferro-concrete frames he designed and championed were the conservative choice, and success, in the aftermath of the Nōbi disaster, was more important to his generation of architects than risk-taking. There was a sense, perhaps not unfounded, that architecture's very survival as a Japanese profession depended on the performance of its designs during the next great earthquake.

Making the foreign technology of ferro-concrete Japanese involved more than rhetorical deployment, however, and this also contributed to its attraction. Like masonry and carpentry before it, ferro-concrete arrived in Japan as an incomplete box of parts, with no instructions on how to resist seismic waves. Despite Sano's discovery of its aseismic qualities in San Francisco, intense work by countless Japanese had to occur before the promise of reliable earthquake resistance became reality, work that further inscribed the technology "made in Japan." Thus did ferro-concrete frames come to be invested, as masonry walls never had been, with a certain nativeness. It helped that in Europe and the United States the steel industry was much more powerful than in metals-starved Japan; in Tokyo, concrete absorbed almost all of the enthusiasm that in the West it shared with steel framing. The relatively low, rigid, and strong ferro-concrete office buildings of early Taishō Tokyo seemed a different species of modern architecture than the steel-frame skyscrapers of Manhattan, despite their similar external adornment. The Japanese structures seemed, to Japanese architects, to have a peculiar and vital relationship with their own unstable earth, further localizing and domesticating what, from the perspective of the European avant-garde, was the most international of building technologies.[9]

Concrete, like masonry before it, also had the virtue of not being wood; it was just as amenable to construction as the opposite of wood, and of everything that was wrong, deficient, and above all naturalistic in the life of the Japanese, past and present. Through ferro-concrete, the architectural campaign against *daiku* knowledge was extended into other areas of traditional Japanese life. Sano and other Taishō-era architects linked the artifactual to the social at a number of important nodes; concrete came to seem the shell of a new Japanese body politic. In the concrete Japan, the citizen-inhabitant would not only be finally safe from destructive nature, but would rise from *tatami* floors and sit in chairs, and live communally (in apartment blocks) rather than in individual houses. This technosocial imaginary (eventually contributing to the lived reality of urban Japan) was not a pastiche of random elements. Ferro-concrete was most (perhaps only) economical if used on large building projects (i.e., apartment blocks), a type of housing alien to Japanese experience. In order to interest the existing Japanese housing reform culture in concrete apartment buildings, links were extended to longstanding social goals, such as promoting the "chair style" (i.e., Euro-American daily life) among common people. Skilful linkages between concrete and social change had also been made in Europe, but in Japan they were uniquely framed within the nation's vulnerability to an unstable nature, and, in a deeper sense, the continuing "evolution" of the Japanese as a virtually distinct human species.[10]

The very way seismicity was discussed changed in the Taishō and early Showa periods. Before the Meiji Restoration, as we have seen, earthquakes were considered the consequence of the movements of a giant catfish. In fact they were not easily separable from "Japan" itself, an archipelago that rested directly on that animal's back. Like many figures in Japanese folklore, the catfish maintained a dual character, sometimes terrible and ferocious, but other times benign (a recognition that natural disaster always benefits someone). Other than focusing on "resistance" and "protection," neither architects nor seismologists of the Meiji period had invented a way of discussing earthquakes that radically broke from folkloric depiction. Theirs was, after all, an age that made much of "the sublime" and which was not above using folklore and folk tradition as a springboard for modern research programs. With Sano, however, earthquakes began to be discussed in a more clinico-military language: "Our country has long been attacked by earthquakes . . . and continues to fight against them." And again: "There threatens Japan a most formidable enemy of most destructive nature—the earthquake, which has its equal in few other parts of the world. And among the manifold efforts of our architects that which is directed against this deadly enemy is indeed incalculable."[11] Sano seems in these passages to have declared war on earthquakes, which were now quite isolated from the rest of Japanese nature and, particularly, the Japanese nation.

BEATING THE CATFISH:
EARTHQUAKE PREDICTION

While Sano and Japanese architecture were working to fortify the country against the next great earthquake, Ōmori Fusakichi and Japanese seismology were attempting to beat the catfish in another way: by honing the art of earthquake prediction. Prediction had always been first among the official goals of the Imperial Earthquake Investigation Committee, and by studying everything from seismograms, to changes in magnetic fields, to the reactions of animals, to historical records of earthquakes and maps of fault lines, Japanese seismologists of late Meiji and early Taishō believed they were hastening the day their warning voices would be essential to the lives of cities and nations. Though instrumentation always held the promise of becoming predictive, Ōmori increasingly focused on historical cartography as the most fruitful technique. This put a premium on the gathering and comparison of historical data, which, because it was particularly abundant in Japan, seemed to constitute a local methodological strength. The key to determining when and where major shocks would occur next, it was reasoned, was discovering where they had occurred before, and then calculating their cycles or periodicity. As a rule, the longer an earthquake zone had remained quiet, the more suspect it became. "The popular idea of repetition of destructive shocks necessarily at one and the same point is a great fallacy," declared Ōmori in a paper of 1920. Behind this "gap theory"—which Ōmori was the first to propose—lay the example of the Nōbi earthquake itself, which had occurred along a fault comparatively quiet for hundreds of years.[12]

While this cartographic method of earthquake monitoring sometimes yielded results, its necessary imprecision and the stakes involved if it turned out wrong, made it conducive to bitter disagreement. The most notorious Japanese prediction controversy began as the country was absorbing the mixed blessings of victory in the Russo-Japanese War. In 1905, Ōmori's younger colleague Imamura Akitsune, assistant professor of seismology at Tokyo Imperial University, wrote an article in the popular journal *Taiyō* warning that Tokyo could be subject to a destructive earthquake within the next fifty years. Imamura's pessimism was based on the absence of seismic records for Sagami Bay to the south of city, the only area of a major north/south fault that, being under water, seismologists could not adequately monitor through historical mapping procedures. Because the fault line under the bay constituted an unknown factor or gap in seismological records, Imamura advised that Tokyo should prepare for a worst-case scenario. Given that the city was built largely of wood, he further argued that casualties could exceed 100,000 were Tokyo to burn.[13]

Imamura's prediction would of course turn out to be prescient, but because it was based on an absence of records rather than their compilation, it invited strong criticism from Imamura's titular boss, Ōmori. The senior seismologist went so far as to publish his own article denouncing Imamura's theory in the same popular journal the following year. Under the title "Rumors of Tokyo and a Great Earthquake," Ōmori likened Imamura's prediction to the popular legend of *hinoe uma* (the fire horse), which held that those years in which the astrological symbols of "fire" and "horse" aligned would be rife with conflagrations. Because 1906 happened to be such a year, wrote Ōmori, Imamura's "rumor" (*fūsetsu*, or "floating theory") recklessly added to an existing superstition-based anxiety about Tokyo's fate. "The theory that a large earthquake will take place in Tokyo in the near future," he concluded, "is academically baseless and trivial."[14]

The Ōmori-Imamura rift, which remains legendary among contemporary Japanese seismologists, likely involved more than a simple disagreement over evidence. Although Ōmori held the chair in seismology at Tokyo Imperial University, and was thus Imamura's senior, the men differed in age by only two years. Although still an assistant professor Imamura was ambitious enough to have published a seismological textbook (in 1905, the same year he delivered his Tokyo prediction), to which Ōmori responded by publishing his own lecture notes the following year.[15] This and other incidents related by Imamura's biographer suggests a rivalry between the two men that could not be contained by professional or departmental hierarchies. That Imamura chose to publish his warning about Tokyo in a popular journal might even indicate that Ōmori or others had blocked its publication in a scientific one, though we have no evidence of this. In any case, Imamura would suffer for overstepping personal and professional boundaries. He became something of a pariah within the community of Japanese scientists, especially after a second public clash with Ōmori in 1915, again on the subject of the predicted Tokyo earthquake. He was forced to retreat from the university for a time and, on returning to his home village, was even censured by his father.[16]

Given what would eventually happen to Tokyo, Ōmori is remembered in the annals of Japanese geophysics as the archetype of the unimaginative and risk-averse scientist, perhaps jealous of his younger and brighter colleague.[17] But Ōmori's penchant for predictive declarations was actually just as strong. In the wake of the San

Francisco earthquake, which occurred the very month of Imamura's public censure, Ōmori predicted that similar events would soon occur elsewhere on the Pacific coast of the Americas. He was seemingly vindicated when great earthquakes struck the Aleutians and the Chilean city of Valparaiso on the same day that August.[18] Imamura himself would posthumously credit Ōmori with having predicted the locations (though not the times) of the destructive Messina-Reggio (1908) and Avezzano (1915) earthquakes in southern Italy, a feat remembered to the present day within Italian seismology.[19] In 1920, Ōmori would take credit in a scientific paper for having predicted the occurrence of the horrific Kansu earthquake in China, citing as evidence an interview he gave the *South China Post* two years before.[20]

In a sense, both Ōmori and Imamura were continuing the tradition of the first occupant of the chair of seismology at Tokyo Imperial University, Sekiya Seikei, who had "calmed the people's nerves" following the Nōbi disaster by ruling out the occurrence of a second large shock. And because Japanese scientists were explicitly tasked with prediction by the state, while their colleagues in most European countries were not, this likely seemed another important research niche that Japanese science could fill. In a paper read before the Pan-Pacific Science Conference in 1920, Ōmori posited the existence of "earthquake zones," "weak links in the earth's crust" tens of thousands of miles long, one of which circumnavigated the Pacific Ocean while another linked Japan with the Mediterranean Basin through India and Persia (see chapter 6 for Ōmori's maps). By compiling seismic histories of each segment of these linear zones, places where earthquakes were likely to occur (based on periodicity) could potentially be mapped.[21] Hence Ōmori's willingness to deploy prediction as far afield as China, Chile, and Italy: he was compiling, and mapping, an earthquake history of the world. The problem with Tokyo was that the "earthquake zone" to the east of the city lay on the ocean floor, and hence remained terra incognito.

Ōmori's methodology was put to its ultimate test when the Kantō Plain around Tokyo entered a period of unusual seismicity in the early 1920s. On December 8, 1921, and again on April 26, 1922, there were "semidestructive" earthquakes in the capital, followed by a third, less severe one on January 14, 1923 (which nonetheless took one life). The 1921 earthquake, the strongest to have occurred in Tokyo for 28 years, damaged an important conduit and nearly cut the city off from its water. The even stronger 1922 earthquake damaged buildings, cut phone service, and stopped the railroad. In the aftermath of the second quake, chief seismologist Ōmori proceeded to calm the government's nerves. He noted in a hastily published scholarly paper that "the successive occurrences of two earthquakes felt strongly in Tokyo is not rare," noting that twin shocks occurred once before, in 1894 (although at that time the second one was the weaker). In other words, there was some basis to have predicted, if one read the evidence of previous earthquakes, that there would be a second shock in Tokyo in 1922. Now Ōmori believed that the cycle had run its course. In the same paper he wrote that "probably the semidestructive earthquake on April 26, 1922, has finished the activity epoch succeeding the period of the seismic rest during the last half a dozen years."[22] In other words, Tokyo could return to normal.

When the third (though less severe) shock struck the city in early 1923, Ōmori was proven wrong in detail, though not, he believed, in theory. He made the educated guess that the occurrence of three semidestructive earthquakes in a short time frame meant that whatever latent seismic energy existed in the vicinity of Tokyo had now been released. If the second earthquake had made this likely, then the occurrence of a third, and lesser, earthquake had made it nearly certain. Thus did he state his original case more strongly in another paper, destined for posthumous publication the following year: "Tokyo may be assumed to be free in future from the visitation of a violent earthquake like that of 1855, as the later shock originated right under the city itself, and as destructive earthquakes do not repeat from one and the same origin, at least not in the course of 1,000 or 1,500 years."[23]

But Ōmori had read the catfish very wrong. He did not survive (by very much) the sublimely catastrophic Great Kantō Earthquake later that year.

THE GREAT KANTŌ EARTHQUAKE

Just before noon on September 1, 1923, Tokyo was shaken to its depths by a massive earthquake that rolled through the city from the direction of Sagami Bay. Ten thousand buildings collapsed almost immediately and more than 140,000 people would be dead by the following dawn, most killed in the fires that burned the still largely wooden city to the ground. In scale and horror, the catastrophe was unparalleled in Japanese history, although its basic development—a shock followed by a series of increasingly convergent fires—was terribly familiar. As in the 1855 Ansei earthquake, the high ground suffered less than the densely populated low ground, which was now more densely populated than ever before. The modern parts of the city, however, were not immune. A structural steel frame collapsed in the course of building, carrying down with it more than two hundred workmen. Yokohama, that Western-style landmark feature whose alluvial soil always shook more than that of the capital itself, was subject to near-total devastation. At Tokyo Imperial University, the seismographs were overturned, the brick walls of laboratories and class-rooms began collapsing, and the seismologists were reduced to fighting fires that burned through half a century's worth of earthquake records.[24]

Attending the Second Pan-Pacific Science Conference in Australia, Ōmori was being shown a seismograph in Sydney when the instrument suddenly began to stir, graphically recording, he soon learned, the distant destruction of the Japanese capital. In an interview he gave the Melbourne *Age* following initial news dispatches—which placed the casualties in the tens of thousands—Ōmori, in the words of the interviewer, "thought reports of the disaster had been exaggerated." He noted that early accounts of the Ansei earthquake of 1855 had mentioned one hundred thousand deaths though the actual total was closer to seven thousand. That earthquake, moreover, had originated right under the city, while the recent one was likely centered a hundred miles to the southwest. The Australian reporters, however, were not only unconvinced but in a judgmental frame of mind: "For thirty-five years this devoted seismologist has labored at research to be able to predict these disasters. Though he has had only a small measure of success—and therein lays the weakness of seismology, regarded as an economically useful science—he has done grand primary work that may well form the basis for prediction in the future." Japanese seismologists "have given their best," the newspaper went on, but "the present horror is a sad commentary on their labors."[25] Thus even before setting sail for Japan, Ōmori was provided a foretaste of his likely reception.

Ōmori boarded the first available ship, and became seriously ill on the return passage. He was nonetheless induced to deliver a short lecture on earthquakes to the ship's passengers as the vessel approached Tokyo. Imamura, who had not only survived the earthquake but became the "man on the spot" for the Japanese government and the world press in Ōmori's absence, met the senior scientist at the dock and reportedly had the satisfaction of an apology.[26] The earthquake had come only eighteen years after Imamura's prediction and, as he anticipated, from the direction of Sagami Bay. Ōmori was soon hospitalized among the city's thousands of earthquake victims, and in the words of his architect-pupil Sano, "he passed away in the turmoil" of postdisaster Tokyo.[27] It was the end of a life and career hardly capable of continuing as before.

Like the wreckage on the Nōbi Plain three decades before, Tokyo's postdisaster landscape echoed with conflicting arguments and explanations, many predating the earthquake but seeming to arise out of the ashes through sudden amplification. The new concrete office quarter of Marunouchi, the flagship of the resist-earthquakes regime, survived the earthquake largely unharmed, while the wooden residential city around it disappeared in flames. The post-Nōbi generation of Japanese architects had now proven beyond a reasonable doubt that they knew how to meet destructive nature. The older generation of Anglo-Japanese architects, it now seemed just as clear, had underestimated those same forces. The Ginza, Conder's Ueno Museum, Tatsuno's buildings at the Imperial University, and much of the rest of Meiji-period masonry Tokyo was shaken to pieces.[28] Brick and stone were virtually banned from the reconstruction, and new building laws—drawn up by Sano Toshikata and his colleagues—were predicated on the extended future use of ferro-concrete.[29] The vast majority of the city would be rebuilt as it always had been, however: in wood, by *daiku*. Even they would be subject, however, to new building regulations mandating metal fittings and other details of the "Western carpentry" that had its origin in the Japanese academy.[30]

Frank Lloyd Wright announced to the world in 1923 that his Imperial Hotel had survived the Great Kantō Earthquake. The world remembers still, although the Japanese-designed buildings in Marunouchi survived just as well. The Japanese architectural world was less impressed with the survival of Wright's hotel than with the damage to another American-designed landmark in the center of Marunouchi itself, the Marunouchi Building, or Maru-Biru. In 1919, Mitsubishi had given the contract for this huge office block—the largest in Tokyo—to the Fuller Construction Company of the East, an American design-build firm then selling efficiency, economy, and other famous American qualities. The Fuller Co. eschewed local knowledge and faith in ferro-concrete and used an American-fabricated steel frame. This classic case of "technology transfer"—the purest one to appear in this book so far—was partly a challenge by Mitsubishi to the knowledge monopoly of the university-centered resist-earthquakes regime. Customizing ferro-concrete to Japanese nature made it hugely expensive.[31]

While still under construction, the Maru-Biru was damaged by the less powerful Tokyo earthquake of April 26, 1922. Although the damage had occurred to an unfinished structure, it frightened Mitsubishi into consulting Naitō Tachu of Waseda University, who had the steel frame reinforced with concrete in the Japanese style. The Maru-Biru thus faced the Great Kantō Earthquake of 1923 as a Japanese-American hybrid. Again it sustained damage. In the postdisaster writings of Japanese architects and seismologists, the Maru-Biru would inevitably be singled out as the American building that failed, and one that would have failed utterly had it not been rescued through Naitō's intervention the year before.[32]

The only modern structure in the Marunouchi quarter to collapse completely, however, had a framework not of steel but of ferro-concrete. The catastrophic failure of the Nagai Building might have constituted a black mark on the reputation of Japanese architecture except that its particular concrete system had been "boldly copied," according to one source, "from that in vogue in an aseismic country."[33] The Nagai Building was thus also isolated from surviving ones in postearthquake accounts on the basis of its foreignness. In fact the failure of this imported ferro-concrete system contributed to a sense that it was not the choice of material (concrete vs. steel) that mattered so much as the exercise of hard-won Japanese technical knowledge and experience.[34]

Without casting doubt on the truth-claims in these accounts, it is noteworthy that "foreign" and "Japanese" elements still mapped out Tokyo's earthquake zone in 1923. Foreign knowledge had again been humbled by Japanese nature, while Japanese knowledge, this time in the form of ferro-concrete office buildings rather than pagodas, had again ridden out the waves. The lesson of Nōbi was thus reinforced for the younger generation of Japanese architect-engineers: Japanese could never be safe in the shell of imported (Western) building technologies. Japanese designers had no one to rely on but themselves. Architecture professor Tanabe Heigaku would write that, following the earthquake, "a loud outcry was raised in favor of adopting buildings of *genuine Japanese structure* which were earthquake proof first and foremost."[35]

The story of the Great Nōbi Earthquake largely received its modern form in the wake of the Great Kantō Earthquake, as part of this revived narrative of foreign failure and Japanese tenacity. Engineer Saita Tokitaro's paper "Earthquake-Proof Construction in Japan," delivered at the Third Pan-Pacific Science Conference in 1926, begins with the by-now familiar description of Edo-period aseismic innovations, such as *shinbashira* and parabolic castle walls, and other, newer discoveries made in the wake of the Tokyo catastrophe, such as "earthquake proof rooms" and "refuge doors" in premodern palaces. He then recounts the story of the Great Nōbi Earthquake shorn of Meiji-period caveats: "All the new brick post offices and other European buildings came crashing down [in 1891] like card houses. On that occasion Japanese houses did not fall, except those that were old and frail. In many cases the supports gave way and the roof came down, imprisoning people until they were rescued."[36] Sano Toshikata would likewise write in 1934: "In Meiji 24 [1891] there was a huge earthquake in Nōbi. At that time brick factories, chimneys, and iron bridge supports in the Nagoya area were extremely damaged. Therefore scholars and engineers did detailed research and learned that it was extremely dangerous to use foreign methods in our country."[37]

While these lessons from history were reanimated and streamlined in the aftermath of the Great Kantō Earthquake, their connections to contemporary research programs were increasingly murky or forced. Naitō Tachu was correct in pointing out that Japanese architects had turned to "traditional principles of earthquake-proof construction" in the aftermath of the Nōbi disaster, but this hardly explained Naitō's own strong preference for ferro-concrete.[38] Those most involved in designing modern structures and calculating statics, such as Sano and Naitō, rarely invoked pagodas or parabolic walls, and never the work of *daiku*. In fact Sano tended to write of the Edo period as a "fairyland," a sort of dream from which modern Japan had awoken, and hardly a model or base for contemporary scientific development.[39]

Even the most triumphalist statements of the resist-earthquakes regime, however, have something of a defensive quality. Their larger context, after all, was the destruction of much of Tokyo and the loss of well over a hundred thousand lives. Other Japanese voices noted that it was not the earthquake itself that had destroyed the city, but the fire that followed. Even the Association of Japanese Architects (Nihon Kenchiku Kai) estimated that the seismic shock brought down less than 10 percent of the city's tens of thousands of wooden buildings.[40] If inexpensive *daiku*-work had proven just as aseismic as the extraordinarily expensive work of architect-engineers, then hadn't the investment of so many resources in ferro-concrete been misapplied? The obsession with "resistance," "strength," and "stability" had diverted attention, some voices suggested, from developing new, cheap, lightweight, flexible, and easily installed fireproof materials, materials that might have kept the city's already earthquake-resistant housing stock from burning down. Architecture had produced only concrete palaces for the government and *zaibatsu* while sacrificing the homes of regular people. The very expense of ferro-concrete made "the concrete Japan" (like the masonry Japan before it) an idle dream. Such were the arguments crafted in the decade following the earthquake by young Marxist-oriented architects like Ichiura Ken, who wrote in 1932: "Architects do not work only for the bourgeois *[usen]*. . . . Today's state is as if people show off their expensive medicine [i.e., ferro-concrete] to poor people. . . ." It was Ichiura and the more outspoken Nishiyama Uzō who, from the early 1930s into the post-war period, would engineer Japanese architecture's turn toward prefabrication, substituting for "earthquake resistance" the American slogan "mass production." Using assembly lines to reduce costs and improve the quality of house production, they reasoned, would allow "even poor people" to "get good inexpensive medicine." Wood framing would be retained in their scheme because it was both inexpensive and reliably earthquake-resistant. *Daiku*, however, were to be sacrificed to the logic of factory-based production. These were, after all, young architects trained largely at elite schools.[41]

Another member of this circle, Makino Masami, launched an even more direct attack on the charisma of Sano's *kōzō* faction in 1932. In an article provocatively entitled "Speaking Ill of Concrete" *(Konkurito henbō ron)*, he wrote, "It is believed that ferro-concrete construction is earthquake proof, but probably this is a misunderstanding or propaganda by scholars who study that material." Makino, though a committed technophile, was frustrated by "architectural regulations which trap us in ferro-concrete only," foreclosing the search for other, potentially cheaper and more nuanced solutions. He would not be the last Japanese architect or engineer to question such total commitment to steel and cement.[42]

While the architecture establishment weighed its accomplishments and shortcomings, the institution of seismology was restructured root and branch following Ōmori's timely death. The Imperial Earthquake Investigation Committee, whose offices had been burnt along with its records, was eclipsed in 1925 by the more tightly structured Earthquake Research Institute at the University of Tokyo. Its first director, Suyehiro Kyōji, had formerly run the research laboratory of the Mitsubishi *zaibatsu*, whose investment in the Marunouchi quarter had made it the most sustained nongovernmental patron of earthquake-proof construction. Mitsubishi was also Japan's largest shipbuilding firm, and Suyehiro, a naval architect, would bring to seismological research a more sophisticated approach to wave theory and the behavior of structures in the semifluid medium of earthquake-roiled ground. He had won a prize around the First World War for a paper entitled "On the Drift of Ships Caused by Rolling among Waves." Under Suyehiro's guidance, seismology turned more strongly to physics, mathematics, and engineering (modeling the rolling of Japanese cities amongst seismic waves) and away from geology, meteorology, cartography, and the gathering of statistics, which had been Ōmori's particular emphases.[43]

With this institutional and methodological break in Japanese seismology, the legacy of Ōmori Fusakichi—as one of the most internationally respected Japanese scientists of the Meiji and Taishō eras—was not only buried but denigrated. The posthumous publication in a seismology journal of Ōmori's written prediction of Tokyo's safety for the next thousand years was clearly intended, by whoever was responsible, to cement his ignominy. The responsible party was likely his successor at Tokyo Imperial University, the long-suffering Imamura, who would remind the Japanese scientific community in an article of 1924 that "I discussed this view [of Tokyo's vulnerability] in full detail, but people refused to believe me. There was even an eminent scientist who ridiculed my opinion once at that time [1905] and again in 1915 as nothing other than a rumor which might cause general panic."[44]

Ōmori's failure to correctly predict Tokyo's destruction was taken by many to be a failure of his research program. In "A Historical Sketch of the Development of Seismology in Japan," written by physicists Terada Torahiko and Matazawa Takeo for an international scientific audience in 1926, Ōmori is diplomatically credited with having had "some kind of presentiment [of the earthquake], though he did his best to avoid exciting useless and pernicious commotion among the public by giving expression to too positive warnings of the coming catastrophe." But turning to Ōmori's research, the physicists conclude that "the results are not quite [as] decisive as they might have been well expected [sic]." The work of the IEIC had "taken a somewhat one-sided course of development" under his stewardship.[45] Such verdicts would only strengthen as seismology became more mathematical and experimental, and Ōmori's statistical and cartographic accounts of seismicity (delivered in his carefully constructed prose style) came to seem increasingly old-fashioned. "Ōmori seismology" continues even today as shorthand for the dark ages of their science among some Japanese practitioners.[46]

THE SUBMERGENCE OF
THE EARTHQUAKE NATION

The characterization of Japan as an earthquake nation, which had helped construct faith in Japanese science internationally in the Meiji period, became in late Taishō and early Showa a potential source of Japanese embarrassment in that same arena. The sudden, all-too-complete destruction of their capital threatened to erase overnight the image of the Japanese as a people in control of their own nature. Indeed, the aftermath of the earthquake saw a resurgence in global discussion of Japanese fragility, the very discourse that Ōmori, Sano, and others had spent their careers attempting to reverse or deflect.

In 1926, while still in the midst of rebuilding, Tokyo hosted the Third Pan-Pacific Science Conference, a landmark achievement for Japan's scientific research community. Though many of the Japanese papers concerned seismology and earthquake engineering, few of the opening remarks, toasts, and other speeches by senior organizers took the Great Kantō Earthquake as an explicit theme. The only eulogy to Ōmori, who had been attending the Second Pan-Pacific Conference in Sydney when Tokyo was destroyed, and was well known to many of the foreign attendees, came from Sir Gerald P. Lenox-Conyngham, representative of the British delegation. The Tokyo earthquake "cast such a gloom over the last days of the Sydney meeting," remembered Sir Gerald, that it "may have been a contributing case to his [Ōmori's] early death." Turning explicitly to seismology, and reminding his Japanese hosts that that science had its origins with English expatriates Milne and Ewing, Sir Gerald wrote destructive earthquakes into the record of Japanese science in embarrassingly explicit terms: "Though so much has been done for this delightful country by the loving care of countless generations of her people, there remains a most grave drawback from which they have been able to do nothing and in the face of which science is at present powerless. I refer to the earthquake, from which this country has suffered so often and so much." Though Sir Gerald praised his hosts for carrying through with the long-scheduled conference in spite of the catastrophe, his language could only have struck older Japanese participants as little changed from that of nineteenth-century expatriate engineers. Countless generations of effort had, in Sir Gerald's reading, produced so very little. Seismicity remained Japan's Achilles' heel.[47]

Foreign descriptions of the catastrophe often re-created, and assigned responsibility to, a traditional Japan hardly changed since the time of the Ansei disaster. Col. Lester E. Jones, for example, the director of the U.S. Coast and Geodetic Survey (the government coordinating agency for American seismology), would write in 1932 that "the poverty of large masses of people" in Tokyo had "necessitated a type of building [the wooden house] which was absolutely unsuited to meet the earthquake peril in a large city."[48] Had he lived, Ōmori might have answered Jones that the earthquakes' easy destruction of the city's modern (i.e., "Western") water supply system (its reservoirs, electric pumps, and especially its miles of piping), a system that had invited the abandonment of the neighborhood wells and firefighting organizations and techniques that had traditionally kept Tokyo's conflagrations contained within specific neighborhoods, was at least as culpable as poverty or woodenness. Both Ōmori and Imamura had consistently warned of the vulnerability of the fire-protection system. Indeed, it was one of the few things they had agreed on in their bitter exchange of 1905–1906. Tokyo's and Yokohama's water pipes, first laid in 1885 by British engineers, had in succeeding years been repeatedly broken by minor earthquakes. Ōmori even illustrated pieces of broken pipe caused by the earthquake of April 26, 1922, in an article written shortly before the final disaster. He had suggested, to no avail, that they be buried deeper.[49]

Imamura might be expected to have agreed with Jones about the unsuitability of wooden houses in contemporary Tokyo, having repeatedly warned of a catastrophic postearthquake fire. And in the aftermath of 1923 he consistently reminded audiences that it was the firestorm, rather than the shaking, that had caused so much death and destruction. Imamura's emphasis on the conflagration, however, served only to bolster the lesson, which Japanese seismology had attempted to teach since its beginnings, that Japanese wooden houses were comparatively tenacious in the face of seismic waves. Noting that only about ten thousand houses had collapsed in the earthquake, and applying the formula worked out by Ōmori after the Nōbi disaster of one death per eleven collapsed Japanese houses, he concluded in a paper for the 1926 Pan-Pacific conference that only about one thousand people had died due to the shock itself. As if to further complicate the narrative of a "traditional" Japanese defenselessness based on poverty and poor construction, Imamura noted that "there were numerous cases of fire due to chemicals," the authorities estimating that at least forty-four fire centers (out of over two hundred) were actually industrial sites. He also added the collapse of the city's bridges—which prevented easy evacuation from burning districts—to that of the water system as critical engineering failures that contributed to the high death toll. A final critical agent of destruction on Imamura's list was the unusually strong wind, which, absent at the time of the Ansei earthquake of 1855, served in 1923 to fan the flames into an uncontrollable firestorm.[50]

The destruction of Tokyo thus becomes, in Imamura's account, a terrible coincidence of natural and manmade forces of which the earthquake itself was only a trigger.[51] Indeed, some seismologists contended that the earthquake had itself been triggered by a cyclonic storm preceding the subterranean event.[52] This multicausal analysis was of course more nuanced than the way seismologists and others had discussed the Great Nōbi Earthquake: as a contest of strength between seismic waves and two highly symbolic styles of architecture. But the political context of the two events also differed. Eager to put seismology on the scientific map in 1891, Milne and his governmental patrons had not hesitated to broadcast to the world the overwhelming force and destructive power of Japanese earthquakes. After 1923, however, the position of Japanese seismologists was somewhat analogous to that of Japanese architects thirty years before. This time it was Ōmori who had made predictions of safety that had not come true. Imamura may have escaped personal blame, but the light of censure inevitably swung toward the discipline whose leadership he had inherited. It was natural—and not unreasonable—that Japanese seismologists deemphasize seismicity as the sole causative agent of this unparalleled urban and national catastrophe.

Imamura's case would be put even more strongly by the British seismologist Charles Davison, who, following Milne, would prove a consistent friend of Japan and Japanese science. It was Davison who, in his 1927 book *Founders of Seismology*, would anoint Ōmori as a founder of their mutual profession, a recognition that few Japanese at the time would have been inclined to extend. In his subsequent *The Japanese Earthquake of 1923*, published in 1931, Davison is intent on countering the image of unmitigated failure on the Kantō Plain and the implications which that carried for the reputations of his Japanese colleagues. Statistics gathered by Japanese researchers following the earthquake, he tells his readers, show that "less than 1 percent of the houses were completely demolished [by the shock] and about 10 percent were badly damaged. Nor was the loss of life excessive if we take the total population into account . . . including those who were burned and counting all the missing as killed, only 2.7 percent of the inhabitants [of the city of Tokyo itself] lost their lives."[53] This he contrasts with the situation in Italian earthquakes of similar magnitude, in which commonly 50 to 97 percent of the inhabitants of towns and cities were killed. Davison thus salvages at least one of Ōmori's Nōbi lessons from the event that had overturned so many others. As for the susceptibility of the *daiku*-built city to its age-old enemy, fire, Davison amplifies and extends Imamura's list of failures to the newer, engineer-designed infrastructure: "The water mains were dislocated, the gas supply failed, telegraph and telephone wires were down, all the traffic by railway or tram-line ceased."[54] In addition to the combustion of chemicals mentioned by Imamura, he adds the explosion of motorcars in the streets. In the more Western-style city of Yokohama, he tells us, not only did most of the masonry structures collapse, but also the bridges, harbor piers, and even breakwaters. Thus does Davison's circle of responsibility extend much wider than the nexus of seismologists and *daiku*, or seismicity and wood, on which many foreign accounts were inclined to dwell.[55]

Suyehiro Kyōji, the director of Tokyo Imperial University's Earthquake Research Institute, would deploy a different but related strategy of presentation during an American lecture tour in 1931, the same year Davison's book was published. Praising the accomplishments of the ferro-concrete regime and emphasizing the survival of the Marunouchi quarter, Suyehiro made no excuse for the rest of Tokyo's destruction. He rather attempted to modify Japan's identity as an "earthquake nation": "I wish to call your attention to the fact that my country, Japan, is generally believed to be one of the most seismic countries in the world. The late Professor J. Milne, a famous British seismologist, said in a joke that we have earthquakes for breakfast, dinner, supper, and earthquakes to sleep upon. Needless to say, this is merely a joke and is far from the truth. As a matter of fact, seismicity in my country is somewhat exaggerated."[56] Suyehiro pointed out that an equally powerful earthquake had taken place in northern Nevada in 1915, but "only one ranch house close to the fault line was seriously injured."[57] In other words, it was population density as much as seismicity that gave Japan its reputation for upheaval.

Tokyo's reconstruction was now emphasized in foreign venues, and destructive geologic forces made somewhat less prominent or unique. References to earthquakes would henceforth be relatively sparse across the range of Japanese books and articles directed abroad, in comparison, for example, to claims that the chief determinant of Japanese national and racial development was climate and geographic location. While Meiji intellectuals like Shiga Shigetaka had grounded arguments about Japan amidst volcanoes and mountain peaks, the early Showa intellectual Watsuji Tetsuro located his Japan among meteorological phenomena, namely humidity, rainfall, and typhoons. In his book *Fūdo* (translated and published as *Climate and Culture* in 1961; originally published in 1935 from material drafted in the late 1920s), Watsuji assigns to Japanese culture a "typhoon nature" and declares that "it is humidity that brings out most of all the differences between East and West." The book invents and reinvents a vocabulary of environmentally grounded social and political unity whose locus is not landscape, but the more flexible (and intimate) realm of water, air, and temperature. For a writer so concerned with the influence of environment on national character, however, Watsuji is notably silent on the matter of seismicity. The omission is more striking in that his reflections on racial temperament began with an earlier work, *Pilgrimages to the Ancient Cathedrals in Italy*, in which he drew similarities, based on climate, between Japanese and southern Italians. Here is the central geographic axis of Milne's "earthquake countries," along with many of the same ethnological arguments, transposed from the subterranean to the atmospheric.[58]

This ironic submergence of Japan as an "earthquake nation" following the destruction of Tokyo would find its echo in the architectural world as well. In the 1930s, European modernism began to map Japan as its spiritual homeland, having been guided there by Horiguchi Sutemi and other Japanese avant-garde architects whose names it never learned.[59] The European reconnaissance was led by architect-ethnographer Bruno Taut, one of the original German fathers of the Modern movement. While zoologist-ethnographer Edward Morse had reveled in the diversity of Japanese homes, based on extensive travels, Taut wrote of The Japanese House, an object-type based mainly on his own rented example. In two influential books about Japan published in the later 1930s, Taut threw out the temples, pagodas, most of the shrines, the castles, and most of the houses and palaces, and distilled "the essence" of Japanese architecture from a few carefully chosen examples, including the Ise shrine and Katsura Villa. The work, even the existence, of a professional Japanese architecture from Tatsuno to Sano was sidestepped in Taut's books, and *daiku* were restored as the native inhabitants of the new/old modernist archipelago.[60]

This new mapping of Japan by European modernists, which Taut's extended residence both signified and furthered, was met half-way by the Japanese desire, intensified by the Kantō earthquake and the capital's rebuilding, to project positive images of art and culture abroad. Wrote architecture professor Itō Chūta in 1936: "Western critics used to regard our architecture with contempt. The number of Western experts who appreciate our architecture has increased in recent times. . . . it is premature for us to expect any real understanding of the essence of our architecture abroad, but it is important to assist the Occident in understanding it." Itō, who as a young man had defended masonry in the aftermath of the Nōbi earthquake, and had only recently designed a ferro-concrete memorial to the victims of the Great Kantō Earthquake, now saw the foreign turn toward Japanese architecture as an opportunity for native design to "emerge from the fetters of foreign tradition" (by which he meant ancient China as well as modern Europe), and "revolutionize the architecture of the world." Foreign modernists were thus assisted in seeing what they had indeed come looking for: Japanese architecture as purified form, the organic product of an ahistorical nation and race, influenced by "nature," but not any peculiarly local manifestation. "Let us create a pure, chaste, and beautiful architecture," wrote Itō, "by adopting the pristine spirit of our ancient architecture."[61] Such statements found reverberation among Western modernists like Antonin Raymond, who wrote: "An architect working in Japan has the advantage of seeing materialized before him in Japanese architecture and civilization, fundamental principles, the rediscovery of which is the goal of the modern architect. Occidentals, hampered as they are by deep-rooted materialism, have not yet realized these principles in all their purity, for this would demand a spiritual outlook."[62] These principles expressed themselves to Raymond with great clarity in "the Japanese house," which "resembles the evolution of a natural form."[63]

Despite the persistence of the evolutionary metaphor from Milne through Raymond, earthquakes had little place in the new modernist schema because "Japanese architecture" (now meaning *daiku*-work) could not be the product of peculiarly local crises. As Taut put it in *Fundamentals of Japanese Architecture*, "That which is peculiar to Japan, the local, is insignificant."[64] Japanese architecture was now to be fundamental and worldly-wise, or "a standard Japanese architecture for the world." In a list Itō Chūta drew up in 1936 of "native factors" that Japanese architecture had developed "in consonance with," the previously popular factors of seismicity and fire were missing. What remained was "latitude, temperature, humidity, rain, snow, soil, and building material."[65]

In the same way, architectural modernists largely ignored traditional house frames (the locus of longstanding arguments about *daiku* knowledge) to concentrate on open floor plans, sliding screens, and the standardized measurements of *tatami* mats, all of which became prototypes for the new international project of prefabricated housing. When Taut's writing touches on *daiku* framing technique, it is in order to dismiss it, in the spirit of early Meiji engineers as "contrary to all logic," "total nonsense," and even "mere whim." "The architect who comes [to Japan] searches in vain," he writes, "for structural and technical devices against storms, earthquakes, and fires." Taut discovers, in the spirit of Watsuji and Itō, that "it was the climate that built the Japanese house, more especially the summer." When *daiku* are praised in his or other modernist writings, it is for inventing a standardized or modular system of construction, finely proportioned, that in the logic of avant-garde architecture virtually negates the need for artisanal skill, novelty, or thought. "This specialization and the accompanying standardization of all the various components," writes Taut, "were achieved at the expense of reason."[66] Taut, Raymond, and other foreign modernists also went beyond nineteenth-century expatriates in consistently using "the Japanese" and often just "he" and "him" in praising indigenous architecture (as in "He understands the quality of the eternal").

This ancient-modern and Japanese-international synthesis was not universally approved of within the Japanese architectural world. Wrote architecture professor Kishida Hideto in 1936: "Generally, visitors from abroad, among whom are included a number of architects, concentrate their attention one-sidedly upon the classical aspects of Japanese buildings. They possess amazingly child-like ideas regarding our modern architecture. . . . Among the visitors to Tokyo and Osaka, we often meet those who express not only surprise over the fact that those cities are so Europeanized but disappointment in not having found Japan a fairyland in keeping with their preconceived notions."[67] He could well have been referring to Taut, who, on first arriving in Japan, claimed to have become physically ill at the sight of modern Tokyo as he traversed it to reach the countryside, where he remained for the rest of his sojourn. By "our modern architecture," Kishida meant the concrete and earthquake-resistant monuments in the Marunouchi quarter and elsewhere, which in the 1930s were being ignored or denigrated by young Japanese and foreign modernists alike. Already in 1931, just eight years after the destruction of Tokyo, seismologist Suyehiro Kyoshi would complain of "the present indifference of the majority of architects and engineers to earthquake problems."[68] The old project of national resistance could not be converted into national projection in the new theater of international design.

With the outbreak of war with China in 1937, the government banned ferroconcrete for nonmilitary applications, and Japanese architecture entered a period of crisis, neglect, and eventual reconstruction. The resist-earthquakes regime became a resist-aerial-bombardment one, and for the duration of the war emergency there was little time or inclination to think about seismicity, even as destructive earthquakes continued to happen around the archipelago. The eventual obliteration of Tokyo, Hiroshima, Nagasaki, and the rest of urban Japan by the U.S. Army Air Force and its assisting scientists in 1944–1945 would forever overshadow anything that the proverbial catfish could do or had ever done to the Japanese. Nagoya Castle, for example, had survived the Nōbi Earthquake only to burn in the American firestorm. The ferro-concrete governmental and bank buildings of Sano's *kōzō* faction, which had peppered the still largely wooden cityscapes of pre-war Japan, became solitary icons to catastrophe in the war's immediate aftermath. Their shattered cementious bodies, barely held together by veinlike iron ribbing, studded the postwar urban plains like sculpted lessons in the futility of aggressive resistance.

Tokyo was largely rebuilt, as it always had been, by *daiku* using lumber and hand tools. But the reconstruction of urban Japan (and the world beyond) following the Second World War would give the new architecture of purity and essence its modern day. In the course of the Showa era, Japan would cease by common consent to be an earthquake nation, while its old identity as an art nation was captured and run with by a newly internationalizing architecture and design community. It was architecture and design, in the years and decades following the Second World War, that as much as any single force projected a positive, universalist view of Japan to a previously hostile world. Japanese seismology and earthquake engineering would continue to grow in skill, application, and prestige in the postwar period, but mitigating earthquakes and other natural disasters became a technical concern with less obvious cultural meaning or import. Both the low concrete buildings of the Hiroshima Peace Memorial and the soaring yet fragile constructions of the postwar Metabolism Group seemed to signal above all an exhaustion with the specter of apocalypse.[69]

NOTES

INTRODUCTION

1. There is not just one Japanese story of the Great Nōbi Earthquake. The one I tell here is pieced together from a number of sources, written and verbal, and some points made explicit in my version are merely implied in Japanese narration. With these caveats, the reader will find modern treatments of the 1891 earthquake in Muramatsu Teijirō, *Nihon kindai kenchiku gijutsushi* (Tokyo: Shōkokusha, 1976), pp. 75–76; Nihon Kenchiku Gakkai, *Kindai Nihon kenchiku-gaku hattatsushi* (Tokyo: Maruzen Kabushiki Gaisha, 1972), p. 268; and Yamaguchi Hiroshi, *Nihon no kindai gendai kenchiku shi [Shin kenchiku-gaku taikei]*, vol. 5 (Tokyo: Shōkokusha, 1993), p. 268. Most contemporary accounts follow a version of the story crafted in the aftermath of the Great Kantō Earthquake of 1923 by Sano Toshikata and other practicing architects, which I contextualize in the last chapter. These Taishō-period versions were in turn based on narratives by late-Meiji-period seismologists and journalists, which I discuss in chapter 5.

2. The Nōbi earthquake does receive a single line in Bannister Fletcher's *History of Architecture*, 20th ed. (Oxford: Architectural Press, 1996), p. 1239, which reports that the Japanese "fully realized the weakness of brick structures" following the catastrophe. This is a rather faithful distillation of the lesson presented in the Japanese accounts cited above.

3. This is not to criticize even "classical" accounts, but to point out how rarely we encounter natural disaster in stories about technological change. This is true even in en-

vironmental histories, which in Japan often begin with the Ashio Copper Mine pollution scandal, an event that first came to public notice the year of the Nōbi earthquake (1891). That the many chroniclers of the pollution scandal have not been interested in the contemporaneous earthquake—also a rural disaster of unprecedented scale—demonstrates how rigidly perceptions of the manmade and the natural disaster color our organization of such events.

4. As Caroline Jones and Peter Galison have pointed out, "There is a history to the perception of difference between science and art, and a parallel history to the attempt to unify the two" (Caroline E. Jones and Peter Galison, eds., *Picturing Science, Producing Art* [New York; London: Routledge, 1998], p. 2). "Architecture" and "technology" are an even more complex dyad, but I would agree with Reyner Banham that even at their point of greatest discursive overlap in the mid-twentieth century there was always a need to maintain coded boundaries. Those who dwell closest to borders are of course most aware of them, and often have the greatest stake in border patrol.

5. This is particularly evident in the work of the late architectural historian Muramatsu Teijirō, whose equal fascination with design and technology, design professionals and craftspeople, academics and businessmen, has little counterpart in Anglo-American historiography, where such interests are usually parceled out among historians of architecture, art, labor, technology, and business. Representative of his work (in addition to *Nihon kindai kenchiku gijutsushi*) are *Nihon kindai kenchiku no rekishi* (Tokyo: Nihon Hōsō Shuppan Kyōkai, 1977) and *Yawarakai mono e no shiten* (Tokyo: Iwanami Shoten, 1994).

6. The problem is well stated by Mark Jerzombek, "Meditations on the Impossibility of a History of Modernity: Seeing beyond Art's History," in Martha Pollak, ed., *The Education of the Architect: Historiography, Urbanism, and the Growth of Architectural Knowledge* (Cambridge, MA: MIT Press, 1997), pp. 195–216. Only within the last few years have we begun to get a history of modern Japanese architecture, in English, based largely on Japanese texts. See especially Jonathan Reynolds, *Maekawa Kunio and the Emergence of Japanese Modernist Architecture* (Berkeley: University of California Press, 2001); and Jordan Sand, *House and Home in Modern Japan: Architecture, Domestic Space, and Bourgeois Culture, 1880–1930* (Cambridge, MA: Harvard University Asia Center, 2003).

7. I mean classical accounts. Historians of science have now mostly embraced the position, well stated by Peter Galison, that "there is something local about scientific knowledge" (Peter Galison and David Stump, eds., *The Disunity of Science: Boundaries, Contexts, and Power* [Stanford: Stanford University Press, 1996], p. 2). The term *style* has even achieved a degree of usage among historians of technology following

Thomas Hughes's *Networks of Power: Electrification in Western Society, 1880–1930* (Baltimore: Johns Hopkins University Press, 1983).

8. This is Nakatani Norihito, who first used that phrase, in my presence, at his incomparable *Meiji zemi* at Waseda University when we were both graduate students in Tokyo.

9. The key work on Japanese cultural nationalism in this period remains Kenneth Pyle, *The New Generation in Meiji Japan: Problems in Cultural Identity, 1885–1895* (Stanford: Stanford University Press, 1969).

10. For lively accounts of how scientists speak for nature, see Bruno Latour, *Science in Action: How to Follow Scientists and Engineers through Society* (Cambridge, MA: Harvard University Press, 1987) and *The Pasteurization of France* (Cambridge, MA: Harvard University Press, 1988). The increasingly abstract use of Latour's "actor-network theory" (crafted with Michel Callon and John Law) risks sidelining his ironic, literary, and politically insightful contributions to science and technology studies, which actually concern me more in the present account. In rediscovering the contingent event or revealing moment within the often-obscuring "process," sci-tech studies has also generated a small but insightful body of literature on accidents. See particularly Harry Collins and Trevor Pinch, *The Golem at Large: What You Should Know about Technology* (Cambridge: Cambridge University Press, 1998); and Diane Vaughan, *The Challenger Launch Decision: Risky Culture, Technology, and Deviance at NASA* (Chicago: University of Chicago Press, 1996).

11. See, for example, Julia Adenay Thomas, *Reconfiguring Nature in Japanese Political Ideology* (Berkeley: University of California Press, 2002).

12. Excepting studies of key droughts, famines, and pandemics, natural disaster has remained a strangely underdeveloped theme in modern history, in contrast to the centrality accorded such phenomena by many premodern historians. That said, there was a significant increase in book-length studies of disaster at the turn of the millennium, many bringing new political and theoretical sophistication to a topic too easily sensationalized. Among English-language books by historians (the journal literature is too large to be summarized here) are Theodore Steinberg, *Acts of God: The Unnatural History of Natural Disasters in America* (Oxford: Oxford University Press, 2000); Ann Larabee, *Decade of Disaster* (Champaign: University of Illinois Press, 1999); Steven Biel, *American Disasters* (New York: New York University Press, 2002); Alessa Johnson, ed., *Dreadful Visitations: Confronting Natural Disaster in the Age of Enlightenment* (New York: Routledge, 1995); Carl S. Smith, *Urban Disorder and the Shape of Belief: The Great Chicago Fire, the Haymarket Bomb, and the Model Town of Pullman* (Chicago: University of Chicago Press, 1996); and Karin Sawislak, *Smoldering City: Chicagoans*

and the Great Fire (Chicago: University of Chicago Press, 1996). As the titles indicate, natural disaster seems particularly compelling to historians of America. Despite the historic overdetermination of Asian nature as sublime and uncontrolled—or, more likely, because of it—catastrophic events have drawn less interest from historians of Asia than developmental processes (notable English-language exceptions include Gregory Bankoff, *Cultures of Disaster: Society and Natural Hazards in the Philippines* [London: RoutledgeCurzon, 2003]; and Hameeda Hossain, Cole Dodge, and F. H. Abel, eds., *From Crisis to Development: Coping with Disasters in Bangladesh* [Dhaka: University Press Limited, 1992]; see the following note for Japanese-language works). There is also a well-developed anthropology of disaster (much of it centering on Latin America) discussed in Susanna Hoffman and Anthony Oliver-Smith, *Catastrophe and Culture: The Anthropology of Disaster* (Santa Fe, NM: School of American Research Press, 2002) and *The Angry Earth: Disaster in Anthropological Perspective* (New York: Routledge, 1999). For the geography of disaster, see Kenneth Hewitt, *Regions of Risk: A Geographical Introduction to Disasters* (London: Addison, Wesley, Longman, 1997); Cesar N. Caviedes, *El Niño in History: Storming through the Ages* (Tallahassee: University of Florida Press, 2001); and David Alexander, *Natural Disasters* (New York: Chapman and Hall, 1993). The trope of disaster has perhaps received its highest profile in the works of public intellectual Mike Davis, namely *Ecology of Fear: Los Angeles and the Imagination of Disaster* (New York: Vintage Books, 1999), *Late Victorian Holocausts: El Niño Famines and The Making of the Third World* (New York: Verso, 2002), and, more recently, *Dead Cities and Other Tales* (New York: New Press, 2002). At the same time, the numbers of book-length accounts of disaster by serious journalists and nonfiction writers have also increased: e.g., Philip Fradkin, *Magnitude 8* (Berkeley: University of California Press, 1999); and Simon Winchester, *Krakatoa: The Day the World Exploded, August 27, 1883* (New York: HarperCollins, 2003).

13. There is a substantial Japanese-language historical literature on natural disaster, although it has yet to achieve (with some exceptions) the academic status increasingly accorded such work in the West. This is partly a function of its production by working scientists. Key titles include Miyazawa Seiji, *Kin-gendai Nihon kishōsaigaishi* (Tokyo: Ikarosu Shuppan, 1999); Kitahara Itoko, *Bandaisan funka: saii kara saigai no kagaku e* (Tokyo: Yoshikawa Kobunken, 1998); Nakajima Chōtarō et al., *Rekishi saigai no hanashi* (Kyoto: Shibunkaku Shuppan, 1992); Kikuchi Kazuo, *Nihon no rekishi saigai. Meiji hen* (Tokyo: Kokon Shoin, 1986); and Sasamoto Shōji, *Saigai bunkashi no kenkyū* (Tokyo: Takashi Shoin, 2003). The Great Kantō Earthquake is the subject of Ogawa Masuo, *Tokyo shōshitsu: Kantō daishinsai no hiroku* (Tokyo: Koseido, 1974); and Nakajima Yoichiro, *Kantō daishinsai* (Tokyo: Yūzankaku, 1973).

14. Sharon Traweek's work on modern Japanese physicists—*Beamtimes and Lifetimes: The World of High Energy Physicists* (Cambridge, MA: Harvard University Press, 1992)—has influenced my consideration of how academic communities reproduce themselves across both geographies and generations. I'm not as concerned with how my groups coordinated, however, as in how they arranged their quarrels. The fabled Japanese instinct for consensus—continually critiqued and qualified by Traweek—is likewise difficult to locate in the Meiji academy.

15. The "transfer" model as applied to Japan has already been critiqued and complicated by Tessa Morris-Suzuki, *The Technological Transformation of Japan: From the Seventeenth to the Twenty-First Centuries* (Cambridge: Cambridge University Press, 1994); and Graeme Gooday and Morris Low, "Technology Transfer and Cultural Exchange: Western Scientists and Engineers Encounter Late Tokugawa and Meiji Japan," *Osiris*, 2nd ser., vol. 13 (1998–99): 99–128, which demonstrates that "cultural exchange" is the more revealing frame. A host of Japanese-authored accounts have also detailed indigenous adaptation of borrowed technologies, making the issue much less straightforward than previously conceived. See, for example, Takamatsu Tōru, "The Way Japan Joined Mechanized Civilization," in Tadao Umeseo et al., *Japanese Civilization in the Modern World* (Osaka: National Museum of Ethnology, 1998).

16. Bruno Latour, *We Have Never Been Modern* (Cambridge, MA: Harvard University Press, 1993), p. 3.

17. Itō Tamekichi, *Shinshiki daiku ho* (Tokyo, 1934).

ONE • STRONG NATION, STONE NATION

1. An exception is James Bartholomew, whose *The Formation of Science in Japan: Building a Research Tradition* (New Haven: Yale University Press, 1989) remains the standard English-language account of the history of modern Japanese science. More recently, the issue of samurai lineage among Japanese scientists has been addressed by Morris Low (in a paper presented at the symposium "A Discussion on the Future History of East Asian Science, Technology, and Medicine," Johns Hopkins University, September 2003). Identity-construction among scientists and engineers in the West has been better explored. See, for example, Steven Shapin, *A Social History of Truth: Civility and Science in Seventeenth-Century England* (Chicago: University of Chicago Press, 1994); Mario Biagioli, *Galileo, Courtier: The Practice of Science in the Culture of Absolutism* (Chicago: University of Chicago Press, 1993); and M. R. Smith, "Becoming Engineers in Early Industrial America" (STS Working Paper no. 13, Science, Technology, and Society Program, MIT, 1990).

2. On physicians, see Bartholomew, who points out that medicine was dominated by commoners both before and after the Restoration. Regarding architecture, the samurai class had occasionally made excursions into design, as had Buddhist priests and others, but never consistently enough to inscribe that practice onto their social identities.

3. A tradition of shipbuilding for the coasting and fishing trades continued even after the "closing" of Japan by the Tokugawa regime in the early seventeenth century.

4. Or managed so many subsidiary artisans. The central or directing role of *daiku* within vast artisan networks was arguably as important to their identity as the ability to understand and manipulate wood, although the two were fully related. Whoever controlled the structure of a building structured the work that went on there. *Daiku* built the framework within which, quite literally, dozens of other types of artisans plied their trades.

5. William H. Coaldrake, *The Way of the Carpenter* (New York: Weatherhill, 1990), p. 15. Other historical discussions of *daiku* include Kiyoshi Seike, *The Art of Japanese Joinery* (New York: Weatherhill, 1977), with a good introduction by translators Yuriko Yobuko and Rebecca M. Davis; Endō Motoo, *Nihon shokuninshi no kenkyū 5: kenchiku, kinko shokuninshiwa* (Tokyo: Yuzankaku, 1961); Endō, *Shokunin-tachi no rekishi* (Tokyo: Shibundō, 1965), which like the previous book covers a range of urban artisans, especially prior to Meiji; Muramatsu Teijirō, *Daiku dōgu no rekishi* (Tokyo: Iwanami Shoten, 1973), the most detailed discussion in Japanese of *daiku* tools; and Muramatsu, *Waga kuni daiku no kōsaku gijutsu ni kansuru kenkyū* (Tokyo: Rōdō Kagaku Kenkyujo Shuppanbu, 1984).

6. For a good discussion of the various building trades in this period, see Hatsuda Tōru, *Shokunin-tachi no seiyō kenchiku* (Tokyo: Kōdansha, 1997).

7. The Japanese method of building stone retaining walls did not involve the use of mortar or the laying of ashlar (square cut pieces of stone); rather, pyramid-shaped stones were pressed into the faces of earthen embankments. This resulted in dramatic stone skirtings of parabolic shape, most famously seen at the base of Japanese castles. The technique differed substantially from Eurasian methods of masonry construction; it was not transferable, in other words, from landscaping to architecture. Exceptions to this rule were approximately forty arched stone bridges constructed in Kyushu in the Edo period, the earliest in the seventeenth century but most in the nineteenth. Kyushu is the part of Japan closest to China and thus, traditionally, Europe (*Kodansha Encyclopedia of Japan* [Tokyo: Kōdansha, 1983], p. 170).

8. Muramatsu Teijirō, *Nihon kindai kenchiku gijutsushi* (Tokyo: Shōkokusha, 1976), p. 74. The reconstruction plan seems to have originated with the governor of Tokyo, whose own house fell victim to the flames.

9. For Waters and the Ginza, see Muramatsu, *Nihon kindai kenchiku no rekishi* (Tokyo: Nihon Hōsō Shuppan Kyōkai, 1977), ch. 3; Fujimori Terunobu, *Meiji no Tokyo keikaku* (Tokyo: Iwanami Shoten, 1982), ch. 1; Fujimori, *Nihon no kindai kenchiku* (Tokyo: Iwanami Shoten, 1993), vol. 1, chs. 1 and 3; David B. Stewart, *The Making of a Modern Japanese Architecture* (Tokyo: Kōdansha, 1987), ch. 1; and Dallas Finn, *Meiji Revisited* (New York: Weatherhill, 1995), ch. 2.

10. Henry D. Smith II, "The Edo-Tokyo Transition: In Search of a Common Ground," in Marius B. Jansen and Gilbert Rozman, eds., *Japan in Transition: From Tokugawa to Meiji* (Princeton: Princeton University Press, 1986), pp. 347–74. Smith notes that Tokyo did not recover Edo's prerevolutionary population until about 1890, or more than two decades after the Imperial restoration (p. 347). He also notes that among the arguments made in favor of locating the Imperial capital in Edo was "the availability of broad tracts of land vacated by the daimyo [feudal lords] that could serve as convenient sites for the offices and institutions of the new regime." Osaka, the other possibility, was intensively settled (p. 355).

11. For Waters in Satsuma, see Stewart and Finn above; for Itō and Yamao, see W. H. Brock, "The Japanese Connexion: Engineering in Tokyo, London, and Glasgow at the End of the Nineteenth Century," *The British Journal for the History of Science* 14 (1981): 229–34.

12. Smith has pointed out that the plans for rebuilding sections of Edo in Western-style brick and stone were discussed even in the late Tokugawa period, based on descriptions of European brick cities in Dutch books. Henry D. Smith II, "Tokyo as an Idea: An Exploration of Japanese Urban Thought until 1945," *Journal of Japanese Studies* 4, no. 1 (Winter 1978): 50.

13. *Kōbu* is variously translated by historians as "technology," "engineering," "industry," and "public works." One of many new Meiji-period words, it encompassed all these Anglo-American meanings and more. Englishmen who worked for the Meiji government generally translated Kōbushō as the Ministry of Public Works (being keenly aware of distinctions between "public" and "private," although in Japan the "private" scarcely existed), while Kōbudaigakkō was the College of Engineering. The word "technology" was only just beginning its modern career, and primarily within American English, but better fits the sense of the school's mission. Kōbushō was founded in 1870, and Kōbudaigakkō in 1871 (the latter was called Kōgakuryo or Kōgakkō until 1877). For descriptions of the college in English, see Brock; Graeme Gooday and Morris Low, "Technology Transfer and Cultural Exchange: Western Scientists and Engineers Encounter Late Tokugawa and Meiji Japan," *Osiris*, 2nd series, vol. 13 (1998–99): 99–128; Henry Dyer, *Dai Nippon* (London: Blackie and Son, 1904), pp. 3–7; and Taka-

hashi Yūzō, "William Edward Ayrton at the Imperial College of Engineering in Tokyo . . . ," *IEEE Transactions on Education* 33, no. 2 (May 1990): 198–205. On the phenomenon of *yatoi*, see H. J. Jones, *Live Machines: Hired Foreigners and Meiji Japan* (Vancouver: University of British Columbia Press, 1980).

14. The other six were civil engineering, mechanical engineering, telegraphy, practical chemistry, mining, and metallurgy. Naval architecture was added a few years later.

15. Historian of science Nakayama Shigeru notes that "almost all the early graduates of the engineering college were samurai." As late as 1890, 86 percent of Imperial University engineering graduates (the Imperial University absorbed Kōbudaigakkō in 1886) were from samurai families. His figure for the university's science courses is 80 percent. Samurai at the beginning of the Meiji period constituted only the top 5 percent of the population as a whole (Nakayama Shigeru, "Japanese Science," in Helaine Selin, ed., *The Encyclopedia of the History of Science, Technology, and Medicine in Non-Western Countries* [Dordrecht, The Netherlands: Kluwer Academic Publications, 1997], p. 469). In humanities programs the percentage of elite entrants was lower. Richard Rubinger notes that in 1885, those from samurai families constituted only 51.7 percent of the student body of the Imperial University as a whole, but further notes that "the bottom 25% of the income scale" was effectively excluded from competition by being unable to enroll in middle schools (Richard Rubinger, "Education: From One Road to One System," in Jansen and Rozman, p. 226). Bartholomew finds that, among Meiji-period scientific and technical fields, only medicine contained higher numbers of commoners than descendents of samurai, although doctoral students with common and samurai origins reached parity in certain other specialties, such as mathematics and geology, by the Taishō period (Bartholomew, *The Formation of Science in Japan*, ch. 3). See also Bartholomew, "Japanese Modernization and the Imperial Universities, 1876–1920," *Journal of Asian Studies* 37, no. 2 (February 1978): 251–71. Accepting the various differentiations in status within the category "samurai," higher education in engineering and science in Japan was hardly the path of upward mobility it is often portrayed as having been in Britain and the United States.

16. *"Kōbudaigakkō* Calendar, 1879," in Nihon Kenchiku Gakkai, *Kindai Nihon kenchiku-gaku hattatsushi* (Tokyo: Maruzen Kabushiki Gaisha, 1972), pp. 1804–5.

17. *"Kōbudaigakkō* Examination for Diploma (Architects), 1879," in Nihon Kenchiku Gakkai, pp. 1806–7.

18. A common construction was *bunmei kaika*, or "[Western] civilization and enlightenment."

19. Wrote Japan scholar Edward Strange in 1897: "The edifices which form the landmarks of his [the European architect's] progress, have been built almost invariably

of stone or brick; wood being—naturally, as we should say—merely an accessory of comparatively trivial importance" (Strange, "Architecture in Japan," *Architectural Review* 1 [1897]: 126).

20. See, for example, James Fergusson's *History of Architecture* (1865), which defines "architecture" as masonry monuments, equates monumentality with civilization, and orders civilizations hierarchically on the basis of stone ruins. Even earlier, British critic John Ruskin's *The Stones of Venice* (1853) suggested the same relationship.

21. Michael Adas, *Machines as the Measure of Men* (Ithaca: Cornell University Press, 1989), pp. 156–58.

22. Speaking in Tokyo in 1891, architect Conder said that "one often hears exampled the wooden buildings of America" as a model for the future development of wooden architecture in Japan. He dismissed the comparison, however, by calling the American buildings "the temporary work of pioneers, early settlers, and speculators." When American cities had become "established centers of commerce," he continued, "the change from timber structures to those of brick, stone, and iron goes on rapidly and surely." Josiah Conder, "The Effects of the Recent Earthquake upon Buildings," *The Japan Weekly Mail*, December 12, 1891, p. 725.

23. Eugene Emmanuel Viollet-le-Duc, *Discourses on Architecture* (Boston: James R. Osgood & Co., 1875), pp. 21, 34–45.

24. For a discussion of how the Earth and its minerals were transformed from a "living" part of nature in classical and medieval Europe to a "dead" part in the Renaissance, see Carolyn Merchant, *The Death of Nature* (San Francisco: Harper & Row, 1980).

25. Suzuki Hiroyuki and Yamaguchi Hiroshi, *Nihon no kindai gendai kenchiku shi [Shin kenchiku-gaku taikei]*, vol. 5 (Tokyo: Shōkokusha, 1993), p. 241.

26. Sone Tatsuzō, "A Thesis on the Future Domestic Architecture of Japan" (September 1879, Architecture Course, Kōbudaigakkō), handwritten manuscript in Architecture Library, Faculty of Engineering, Tokyo University.

27. George Cawley, "Some Remarks on Constructions in Brick and Wood and Their Suitability for Japan," *Transactions of the Asiatic Society of Japan* (hereafter *TASJ*) 6 (1877–78): 314.

28. Anonymous, "Japanese Houses," *American Architect and Building News*, January 22, 1876, p. 26.

29. Ralph Adams Cram, *Impressions of Japanese Architecture and the Allied Arts* (New York: Baker & Taylor, 1905), pp. 35–36. The 1888 edition of Joseph Gwilt's *An Encyclopedia of Architecture*, although prepared at the very height of British interest in Japanese art, has sections on India and China, but not Japan. Well into the twentieth

century, British architects in particular argued over whether to apply the word "architecture" to Japanese buildings. Wrote architect H. H. Stratham in 1912: "Whether Japanese building has properly a claim to be called 'architecture' is a question which may be debated. The word is usually associated in our minds with monumental erections composed of solid and durable materials—granite, marble, stone, and brick" (H. H. Stratham, "Japanese Architecture," *Architectural Review*, October 1912, pp. 177–88).

30. Conder spoke in 1887 of "the very temporary character of the present buildings in the Capital" ("Domestic Architecture in Japan," *Proceedings of the Royal Institute of British Architects* [hereafter *PRIBA*] 3, no. 10 [March 1887]: 198).

31. Quoted in Muramatsu, "Mokuzō kōzō no kindaika," in Nihon Kenchiku Gakkai, pp. 7–10 (quotation, p. 8).

32. J. M. Richards, *An Architectural Journey in Japan* (London: Architectural Press, 1963), p. 158.

33. Rather, Kōbudaigakkō became the direct model for a British engineering institution, the Glasgow and West of Scotland Technical College, which principal Henry Dyer helped found on his return to Britain. "I was able to transfer from Japan," wrote Dyer, "the programme of studies of the Imperial College of Engineering to the Glasgow Institution" (Dyer, p. 11).

34. Conder was actually unusual for having attended lectures on architecture, given by T. Roger Smith at University College in the 1870s. These can also be seen, however, as an extension of his studio-based apprenticeship to Smith. See J. Morduant Crook, "Josiah Conder in England: Education, Training, and Background," in Suzuki Hiroyuki, ed., *Josiah Conder: A Victorian Architect in Japan* (Tokyo: Bijutsu Shuppan, 1997), p. 26.

35. Barrington Kaye, *The Development of the Architectural Profession in Britain* (London: George Allen & Unwin Ltd., 1960), and Frank Jenkins, *Architect and Patron* (London: Oxford University Press, 1961). According to Jenkins, King's College, London, was the first to institute a three-year, full-time course in architecture leading to a diploma, in 1892. Previously a handful of schools had offered part-time (mostly night) courses. Even as late as 1960, 30 percent of entrants to the British architectural profession were trained primarily in architects' offices or by attending night schools.

36. The École des Beaux-Arts, the French government art school founded in the late eighteenth century, shared the training and titling of architects with the ateliers of Parisian architects, which were the real centers of daily learning. Student attention centered not so much on instruction as the competition for government-sponsored prizes.

The United States had, of course, no national university system, although the land-grant colleges established after the Civil War were nationally chartered. In 1877, when Conder began to teach the *zōka* course, there were three university-level architecture departments in the United States (at MIT, Cornell, and Michigan, the latter founded the previous year).

37. Fujimori Terunobu, "Josiah Conder and Japan," in Suzuki, ed., *Joseph Conder*, p. 18.

38. Nihon Kenchiku Gakkai, p. 1950. By the end of the Meiji period (1912), the *zōkagaku* course had a total of 175 alumni (Muramatsu, *Nihon kindai kenchiku gijutsushi*, p. 100).

39. Kaye, p. 173.

40. Harold Perkin, *The Rise of Professional Society in England since 1880* (London: Routledge, 1989); Margali S. Larson, *The Rise of Professionalism* (Berkeley: University of California Press, 1977).

41. Nihon Kenchiku Gakkai, p. 1950.

42. Conder set an example of what a professional architect was by establishing a private practice after his teaching contract expired in 1884. His most prominent student and successor, Tatsuno Kingo, would eventually do the same (at the end of his own government career). But that was as far as the "professional" identity was developed, at least at the top; the private designer and design firm never became prominent in Japan until after the Second World War.

43. For a full discussion see Jonathan Reynolds, *Maekawa Kunio and the Emergence of Japanese Modernist Architecture* (Berkeley: University of California Press, 2001).

44. Encouraged by their teacher, however, fifteen of the first graduates formed the Japan Architectural Institute (Nihon Zōka-Gakkai) in 1886. The Zōka-Gakkai (now Kenchiku-Gakkai) may have been intended, at least by Conder, as a catalyst for private practice and professionalization on the model of the Royal Institute. But it thrived instead as a sort of alumni club. Its members were sufficiently credentialed as Kōbu-daigakkō graduates that they were unneedful of the additional proof they were architects that "RIBA" at the end of one's name provided their British counterparts (the initials stand for the Royal Institute of British Architects).

45. Josiah Conder, "The Practice of Architecture in Japan," *Japan Weekly Mail*, August 28, 1886, p. 215. I am indebted to Dr. Suzuki Hiroyuki for calling my attention to this article.

46. Satachi Shichijirō, "The Future Domestic Architecture of Japan" (September 1879, Architecture Course, Kōbudaigakkō), handwritten manuscript in Architecture Library, Faculty of Engineering, Tokyo University.

47. Nakatani Norihito et al, "'Zōka' kara 'kenchiku' e," *Kenchiku ₹asshi* 112, no. 1410 (August 1997): 13–21.

48. As Joseph Gwilt had put it in the introduction to his *Encyclopedia of Architecture* (London, 1842): "The mere art, or rather science, of construction, has no title to a place among the fine arts [which Gwilt hoped architecture might have]. . . . It is only when a nation has arrived at a certain degree of opulence and luxury that architecture can be said to exist at all." Gwilt's book would often appear in the bibliographies of Meiji-period Japanese architectural texts.

49. The doctrine that art cannot be learned, but is a "talent" that one "is born with," so often expressed in the last quarter of the nineteenth century and later, would seem to be contradicted by the burgeoning of art and architectural schools in that same period. Yet prominent spokesmen for this position were often architectural school professors. The gothicist and Japanophile Ralph Adams Cram, for example, remembered in his later years that, while teaching at MIT, "my function . . . was not to get men into the profession, but to keep them out." Cram believed that "about sixty percent of the men in the Department at any given time were absolutely unfitted to become architects or even good draftsmen" (Ralph Adams Cram, "Can We Produce Architects by Education?" *The Architect's World* 1, no. 1 [February 1938]: 27–28). More than departments of science and engineering, architectural courses were full of culling devices, such as competitions, prizes, and study trips, designed to construct hierarchies all the way down. Levy notes that although 3,400 to 4,000 students enrolled in the architecture course at MIT (the largest American architecture school) in the second half of the nineteenth century, only 600 to 700 actually received diplomas (Richard Levy, "The Professionalization of American Architects and Civil Engineers, 1865–1917," Ph.D. diss., University of California, Berkeley, 1980, p. 170).

50. Nakatani et al.

51. Ibid.

52. This was the name of Japan's second architectural journal, founded in 1907 and intended primarily for "middle-level architectural engineers," or the new foreman class that included many former *daiku*.

53. This instinct for restricting the use of "architecture" in Britain and the United States was at once linguistic and institutional. As "architecture" was a descriptor applied to a comparatively few buildings, so the institutions of the profession sought to limit the title "architect" to a comparatively few practitioners. All professions seek to limit the number of entrants, but architecture in the later nineteenth century represented the extreme case. Richard Levy notes a pattern in the American Institute of Architects (AIA) of erecting barriers to the entry of younger practitioners, with the result

that the mean age difference between graduates of architectural schools and members of the AIA by 1910 was thirty years (Levy, pp. 72–73). While architects invariably pointed to practical (economic) reasons for limiting professional membership, the cult of natural talent was more powerful in the developing fine-art discourse than in the developing scientific one, where a greater premium was placed on industrial concepts like "sacrifice" and "work."

54. Nakamura Tetsutarō, ed., *Nihon kenchiku ji* (Tokyo: Maruzen, 1904), pp. 1–2.

55. Conder, Address to the Meiji Art Society (Meiji Bijutsu Kai), *Japan Weekly Mail*, December 14, 1889, quoted in Yamaguchi Seiichi, "Josiah Conder on Japanese Studies," in Suzuki, ed., *Josiah Conder*, p. 56. Conder, "The Practice of Architecture in Japan," pp. 213–14.

56. Another aspect of the process was the architect's abandonment of the building site for the office/studio. Levy notes that refinements in contracting in the last quarter of the nineteenth century "made it possible for the architect to no longer be in strict attendance" during the constructive act (p. 84).

57. Conder, "The Practice of Architecture in Japan," p. 215; Kaye locates the importance, within British architecture, of having only limited knowledge about building, in the eighteenth-century emergence of "the architect" as a gentleman's role. He thus quotes Lord Chesterfield, writing to his son in 1749: "You may soon be acquainted with the considerable parts of Civil Architecture; and for the minute and mechanical parts of it; leave them to masons, bricklayers, and Lord Burlington; who has, to a certain degree, lessened himself by knowing them too well" (p. 46). Gentleman-architect Lord Burlington was even lampooned in a famous engraving by William Hogarth as a mason carrying a hawk of mortar (reproduced in Jenkins, plate 5). In the late nineteenth century, as engineers assumed the role of masons and bricklayers, it was skills like mathematics that architects had to be careful to not know too well. Wrote Ralph Adams Cram in 1938: "Nearly all the great architects I have known during the past fifty years made no boast of their mathematical proficiency, or used it to any great degree—when they had it . . . the creative designer, by his very nature, can hardly function as a structural engineer, and vis versa" (Cram, "Can We Produce Architects by Education?" p. 30).

58. Satachi.

59. Ibid.

60. Muramatsu tells this story of the construction of the Temporary Diet Building in 1891 ("temporary" because it was built in wood, although the legislature would be housed there for nearly half a century): two *zōkagaku-shi*, Yoshi Shigenori and Yoshizawa Tomotarō, took on the roles of "architect" and "general contractor" respectively. Yet because both were graduates of the same course, each refused to recog-

nize the other's authority. They finally settled the matter with a sumo match, which Yoshi won (Muramatsu, *Nihon kindai kenchiku gijutsushi,* p. 50).

61. Conder, "The Practice of Architecture in Japan," p. 216.

62. See Levy, esp. pp. 243–76. Said William Ware, the first director of the architecture program at MIT, in 1873, "The too extended study of geometry and statics naturally induces a habit of mind that is precisely opposed to the architectural turn of mind . . ." (Levy, p. 253).

63. On the title pages of Meiji-period books and articles, architect-authors were commonly titled either "engineer" or "professor of engineering," the second term having the higher status. When Japanese universities began to proliferate in the Taishō period (after 1912), the name of the university was often added to the title "engineering professor" that preceded the author's name. The additional title "Member of the Association of Japanese Architects," equivalent to the British RIBA or American AIA, was a strictly secondary title whose use remained optional. The nomenclature of engineering still orders the Japanese architectural world to an extent unusual in Europe and the United States. Architectural historians at Japanese universities and their students, for example, are organized into "research labs" *(kenkyū-jo)* in the same manner as engineering professors and students, although what actually goes on there is not fundamentally different from what occurs in departments of architecture and art history around the world.

64. Funakoshi Kinya, "The Adaptation of European Architecture in Japan" (1883, Architecture Course, Kōbudaigakkō), handwritten manuscript in Architecture Library, Faculty of Engineering, Tokyo University.

65. Taki Daikichi, *Kenchiku kōgi ron* (Tokyo: Kenchiku Shoin, 1890), p. 1.

66. Muramatsu Teijirō, *Yawarakai mono eno shiten* (Tokyo: Iwanami Shoten, 1994), p. 53.

67. Sone, "A Thesis on the Future Domestic Architecture of Japan."

68. Josiah Conder, "The Effects of the Recent Earthquake upon Buildings," *Japan Weekly Mail,* December 12, 1891, p. 725. On the commonality of truss-related knowledge among American carpenters, see any issue of the journal *Carpentry and Building,* which from 1879 onward had an extensive correspondence section in which carpenters from all over the country would elicit and respond to queries. Even in the late eighteenth century trusses were a standard technology for the construction of rural meetinghouses, urban factories and warehouses, local government buildings, and the like.

69. Kenchikugaku Kenkyūkai, *Kenchikugaku kōhon* (Tokyo, 1905).

70. Muramatsu, *Nihon kindai kenchiku gijutsushi,* p. 81. For the trend in American schools, see Levy.

71. For *daiku* ritual, see Coaldrake, *Way of the Carpenter*; Endō, *Nihon shokuninshi no kenkyū.*

72. Sunami Takashi, "Architecture of Shinto Shrines," in *Architectural Japan* (Tokyo: Japan Times & Mail, 1936), p. 13.

73. Coaldrake; Endō.

74. Ibid.

75. The late Tokugawa and Meiji period *kikujustu-sho,* for example, became a subject of serious scholarship only in the 1990s. See Nakatani Norihito, "Bakumatsu, Meiji ki kikujutsu no tenkei katei no kenkyū" (Ph.D. diss., Waseda University, Tokyo, March 1998).

76. There is a relatively large and growing literature, in English as well as Japanese, about the phenomenon of *wayō setchū,* much of it illustrated with photographs and floor plans. The discussion below draws particularly on Fujimori Terunobu, *Nihon kindai kenchiku,* vol. 1; Suzuki Hiroyuki and Hatsuda Tōru, *Zumen de miru: toshi kenchiku no Meiji* (Tokyo: Kashiwa Shobō, 1990); Hatsuda, *Shokunin-tachi no seiyō kenchiku;* Muramatsu, *Nihon kindai kenchiku no rekishi,* chs. 1 and 2; Uchida Seizō, *Nippon no kindai jūtaku* (Tokyo: Kashima Shuppankai, 1992), ch. 1; Stewart, *The Making of a Modern Japanese Architecture;* and Finn, *Meiji Revisited.* The term *wayō,* combining the characters for "Japanese" and "Western," was common in the Japanese architectural world by the late Meiji period, judging from the number of style books that incorporate it into their titles. This type of architecture has more commonly been called in contemporary Japanese *giyōfu,* or "imitation Western style," a term that I reject here because it assumes an ideal original that Japanese craftsmen were simply copying.

77. To what extent *daiku* incorporated the constructive (as opposed to ornamental) details of "Western" carpentry into their own practices is a complex one, and has never been subjected to more than case-study investigation. Existing studies show tremendous variation. My own examination of the frame of a convincingly "Western-style" house at Meiji Gakuin in Tokyo (the Imbry-kan), constructed for a foreign missionary by *daiku* from Niigata in 1880, revealed an exceedingly complicated arrangement of Japanese, British, and American details. Yet even the act of isolating a "detail" and naming it "British" or "American" is fraught with difficulty, as we are dealing here with continuous systems. The roof of the Imbry-kan for example, shaded from purely Japanese areas to purely British ones, yet the particular British choices were carefully chosen for their compatibility with, if not similarity to, the Japanese ones. The details of the outer wall system were all American, yet put together in a way no American carpenter had ever seen. If the Imbry-kan is taken as an extreme example of Euro-

American influence extending even to the interior structure, it is still far from a pure or textbook example of technology transfer. For further discussion, see Gregory Clancey, *Meiji Gakuin senkyoshi-kan (Imbry-kan) no kōzō: kenchiku chosa hokoku* (Tokyo: Meiji Gakuin, 1996).

78. My information about the history of these family-owned companies comes mainly from Kikuoka Tomoya, *Kensetsugyō o okoshita hitobito* (Tokyo: Shōkokusha, 1993). The stories of the Shimizu and Takenaka firms in particular have been absorbed into the master-narrative of Japanese architectural history in a way that the histories of general contracting firms have not been in the United States and Europe.

79. Muramatsu Teijirō, "History of the Building Design Department of Takenaka Kōmuten," in Building Design Dept. of Takenaka Kōmuten, *Takenaka kōmuten sekei bin* (Tokyo: Shinkenchiku-sha, 1987); Muramatsu, "The Japanese Construction Industry IV," *The Japan Architect*, no. 318 (January–February 1968): 139–46; Takenaka Kōmuten Shichijūnenshi Hensan Iinkai, ed., *Takenaka Kōmuten shichijūnenshi* (Tokyo: Takenaka Kōmuten, 1969).

80. I am not making a naive argument that the modern-day firms of Shimizu-gumi and Takenaka Kōmuten are just Meiji-period *daiku* writ large. My point is only that it is impossible to identify a moment when such companies stop being *daiku*, or lose their "*daiku*-ness."

81. Muramatsu believes that Takenaka's coining of the new word *Kōmuten* as its name for "firm" or "company" around 1909 sought to express the sense of a "design-build" entity (Muramatsu, "History of the Building Design Department of Takenaka Kōmuten," p. 35).

82. Initially the design and construction offices within these firms were strictly separated, and architects did not supervise building sites *(gemba)*, which would have meant managing *daiku* and other artisans. The first company architect to cross this line and manage the building process itself was Kitamura Kōzō, when he became the Osaka branch head of Shimizu-gumi in 1913 [Nihon Kenchiku Gakkai, ch. 11]. The fact that this "crossing" is recorded at all suggests its cultural import. Even today these companies have not "evolved" into firms fully complementary to a professional architecture. In the case of Takenaka Kōmuten, for example, 60 percent of its work was designed in-house in 1985.

83. Author's interview with architect Yanagida Ryōzō of Yanagida, Ishizuka, and Associates, Sapporo and Tokyo, 1994.

84. Conder, "The Practice of Architecture in Japan," p. 215.

85. Kikuoka, p. 229.

86. Even the Imperial University professors who succeeded Conder, such as Naka-mura Tetsutarō in 1889, often found part-time employment with Shimizu and its competitors (Kikuoka, p. 229).

87. This is not to say that being a *daiku*, even a *daiku*-capitalist, erased the many differences constructed around artisan and samurai ancestry. According to Muramatsu, "Construction . . . until after the Second World War, went under a set of names which implied scorn, and some people went so far as to joff, 'scratch a construction worker and find a thief.' The fact is that until 1925, members of the construction industry were not eligible to run for the Diet" (Muramatsu, "The Japanese Construction Industry IV," p. 141).

88. Stewart, p. 31; Hatsuda, pp. 206–8.

89. Kajima Iwakichi, one of the *daiku* we encountered in Yokohama, did so much work for the railroad bureau that he was nicknamed "Tetsudō [Railroad] Kajima" (Kikuoka, p. 35).

90. Hatsuda quotes Conder's student Tatsuno Kingo as saying, in a eulogy to an architect who entered ministerial service in this period, that the latter had helped "break the bad habits of the Edo period, such as the *sakujikata* habit," by which was meant the ministerial employment of *daiku* in design/build positions. "An honest wind blew into the architectural world," continued Tatsuno. Japanese architects, like their British and American counterparts, would view the world of building artisans as essentially corrupt.

91. Endō Akihisa, *Hokkaido jōtakushiwa* (Tokyo: Sumai no Toshokan Shuppankyoku, 1994); Endō, "Kaitakushi eizenjigyō no kenkyū" (unpublished manuscript in author's possession, 1961); Koshino Takeshi, *Hokkaido ni okeru shoki yōfū kenchiku no kenkyū* (Sapporo: Hokkaido Daigaku Toshokankakai, 1993). For an overview of the use of American experts in the colonization of Hokkaido, see Fujita Fumiko, *Hokkaido o kaitakushita amerikajin* (Tokyo: Shinchosha, 1993).

92. Endō, "Kaitakushi eizenjigyō no kenkyū."

93. A literature that symmetrically considers "wa" and "yō" in the work of Meiji period *daiku* awaits production. One recent step in that direction, however, is a master's thesis by Yoshimoto Makiko, "Echigo mazedaiku" (M.A. thesis, architecture, Hokkaido University, 1994), which follows Meiji-period *daiku* from Niigata prefecture as they move back and forth from Hokkaido to Niigata to Tokyo constructing *yōkan* (Western-style buildings) and traditional temples and shrines. A privately published history of a daiku family in Gifu prefecture, *Waʒa takumi hito Sakashita Jinkichi* (Takayama, 1994) by Sakashita Yukari, discusses and illustrates the full corpus of their work from Edo to

early Showa, demonstrating their movement from "wa" to "yō" depending on the commission.

94. In applying the linguistic concept of pidgin to the artifactual world, I am following the discussion in Peter Galison, *Image and Logic* (Chicago: University of Chicago Press, 1997), pp. 48–51, 831–37.

95. Nakatani, "Bakumatsu, Meiji ki kikujutsu no tenkei katei no kenkyū"; Nakatani, *Kinsei kenchikuronshū* (Osaka: Henshū Shuppan Soshikitai Asetate, 2004).

96. Ibid.

97. Galison. The best examples of the creolization of "Western" architecture in Japan are the numerous school buildings, most constructed by local *daiku*, built in every area of the Empire beginning in the 1870s–1880s.

TWO • EARTHQUAKES

1. Said Hattori Ichizō, the first president of the Japan Seismological Society, in 1878: "It seems strange that in Japan, which is subject to very frequent earthquakes, so little notice has been taken of the subject" ("Destructive Earthquakes of Japan," *Transactions of the Asiatic Society of Japan* [hereafter *TASJ*] 6, part 2 [1878–79]: 249). The degree to which Japanese did or did not "notice" earthquakes had become an issue among the foreigners Hattori was addressing. Other Japanese scholars, speaking at a later date to foreign audiences, would reach different conclusions. But always it was the foreign focus on earthquakes that made this question of Japanese notice or concern pressing.

2. R. H. Brunton, "Constructive Art in Japan, Part II," *TASJ* 3 (1875): 72. In addition to constructing lighthouses, Brunton also laid out the first Japanese telegraph line in 1869 (Henry Dyer, *Dai Nippon* [London: Blackie and Son, 1904], p. 145), and recommended the construction of the Ginza to the government in 1872 (Muramatsu Teijirō, "Mokuzō kōzō no kindaika," in Nihon Kenchiku Gakkai, *Kindai Nihon kenchiku-gaku hattatsushi* [Tokyo: Maruzen Kabushiki Gaisha, 1972], p. 11).

3. Josiah Conder, "The Practice of Architecture in Japan," *Japan Weekly Mail* (August 28, 1886), p. 214.

4. Conder, "Domestic Architecture in Japan," *Proceedings of the Royal Institute of British Architects* 3, no. 10 (March 3, 1887): 198.

5. M. J. Lescasse, "Earthquakes and Buildings" (serialized in four parts), *Japan Gazette*, March 2–15, 1877.

6. Brunton, "Constructive Art in Japan, Part I," *TASJ* 2 (1873–74).

7. Henry Dyer, Comments regarding Milne's "On Construction in Earthquake Countries," *Minutes of the Proceedings of the Institution of Civil Engineers* 83, session 1885–86, part 1, paper 2108, pp. 309–13.

8. C. A. W. Pownall, "Notes on Recent Publications Relating to the Effect of Earthquakes on Structures," *Transactions of the Seismological Society of Japan* (hereafter *TSSJ*) 16 (1892): 1–18. This was originally delivered as a lecture in 1891.

9. Brunton, "Constructive Art in Japan, Part I," p. 66.

10. George Cawley, "Some Remarks on Construction in Brick and Wood and Their Relative Suitability in Japan," *TASJ* 6 (1877–78): 315.

11. Brunton, "Constructive Art in Japan, Part I," p. 71.

12. Cawley, "Some Remarks on Construction in Brick and Wood," p. 297.

13. For Japanese joinery, see Kiyoshi Seike, *The Art of Japanese Joinery* (New York: Weatherhill, 1977). Cawley, "Some Remarks on Construction in Brick and Wood," p. 296–98.

14. Conder, "The Effects of the Recent Earthquake upon Buildings," *Japan Weekly Mail* (December 12, 1891), p. 725.

15. Edward Morse, *Japanese Homes and Their Surroundings* (Rutland, VT: Charles E. Tuttle Co., 1972), p. 11 [originally published 1886].

16. Earthquakes of the nondestructive kind occasionally occurred in Great Britain, and from the eighteenth century onward were a subject of scientific investigation. The almost total destruction of Lisbon in the catastrophic earthquake of 1750 (and of a number of large Italian towns in the late eighteenth and early nineteenth centuries) demonstrates that European masonry's record as an earthquake-resistant material was at best mixed. Indeed, the aseismic qualities of masonry—particularly English masonry—was in no sense as solid a fact in Europe as it became among Europeans in Japan.

17. These characteristics were often linked, positively, to Shinto and Buddhism, and negatively to "Japanese superstition." Henry Dyer invokes the latter in describing how the first telegraph line (which had been designed by Brunton) "suffered from the ignorant masses, who looked upon the telegraph as a species of witchcraft and frequently broke down the line, so that the guarding of it was no easy matter" (Dyer, *Dai Nippon*, p. 145).

18. See Yokoyama Toshio, *Japan in the Victorian Mind: A Study of Stereotyped Images of a Nation, 1850–80* (London: Macmillan, 1987). Yokoyama found that the Japanese were already being discussed as "strangely imitative" in British journals of the early 1870s (pp. 106–7).

19. Remarks by Sir Harry Parkes following a lecture at the Asiatic Society of Japan (*TASJ* 3, part 2 [1875]: 32). Resident engineer C. A. W. Pownall agreed, writing in 1891 that "the Japanese type of house was probably adopted for other reasons" than earthquakes (Pownall, p. 2). Architect Josiah Conder wrote that same year (1891) that Japanese carpentry methods "have certainly not been devised with a view to security during earthquakes" (Conder, "The Effects of the Recent Earthquake upon Buildings," p. 726).

20. Brunton, "Constructive Art in Japan, Part I," pp. 78–79.

21. Ibid.

22. This story was related to me in conversation by Dr. Suzuki Hiroyuki.

23. On this phenomenon, which art historians call "Japonisme," see Gabriel Weisberg and Yvonne Weisberg, *Japonisme: An Annotated Bibliography* (New York: Garland Publishing Co., 1990), especially the introductory essay; Elizabeth Aslin, *The Aesthetic Movement, Prelude to Art Nouveau* (New York: Frederick A. Praeger, 1969); and Sigfried Wichman, *Japonisme: The Japanese Influence in Western Art since 1858* (London: Thames and Hudson, 1981).

24. See particularly Joshua Rose, "The Japanese Government Building at the Centennial Grounds in Fairmount Park," *Scientific American Supplement*, no. 11, March 11, 1876, p. 169; and "The Japanese at the Centennial," *Scientific American Supplement*, no. 25, June 17, 1876.

25. Ibid.; Lavan, "Are the Japanese Workmen Slow?" *Scientific American Supplement*, no. 20, May 13, 1876, p. 309.

26. *American Architect and Building News*, January 8, 1876, p. 2; and January 22, 1876, p. 26.

27. *American Architect and Building News*, February 5, 1876, pp. 42–43.

28. *American Architect and Building News*, February 12, 1876, pp. 50–51.

29. Ibid., p. 55.

30. T. Jackson Lears, *No Place of Grace* (New York: Pantheon Books, 1981).

31. Remarks of A. Diosy, *Transactions and Proceedings of the Japan Society, London* (hereafter *TPJSL*), vol. 2, second session, 1892–93, p. 227.

32. Ibid.

33. Sir Rutherford Alcock, *The Capital of the Tycoon. A Narrative of a Three Year's Residence in Japan* (New York: Greenwood Press, 1969), vol. 1, p. 414. For an excellent discussion of British tropes, including Alcock's "curiously reversed" Japan and its influence on subsequent writers, see Yokoyama.

34. Cawley, "Wood and Its Application to Japanese Artistic and Industrial Design," *Transactions and Proceedings of the Japan Society of London* 2 (1892–93): 206–23.

35. Ibid.

36. "Joinery"—the making of interior woodwork, doors, and windows—was the least "constructive" part of Anglo-American building-carpentry. Cawley's compliment to the British ability to construct large objects, even if meant to apply to carpenters, would have but weakly reflected onto the man on stage.

37. Cawley, "Wood and Its Application to Japanese Artistic and Industrial Design."

38. Ibid.

39. "The Britain of the East" occurs again as the subtitle of Henry Dyers's *Dai Nippon*. Dyer was the first principal of Kōbudaigakkō, and Cawley's former boss.

40. Alcock, p. 109.

41. Cawley, "Wood and Its Application to Japanese Artistic and Industrial Design," p. 219.

42. Ibid., p. 207.

43. Yokoyama, surveying English journal articles of the 1870s, finds that already the love of certain writers for "Old Japan" was "counterbalanced by their hatred of New Japan, which was, in their eyes, not at all Japan but industrialized Britain." One writer spoke of "an eruption of Birmingham into Arcadia" (p. 104).

44. The most complete account of Dresser in English is Stuart Durant, *Christopher Dresser* (London: Academy Group, 1993), and in Japanese, Suzuki Hiroyuki, *Victorian gothic no hōkai* (Tokyo: Chūō Kōron Bijutsu Shuppan, 1996), pp. 63–93. I have relied equally on both accounts. Dresser held appointments as art advisor and chief designer at several large manufacturing firms in the early 1870s. He remained an outsider in the mainstream English art world because of his collaboration with industry and his close association with the government design school at South Kensington.

45. Suzuki, *Victorian gothic no hōkai*, pp. 72–78.

46. Christopher Dresser, *Japan: Its Architecture, Art, and Manufactures* (New York: Garland Publishing Co., 1977), pp. 236–37 [originally published 1882].

47. Ibid., pp. 235–36.

48. Ibid., pp. 237–38. According to Suzuki, Dresser visited two pagodas, at Asakusa and Kofukuji (p. 80).

49. Suzuki, *Victorian gothic no hōkai*, pp. 78–84, 123–26.

50. Ralph Adams Cram, "The Early Architecture of Japan," *The Architectural Review*, 1893.

51. H. H. Stratham, "Japanese Architecture," *Architectural Review*, October 1912, pp. 177–88.

52. Ibid.

53. Ibid.

54. Cram, *Impressions of Japanese Architecture and the Allied Arts* (Boston: Marshall Jones Co., 1905), p. 39.

55. Crane, quoted in David B. Stewart, *The Making of a Modern Japanese Architecture* (Tokyo: Kōdansha, 1987), p. 74.

56. Stratham, p. 188.

57. Strange, "Architecture in Japan," *Architectural Review* 1 (1897): 132.

58. Portions of this letter from Kozima to Conder were quoted during remarks by Roger T. Conder, Josiah's brother, in *Proceedings of the Royal Institute of British Architects* 3 (June 1886): 255.

59. M. J. Lescasse, "Description of a System Intended to Give a Great Security to Buildings in Masonry Against Earthquakes," in John Milne, ed., *Construction in Earthquake Countries* (Tokyo: Seismological Society of Japan, 1889), pp. 85–86; the volume was published as a special issue (vol. 14) of the Society's *Transactions*. This is an English abstract of Lescasse's article, which had originally appeared in French in *Memoires de la Société des Ingenieurs civils*, April 6, 1887, p. 212. The report of Japanese dissent by the Frenchman Lescasse was itself part of a dissent (albeit limited) from the opinions of his British colleagues. Partly because the French had provided so much technological and political support to the Tokugawa government, technical education and the construction of railroads and other public works in Japan following the overthrow of the Shogunate was dominated by British *yatoi*. Although equally committed to a masonry Japan, Lescasse, as a French engineer, was enough of an outsider to take seriously accounts of Japanese doubt. He became one of the few foreign engineers to advocate, at least in print, reforming northern European "constructive science" to meet what he regarded as a new and exceptional natural threat. Lescasse developed a way of reinforcing European masonry by embedding iron rods in the joints. The method was not only expensive, but constituted an admission that European practices could not be transferred to Japan without adaptation. It was Tachikawa's discovery of just such reinforcement in Yokosuka and Osaka that had led him to doubt the veracity of British claims of masonry's aseismic nature.

60. Tachikawa Tomokata, "Kōbushō yontō gishu Tachikawa Tomokata shoshin," in Nihon Kenchiku Gakkai, *Kindai Nihon kenchiku-gaku hattatsushi* (Tokyo: Maruzen Kabushiki Gaisha, 1972), p. 14. This is also discussed in Muramatsu, *Nihon kindai kenchiku gijutsushi* (Tokyo: Shōkokusha, 1976), p. 75. Muramatsu, who also edited the Tachikawa article in the Nihon Kenchiku Gakkai book cited above, dates it differently in each place. The first citation has it written in 1889, and the second in 1879. The second book is the later of the two, so he may have been correcting an earlier mistake.

61. Ibid.

62. John Milne, "Preliminary Report on Earthquake Motion," *TSSJ* 14 (1891): 26.

63. Muramatsu, *Nihon kindai kenchiku gijutsushi*, p. 79. On Kigo and the Imperial Palace project, see Cherie Wendelken, "The Tectonics of Japanese Style: Architect and Carpenter in the Late Meiji Period," *Art Journal* 55 (Fall 1996): 28–37.

64. Muramatsu, *Nihon kindai kenchiku gijutsushi*, p. 75.

65. Fujimori, *Nihon no kindai kenchiku* (Tokyo: Iwanami Shoten, 1993), vol. 1, pp. 47–56.

66. Brunton, "Constructive Art in Japan, Part II," pp. 22–23, mentions the Customs House and Town Hall at Yokohama, and "new government offices" in Tokyo, as having been built with such a system. He also suggests that is was a collaborative invention of *daiku* and foreigners in the Treaty ports, a claim that Dr. Fujimori's research has substantiated; Cawley noted that the system was "now being largely used by the government for the numerous departmental offices in Tokyo and other places" (Cawley, "Some Remarks on Construction in Brick and Wood," p. 306).

67. Ibid.

68. Fujimori, *Nihon no kindai kenchiku*, pp. 47–56.

69. Hatsuda, *Shokunin-tachi no seiyō kenchiku* (Tokyo: Kōdansha, 1997).

70. Funakoshi Kinya, "The Adoption of European Architecture in Japan" (1883, Architecture Course, Kōbudaigakkō), handwritten manuscript in Architecture Library, Faculty of Engineering, Tokyo University.

71. Ibid.

72. Sone, "A Thesis on [the] Future Domestic Architecture of Japan" (September 1879, Architecture Course, Kōbudaigakkō), handwritten manuscript in Architecture Library, Faculty of Engineering, Tokyo University.

73. Ibid.

74. Ibid.

75. Tatsuno Kingo, "Graduation Thesis" (1879, Architecture Course, Kōbudaigakkō), handwritten manuscript in Architecture Library, Faculty of Engineering, Tokyo University.

76. Ibid.

77. Ibid.

78. Funakoshi.

THREE • THE SEISMOLOGISTS

1. The only biography of Milne, from which I have taken my general outline of his life and career, is A. L. Herbert-Gustar and P. A. Nott, *John Milne: Father of Modern*

Seismology (Tenterden, UK: Paul Norbury, 1980). There are briefer but more critical accounts of Milne in Charles Davison, *The Founders of Seismology* (Cambridge: Cambridge University Press, 1927); Gooday and Low, pp. 121–27; and Robert Muir Wood, "Robert Mallet and John Milne—Earthquakes Incorporated in Victorian Britain," *Earthquake Engineering and Structural Dynamics* 17 (1988): 107–42.

2. The Seismological Society was racially mixed from the beginning, with thirty-six Japanese members in 1881 out of the ninety-nine resident in Japan (eighteen members lived abroad). Most of the non-Japanese were British, but there were also eight Italians and a handful of Americans, including the philosopher and art critic Ernest Fenollosa. The society always had a Japanese president, and became more accommodating to the Japanese membership over time, publishing its journal in both languages starting in 1883, and at the same time instituting Japanese and foreign officer positions (*Transactions of the Seismological Society of Japan* [hereafter *TSSJ*], vol. 2, July–December 1880, and vol. 5, May–December 1882). But overwhelmingly, the largest number of articles in the Seismological Society journal were always by foreign members of the Kōbudaigakkō and Imperial University faculties, particularly Milne.

3. Robert Mallet, who coined the word "seismology" and published *The Great Neapolitan Earthquake of 1857: The First Principles of Observational Seismology . . .* in 1862, was a civil engineer. He was still the most influential spokesman for earthquakes when Milne went to Japan, but never attempted to institutionalize seismology as a discipline. See the chapter on Mallet in Davison, *Founders of Seismology*, pp. 65–86, and also Wood. Wood points out that a number of Germans were publishing seismological research at the same time. Italy, Switzerland, and France also contained earthquake research clusters.

4. Milne, "The Earthquake in Japan of Feb. 22, 1880," *TSSJ* 1, part 2 (1880): 1–115 (quotation p. 1).

5. Quoted in Davison, p. 76.

6. Milne, "The Earthquake in Japan of Feb. 22, 1880," p. 2.

7. Ibid.

8. Milne, "Notes on the Recent Earthquakes of Yedo Plain, and Their Effects on Certain Buildings," *TSSJ* 2 (July–December 1880): 27–35.

9. Ibid.

10. Remarks by W. E. Ayrton following Brunton, "Constructive Art in Japan, Part II," *Transactions of the Asiatic Society of Japan* (hereafter *TASJ*) 3 (1875): 33–34. In 1878, after another discussion on earthquakes at the Asiatic Society in Tokyo, the American education specialist Dr. David Murray defended the aseismic qualities of temple

buildings and warned that *yatoi* must "look forward both with interest and concern to the effect of a destructive earthquake upon the brick buildings which had been recently erected in this city" (quoted from George Cawley, "Some Remarks on Constructions in Brick and Wood and Their Relative Suitability for Japan," *TASJ* 6 [1877–78]).

11. J. Perry and W. E. Ayrton, "On a Neglected Principle That May Be Employed in Earthquake Measurement," *TASJ* 5 (1876–77). "Terrestrial physics," a term with an ancient pedigree, would increasingly give way in the late nineteenth and early twentieth centuries to "geophysics." Although seismology is conventionally considered a subcategory of geophysics, not only did the first term precede the second, but it helped in some sense to construct it. The invention of more sophisticated instruments for exploring the earth's crust—including the seismograph—in the later nineteenth century clearly helped reinvigorate "terrestrial physics" to the extent that a new nomenclature seemed desirable, if not necessary.

12. The pamphlet is quoted in remarks by Ayrton following a paper by Hattori Ichizō (*TASJ* 6, part 2 [1878]: 289).

13. Herbert-Gustar and Nott, p. 45.

14. Ibid., p. 13.

15. A complete merger with one's research was of course one mark of a late nineteenth-century "man of science." Milne was so marked by his nickname among *yatoi* ("Earthquake" Milne) and also by the comment of his friend John Perry, to the Institution of Civil Engineers in London, that Milne appeared "actually to love earthquakes while others feared them" (*TSSJ* 11 [1887]: 139).

16. Milne, *Seismology* (London: Kegan, Paul, Trench, Truber & Co., 1898), pp. 166–67.

17. Milne, remarks following Walter Weston's lecture "Exploration in the Japanese Alps, 1891–1894," *Geographical Journal* 7, no. 3 (February 1896): 146–49.

18. Ibid.

19. See George H. Ford, "The Felicitous Space: The Cottage Controversy," in U. C. Knoepflmacher and G. B. Tennyson, *Nature and the Victorian Imagination* (Berkeley: University of California Press, 1977), pp. 29–48.

20. Wooden Japanese houses after a minor or "semidestructive" earthquake were of course often covered with cracks on exterior stucco or internal plaster, but these were of so different an order than the masonry cracks that Mallet had examined and recorded in Naples that no "science" of reading them ever developed.

21. Milne, "The Earthquake in Japan of Feb. 22, 1880," p. 115.

22. Quoted in Herbert-Gustar and Nott, p. 80.

23. James Dewey and Perry Byerly, "The Early History of Seismometry (to 1900)," *Bulletin of the Seismological Society of America* 59, no. 1 (February 1969): 183–227.

24. Milne, "Notes on the Recent Earthquake of Yedo Plain," p. 35. A mercury-based seismograph invented by the Italian physicist and meteorologist Luigi Palmieri (who also invented the word in 1859) was actually operating in Tokyo's meteorological observatory when Milne arrived in 1876. Palmieri's interest in seismicity came mainly through his monitoring of volcanic Mount Vesuvius. The seismographs invented by Ewing and Gray operated on a different principle than Palmieri's, however, and provided a new level of sensitivity (as well as a real graphic record or "seismogram"). Tokyo's expatriates thereafter downgraded Palmieri's device by reclassifying it as a "seismoscope" and eventually had it replaced at the Tokyo observatory with an Ewing-Gray-Milne machine. Italian seismometry, which remained vigorous, would eventually adopt the principle of the Japanese machines. For a detailed discussion of European seismometry, see Dewey and Byerly.

25. Wrote the Swiss earthquake investigator F. A. Forel in 1887: "More had been learnt from the seismograph-tracer of the Anglo-Japanese observers in two years, than twenty centuries of European science had been able to show" (*TSSJ* 11 [1887]: 165). "Seismometry," as the invention of seismic recording devices was called in Tokyo, was at least indirectly influenced by the Kōbudaigakkō interest in telegraphy. The new seismographs and telegraphs were in effect siblings, as Thomas Gray, one of the seismograph's three "fathers," and the one most responsible for the construction and actual workings of the final prototype, was Kōbudaigakkō professor of telegraphic engineering. Seismographs were mechanical rather than electrical devices although, like telegraphs, clocks were integral to their working. James Ewing seems to have been the most committed of Tokyo's seismometrists, however, contributing no less than eight articles on the construction and operation of seismographs to *TSSJ* between 1880 and 1883, when he returned to Britain. Representative papers by Ewing include: "A New Form of Pendulum Seismograph," *TSSJ* 1 (1880): 38–43; "On a New Seismograph for Horizontal Motion," *TSSJ* 2 (1880): 45–49; and "Earthquake Measurement," *Memoirs of the Science Dept., Tokyo Daigaku* 9 (1883). Milne and Gray published research related to seismometry in the same period, sometimes in British journals, and the cooperation between them and Ewing seems to have been tinged with some rivalry.

26. On Ayrton and Perry in Japan, see Takahashi Yūzō, "William Edward Ayrton at the Imperial College of Engineering in Tokyo . . . ," *IEEE Transactions on Education* 33, no. 2 (May 1990): 198–205; for Ewing, see Sigalia Dostrovsky, "James Alfred Ewing," in Charles Gillispie, ed., *Dictionary of Scientific Biography* (New York: Scrib-

ner, 1970). Both Ayrton and Ewing had studied under Thomson (later Lord Kelvin) in Scotland. Ewing would eventually become principal and vice chancellor of the University of Edinburgh, and Ayrton and Perry would also maintain distinguished careers on returning to Britain (see Graeme Gooday, "Teaching Telegraphy and Electrotechnics in the Physics Laboratory: William Ayrton and the Creation of an Academic Space for Electrical Engineering in Britain, 1873–1884," *History of Technology* 13 [1991]: 73–111). Milne's career as a seismologist probably benefited from the early departure from Japan of Ayrton, Perry, Ewing, and Gray, who necessarily turned to other research interests.

27. For the triangular relationship between geology, biology, and physics (or Charles Lyell, Charles Darwin, and Lord Kelvin), see Joe E. Burchfield, *Lord Kelvin and the Age of the Earth* (Chicago: University of Chicago Press, 1975). Earthquakes had been "put on the map" of geology by Lyell, for whom they were important evidence for uniformatarianism. Darwin was also a geologist and a devotee of Lyell, and even became a student of earthquakes after experiencing a couple in South America during the voyage of the *Beagle*. Kelvin's interest in earthquakes would come later, and would have to do with the use of seismic waves to characterize material at the earth's core.

28. George Cawley, "Some Remarks on Constructions in Brick and Wood and Their Suitability for Japan," *TASJ* 6 (1877–78): 317.

29. Milne, "On Construction in Earthquake Countries," *Minutes of the Proceedings of the Institution of Civil Engineers* 83, session 1885–86, part 1, paper 2108, pp. 278–320.

30. Milne, "Seismology," *Kagaku zasshi* 20 (1883): 313–18.

31. Milne, "On the Earthquake Phenomena of Japan," *Report of the 54th Meeting of the British Association for the Advancement of Science* (London, 1885), pp. 248–49.

32. Ibid.

33. Milne, *Earthquakes and Other Earth Movements* (New York: D. Appleton, 1886); Milne, *Seismology*, p. 158.

34. At one point in *Earthquakes and Other Earth Movements*, Milne even criticizes the introduction of triangularity (diagonal braces) into roof construction, noting that some parts of Kōbudaigakkō's roofs "have suffered for their rigidity, being twisted and bent" (p. 125).

35. Milne, *Earthquakes and Other Earth Movements*, pp. 128–29. Milne had made certain of these suggestions for reforming masonry construction as early as 1880 ("The Earthquake in Japan of Feb. 22, 1880," *TSSJ* 1, part 2). He attributed the suggestion of arranging windows along a diagonal line to Perry.

36. Ibid.

37. Milne, "On Construction in Earthquake Countries."

38. Dyer, Comments regarding John Milne's "On Construction in Earthquake Countries," in *Minutes of the Proceedings of the Institution of Civil Engineers* 83, session 1885–86, pp. 309–13.

39. Ibid.

40. Ibid.

41. Ibid.

42. Josiah Conder, "The Practice of Architecture in Japan," *Japan Weekly Mail*, August 28, 1886, pp. 213–16.

43. Ibid.

44. Taki Daikichi, "Future Architecture in Japan" (1883, Architecture Course, Kōbudaigakkō); handwritten manuscript in Architecture Library, Faculty of Engineering, University of Tokyo.

45. Milne, *Earthquakes and Other Earth Movements*, pp. 123–24.

46. Yamao Yōzō, who had been influential in founding Kōbudaigakkō, eventually became Viscount Yamao and Controller of the Imperial Household. Although Yamao had declined the presidency of the Seismological Society, he had, at Dyer's instigation, accepted the same post in the Japanese Institution (or Society) of Engineers, which likely contributed to his value as an ally in Milne's text (Dyer, *Dai Nippon* [London: Blackie and Son, 1904], p. 26).

47. Brunton had left Japanese employment in 1876, the year that Milne and Conder both arrived (Muramatsu Teijirō, "Mokuso no kindaika," in Nihon Kenchiku Gakkai, *Kindai Nihon kenchiku-gaku hattatsushi* [Tokyo: Maruzen Kabushiki Gaisha, 1972], p. 11).

48. As early as the first meeting of the Seismological Society of Japan, in 1880, Milne had said, "Should we, for instance, wish to know the reasons why the people of Japan or England are as we see them now, we shall find ourselves driven back from history to geology" (*TSSJ* 1 [April–June 1880]: 6).

49. Milne, "Earthquake Effects[,] Emotional and Moral," *TSSJ* 11 (1887): 94, 109.

50. Ibid., p. 109.

51. Ibid.

52. Kenneth Pyle's discussion of young intellectuals in this period excavates a language rich in Darwinian metaphors. Even the nativist Shiga Shigetaka's "Declaration of Principles Held by *Nihonjin*" (the newspaper of the Seikyosha movement), published in 1888, describes *kokusui* (national essence) as a force that "germinated, grew, and developed through adaptation to the influence of all environmental factors." The "future evolution" of *kokusui*, continued Shiga, "will be no more than the proper application of the fundamental principles of biology" (Kenneth Pyle, *The New Generation*

in Meiji Japan: Problems in Cultural Identity, 1885–1895 [Stanford: Stanford University Press, 1969], p. 68). Also see Pyle, pp. 36–37, 61, 110–11, 150.

53. For a discussion of the influence of social Darwinism in Meiji Japan, and on Katō in particular, see Watanabe Masao, *The Japanese and Western Science* (Philadelphia: University of Pennsylvania Press, 1976), pp. 65–83. Pyle calls Katō "perhaps the best-known exponent of Darwinian theories in Japan" (Pyle, p. 111n). See also Morris Low, "The Japanese Nation in Evolution: W. E. Griffis, Hybridity, and the Whiteness of the Japanese Race," *History and Anthropology* 11 (1999): 2–3.

54. Katō's long patronage of seismology was partly a function of his Imperial University presidency, but his name is met with so consistently in the writings of seismologists that it seems to have extended beyond that. In an 1883 monograph on seismometry, for example, James Ewing thanks Katō "for providing me with the means of establishing a Seismological Observatory."

55. Pyle, p. 23.

56. According to Watanabe, Katō learned from Buckle that, in Katō's own words, "any statement is meaningless if it is not based on science" (p. 71).

57. Milne, "Earthquake Effects[,] Emotional and Moral," p. 109.

58. Pyle, pp. 23, 89. There is a good but brief discussion of Buckle in Theodore Porter, *The Rise of Statistical Thinking, 1820–1900* (Princeton: Princeton University Press, 1986), pp. 60–61.

59. Milne, "Earthquake Effects[,] Emotional and Moral," p. 111. Historian Richard Minear classes Chamberlain among the three "most influential Japanese scholars of the last hundred years" and one of the best examples, in Japanese studies, of Edward Said's "orientalist" (Richard Minear, "Orientalism and the Study of Japan," *Journal of Asian Studies* 39, no. 3 [May 1980]: 507–10). "The Orient," as we have seen, could be mapped in many ways, but Chamberlain was particularly consistent (and insistent) in applying the geographic (East-West) dyad. President and longtime member of Tokyo's Asiatic Society, Chamberlain was also one of few *yatoi* with a command of Japanese. In his later cataloging of Japanese earthquake records, Milne relied upon Chamberlain's linguistic skills.

60. Milne, "Earthquake Effects[,] Emotional and Moral," p. 112.

61. Andrew Markus, "Gesaku Authors and the Ansei Earthquake of 1855," in Dennis Washburn and Alan Tansman, eds., *Studies in Modern Japanese Literature: Essays in Honor of Edwin McClellan* (Ann Arbor: Center for Japanese Studies, University of Michigan, 1997), pp. 54–59.

62. Although Sekiya and Ōmori were the drivers of this project, the collection was edited for publication by their colleague Toyama Minoru ("Dainihon Jishin Shiryo,"

Reports of the IEIC 46 [1904]; Kikuchi Dairoku, *Recent Seismological Investigations in Japan* [Tokyo, ca. 1904], p. 9).

63. Milne, "Earthquake Effects[,] Emotional and Moral," p. 113.

64. Ibid., p. 92.

65. Ibid., p. 93.

66. Ibid., pp. 93–94.

67. Dyer, Comments regarding Milne, p. 311.

68. Cawley, "Some Remarks on Constructions in Brick and Wood," p. 316.

69. Conder, "Domestic Architecture in Japan," *Proceedings of the Royal Institute of British Architects* 3, no. 10 (March 3, 1887): 198.

70. Brunton, "Constructive Art in Japan, Part II," *TASJ* 3 (1875): 72.

71. Stuart Durant, *Christopher Dresser* (London: Academy Group, 1993), p. 11. Sand notes that *yokan*, or Western-style wings built on Japanese houses as formal reception rooms, were being constructed as early as 1874 (Jordan Sand, *House and Home in Modern Japan: Architecture, Domestic Space, and Bourgeois Culture, 1880–1930* [Cambridge, MA: Harvard University Asia Center, 2003], p. 41). Designs for such hybrid structures were published in Japanese pattern-books into the late Meiji period; see for example Yoshihara Yonejiro, ed., *Wayō jūtaku kenchiku ʐushū* (Tokyo: Kenchiku Shoin, 1910).

72. Edward Morse, *Japanese Homes and Their Surroundings* (Rutland, VT: Charles E. Tuttle Co., 1972).

73. Cherie Wendelken notes that "the [Japanese] house, particularly the common house, does not appear as a significant object of interest to the architect as historian, practitioner or restorationist until the Taisho Period (1912–26)" ("Living with the Past: Preservation and Development in Japanese Architecture and Town Planning," Ph.D. dissertation, MIT, 1994, p. 28).

74. Morse, p. 10.

75. It may have been not only Morse's nationality, but also his having been a member of the science faculty of the Imperial University (rather than Kōbudaigakkō), that allowed him so comfortably to attack British architects and engineers.

76. Morse, pp. 12–13.

77. On dismantling as a firefighting technique, see Kawagoe Kunio et al., *Kenchiku anʐenron (Shin kenchikugaku Taikei 12)* (Tokyo: Shōkokusha, 1983), pp. 320–24. Kawagoe notes that dismantling disproportionately affected the rented houses of the poorest class (called *nagaya*), which densely packed the interiors of city blocks in Edo/Tokyo and other Japanese cities. Merchants' houses and shops not only faced major streets (which served as firebreaks) but were often of *dōʐō-ʐukuri* construction and so relatively safer from fire and immune from dismantling.

78. Sand, p. 136.

79. Sir Rutherford Alcock, *The Capital of the Tycoon. A Narrative of a Three Year's Residence in Japan* (New York: Greenwood Press, 1969), vol. 1, p. 124.

80. Wendelken, "Living with the Past," pp. 25–26. This was one of a number of such regulations enacted after the Meireki Fire, which destroyed the greater portion of Edo (Tokyo) in 1660. The Meireki Fire would not be matched in ferocity or extent of damage until the fire following the Great Kantō (Tokyo) Earthquake of 1923.

81. Kawagoe notes that the use of *dozō-zukuri* in Edo greatly increased following the Meireki Fire of 1660. Two centuries later, when the city of Tokyo issued building regulations following a significant fire in 1881, the law gave *dozō-zukuri* equal status with brick and stone as a fire-resistant material (pp. 322, 324).

82. A second method of fireproofing wooden walls, called *namako*, was also invented in the Edo period but became much more common in the Meiji, and was particularly associated with *wayō setchū* buildings in Yokohama. It used square stone tiles placed diagonally, with thick white raised plaster joints run over and between them, creating a unique visual effect.

83. Morse, pp. 10–11.

84. Conder, "The Practice of Architecture in Japan," p. 215.

FOUR • THE NATIONAL ESSENCE

1. Kenneth Pyle, *The New Generation in Meiji Japan: Problems in Cultural Identity, 1885–1895* (Stanford: Stanford University Press, 1969).

2. Julia Adenay Thomas, *Reconfiguring Nature in Japanese Political Ideology* (Berkeley: University of California Press, 2002), p. 173. See particularly Thomas's discussion of Karatani Kojin's claim for a *fukei no hakkan* (discovery of landscape) in Japanese literature of mid- to late Meiji (pp. 174–76).

3. *Japan Weekly Mail*, April 23, 1889.

4. An article by Yokohama journalist H. S. Palmer suggests that the change in Japanese "female costume" was as unpopular with male expatriates as with Japanese men. "This grievous change, now in progress, is loudly deprecated by all on-lookers. With most of us the first feeling is one of wrathful indignation" (H. S. Palmer, "Social Problems in Japan" [Tokyo], April 14, 1887, accessed on Higuchi Jiro and Higuchi Yoichiro's Web site for the Henry Spencer Palmer Museum: http://homepage3.nifty.com/yhiguchi/).

5. Masako Gavin, *Shiga Shigetaka, 1863–1927: The Forgotten Enlightener* (Richmond, UK: Curzon Press, 2001).

6. For discussions of the Rokumeikan and what went on there, see Watanabe Toshio, "Josiah Conder's Rokumeikan: Architecture and National Representation in Meiji Japan," *Art Journal* 55 (Fall 1996): 21–27; and Donald H. Shively, "The Japanization of the Middle Meiji," in Shively, ed., *Tradition and Modernization in Japanese Culture* (Princeton: Princeton University Press, 1971), pp. 94–96. Shively captures the Rokumeikan's epicentral character, noting that after its opening in 1883, which was attended by 1,100 people, "dance studios mushroomed throughout the capital" (p. 95). The phrase "end of the *Rokumeikan* era" is taken from Reynolds, p. 81, but variations appear in many historical texts. Fujimori writes that it was the dream of Foreign Minister Inoue Kaoru "to convert the whole of Tokyo into a kind of gigantic *Rokumeikan*" (Fujimori Terunobu, "Josiah Conder and Japan," in Suzuki Hiroyuki, ed., *Josiah Conder: A Victorian Architect in Japan* [Tokyo: Bijutsu Shuppan, 1997], p. 19).

7. The first generation of Western teachers was, by and large, the only one, their Japanese students taking their places as early as the following decade. By the end of the 1880s, the technical ministries and their educational system had become self-generating.

8. Kōbudaigakkō would be rehoused on the new Imperial University campus in a brick building designed by Tatsuno (Henry Dyer, *Dai Nippon* [London: Blackie and Son], p. 90).

9. Suzuki Hiroyuki, *Josiah Conder: A Victorian Architect in Japan*. Conder was also appointed, in 1886, to a position in the government's new Rinji kenchikukyoku (Temporary Architecture Bureau), which carried out major government building projects through the end of the decade (Muramatsu Teijirō, *Nihon kindai kenchiku gijutsushi* [Tokyo: Shōkokusha, 1976], p. 47).

10. Cherie Wendelken, "The Tectonics of Japanese Style: Architect and Carpenter in the Late Meiji Period," *Art Journal* 55 (Fall 1996): 30–34.

11. H. S. Palmer, "The Story of an Earthquake," unpublished article for *Times* of London (Tokyo, March 1, 1887), accessed on Higuchi and Higuchi Web site.

12. Wendelken, "The Tectonics of Japanese Style."

13. Kōda Rohan, *Gojūnotō* (Tokyo: Iwanami Shoten, 1953).

14. Lawrence W. Chisholm, *Fenollosa: The Far East and American Culture* (New Haven: Yale University Press, 1963), p. 46.

15. John M. Rosenfield, "Western-Style Painting in the Early Meiji Period and Its Critics," in Shively, pp. 181–219. For more recent discussion of Okakura, see two works by Stefan Tanaka: *Japan's Orient: Rendering Pasts into History* (Berkeley: University of California Press, 1993) and "Imaging History: Inscribing Belief in the Nation," *The Journal of Asian Studies* 53, no. 1 (February 1994): 24–44.

16. *Japan Weekly Mail*, August 28, 1886, p. 213.

17. The Imperial Ministry would eventually become a major patron of Western-style architecture, even hiring one of Conder's students, Katayama Tōkuma. Near the end of the Meiji period Katayama would design and oversee the construction of a perfectly European-looking, steel-reinforced masonry palace (the Akasaka Detached Palace, constructed between 1897 and 1908), which was made hugely expensive by the need for seismic reinforcements. The Emperor, in the end, would decline to live there. For a good account of Tatsuno and Katayama (including a discussion of the Akasaka Detached Palace project), see William Coaldrake, *Architecture and Authority in Japan* (New York: Routledge, 1996), pp. 218–22, 233.

18. J. Morduant Crook, "Josiah Conder in England: Education, Training, and Background," in Suzuki Hiroyuki, ed., *Josiah Conder: A Victorian Architect in Japan* (Tokyo: Bijutsu Shuppan, 1997), p. 27.

19. Conder, "The Effects of the Recent Earthquake upon Buildings," *Japan Weekly Mail*, December 12, 1891, p. 725.

20. Conder, "The Condition of Architecture in Japan" (paper to be read before the International Congress of Architects, World's Columbian Exposition, August 2, 1893), *Japan Weekly Mail*, September 30, 1893, p. 392.

21. Suzuki Hiroyuki, *Victorian Gothic no Hōkai* (Tokyo: Chūō Kōron Bijutsu Shuppan, 1996), p. 109. Watanabe Toshio, "Josiah Conder's Rokumeikan," pp. 25–26.

22. Suzuki, private correspondence; see also the chapter on Conder in Suzuki, *Victorian Gothic no Hōkai*, pp. 95–153. Pyle, p. 105.

23. Conder wrote in his paper for the World's Columbian Exposition in Chicago (1893): "I do not go so far as some eminent members of the profession, who assert that [Japanese architecture] is not entitled to be termed Architecture . . . on the score of artistic qualities, the Japanese method can hardly be denied the title of Architecture. . . . Notwithstanding the comparatively perishable nature of the material employed, these buildings can hardly be regarded as other than monumental" (Conder, "The Condition of Architecture in Japan," p. 392).

24. Fujimori, "Josiah Conder and Japan," p. 21.

25. Quoted in Kawanabe Kusumi, "Josiah Conder and Kawanabe Kyosai," in Suzuki, *Josiah Conder*, pp. 62–63.

26. Said Conder before the Association of Japanese Architects in 1886: "The perishable and inflammable nature of the ancient buildings in this country renders it impossible that, even with the greatest care, we should preserve them long" (Conder, "The Practice of Architecture in Japan," *Japan Weekly Mail*, August 28, 1886, p. 213).

27. Conder, "The Condition of Architecture in Japan," p. 394.

28. Conder, "The Effects of the Recent Earthquake upon Buildings," p. 725.

29. Conder, "The Practice of Architecture in Japan," pp. 213–14.

30. Charles Davison, *The Founders of Seismology* (Cambridge: Cambridge University Press, 1927), p. 210.

31. A. L. Herbert-Gustar, and P. A. Nott, *John Milne: Father of Modern Seismology* (Tenterden, UK: Paul Norbury, 1980), p. 84.

32. Ibid., pp. 186–87.

33. Ibid., p. 82.

34. Milne, "Seismic Science in Japan," *Transactions of the Seismological Society of Japan* (hereafter *TSSJ*) 1, part 1 (April–June 1880): 3–37 (quotation p. 28).

35. Milne, "Suggestions for the Systematic Observance of Earthquakes," *TSSJ* 4 (January–June 1882): 85–117 (quotation p. 110).

36. Ibid., pp. 87–111; Kikuchi Dairoku, *Recent Seismological Investigations in Japan* (privately published, Tokyo, ca. 1904), p. 3.

37. One of the most valuable tasks that the Meteorological Department would perform for Milne and subsequent seismologists was constructing maps from seismic data. In 1895 Milne mentions that seismic maps had been created by the department from 80,000 to 100,000 individual documents, mostly postcards. The mapping project was temporarily terminated in 1892 because the mapmakers were simply overwhelmed with data. Milne, "A Catalogue of 8331 Earthquakes Recorded in Japan 1885–1892," *Seismological Journal of Japan* 4 (1895).

38. Latour, *Science in Action: How to Follow Scientists and Engineers through Society* (Cambridge, MA: Harvard University Press, 1987), p. 134.

39. Herbert-Gustar and Nott, p. 94.

40. Milne's "Catalogue of 8331 Earthquakes" states that a single earthquake could elicit several hundred postcard responses from the 968 reporting stations that were in touch with Tokyo by 1892 (p. 3). In 1904, according to Kikuchi, 71 local meteorological stations were equipped with seismographs linked to nearby telegraph offices, and another 1,437 stations were available for other sorts of data recording (Kikuchi, p. 9).

41. Hattori, who was from Chōshū, had gone to the United States in the late 1860s to take a degree at Rutgers. Following his early career as an Imperial University scholar (where he rose to become vice president), he was appointed governor of various prefectures and eventually became an aristocrat and member of the House of Peers (Hashimoto Manpei, *Jishingaku koto hajime: kaitakusha Sekiya Kiyokage no shōgai* [Tokyo: Asahi Shimbunsha, 1983], p. 68). Coincidentally, in 1896 he was governor of one of the northern prefectures most affected by the Great Sanriku Tsunami (the worst seismic disaster of the Meiji period) and became celebrated for his relief efforts. As a

parliamentarian in 1923, Hattori would help lead the effort to increase funding for seismology in the wake of the Great Kantō Earthquake.

42. Herbert-Gustar and Nott, p. 91.

43. John Milne, ed., *Construction in Earthquake Countries* (Tokyo: Seismological Society of Japan, 1889); the volume was published as a special issue (vol. 14) of the Society's *Transactions*.

44. After writing Lord Kelvin about his finding that seismic waves travel "round the world," Milne published Kelvin's reply in *Transactions of the Seismological Society of Japan,* in which the famous physicist stated: "I earnestly hope that the Japanese authorities will do all that can be done to promote your work and to allow you all the possible opportunities for carrying it out" (*TSSJ* 19 [1894]: 87).

45. H. M. Paul, "Measuring Earthquakes," *Science* 4, no. 96 (1884): 516–18 (quotation p. 516); H. S. Palmer, "Earthquake Research in Japan" (Tokyo, November 23, 1886), accessed on Higuchi and Higuchi Web site.

46. Milne, "Seismological Work in Japan," *Nature,* October 31, 1889, p. 657.

47. Milne, "Seismological Observations and Earth Physics," *The Geographical Journal* 21, no. 1 (January 1903): 1–22.

48. Milne, "Catalogue of 8331 Earthquakes." As late as 1886, Yokohama journalist H. S. Palmer could write that Japan "has been thus far free from fierce terrestrial disturbances of the class manifested during the last few years in so many other parts of the world" (H. S. Palmer, "Earthquake Research in Japan" [Tokyo, November 23, 1886], accessed on Higuchi and Higuchi Web site).

49. H. S. Palmer, "The Story of an Earthquake."

50. Kotō Bunjirō, "The Scope of the Vulcanological Survey of Japan," *Publications of the Imperial Earthquake Investigation Committee in Foreign Languages* 3 (1900): 89.

51. The photograph is reproduced in James L. Huffman, *Creating a Public: People and Press in Meiji Japan* (Honolulu: University of Hawaii Press, 1997).

52. H. S. Palmer, "The Recent Volcanic Explosion in Japan" (Tokyo, July 28, 1888), and "The Bandai-san Eruption" (Tokyo, October 12, 1888), both accessed on Higuchi and Higuchi Web site.

53. Milne, Sekiya, and Ōmori would all visit volcanoes and write extensive articles on eruptions. See for example Milne, "Volcanoes of Japan," *TSSJ* 9, part 2 (1886). Unlike earthquakes, however, the seismologists' "ownership" of vulcanology would come to be disputed with Japanese geologists, such as Kotō Bunjirō.

54. S. Brantley and H. Glicken, "Volcanic Debris Avalanches," *Earthquakes and Volcanoes* 18, no. 6 (1986): 195–206.

55. H. S. Palmer, "The Bandai-san Eruption" (Tokyo, October 12, 1888), accessed on Higuchi and Higuchi Web site.

56. Sekiya Seikei, "The Severe Earthquake of the 15th of January, 1887," *TSSJ* 11 (1887): 83.

57. Ibid., p. 87.

58. Sekiya Seikei and Kikuchi Y., "The Eruption of Bandai-san," *Journal of the College of Science, Imperial University of Japan* 3, no. 2 (1889): 1–172. The *Japan Weekly Mail* issued a 24-page special edition, "The Eruption of Bandai-san with a Coloured Plate," which is preserved in the collection of the National Diet Library, Tokyo (B-203, JP 41–23 943).

59. Quoted in Gavin, pp. 32–33.

60. Shiga Shigetaka, *Nihon fūkeiron* (Tokyo: Seikyōsha, 1894), p. 52.

61. Ibid., p. 98.

62. "Extract from the Report of the Committee Appointed to Propose Building Regulations for Ischia," in Milne, *Construction in Earthquake Countries*, pp. 140–43.

63. Conder to the Editor of the *Japan Weekly Mail*, June 18, 1889 (published June 23, 1889), p. 605.

64. This was the commission sent to Europe and America to study art education from 1886 to 1888, whose report resulted in the founding of the Tokyo Bijutsu Gakkō in 1889 (Dyer, p. 95).

65. Ibid. As he did in responding to Dresser over the issue of pagodas, Conder styles himself at the end of this letter as "Architect to the Japanese Government."

66. "Extract from the Report of the Committee Appointed to Propose Building Regulations for Ischia," in Milne, *Construction in Earthquake Countries*, p. 142.

67. Quoted in R. H. Brunton, "Constructive Art in Japan, Part I," *Transactions of the Asiatic Society of Japan* 2 (1873–74): 70.

68. Ibid. In a paper defending the aseismic properties of masonry read in Tokyo in 1891, civil engineer C. A. W. Pownall included a bibliography pertaining to the architecture of European antiquity, compiled at his request by an anonymous European correspondent. In the correspondent's attached note, which Pownall also published, the bibliography is described as being "about old works which were built before seismology was even thought of" (Pownall, "Notes on Recent Publications Relating to the Effect of Earthquakes on Structures," *TSSJ* 16 [1892]).

69. *Japan Weekly Mail*, June 22, 1889, p. 597.

70. This was Frank Brinkley. Dyer mentions their relationship in *Dai Nippon*, p. 4.

71. *Japan Weekly Mail*, p. 597.

72. Ibid.

73. Ibid.

74. Tatsuno Kingo, "Itariakoku isukiya-tō jishin kenchiku," *Kenchiku zasshi* 4, no. 43 (1891).

75. Ibid.

76. Ibid.

77. Milne, *Construction in Earthquake Countries*, p. 11.

FIVE • A GREAT EARTHQUAKE

1. I take most of these figures from tables 1–2, "Recent World Large Earthquakes," in Minoru Wakabayashi, *Design of Earthquake-Resistant Buildings* (New York: Mc-Graw Hill, 1986). According to Charles Davison, the land area "disturbed" by the Nōbi earthquake was a remarkable 330,000 square miles, which is larger than the Japanese archipelago itself (Davison, "The Great Japanese Earthquake of Oct. 28, 1891," *Geographical Journal* 17, no. 6 [June 1901]: 637). He also notes that land waves as high as a foot were observed rolling down certain streets (639).

2. The Nōbi earthquake was (and is) sometimes called the Mino-Owari Earthquake after the two provinces most affected. The term "great earthquake" is a direct translation of the Japanese *daijishin*, but had also been used by Mallet to describe the 1857 earthquake in Naples. An equally common Japanese name for such events was (and is) *dai-shin-sai*, or "great earthquake disaster," which puts greater stress on the human nature of the catastrophe.

3. Another large railroad bridge, at Kiso, had its arched supports so damaged that it had to be dynamited (John Milne, *Seismology* [London: Kegan, Paul, Trench, Truber & Co., 1898], p. 165).

4. *Asahi shimbun*, October 29, 1891, p. 1.

5. *Asahi shimbun*, October 30, 1891, p. 1.

6. Excerpted in *Japan Weekly Mail*, October 31, 1891, pp. 537–38.

7. *Asahi shimbun*, November 3, 1891, p. 1.

8. Ishihara Ken, ed., *Nōbi sanjō jishin jikki* [Factual Record of the Miserable Nōbi Earthquake] (Tokyo, 1891), pp. 17–18, gives a list of damaged brick buildings. A more detailed description of damage to the city's masonry structures is given by Conder, who notes that the only brick building "which had received no injury whatever" was a large powder magazine at the local garrison ("An Architect's Note on the Great Earthquake of 1891," *Seismological Journal of Japan* 18 [1893]: 11).

9. Suzuki Sakujirō, ed., *Aichi gifu daijishin no sanjō* [The Aichi-Gifu Great Earthquake's Miserable Spectacle] (Nagoya, 1891), p. 7; Miyawaki Hikozaburō, ed., *Daijishin*

jichi kenbunroku [On-the-Spot Record of Great Earthquake Experiences] (Nagoya, 1891), p. 10; Ishihara, p. 18.

10. Suzuki Sakujirō, p. 6.

11. Mori Takayuki, ed., *Jishinjuhō* (Nagoya, 1891); Kizawa Noritoshi and Yamawa Yoshihiko, *Meiji shinsai shūroku* [Collection of Records of Meiji Earthquake Disaster] (Nagoya, 1891).

12. Quoted in *Japan Weekly Mail*, November 14, 1891, p. 581.

13. *Japan Weekly Mail*, "Professor Sekiya on the Earthquake," November 7, 1891, p. 546.

14. *Japan Weekly Mail*, November 21, 1891, p. 617.

15. *Nichi nichi shimbun* (Gifu), November 2, 1891.

16. Ishihara, p. 16.

17. Quoted in *Japan Weekly Mail*, November 7, 1891, p. 542.

18. Conder traveled with his former student Kawaii Kōzō. Milne was accompanied by his student Ōmori Fusakichi, Nakamura Tetsutarō, the chief of the Interior Ministry observatory, and Shimizu from the Interior Ministry (*Japan Weekly Mail*, November 14, 1891, p. 591).

19. Quoted in Hara Tokuzō, "Josiah Conder and His Patrons," in Suzuki Hiroyuki, ed., *Josiah Conder: A Victorian Architect in Japan* (Tokyo: Bijutsu Shuppan, 1997), p. 45.

20. *Japan Weekly Mail*, November 7, 1891, p. 558.

21. Ibid., p. 556.

22. The photo of the Nagoya post office and neighboring *ryokan* is reproduced in Nagoya-shi Bōsai Kaigi Jishin Taisaku Senmon Iinkai, *Nōbi jishin bunken mokuroku* [Nōbi Earthquake: List of Materials] (Nagoya: Nagoya-shi Shiminkyoku Saigai Taisakuka, 1978), p. 40. Conder himself noted that except for the damage from the collapsing post office, the inn was little injured.

23. *Japan Weekly Mail*, November 7, 1891, p. 556.

24. Ibid., p. 558.

25. Ibid., p. 559.

26. *Japan Weekly Mail*, November 14, 1891, p. 591.

27. Ibid., p. 593.

28. Ibid., p. 591.

29. Ibid., p. 587.

30. *Japan Weekly Mail*, November 21, 1891, p. 619. Smedly also observed that an all-wooden, *daiku*-built cotton textile mill in Nagoya, unlike the brick Owari Spinning Mill, "stood intact and was in full working order."

31. *Jiji shimpō*, quoted in *Japan Weekly Mail*, November 14, 1891. The story of the hundred or more people killed in the temple collapse may have been apocryphal, as other sources changed its location. According to Miyowaki's *Daijishin jichi kenbunroku*, the temple was in Kotokuji, Sagachō town, Aichi prefecture, and the "more than 100 people" who died in its sudden collapse had just finished listening to a fatalistic sermon (Miyowaki, p. 9).

32. Ibid.

33. Min'yusha leader Tokutomi Sohō described in 1888 the "new conservative group," which he opposed, as including (among others) "confucianists, shinto and buddhist priests, [and] Chinese-style doctors," while Yamaji Aizan noted that "many backwoods priests and confucianists were delighted to plunge into the [conservative] movement" although it remained controlled by urban intellectuals. (Kenneth Pyle, *The New Generation in Meiji Japan: Problems in Cultural Identity, 1885–1895* [Stanford: Stanford University Press, 1969], pp. 107, 108).

34. *Japan Weekly Mail*, November 14, 1891, p. 581.

35. Most of the woodblock prints I refer to here are in the collection of the Nagoya City Museum. The key prints have been reproduced, along with many other illustrations of the Nōbi earthquake from other sources, in *Nōbi jishin bunken mokuroku*. I am particularly referring to the following three-part prints: "Meiji 24 nen 10 gatsu 28 nichi daijishinzu" by Baidō Kokunimasu; "Meiji 24 10 gatsu daijishingo" by Toyohara Kuniteru; "Gifu shigai daijishin no zu" by Utagawa Kinitoshi (a.k.a. Baiō); and "Gifuken aichiken daijishin jikkyo" by an anonymous artist. The three signed works are by artists resident in Tokyo. The lithographic illustration of the overturned train, with Mount Fuji in the background, forms the cover of Katsugame Shigetarō, ed., *Nōbi shinsai zue hyōshi* [Pictures of the Actual Places of the Nōbi Earthquake] (Tokyo, 1891).

36. The derailed train, which was of such interest to the woodblock artists, was likely based on an early news report or rumor. I have been unable to find reference to it in the larger newspapers or book-length accounts that appeared within weeks of the disaster. The reference to destroyed track comes from Davison, "The Great Earthquake in Japan of Oct. 28, 1891," p. 637.

37. Ishihara, p. 17.

38. Conder reported in 1893 that, although he had thought the castle uninjured during his own inspection, "close examination afterwards" revealed it "had been thrown about a foot out of the perpendicular and extensive repairs were consequently undertaken" (Conder, "An Architect's Note on the Great Earthquake of 1891," p. 60). A short note in the journal *Kenchiku zasshi* (vol. 7, no. 12 [1892]: 379) reported that one year after the earthquake, 580 workers were busy repairing damage to the castle's inte-

rior. The anonymous author was proud that the supervising architects "did not borrow foreign ideas" in the restoration.

39. The undamaged nature of Ōgaki Castle was testified to by Conder himself, who found it "one of the few structures remaining" in postdisaster Ōgaki (Conder, "An Architect's Notes on the Great Earthquake of 1891," p. 60).

40. I thank Barry Steben for his translation of the cursive script in the four prints "Meiji 24 nen 10 gatsu 28 nichi daijishinzu" by Baidō Kokunimasu; "Meiji 24 10 gatsu daijishingo" by Toyohara Kuniteru; "Gifu shigai daijishin no zu" by Utagawa Kinitoshi (a.k.a. Baiō); and "Gifuken aichiken daijishin jikkyo" by an anonymous artist, all in the collection of the Nagoya City Museum.

41. Suzuki Sakujirō, pp. 11, 23. Artists rushing multicolored woodblocks into print immediately following the earthquake may not have had access to news from towns and villages, which came in more slowly than reports from Nagoya. It may be, then, that they interpreted the earthquake through the lens of Edo's destruction in 1855. The black-and-white woodblocks in books written weeks or months after the catastrophe more often included changes to the landscape, such as ground-cracks and the creation of new lakes, as well as scenes of mayhem in the countryside. Indeed, the emphasis in these later books shifts away from Nagoya and toward the area around Gifu, Ōgaki, and in the Neo Valley, where most of the worst destruction happened.

42. For the Ansei earthquake, see Andrew Markus, "Gesaku Authors and the Ansei Earthquake of 1855," in Dennis Washburn and Alan Tansman, ed., *Studies in Modern Japanese Literature: Essays in Honor of Edwin McClellan* (Ann Arbor: Center for Japanese Studies, University of Michigan, 1997); and Hashimoto Manpei, *Jishingaku koto hajime: kaitakusha Sekiya Kiyokage no shōgai* (Tokyo: Asahi Shinbusha, 1983). Buildings of the elite did not entirely escape damage or collapse in the Ansei disaster. Edo Castle remained standing in 1855, like Nagoya Castle in 1891, but all thirty-six of its annexes or outbuildings were damaged, and certain of its ceremonial gates collapsed (Ishihara, p. 6, supplement). Nonetheless, the Kabuki actor Nakamura, in his memoirs of the event, noted that "in general, the shrines and temples were not badly damaged," and that the Asakusa pagoda, its bent mast testifying to its tenacity rather than its vulnerability, became a popular attraction in the aftermath of the disaster (Ishihara, p. 14, supplement). An Ansei-period woodblock print depicting the Asakusa pagoda with bent mast forms part of the collection of the Earthquake Research Institute at Tokyo University.

43. Articles on how to stabilize brick chimneys against seismic waves appeared in Japanese engineering and seismology journals into the 1920s.

44. On the sensitivity of Japanese and Chinese rulers to irregularities in the natural order, see Masayoshi Sugimoto and David L. Swain, *Science and Culture in Traditional Japan* (Cambridge: MIT Press, 1978).

45. *Japan Weekly Mail*, "Riots in Gifu," November 28, 1891, p. 6.

46. Milne's reports from Nōbi's epicentral zone reveal glimpses of its hellish aspect. In a note dated November 4, a week after the great earthquake, he writes, "There are continually small earthquakes, generally proceeded by a rumbling sound . . . and there is very frequent rumbling without any shaking afterward." For the next two days and nights, he reports, "it rained severely. The thunder was distant and mingled with the rumbling preceding earthquakes, which were very frequent on this night" (November 6). On November 7 he found the Gifu-Ōgaki road "one weary waste of ruined peasants' houses," with little sign of rebuilding. "The peasants cannot afford, at this time of year, to neglect their agricultural work, and they seem satisfied to find what shelter they can amongst the ruins of their houses, or do without shelter altogether" (*Japan Weekly Mail*, November 14, 1891, p. 592). A Japanese correspondent to the newspaper *Kokkai* telegraphed from Gifu on November 6 that "the people of the location fear that a fall of rain may be followed by another earthquake" (quoted in *Japan Weekly Mail*, November 14, 1891, p. 592). "At Gifu the earthquake shocks occur fifteen times a day or more," wrote another correspondent in mid-November, "and a terrible restlessness is felt by all as to the possibility of further disaster" (*Japan Weekly Mail*, November 28, 1891, p. 653). In fact violent aftershocks would continue until January 1892, and less powerful ones would be felt for two years after the earthquake. At least thirty of these were strong enough to register in Tokyo (Davison, "The Great Japanese Earthquake of Oct. 28, 1891," p. 645).

47. *Nichi nichi shimbun*, November 2, 1891 (notice dated October 30 and 31).

48. *Japan Weekly Mail*, November 7, 1891, p. 546.

49. Hashimoto notes that "calming the people's nerves" was a principal purpose of postearthquake scholarship from at least the thirteenth century. It became particularly notable from the seventeenth century onward, the Tokugawa regime making social stability into a near science (Hashimoto, pp. 1–28, 54–57).

50. Ibid., pp. 27–33.

51. Ishihara provided a supplement in his 1891 book on the Nōbi disaster *(Nōbi sanjō jishin jikki)*, recalling incidents and themes from the Ansei earthquake. The bulk of this appendix is a firsthand account of the 1855 disaster by the Kabuki actor Nakamura (who died in 1890, the year before Nōbi); I take the quotation from p. 14. The political implications of the 1855 Ansei earthquake are also discussed in Markus.

52. According to a Japanese reporter who traversed the epicentral zone, "The people are thoroughly frightened, the terrible incidents of the earthquake of 37 years ago being still fresh in the memory of old folks" (Letter of Y. Takenobu, *Japan Weekly Mail*, November 7, 1891, p. 556). Many reminiscences of the Ansei earthquake, even journals kept at the time, were published in newspapers following the Nōbi quake, testifying to the narrative merger of the two events (*Japan Weekly Mail*, November 7, 1891, p. 51). Sugimoto and Swain note that portent astrology, which entered Japan from China in classical times, "sought to correlate celestial, meteorological, and seismological portents with the social phenomena related to imperial rule or major political events" and that emperors since the seventh century were thus "quite sensitive to irregularities in the natural order" (pp. 53–54).

53. The *namaʒu-e* described here are from a series owned by the Earthquake Research Institute of Tokyo University. For a full discussion of these prints, see Miyata Noboru and Takata Mamoru, eds., *Namaʒu-e: jishin to Nihon bunka* (Tokyo: Satofumi Shuppan, 1995); and in English, Cornelis Ouwehand, *Namaʒu-e and Their Themes: An Interpretative Approach to Some Aspects of Japanese Folk-Religion* (Leiden: Brill, 1964). A few examples have also been published, along with a short essay on the history of Japanese earthquakes, in *Tokyo and Earthquakes* (Tokyo: Metropolitan Government, 1995), pp. 1–26. This book was itself part of a nerve-calming project following the Great Hanshin Earthquake of 1995 in Kobe. Markus (pp. 58–59) also cites popular accounts of the earthquake that highlight its beneficiaries as well as victims.

54. On *yonaoshi* (world rectification) as it related to earthquakes in the pre-Meiji era, see Miyata and Takata. According to the authors, the identification of catfish with earthquakes, and both with *yonaoshi*, grew particularly strong in the late Edo period.

55. The catfish as symbol appears occasionally in graphics of the Nōbi catastrophe, but as a one-dimensional image shorn of the anthropomorphism and often rich story lines accompanying the Ansei prints. A catfish on the cover of one of the popular accounts of the 1891 disaster, for example, is anatomically correct, as though sketched in a fish market.

56. Markus's examples of the multilayered, ironic, and often playfully morbid character of Ansei earthquake literature, which included joke books, comic verse, and humorous monologues, have few counterparts in the literature of the 1891 catastrophe, where the emphasis is on earnest, factual reportage and the dramatization of sublimity, surprise, and suffering.

57. The Hokkaido resettlement project is mentioned in *Japan Weekly Mail*, November 7, 1891, p. 550. Newspaper reports from the epicentral zone demonstrate the disjuncture between the geography of misery and the isoseismal lines of the earth-

quake itself. "The scene of destruction has become a scene of construction," wrote B. Howard from Nagoya on November 6, and "hundreds of workmen come by the daily train" (*Japan Weekly Mail*, November 14, 1891, p. 588). In the smaller town of Ōgaki at nearly the same time Milne found everyone "in little temporary huts" and "signs of starvation in the faces of some" (*Japan Weekly Mail*, November 14, 1891, p. 593). A. A. V., a Japanese Christian wandering rural hamlets dispensing bibles and small amounts of money, wrote that along the river Kiso, where wounded people were sleeping on bare ground, "the banks . . . are destroyed and the people expect to die of a flood before spring if they live so long" (*Japan Weekly Mail*, November 28, 1891, p. 653).

58. *Nichi nichi shimbun* (Gifu), November 1 and 2; Kizawa and Yamawa, pp. 11–13.

59. Kizawa and Yamawa, pp. 178–79.

60. Ishihara, pp. 5, 18. According to Ishihara, the story about Gotō, which was circulating around Tokyo, had its source in a household servant.

61. Kizawa and Yamawa, pp. 172–73.

62. Ibid.

63. Ibid., p. 169.

64. Ibid., p. 157; *Nichi nichi shimbun* (Gifu), p. 157.

65. Kizawa and Yamawa, p. 174.

66. Ibid., pp. 61–66.

67. Suzuki Sakujirō, p. 2.

68. Miyawaki, pp. 1, 3, 5.

69. Suzuki Sakujirō, pp. 20–21; *Nichi nichi shimbun* (Gifu), November 3, 1891; Katō Yoichi, *Daijishin no jikkyō* (Nagoya: Morishima Mizutarō, 1891), pp. 3–7.

70. Nagoya Ukiyochinbunsha, *Meiji jishin shōhō* (Nagoya, 1891), p. 10. It is noteworthy that this account reports both indigenous European and Asian earthquake myths as "superstitions," nor does it privilege the theories of ancient Greeks over those of Confucians. Two articles by Sekiya Seikei are appended to the same volume.

71. John Milne and W. K. Burton, *The Great Earthquake in Japan, 1891* (London and Yokohama: Standford, 1892). The prospectus for the book described it as a "handsomely bound volume suitable for the drawing-room table" (*Japan Weekly Mail*, November 28, 1891).

72. Sir Frederick Bramwell, Remarks on John Milne's "Construction in Earthquake Countries," *Minutes of Proceedings of the Institution of Civil Engineers* 83 (1886): 296.

73. Milne would return to the theme of astronomy vs. seismology in a 1911 *Nature* article: "Astronomers have received the support of nations since the days of astrology, while seismology is in its childhood seeking for more extended recognition" (quoted in

A. L. Herbert-Gustar and P. A. Nott, *John Milne: Father of Modern Seismology* [Tenterden, UK: Paul Norbury, 1980], p. 164). Yet Milne may have made a strategic mistake in recording the Nōbi earthquake as photographs. As a later English seismologist (Charles Davison) would write in 1926: "Even at the present day, when seismographs are so common, it is the registration of a distant earthquake, not the havoc wrought by it, that appeals to the public with unfailing interest." Not only the public, he might have added, but other seismologists. Davison, who completely ignores the photograph book in his own account of Milne's career, suggests that Milne's reputation as a seismologist is somewhat diminished for his having never made "a careful investigation of a great earthquake" (Davison, *The Founders of Seismology* [Cambridge: Cambridge University Press, 1927], p. 88).

74. Milne and Burton, *The Great Earthquake*, plate 7.

75. Ibid., plate 25.

76. Ibid.

77. It was Pownall who had argued in a lecture in January of that year that "no form of architecture would appear, prima facie, to be less adopted" to resist earthquakes than a Japanese house (see chapter 2, n8).

78. Milne, *Seismology*, p. 190.

79. Milne seems to have maintained a closer dialogue with railroad engineers than other types of civil engineers or architects. In his 1898 textbook on seismology, he used the same photos of the collapsed Nagara bridge, but three pages beyond, illustrated a new and different railroad bridge designed by the same engineer, C. A. W. Pownall. The second bridge was based on principles experimentally arrived at by Milne's own shaking-table experiments.

80. Milne, "Seismometry and Engineering in Relation to the Recent Earthquake in Japan," *Nature* 45, no. 1154 (December 10, 1891): 127.

81. Milne, "On the Earthquake Phenomenon of Japan," *Report of the 54th Meeting of the British Association for the Advancement of Science* (London, 1885), pp. 248–49.

82. Milne, *Seismology*, pp. 135–36.

83. Conder, "Earthquakes versus Buildings" (read before the Society of Japanese Architects, January 27, 1892), in *Japan Weekly Mail*, January 30, 1892, p. 153.

84. Conder, "The Effects of the Recent Earthquake upon Buildings," *Japan Weekly Mail*, December 12, 1891, p. 725.

85. Conder, "Earthquakes versus Buildings."

86. Ibid.

87. Ibid.

88. Milne repeated this metaphor, which he had used since at least the mid-1880s, in an article in the *Japan Weekly Mail*, November 28, 1891, p. 660.

89. Conder, "Earthquakes versus Buildings."

90. Ibid.

91. Conder, "Effects of the Recent Earthquake upon Buildings," p. 726.

92. Ibid.

93. Ibid.

94. Ibid.

95. Conder, "Earthquakes versus Buildings."

96. Ibid.

97. *Japan Weekly Mail*, November 28, 1891, p. 647, and December 5, 1891, pp. 666, 694.

98. Milne's ability to discount the venerable theory that earthquakes were triggered by electrical phenomenon, something no European scientist had been able to do, was another instance of his using evidence collected by the Imperial bureaucracy. In an article of 1894 he would discount the "electrical trigger" by comparing data gathered by the Telegraph Department on earth currents with his own records on earthquake frequency (Milne, "Seismic, Magnetic, and Electrical Phenomenon," *Transactions of the Seismological Society of Japan* [hereafter *TSSJ*] 19 [1894]: 29).

99. "Professor Milne on the Great Earthquake," *Japan Weekly Mail*, November 28, 1891, pp. 659–60; "The Great Earthquake," *Japan Weekly Mail*, December 5, 1891, pp. 694–96. Conder prefaced one of his own talks that winter by saying, "It is very difficult to treat such a subject [architecture] in a popular and attractive manner" (Conder, "Effects of the Recent Earthquake upon Buildings," p. 725).

100. Milne actually conducted experiments into the 1890s to disprove the theory that the construction of railroads in Japan had lessened the incidence of earthquakes (by affecting the electrical charge of the ground). There was statistical evidence of this effect for both Japan and California (Milne, "Seismic, Magnetic, and Electrical Phenomena").

101. "Professor Milne on the Great Earthquake."

102. Hashimoto, p. 22.

103. As late as 1898 Milne had not discounted changes in barometric pressure as having possible subterranean effects (*Seismology*, p. 218).

104. "Professor Milne on the Great Earthquake," p. 660.

105. "The Great Earthquake," p. 696.

106. Ibid.

107. Ibid.

108. Ibid.

109. Milne was aware that many temples in the epifocal region had fallen; he mentions this in *Seismology* (1898). But the passage follows a strong endorsement of the survivability of temples generally: "In the great earthquake of Ansei, 1855, so far as I am aware, the whole of these buildings remained intact" (p. 158).

110. "The Great Earthquake," p. 696.

111. Herbert-Gustar and Nott, p. 118.

112. Edward F. Strange, "Architecture in Japan," *Architectural Review* 1 (1897): 126–35.

113. Ibid.

114. Cawley, "Wood and Its Application to Japanese Artistic and Industrial Design," *Transactions and Proceedings of the Japan Society of London* 2 (1892–93): 221.

115. Stratham, "Japanese Architecture," *Architectural Review* (October 1912): 188.

116. Conder, "The Condition of Architecture in Japan" (paper to be read before the International Congress of Architects, World's Columbian Exposition, August 2, 1893), in *Japan Weekly Mail*, September 30, 1893, p. 392.

117. Ibid., p. 394.

SIX · JAPAN AS EARTHQUAKE NATION

1. Hashimoto Manpei, *Jishingaku koto hajime: kaitakusha Sekiya Kiyokage no shōgai* (Tokyo: Asahi Shimbunsha, 1983), pp. 29, 55.

2. Ishihara Ken, ed., *Nōbi sanjō jishin jikki* (Tokyo, 1891), p. 5.

3. Umehara Chūzō, *Shin-u shinsairoku* [Record of the Disaster] (Osaka, 1891), p. 26.

4. *Nichi nichi shimbun* (Gifu), November 1, 1891.

5. John Milne, quoted in *Japan Weekly Mail*, November 7, 1891, p. 559.

6. Ōmori Fusakichi's research on pheasants, for example, is mentioned in an obituary by Charles Davison (*Nature* 113, no. 2830 [1924]: 133). Ōmori also published articles on the relation of earthquakes to weather, claiming to have proven statistically that seismicity occurred when the air was still, and almost never in windy conditions (Ōmori, "Notes on the Secondary Causes of Earthquakes," *Bulletin of the Imperial Earthquake Investigation Committee* [hereafter *BIEIC*] 2, no. 2 [October 1908]: 101–35). For recent Japanese research on "precursor phenomena," see, for example, Ikeya Mataji et al., "Reproduction of Mimosa and Clock Anomalies before Earthquakes: Are They 'Alice in Wonderland' Syndrome?" *Proceedings of the Japanese Academy* 74, series B (1998): 60–64. The "Alice in Wonderland syndrome" refers to the phenomena of clock hands

suddenly moving backward, which apparently was observed prior to the Kobe earthquake. Ikeya also describes experiments with eels and other animals. His bibliography refers to work conducted by Japanese scientists as early as the 1930s, though in fact such research began even earlier with Ōmori.

7. Ishihara, pp. 17–18. According to Hashimoto (p. 32), this machine was called a *jishintokei* (earthquake clock) and a second example was constructed sometime after the earthquake by the Dutch Studies scholar (and later martyr) Sakuma Shozan.

8. Ishihara, pp. 17–18.

9. I am relying on the 1883 version of the Rossi-Forel scale printed in Charles Davison, *A Manual of Seismology* (Cambridge: Cambridge University Press, 1921).

10. In this and the following paragraphs I am relying on Ōmori's own English translation of his scale in Ōmori Fusakichi, "Seismic Experiments on the Fracturing and Overturning of Columns," *Publications of the Imperial Earthquake Investigation Committee* (hereafter *PIEIC*) 4 (1900): 138–41. It is likely that Ōmori was building on an earlier scale developed by Sekiya in 1884.

11. Ōmori is credited with the first earthquake scale of "absolute" (that is, quantifiable) intensity by Davison, *A Manual of Seismology,* pp. 53–54.

12. Milne, *Seismology* (London: Kegan, Paul, Trench, Truber & Co., 1898), p. 136.

13. Ōmori, "Seismic Experiments," pp. 138–41.

14. I take these translations of the Mercalli scale from Alfredo Montel, *Building Structures in Earthquake Countries* (London: Charles Griffin & Co., 1912), pp. 9–11. Montel also publishes Ōmori's scale and attempts to reconcile it with Mercalli's in the form of a chart.

15. *Japan Weekly Mail,* November 7, 1891, p. 559.

16. Charles Davison, *The Hereford Earthquake of Dec. 17, 1896* (Birmingham, UK: Cornish Bros., 1899), p. 266.

17. William H. Hobbs, *Earthquakes: An Introduction to Seismic Geology* (New York: D. Appleton, 1907), p. 227.

18. Davison, *Great Earthquakes* (London: Thomas Murby & Co., 1936), pp. 140–41.

19. Ibid.

20. "Japan," wrote Baron Kikuchi in 1904, "is preeminently a land of earthquakes" (Kikuchi Dairoku, *Recent Seismological Investigations in Japan* [Tokyo, 1904], p. 1).

21. *Japan Weekly Mail,* November 28, 1891, p. 647.

22. Kikuchi, p. 3.

23. The first chairman of the IEIC, President Katō of Tokyo University, was also a longtime Seismological Society member. Kikuchi was chairman of the IEIC from 1893 to 1901. Ōmori was the secretary of the organization from 1897.

24. Tanakadate Aikitsu, "A Magnetic Survey of All Japan," *Journal of the College of Science, Imperial University* 14 (1904): 1–180; Tanakadate Aikitsu and Nagaoka Hantaro, "The Disturbance of Isomagnetics Attending the Mino-Owari Earthquake of 1891," *Journal of the College of Science, Imperial University* 5, part 3 (1892): 149–96. The survey of 1893 was conducted mostly by the physics students of the Imperial University, according to a retrospective account of 1926, "among whom we find the names of the prominent physicists of the present days." Terada Torahiko and Matuzawa Takeo, "A Historical Sketch of the Development of Seismology in Japan," in National Research Council of Japan, *Scientific Japan* [prepared in connection with the Third Pan-Pacific Science Congress] (Kyoto, 1926), pp. 251–310 (quotation p. 301).

25. Kotō Bunjirō, "On the Cause of the Great Earthquake in Central Japan, 1891," *Journal of the College of Science, Imperial University* 5, part 3 (1892): 295–353.

26. Ibid., "The Scope of the Vulcanological Survey of Japan," *Publications of the Imperial Earthquake Investigation Committee in Foreign Languages* (hereafter *PIEIC in Foreign Languages*) 3 (1900): 89–93 (quotations from pp. 93, 89).

27. Ibid., p. 89.

28. Kikuchi, p. 3.

29. Monbushō (Ministry of Education), *Catalog of Objects Exhibited at the World's Columbian Exposition, Chicago, U.S.A., 1893, by the Department of Education, Japan* (Tokyo, 1893), pp. 53–55.

30. Ibid.

31. Ibid.

32. The most complete discussion of the Hō-ō-den in English is chapter 8 of Clay Lancaster, *The Japanese Influence in America* (New York: W. H. Rawls, 1963). The building was designed by Kuru Masamichi, a graduate of the *zōka* course at the Imperial University.

33. Milne, having returned to his home country in 1895, was attempting to direct world seismological study from his new laboratory at Shide on the Isle of Wight. The International Association that Japan hoped to join in 1904 was a German-created entity that Milne opposed.

34. In Davison's *Founders of Seismology* (Cambridge: Cambridge University Press, 1927), Ōmori would follow Milne as the last "founder" of the science.

35. Ōmori also published in European journals, beginning with an article on the Tokyo earthquake of 1894 in *Nature*, the journal of Milne's patrons, the British Association for the Advancement of Science, in 1897 (*Nature* 56).

36. Milne, "A Catalog of 8331 Earthquakes Recorded in Japan 1885–1892," *Seismological Journal of Japan* 4 (1895): 21.

37. Ōmori, "Preliminary Notes on the Cause of the San Francisco Earthquake of Apr. 18, 1906," *BIEIC* 1, no. 1 (January 1907).

38. Asahi Shōgakkō PTA, *Watashitachi no daisenpai jishingakusha no chichi Ōmori Fusakichi* (Tokyo, 1972).

39. Davison, *Founders of Seismology*, p. 207.

40. Ernst von Rebeur-Paschwitz, "The Earthquake of Tokio, April 18, 1889," *Nature* 40 (1889): 294–95. The Prussian scientist was using his seismograph-like instrument to study "the gravitational influence of the moon," not earthquakes, and his detection of seismic waves from Japan was accidental. The new project launched by von Rebeur-Paschwitz's discovery is apparent in article titles like "The Constitution of the Interior of the Earth as Revealed by Earthquakes" (R. D. Oldham, *Quarterly Journal of the Geological Society* 62 [1906]: 456–73). The seismograph and seismic waves informed a new phase in an old debate between Lord Kelvin and geologists over the age of the earth. Both sides hoped that seismic evidence would prove whether the interior was solid (Kelvin) or liquid (the geologists), a question that had a major bearing on, among other things, the validity of Darwin's theory of evolution (see Joe E. Burchfield, *Lord Kelvin and the Age of the Earth* [Chicago: University of Chicago Press, 1975], ch. 5).

41. The British Association for the Advancement of Science began instituting a worldwide monitoring system under Milne's direction in 1895. German scientists countered with an International Seismological Association in 1901, which, given the reputation of German physics and other factors, ultimately proved the most successful—that is, the more widely networked—of the two projects (Davison, *A Manual of Seismology*, p. 141).

42. For American seismology, see Hobbs.

43. Kikuchi, p. 117.

44. Ibid.

45. George Carroll Curtis, "Work Going on at Kilauea Volcano," *Science* 38, no. 976 (1913): 355–58; Edmund Otis Hovey, "Geological Society of America" (Report), *Science* 29, no. 746 (1909): 623–39; Augustin Udias and William Stauder, "The Jesuit Contribution to Seismology," *Seismological Research Letters* 67, no. 3 (May/June 1996): 10–19.

46. Ōmori, "Preliminary Notes on the Cause of the San Francisco Earthquake," p. 19; and "Notes on the Secondary Causes of Earthquakes."

47. There is some dispute about these casualty figures, as in any disaster involving so large a number of people. Ōmori and the Italian seismologist G. B. Rizzo both placed initial casualties above 100,000. Davison later called this figure "excessive," and noted that estimates for Messina and Reggio alone (where presumably the most authoritative

figures could be gathered) ranged anywhere between 46,800 and 82,035. My figure of 120,000 comes from Wakabayashi (Minoru Wakabayashi, *Design of Earthquake-Resistant Buildings* [New York: McGraw Hill, 1986]). The percentage of collapsed houses, first reported by Ōmori (see citation in n48 below), was repeated without challenge by Davison in 1936 (*Great Earthquakes*, p. 203).

48. Ōmori, "Preliminary Report on the Messina-Reggio Earthquake of Dec. 28, 1908," *BIEIC* 3, no. 1 (1909). In Charles Davison's bibliography of the Messina earthquake, prepared in 1936, only four of twenty-six scientific articles are in English; the rest are in Italian. Two of the English articles are by Ōmori, and two by relatively obscure American researchers (Davison, *Great Earthquakes*, pp. 210–11).

49. Ōmori, "Preliminary Report on the Messina-Reggio Earthquake," pp. 38–39.

50. Ibid., pp. 39–40.

51. Ōmori, "Notes on the Great Mino-Owari Earthquake of Oct. 28, 1891," *PIEIC in Foreign Languages*, no. 4 (Tokyo: IEIC, 1900), p. 13.

52. Sekiya Seikei, "The Severe Earthquake of the 15th of January, 1887," *Transactions of the Seismological Society of Japan* 11 (1887): 79–90.

53. I take these figures from Charles Davison, *The Japanese Earthquake of 1923* (London: Thomas Murby & Co., 1931), p. 6. It was only with the publication of Davison's book on the Kantō earthquake in 1931 that the disparity between European and Japanese lethality rates was noted by a British seismologist. Davison does not cite Ōmori, however, or ground the discussion in the Nōbi earthquake.

54. Montel, *Building Structures in Earthquake Countries.*

55. Ibid., p. 15.

56. Ibid., pp. 26–27.

57. Ibid.

58. The role of science, technology, and medicine in the Japanese colonization of Asia has been traced in a number of recent monographs and articles, though few focus on geology. See especially Daqing Yang, *Technology of Empire: Telecommunications and Japanese Imperialism, 1930–1945* (Cambridge, MA: Harvard University Press, 2003); Ming-Cheng Miriam Lo, *Doctors within Borders: Profession, Ethnicity, and Modernity in Colonial Taiwan* (Berkeley: University of California Press, 2002); and Tsukahara Togo, "The Japanese Colonial Sciences in the Greater East Asia Co-Prosperity Sphere: Mere Successor of the Europeans or the Initiator of the New Era?" *Journal of the Japan-Netherlands Institute* 6 (1996): 175–88.

59. Ōmori, "Preliminary Note on the Formosan Earthquake of Mar. 17, 1906," *BIEIC* 1, no. 2 (March 1907): 53–69.

60. Ibid., p. 55.

61. Ibid., figs. 8 and 9.

62. Ibid., p. 63.

63. Ibid., pp. 55, 62.

64. We are not told what happened to the railroad line that, according to an accompanying map, traverses the fault itself and crosses at least two bridges in the epicentral zone.

65. Monbushō, p. 54.

66. Ōmori, "The Omachi (Shinano) Earthquakes of 1918," *BIEIC* 10 (1922–1928): 4–5.

67. Ibid., p. 2.

68. Ōmori, "Note on the Form of Japanese Castle Walls," *BIEIC* 9 (1918–1921): 30–32.

69. Ōmori, "Measurement of the Vibration of Gojūnotōs, or 5-Story Buddhist Stupas (Pagodas)," *BIEIC* 9 (1918–1921): 110–52.

SEVEN • JAPANESE ARCHITECTURE AFTER NŌBI

1. *Asahi shimbun*, October 31, 1891, p. 1.

2. Muramatsu Teijirō, *Nihan kindai kenchiku gijutsushi* (Tokyo: Shōkokusha, 1976), p. 76.

3. Tatsuno Kingo, "Report on the Earthquake-Proof House," *Shinsai yobō chōsakai hōkoku 1* (Tokyo: IEIC, 1893).

4. Ibid., p. 98.

5. Milne, *Seismology* (London: Kegan, Paul, Trench, Truber & Co., 1898), pp. 66–67.

6. Conder's student Sone Tatsuzō would go to the United States in 1893 to study iron construction, but iron and steel framing remained impractical for all but the most important projects in a nation still importing those materials. The eventual solution, steel-reinforced concrete, would only begin to be used on a substantial scale during the economic boom of the First World War.

7. For the best recent overview of Itō, see Suzuki Hiroyuki, ed., *Itō Chōta o shite imasu ka* (Tokyo: Okoku, 2003); see also Inoue Shōichi, *Hōryūji e no seishinshi* (Tokyo: Kōbundō, 1994); and Dallas Finn, *Meiji Revisited* (New York: Weatherhill, 1995), pp. 167–68. I take my discussion of the shrine and temple style from Cherie Wendelken, "The Tectonics of Japanese Style: Architect and Carpenter in the Late Meiji Period," *Art Journal* 55 (Fall 1996). Discussion of a modern Japanese architecture had of course

begun as early as the 1870s among Conder and his students, though the first models were explicitly Western.

8. Ibid.

9. Wendelken, p. 32.

10. William Coaldrake, *The Way of the Carpenter* (New York: Weatherhill, 1990), pp. 153–56.

11. Quoted in Mutō Kiyoshi, "Gojūnotō and Earthquakes," paper no. 668, in *Proceedings of the World Engineering Congress, Tokyo 1929*, vol. 7 (Tokyo: World Engineering Congress/Kōgakkai, 1931), p. 269.

12. My outline of Itō's career in this section is greatly informed by Muramatsu Teijirō's biography, *Yawarakai mono e no shiten: itan no kenchikuka Itō Tamekichi* (Tokyo: Iwanami Shoten, 1994).

13. Muramatsu, *Yawarakai mono e no shiten: itan no kenchikuka Itō Tamekichi*, pp. 58–65; Itō Tamekichi, *Shinshiki daikuhō* (Tokyo, 1934), pp. 17–18.

14. Ibid.

15. Itō did not present the finished house as entirely Western. He used sliding screens rather than first floor walls, and the frame rose from round stones rather than a Western foundation and basement. In plan, he preserved open Japanese rooms and ran the corridors around the exterior in the accepted fashion. Itō intended no revolution in how Japanese lived, only how their houses were constructed. His model house was a subtle synthesis of American carpentry, Japanese plan and form, the new concern with disaster resistance, and the reform menu of foreign architects and engineers.

16. Being a "regular" member of the Nihon Zōka Gakkai generally required that one be a *zōkagaku-shi*—a graduate of the Imperial University course. "Secondary" membership was for those "in the same profession," who were required to have competency or practice in at least two departments of the *zōka* course. This effectively excluded most *daiku*.

17. Muramatsu, *Yawarakai mono e no shiten*, p. 48.

18. Itō, *Nihon kenchiku kōzō kairyōhō* (Tokyo: Kyōeki Shosha, 1892).

19. Ibid.

20. Ibid.

21. Even Milne, following the Nōbi earthquake, had faulted Japanese carpenters for "honeycombing their posts and mortises" (*Japan Weekly Mail*, November 14, 1891, p. 591).

22. Itō reprinted this flyer in one of his later books, *Shinshiki daikuhō*, p. 14.

23. Conder, "Earthquakes versus Buildings" (paper read before the Society of Japanese Architects, January 27, 1892), *Japan Weekly Mail*, January 30, 1892, p. 153.

24. Nathan Rosenberg, "America's Rise to Woodworking Leadership," in Brooke Hindle, ed., *America's Wooden Age* (Tarrytown, NY: Sleepy Hollow Press, 1985), pp. 37–62; Paul E. Sprague, "The Origin of Balloon Framing," *Journal of the Society of Architectural Historians* 40 (December 1981): 311–19.

25. Itō, *Mokkō jutsu kyokashō* (Tokyo: Shokko Gundan Sōritsu Jimusho, 1894).

26. In his *Shinshiki daikuhō*, for example, in which Itō addressed each chapter to a different audience (*daiku*, homeowners, architects, etc.), he asked *daiku* to "please consider me an old *daiku*" (p. 12).

27. Itō, *Nihon kenchiku kōzō kairyōhō*, p. 2.

28. Ibid., p. 4; Cherie Wendelken has pointed out how, in Japanese architectural writings, "the interest of the foreign expert" was often made to serve "a sort of mandate" for the author's project. Itō's story is very similar to Tatsuno's explanation of why he introduced the study of Japanese architectural history into the Japanese academy. When asked in England by architect William Burges to describe Japan's existing architecture, he found himself unable to do so. Accepting that these "admittals of ignorance" are partly literary strategies, they also illustrate the degree to which *zōkagaku-shi* were intensely oriented toward Europe (Wendelken, "The Tectonics of Japanese Style: Architect and Carpenter in the Late Meiji Period," *Art Journal* 55 [Fall 1996], p. 31).

29. Itō, *Nihon kenchiku kōzō kairyōhō*, p. 6.

30. Ibid., p. 4.

31. Conder, "The Effects of the Recent Earthquake upon Buildings," *Japan Weekly Mail* (December 12, 1891): 726.

32. Stratham, "Japanese Architecture," *Architectural Review* (October 1912): 128.

33. Itō, *Mokkō jutsu kyokashō*, appendix, pp. 1–2.

34. Ibid.

35. Ibid.

36. Ibid., p. 5. The regulations that form an appendix to Itō's book had been previously published, in November 1892, as "Shokkō Gundan sōritsu" (Worker Corps Prospectus).

37. Ibid., p. 11.

38. Ibid., pp. 9–14.

39. Ibid.

40. Ibid.

41. The unusually successful Shimizu-gumi, still one of the largest construction companies in Japan, employed at that time (1896) just fifty-nine people (Muramatsu, "The Japanese Construction Industry IV," *The Japan Architect* 318 [January–February 1968]: 141).

42. Muramatsu, *Yawarakai mono e no shiten*, pp. 121–22, 131–32.

43. Ibid., pp. 123–24.

44. Ibid., pp. 66–68.

45. For Japanese trade schools, see Shimizu Keiichi, "Meijiki ni okeru shotō-chūtō kenchiku kyōiku no shiteki kenkyū" (Ph.D. diss., Nihon University, 1982).

46. Conder writing as "X" in the *Japan Weekly Mail*, November 27, 1891, p. 616; Muramatsu, p. 66. Itō's unpublished autobiographical narrative, or *shuki*, was finished in 1933, according to Muramatsu, when Itō was seventy years old (p. 181).

47. Muramatsu, *Yawarakai mono e no shiten*, pp. 64–66.

48. Ibid.; Tatsuno Kingo, Katayama Tōkuma, Nakamura Tsutarō, and Sone Tatsuzō, "Models of Buildings for the Seismic Experiments," *Shinsai yobō chōsakai hōkoku* 2 (Tokyo: IEIC, 1895).

49. Muramatsu, *Yawarakai mono e no shiten*, pp. 66–67.

50. Tatsuno Kingo et al., "Models of Buildings," pp. 5–12; photographs of these models were republished in Kikuchi (1904).

51. Kikuchi, *Recent Seismological Investigations in Japan* (Tokyo, 1904), p. 66.

52. The IEIC designs for earthquake-resistant wooden houses, although not resembling any Western houses, were consistent with the most complex types of European roofs. They were similar to the roof systems used in the largest ministerial and urban office buildings following the Tokyo earthquake of 1894.

53. Muramatsu, *Yawarakai mono e no shiten*, p. 68.

54. Conder, "Earthquakes versus Buildings," p. 153.

55. Muramatsu, *Yawarakai mono e no shiten*, pp. 126–27.

56. Ibid.

57. Milne, *Seismology*, pp. 188–89.

58. Thomas Tredgold, *Elementary Principles of Carpentry* (London: Lockwood and Co., 1870 [5th edition; originally published 1828]); Anonymous, *Notes on Building Construction*, part I (London: Rivington, 1875).

59. Tredgold, pp. i–vii.

60. *Notes on Building Construction*, title page.

61. Ibid., pp. v–vii.

62. Ibid., p. 65.

63. Ibid., p. 114, fig. 227; Taki Daikichi, *Kenchiku kōgi roku* (Tokyo: Kenchiku Shoin, 1896), p. 490, fig. 148.

64. Erwin Marx, *Die Hochbau-Constructionen: Des Handbuches der Architectur*, dritter theil, 2 band, 1 heft [Wande und Wand-Oeffnungen] (Darmstadt: Verlag von Arnold Bergstrasser, 1891).

65. Taki Daikichi, "Taishin kōzō," *Kenchiku ₹asshi* 7, no. 74 (1894): 51.

66. Mihashi Shirō, *Dai kenchiku-gaku* (Tokyo, 1915), fig. 185.

67. Kikuchi presents a photograph of an IEIC model (miniature) frame with thatched roof, over the caption "Model of a Farmer's Cottage" (fig. 48). Cross-sectional drawings of the this model were published the same year in the Education Ministry textbook *Kogyogakkō kenchiku sei₹u kyoju yomoku* (Tokyo, 1904), which were intended to be copied by students learning architectural drafting at state technical schools. The frame and its details seem strongly influenced by European (particularly German) heavy carpentry (e.g., figs. 313–315, showing roofs for industrial buildings, in Adolf Opderbecke, *Das Holz̧bau-Buch fur den Shulgebrauch und die Baupraxis* [Hannover: Verlag Th. Schafer, 1909]).

68. IEIC, "Condensed Statement on the Construction of Earthquake-Proof Wooden Buildings," *PIEIC in Foreign Languages* 4 (Tokyo, 1900).

EIGHT • THE GREAT KANTŌ EARTHQUAKE AND THE SUBMERGENCE OF THE EARTHQUAKE NATION

1. Sano Toshikata, *Kaoku taishin kō₹ō ron* (Tokyo, 1915); Fujimori, *Nihon no kindai kenchiku* (Tokyo: Iwanami Shoten, 1993), vol. 2, ch. 10.

2. Sano, *Sano hakase tsuisōroku* (Tokyo: Sano Hakase Tsuisōroku Henshū Iinkai, 1957). Fujimori, *Nihon no kindai kenchiku*, vol. 2, pp. 123–38. For an account of Sano in English, see Jonathan Reynolds, *Maekawa Kunio and the Emergence of Japanese Modernist Architecture* (Berkeley: University of California Press, 2001), pp. 47–49. Sano also represented a break in the Anglocentric orientation of Japanese architecture, having finished his graduate study in Germany. Tenabe Heigaku wrote that when Sano took up teaching at Tokyo Imperial University, "English architectural methods, as theoretically enforced, changed to a Japanese method influenced by German ideas." The English idea had been to train "an architect pure and simple," while the new goal was to train a *bauingeniuer* (building engineer) (Tenabe Heigaku, "Technical Education in Japan," in Japan Times and Mail, *Architectural Japan* [Tokyo, 1936], p. 171).

3. Fujimori, *Nihon no kindai kenchiku*, vol. 2, ch. 10.

4. Ibid.; Reynolds, *Maekawa Kunio*.

5. Sano, *Sano hakase tsuisōroku*, p. 6.

6. Quoted in Fujimori, *Nihon no kindai kenchiku*, vol. 2, ch. 10; Noda's thesis is also discussed in Reynolds, "The *Bunriha* and the Problem of 'Tradition' for Modernist Architecture," in Donald Denoon et al., eds., *Multicultural Japan: Paleolithic to Postmodern* (Cambridge: Cambridge University Press, 1996), p. 236.

7. Quoted in Nishiyama Uzō, "Wagakuni kenchikuka no shōrai ni tsuite," *Kenchiku zasshi* (April 1937), p. 521. Despite these and similar pronouncements, Sano did not see himself as abandoning aesthetics. He was an admirer of Le Corbusier, a fellow worker in concrete, and his statements rejecting "architectural feature or style" sometimes overlap with the language of European modernist manifestos. At base, however, Sano's perspective on aesthetics was colored by racialism ("the artistic nature latent in our race [is] manifested through the spirit of simplicity and naiveté"), which led him to see design creativity as a European ideal alien to Japanese experience. Japanese aesthetics would *naturally* reemerge in modern work, he believed, because "there runs in our veins an unadulterated quality of taste bequeathed to us by our ancestors" (Sano, "Recent Development of Architecture in Japan," *Proceedings of the World Engineering Conference*, vol. 7 [Tokyo: World Engineering Congress, 1931], pp. 3–4).

8. Sano's major critic was the Navy engineer Majima Kenzaburō, who as early as 1924 began to criticize the preoccupation with ferro-concrete among Japanese architects and instead make a case for the superior earthquake-resisting properties of steel frames. Their increasingly personal argument would roil the Japanese architecture and engineering worlds into the 1930s. Majima's position complicated attempts by Japanese architects to name steel framing as an essentially "American" technology unsuitable for use in earthquake countries. See, for example, Majima Kenzaburō, "On the Construction of Earthquake-Proof Buildings" (English abstract of an article that originally appeared in *Reports of the Imperial Earthquake Investigation Committee*, vol. 10, no. 2, 1924), National Research Council of Japan, *Proceedings of the Third Pan-Pacific Science Conference, Tokyo, Oct. 30–Nov. 11, 1926*, vol. 2 (Tokyo, 1928), p. 1453.

9. A story told by the architect/engineer Naitō Tachu about how he came to invent an earthquake-resistant concrete frame emphasizes his lack of debt to foreign knowledge. Naitō, like countless Japanese students before him, studied abroad (in the United States) in order to understand Western science and technology. He claims to have discovered nothing of value, however, in his chosen field of earthquake engineering. While sailing home, he noticed that the vertical separators he had arranged in his luggage swayed with the ship without upsetting their position or function. Here was the kernel of his idea for an earthquake-proof structural system based on concrete walls. (I have taken this story from Fujimori, *Nihon no kindai kenchiku*, vol. 2, pp. 133–34.) By locating the "eureka moment" on a ship sailing away from the West, a West with nothing to teach the young Naitō, the story neatly unsettles the trope of Japanese enlightenment through Western contact.

10. Sano, Naitō and others formed the Shakai Seisakuha (Social Policy Faction) in the early Taishō period, pressing architects to concentrate on four themes: earthquakes,

fires, houses, and cities. Ferro-concrete was so much at the center of their thinking about each problem that they were also known as the *kōzo* (structure) faction. There is an extended discussion of the Shakai Seisakuha in Fujimori, *Nihon no kindai kenchiku*, vol. 2, ch. 10. For the Japanese housing reform culture from early Meiji into the period immediately preceding that of Sano's greatest influence, see Jordan Sand, *House and Home in Modern Japan: Architecture, Domestic Space, and Bourgeois Culture, 1880–1930* (Cambridge, MA: Harvard University Asia Center, 2003).

11. Sano Toshikata and Taniguchi Tadashi, *Taishin kōzō hanron* (Tokyo: Iwanami Shoten, 1934), p. 6; Sano, "Recent Developments of Architecture in Japan," p. 3.

12. Ōmori Fusakichi, "Earthquake Zones in and around the Pacific" (read at the First Pan-Pacific Science Conference, 1920), *Bulletin of the Imperial Earthquake Investigation Committee* (hereafter *BIEIC*) 11, no. 1 (March 1923): 28–32.

13. Imamura's *Taiyō* article and the controversy it generated are summarized in Aki Keiiti, "Possibilities of Seismology in the 1980s" [presidential address], *Bulletin of the Seismological Society of America* 70, no. 5 (October 1980): 1969–76. I've also relied on the account in Yamashita Fumio, *Jishin yochi no senkusha Imamura Akitsune no shōgai* (Tokyo, 1989).

14. Ōmori, "Tokyo to daijishin no fusetsu" *Taiyō* 12, no. 4 (April 1906): 173–77.

15. Imamura Akitsune, *Jishingaku* (Tokyo: Dainihon-Tosho, 1905). The title translates simply, and definitively, as "seismology." Ōmori Fusakichi, *Jishin gaku kōwa* (Tokyo: Kaiseikan, 1907).

16. Yamashita, pp. 7–9.

17. Ibid.

18. Ōmori, "Note on the Valparaiso and Aleutian earthquakes of Aug. 17, 1906," *BIEIC* 1, no. 2 (March 1907): 75–113.

19. Imamura, "The Great Earthquake in SE Japan, Sept. 1, 1923 with two appendices," in National Research Council of Japan, *Scientific Japan, Past and Present* [printed in connection with the Third Pan-Pacific Science Congress, Tokyo, 1926] (Kyoto, 1926), pp. 141–76; Gianluca Valensise and Daniela Pantosi, "The Investigation of Potential Earthquake Sources in Peninsula Italy," *Journal of Seismology* 5 (2001): 287–306. Valensise and Pantosi note that "even though Ōmori had actually foreseen the location of the 1915 earthquake, his views did not gain much recognition because most other scientists maintained that seismicity is essentially a random phenomenon" (p. 287).

20. Ōmori, "Note on the Kansu Earthquake of Dec. 16, 1920," Imperial Earthquake Investigation Committee (hereafter IEIC), *Seismological Notes*, no. 1 (Tokyo, 1921), p. 8.

21. Ōmori, "Earthquake Zones in and around the Pacific," p. 29.

22. Ōmori, "The Semi-Destructive Earthquake of April 26, 1922," IEIC, *Seismological Notes*, no. 3 (Tokyo, 1922), p. 1.

23. Ōmori, "Tokyo Observations of the Strong Earthquake on Jan. 14, 1923," IEIC, *Seismological Notes*, no. 4 (Tokyo, 1924), p. 10.

24. Imamura, "Preliminary Note on the Great Earthquake of SE Japan on Sept. 1, 1923," IEIC, *Seismological Notes*, no. 6 (Tokyo, 1924). Imamura, who was at his desk at Tokyo Imperial University when the earthquake struck, writes, "I can not tell you how desperately I fought against the fire without any water or any help from the outside" (p. 2). The collapse of the unfinished steel frame was reported in John W. Doty and W. W. Johnston, "Modern Steel and Re-enforced Concrete Structures Survive Japanese Earthquake," *Engineering News Record* 91, no. 17 (October 25, 1923): 678–81. For general accounts of the earthquake in English, see O. M. Poole, *The Death of Old Yokohama* (London: George Allen and Unwin, Ltd. 1968); and Bureau of Social Affairs Home Office (Japan), *The Great Earthquake of 1923 in Japan* (Tokyo, 1926).

25. *The Age* (Melbourne), September 4, 1923.

26. Yamashita, p. 9.

27. Sano and Taniguchi, p. 4.

28. While the percentage of fallen or damaged masonry buildings was large (over 80 percent, according to Suyehiro) there were notable exceptions, such as Tatsuno's Tokyo Station, Katayama's Akasaka Detached Palace, and Conder's and Sone's carefully constructed brick buildings for Mitsubishi in the Marunouchi quarter, which suffered "not a single crack" (Suyehiro Memorial Committee, *Scientific and Technical Papers of Suyehiro Kyōji* [Tokyo, 1934], pp. 422, 427).

29. Wrote Naitō in 1936: "One striking change noticeable in this Empire after the Great Earthquake of 1923 is the de facto disappearance of brick buildings and the contradistinctive predominance of steel and reinforced concrete structures" (Naitō Tachu, "Quake Proof Structure," in Japan Times and Mail, *Architectural Japan* [Tokyo, 1936], pp. 210–14, quotation p. 214).

30. See Sand, pp. 271–74.

31. Jeffrey W. Cody, "Erecting Monuments to the God of Business and Trade: The Fuller Construction Company of the Orient, 1919–1926," *Construction History* 12 (1996): 67–81; Naitō Tachu, "Building Construction after the Great Earthquake," in World Engineering Congress, *Proceedings of the World Engineering Congress, Tokyo 1929*, vol. 7 (Tokyo: World Engineering Congress/Kōgakkai, 1931), pp. 95–101; Naitō, "Quake Proof Structure"; Mutō Kiyoshi, "Seismic-Proof Construction," in Japan

Times and Mail, *Architectural Japan* (Tokyo, 1936), pp. 201–7; Suyehiro Memorial Committee, pp. 421–54.

32. The seismologist Suyehiro Kyoji thus told an American academic audience in 1931 that "except for the single case of the Marunouchi Building, which was built by a foreign contractor with slight experience in destructive earthquakes," all of the many Mitsubishi Company buildings in the quarter had survived unharmed (Suyehiro Memorial Committee, p. 422).

33. Ibid., p. 432.

34. A third major building listed as sustaining damage, the NYK Building, was also singled out in one account as "built in the American style," probably meaning with an unreinforced steel frame (Mutō, "Seismic-Proof Construction," p. 207).

35. Tenabe, p. 171 (emphasis added).

36. Saita Tokitarō, "Earthquake Proof Construction in Japan," in National Research Council of Japan, *Proceedings of the Third Pan-Pacific Science Conference Tokyo, Oct. 30–Nov. 11, 1926,* vol. 2 (Tokyo, 1928), pp. 1438–39.

37. Sano and Taniguchi, pp. 12–13.

38. Naitō, "Earthquake Proof Construction," in National Research Council of Japan, *Proceedings of the Third Pan-Pacific Science Congress, Tokyo, Oct. 30–Nov. 11, 1926,* vol. 2 (Tokyo, 1928).

39. Although Sano begins his "Recent Development of Architecture in Japan" with an evocation of the Ise shrine and Hōryūji temple, he concludes that following "the footsteps of our forbears" is "nothing but a dream." With the opening of Japan "we were compelled to awake as if from a long secluded dream in fairyland" (pp. 1–2). He would later write, in relation to the pagoda debate, "I don't think ancient *daiku* thought about earthquake-proof framing," which reflected the dominant opinion among Japanese architects from Condor through Itō Chūta (Sano and Taniguchi, p. 23).

40. Statistically, Tokyo's wooden, *daiku*-built structures fared just as well in the initial shock as its ferro-concrete, engineer-designed buildings. According to generally accepted estimates, about 10 percent of both classes of buildings were destroyed by seismic waves (Suyehiro Memorial Committee, p. 432). New building laws following the earthquake placed as many restrictions on wooden frames as on masonry shells, however, limiting both to two stories (Naitō, "Building Construction after the Great Earthquake," pp. 95–96).

41. Ichiura Ken, Nishiyama Uzō, and other young, radical, and technophilic architects would join the research staff of the Japan Housing Corporation (Jutaku Eidan) during the Pacific War, and actually institute the factory production of Japanese

houses. Their particular circle or faction, to whom much of the postwar obsession with prefabrication and high-tech design work can perhaps be traced, has never been the subject of proper historical scholarship. Among their key articles are Ichiura Ken, "Jōtaku to kanshiki kōzō," *Kokusai kenchiku* 8, no. 3 (March 1932): 117–22 (quotation p. 119); Ichiura, "Kenchiku seisan no gōrika," *Kenchiku ʒasshi* (December 1937): 40–46; and Nishiyama Uzō, "Wagakuni kenchikuka no shōrai ni tsuite," *Kenchiku ʒasshi* (April 1937).

42. Makino Masami, "Konkurito henbō ron," *Kokusai kenchiku* 8, no. 11 (November 1932): 433–42. Makino's skepticism about the earthquake-resistant qualities of ferroconcrete construction would be voiced again after the spectacular collapse of the concrete Hanshin Expressway in the Kobe earthquake of 1995.

43. Suyehiro Memorial Committee.

44. Imamura, "Preliminary Note on the Great Earthquake of SE Japan on Sept. 1, 1923," p. 1.

45. Terada Torihiko and Matazawa Takeo, "A Historical Sketch of the Development of Seismology in Japan," in National Research Council of Japan, *Scientific Japan, Past and Present* (Kyoto, 1926), pp. 251–310.

46. Ōmori lacks a proper biography, for example, although book-length biographies have been prepared for his predecessor, Sekiya Seikei, and his successor, Imamura Akitsune. Sympathetic treatments of Ōmori were for a long time after his death more common in foreign publications than in Japanese ones (e.g., the chapter honoring his contributions to the field in Davison's 1927 *Founders of Seismology*). The seismologist Ikegami Ryōhei wrote in the most extensive Japanese survey of Ōmori's work (1981) that "I would like to point out that Ōmori almost closed his eyes to the analytic (mathematically-based) seismology which developed later in Europe" ("Ōmori jishingaku no nokoshitamono," *Zisin* 34 [September 1981]: 38). Likewise, Japanese seismologist Utsu Tokuji describes Ōmori's research in a recent historical sketch of his discipline as "rather limited in effect" and "the conclusions of many papers by him . . . were invariable questionable in terms of statistical significance" ("Historical Development of Seismology in Japan," in William H. K. Lee, Hiroo Kanamori, Paul C. Jennings, and Carl Kisslinger, eds., *International Handbook of Earthquake and Engineering Seismology*, part B [San Diego: Academic Press, 2003], p. 6). The most commonly cited contribution of Ōmori to contemporary science is his formula for the diminution of aftershocks, still known as "Omori's Law."

47. Sir Gerald P. Lenox-Conyngham, "Remarks," in National Research Council of Japan, *Proceedings of the Third Pan-Pacific Science Conference, Tokyo, Oct. 30–Nov. 11, 1926,* vol. 1 (Tokyo, 1928), pp. 76–78.

48. Col. Lester E. Jones, "Science and the Earthquake Peril" [paper to be read March 17, 1926], privately printed and bound, in Retrospective Collection of MIT Libraries, pp. 570–71.

49. Ōmori, "The Semi-Destructive Earthquake of April 26, 1922," pp. 1–30; Ōmori's *Taiyō* article of 1906 noted that Yokohama's water pipes had already been broken by seismic action. Imamura recalled in 1924 that Ōmori as well as himself "often gave advice to the citizens of Tokyo to improve the construction of their water pipes" (Imamura, "Preliminary Notes on the Great Earthquake of SE Japan on Sept. 1, 1923," pp. 1–21).

50. Imamura, "Preliminary Notes on the Great Earthquake of SE Japan on Sept. 1, 1923."

51. Ibid.

52. Suyehiro Memorial Committee, p. 385.

53. Davison, *The Japanese Earthquake of 1923* (London: Thomas Murby & Co., 1931).

54. Ibid.

55. Ibid.

56. Suyehiro Memorial Committee, p. 355.

57. Ibid.

58. Watsuji Tetsuro, *Climate and Culture [Fūdo]*, Geoffrey Bownas, trans. (New York: Greenwood Press, 1961). My comments on Watsuji's *Pilgrimages to the Ancient Cathedrals in Italy* follow the discussion by Furukawa Tatsushi in the last chapter of the same volume.

59. Inoue Shōichi, in *Tsukurareta Katsura Rikyū shinwa* (Tokyo: Kōbundō, 1986), describes the Japanese social milieu within which Taut and other modernists "discovered" Katsura Villa as a modernist object. For a discussion of Horiguchi Sutemi and what the author calls "the understanding of tradition through the filter of Modernism," see Fujioka Hiroyasu, "Nihonteki na mono o meguru shisaku," in Tajiri Hirohiko, ed., *Horiguchi Sutemi no Nippon* (Tokyo: Shōkokusha, 1997), p. 114. For a discussion of the larger circle around Horiguchi, which included Maekawa Kunio, see Reynolds, *Maekawa Kunio.*

60. Bruno Taut, *Fundamentals of Japanese Architecture* (Tokyo: Kokusai Bunka Shinkokai, 1936); Taut, *Houses and People of Japan* (London: John Gifford, 1938). Adopting the stance of an anthropologist conducting fieldwork, Taut writes of his rented quarters, "It seemed to me best to confine my researches entirely to this little house" as "it contained every Japanese element, and if one had understood these elements here, then the variations would not confuse one, however numerous they might be" (p. 24).

61. Itō Chūta, "On Japanese Architecture," in Japan Times and Mail, *Architectural Japan* (Tokyo, 1936), p. 3. Itō's Memorial Hall to the victims of the Great Kantō Earthquake is discussed and illustrated in Reynolds, *Maekawa Kunio*, pp. 10–11. Perhaps mindful of its status as an aseismic icon, Itō capped his Memorial Hall with a ferroconcrete pagoda.

62. Antonin Raymond, "Notes on Architecture in Japan," *Cultural Japan* 4, no. 2 (July 1936): 177–81. *Cultural Japan* was the organ of the right-wing Japan Cultural Foundation (Nippon Bunka Renmei). The journal's editor, Fujisawa Chikao, shared an appreciation of the spiritual and eternal. "Our Emperor, Tenno," he wrote in a typical essay around the time of Raymond's article, "is the direct and uninterrupted successor of the grandson of the Sun Goddess who embodies the very eternal life pervading the Great Universe." Nothing in Raymond's own text would have contradicted Fujisawa's view of "the singular metaphysical relationship existing between the contemporary modern Japan and the old traditional Japan" or that "the evils of individualism may be peacefully removed by appealing to that national subconscious feeling. . . ."

63. Ibid.

64. Taut, *Fundamentals of Japanese Architecture*, pp. 19–20.

65. Itō, "On Japanese Architecture," p. 1. The first five items on Itō's list also define "Japan" in Watsuji's *Fūdo*, which had been published the previous year. Sano Toshikata would exploit a similar list in arguing, in 1934, that earthquakes had little influence on the Japanese preference for wooden architecture. The "number one reason" that wooden framing had developed in Japan, he claimed, was the abundance of that material, followed by the Japanese "national character" (which prefers simplicity and assimilation with nature), and lastly the mild climate (Sano and Taniguchi, p. 6).

66. Taut, *Fundamentals of Japanese Architecture*, pp. 12–13; Taut, *Houses and People of Japan*, pp. 65, 192, 213–14. In the latter book, Taut devotes a whole chapter to "the carpenter," with significant attention to photographs and descriptions of *daiku* tool and ritual. This ethnographic presentation of *daiku* was likely the most complete to appear up to that time, either in English or Japanese. Except for his novel format, however, Taut is fully within the nineteenth-century tradition of separating *daiku* hand from mind: for example, "he upsets with elegance all reasonable constructive sense" (p. 192). Taut is so certain that climate is the major determining factor in Japanese house-design that he appends to his book maps of currents and winds, and even a weather chart from the Ministry of Health.

67. Kishida Hideto, "Modern Architecture in Japan," in Japan Times and Mail, *Architectural Japan* (Tokyo, 1936), pp. 167–69 (quotation p. 167).

68. Suyehiro Memorial Committee, p. 388. This disinterest in earthquakes within the architectural profession was not yet reflected in the architectural curriculum of Tokyo Imperial University, where in 1934 the study of seismology still dominated the second year (after first-year lessons in math, physics, structural dynamics, the history of architecture, and drawing). The forced nature of this study and its local/national character may have contributed to the indifference of younger designers taken with the comparative freedoms of "international" architecture. There was also the reality that Tokyo had been rebuilt, and was unlikely to experience a second major earthquake in the working life of that generation (Tenabe, p. 172).

69. According to Suzuki Hiroyuki, the exhibit of the plans for Kenzo Tange's Peace Memorial Museum in Hiroshima at the 1951 Congrès Internationaux d'Architecture Moderne conference in Tokyo was "the first time since the war [that] Japanese architecture was introduced to the European architectural community." Likewise, the Metabolism Group, which defined Japanese avant-garde design in the early 1960s, was organized on the occasion of the World Design Conference (1960) in Tokyo. Both moments arguably revived Japanese architecture's Meiji-period diplomatic mission, even as they demonstrated that a certain peace had been made between modern materials and indigenous aesthetics (Suzuki Hiroyuki, Reyner Banham, and Kobayashi Katsuhiro, *Contemporary Architecture of Japan, 1958–1984* [New York: Rizzoli, 1985], pp. 5–6).

BIBLIOGRAPHY

Adas, Michael. *Machines as the Measure of Men*. Ithaca: Cornell University Press, 1989.

Aichiken Keisatsubu, ed. *Meiji nijūyonen jūgatsu nijūhachinichi shinsai kiroku*. Nagoya, 1892.

Aichiken Nagoya Sokkōjo, ed. *Meiji nijūyonen jūgatsu nijūhachinichi Aichiken daishinroku*. Nagoya, 1897.

Aki Keiiti. "Possibilities of Seismology in the 1980s" [presidential address]. *Bulletin of the Seismological Society of America* 70, no. 5 (October 1980): 1969–76.

Alcock, Sir Rutherford. *The Capital of the Tycoon. A Narrative of a Three Year's Residence in Japan*, 2 vols. New York: Greenwood Press, 1969.

Alexander, David. *Natural Disasters*. New York: Chapman and Hall, 1993.

Anonymous. *Notes on Building Construction*, part 1. London: Rivington, 1875.

Asahi Shōgakkō PTA. *Watashitachi no daisenpai jishingakusha no chichi Ōmori Fusakichi*. Tokyo, 1972.

Aslin, Elizabeth. *The Aesthetic Movement, Prelude to Art Nouveau*. New York: Frederick A. Praeger, 1969.

Azuma Kenzaburō, ed. *Fūzokugahō: hachi-gatsu 28 shinsai shinbun jōkan*. Tokyo, 1891.

Bankoff, Gregory. *Cultures of Disaster: Society and Natural Hazards in the Philippines*. London: RoutledgeCurzon, 2003.

Bartholomew, James. "Japanese Modernization and the Imperial Universities, 1876–1920." *Journal of Asian Studies* 37, no. 2 (February 1978): 251–71.

―――. *The Formation of Science in Japan: Building a Research Tradition*. New Haven: Yale University Press, 1989.

Biagioli, Mario. *Galileo, Courtier: The Practice of Science in the Culture of Absolutism*. Chicago: University of Chicago Press, 1993.

Biel, Steven. *American Disasters*. New York: New York University Press, 2002.

Brantley, S., and H. Glicken. "Volcanic Debris Avalanches." *Earthquakes and Volcanoes* 18, no. 6 (1986): 195–206.

Brock, W. H. "The Japanese Connexion: Engineering in Tokyo, London, and Glasgow at the End of the Nineteenth Century." *The British Journal for the History of Science* 14 (1981): 229–34.

Brunton, R. H. "Constructive Art in Japan, Part I." *Transactions of the Asiatic Society of Japan* 2 (1873–74).

―――. "Constructive Art in Japan, Part II." *Transactions of the Asiatic Society of Japan* 3 (1875).

Burchfield, Joe E. *Lord Kelvin and the Age of the Earth*. Chicago: University of Chicago Press, 1975.

Caviedes, Cesar N. *El Niño in History: Storming through the Ages*. Tallahassee: University of Florida Press, 2001.

Cawley, George. "Some Remarks on Constructions in Brick and Wood and Their Relative Suitability for Japan." *Transactions of the Asiatic Society of Japan* 6, part 2 (1877–78).

―――. "Wood and Its Application to Japanese Artistic and Industrial Design." *Transactions and Proceedings of the Japan Society of London* 2 (1892–93): 206–23.

Chisholm, Lawrence W. *Fenollosa: The Far East and American Culture*. New Haven: Yale University Press, 1963.

Clancey, Gregory. *Meiji Gakuin senkyōshi-kan (Imbry-kan) no kōzō: kenchiku chōsa hōkoku*. Tokyo: Meiji Gakuin, 1996.

―――. "The Science of Eurasia: Meiji Seismology as Cultural Critique." In *Historical Perspectives on East Asian Science, Technology, and Medicine*, edited by Alan Chan, Gregory Clancey, and Loy Hui Chieh, pp. 27–40. Singapore: Singapore University Press and World Scientific Publishing, 2002.

―――. "Foreign Knowledge: Cultures of Western Science-Making in Meiji Japan." *Historia Scientiarum* 11, no. 3 (2002): 245–60. Reprinted in *Asia in Europe, Europe in Asia*, edited by Srilata Ravi, Mario Ruttan, and Beng-Lan Goh, pp. 162–83. Leiden, Netherlands: International Institute for Asian Studies, 2004.

————. "Toward a Spatial History of Emergency: Notes from Singapore." In *Beyond Description: Singapore, Space, Historicity,* edited by Ryan Bishop, John Phillips, and Yeo Wei Wei, pp. 30–59. New York: Routledge, 2004.

————. "Modernity and Carpenters: *Daiku* Technique and Meiji Technocracy." In *Building a Modern Japan: Science, Technology, and Medicine from the Meiji Era and Beyond,* edited by Morris Low, pp. 183–206. New York: Palgrave Macmillan, 2005.

Coaldrake, William. *The Way of the Carpenter.* New York: Weatherhill, 1990.

————. *Architecture and Authority in Japan.* New York: Routledge, 1996.

Cody, Jeffrey W. "Erecting Monuments to the God of Business and Trade: The Fuller Construction Company of the Orient, 1919–1926." *Construction History* 12 (1996): 67–81.

Collins, Harry, and Trevor Pinch. *The Golem at Large: What You Should Know about Technology.* Cambridge: Cambridge University Press, 1998.

Conant, Ellen. "Reflections on the Rising Sun: Japan's Participation in International Exhibits, 1862–1910." In *Japan and Britain: An Aesthetic Dialogue, 1850–1930,* edited by Tomoko Sato and Toshio Watanabe, pp. 79–92. London: Lund Humphries, 1991.

Conder, Josiah. "The Practice of Architecture in Japan." *Japan Weekly Mail,* August 28, 1886, pp. 213–16.

————. "Domestic Architecture in Japan." *Proceedings of the Royal Institute of British Architects* 3, no. 10 (March 1887): 198.

————. "The Effects of the Recent Earthquake upon Buildings." *Japan Weekly Mail,* December 12, 1891, p. 725.

————. "Earthquakes versus Buildings" (read before the Society of Japanese Architects, January 27, 1892). *Japan Weekly Mail,* January 30, 1892, p. 153.

————. "The Condition of Architecture in Japan" (paper to be read before the International Congress of Architects, World's Columbian Exposition, August 2, 1893). *Japan Weekly Mail,* September 30, 1893, p. 394.

————. "An Architect's Notes on the Great Earthquake of 1891." *Seismological Journal of Japan* 18 (1893): 1–91.

Cram, Ralph Adams. "The Early Architecture of Japan." *The Architectural Review,* 1893.

————. *Impressions of Japanese Architecture and the Allied Arts.* New York: Baker & Taylor, 1905.

————. "Can We Produce Architects by Education?" *The Architect's World* 1, no. 1 (February 1938): 27–28.

Crook, J. Morduant. "Josiah Conder in England: Education, Training, and Background." In *Josiah Conder: A Victorian Architect in Japan*, edited by Suzuki Hiroyuki, pp. 26–28. Tokyo: Bijutsu Shuppan, 1997.

Curtis, George Carroll. "Work Going on at Kilauea Volcano." *Science* 38, no. 976 (1913): 355–58.

Davis, Mike. *Ecology of Fear: Los Angeles and the Imagination of Disaster*. New York: Vintage Books, 1999.

———. *Dead Cities and Other Tales*. New York: New Press, 2002.

———. *Late Victorian Holocausts: El Niño Famines and The Making of the Third World*. London: Verso, 2002.

Davison, Charles. *The Hereford Earthquake of Dec. 17, 1896*. Birmingham, UK: Cornish Bros., 1899.

———. "The Great Japanese Earthquake of Oct. 28, 1891." *Geographical Journal* 17, no. 6 (June 1901).

———. *A Manual of Seismology*. Cambridge: Cambridge University Press, 1921.

———. *The Founders of Seismology*. Cambridge: Cambridge University Press, 1927.

———. *The Japanese Earthquake of 1923*. London: Thomas Murby & Co., 1931.

———. *Great Earthquakes*. London: Thomas Murby & Co., 1936.

Dewey, James, and Perry Byerly. "The Early History of Seismometry (to 1900)." *Bulletin of the Seismological Society of America* 59, no. 1 (February 1969): 183–227.

Dostrovsky, Sigalia. "James Alfred Ewing." In *Dictionary of Scientific Biography*, edited by Charles Gillispie. New York: Scribner, 1970.

Doty, John W., and W. W. Johnston. "Modern Steel and Re-Enforced Concrete Structures Survive Japanese Earthquake." *Engineering News Record* 91, no. 17 (October 25, 1923): 678–81.

Dresser, Christopher. *Japan: Its Architecture, Art, and Manufactures*. New York: Garland Publishing Co., 1977 (originally published 1882).

Durant, Stuart. *Christopher Dresser*. London: Academy Group, 1993.

Dyer, Henry. Comments regarding John Milne's "On Construction in Earthquake Countries." *Minutes of the Proceedings of the Institution of Civil Engineers* 83 (1886): 309–13.

———. *Dai Nippon*. London: Blackie and Son, 1904.

Endō Akihisa. "Kaitakushi eizen jigyō no kenkyū." Unpublished manuscript in author's possession. 1961.

———. *Hokkaido jūtakushiwa*. Tokyo: Sumai no Toshokan Shuppankyoku, 1994.

Endō Motoo. *Nihon shokuninshi no kenkyū 5: kenchiku, kinko shokuninshiwa.* Tokyo: Yuzankaku, 1961.

———. *Shokunin-tachi no rekishi.* Tokyo: Shibundō, 1965.

Ewing, James. "A New Form of Pendulum Seismograph." *Transactions of the Seismological Society of Japan* 1 (1880): 38–43.

———. "On a New Seismograph for Horizontal Motion." *Transactions of the Seismological Society of Japan* 2 (1880): 45–49.

———. "Earthquake Measurement." *Memoirs of the Science Dept., Tokyo Daigaku* 9 (1883).

Finn, Dallas. *Meiji Revisited.* New York: Weatherhill, 1995.

Fletcher, Bannister. *History of Architecture,* 20th ed. Oxford: Architectural Press, 1996.

Ford, George H. "The Felicitous Space: The Cottage Controversy." In *Nature and the Victorian Imagination,* edited by U. C. Knoepflmacher and G. B. Tennyson, pp. 29–48. Berkeley: University of California Press, 1977.

Fradkin, Philip. *Magnitude 8.* Berkeley: University of California Press, 1999.

Fujimori Terunobu. *Meiji no Tokyo keikaku.* Tokyo: Iwanami Shoten, 1982.

———. *Nihon no kindai kenchiku.* 2 vols. Tokyo: Iwanami Shoten, 1993.

———. "Josiah Conder and Japan." In *Josiah Conder: A Victorian Architect in Japan,* edited by Suzuki Hiroyuki, pp. 17–21. Tokyo: Bijutsu Shuppan, 1997.

Fujioka Hiroyasu. "Nihonteki na mono o meguru shisaku." In *Horiguchi Sutemi no Nihon,* edited by Tajiri Hirohiko, pp. 111–20. Tokyo: Shōkokusha, 1997.

Fujita Fumiko. *Hokkaido o kaitakushita amerikajin.* Tokyo: Shinchosha, 1993.

Funakishi Kinya. "The Adaptation of European Architecture in Japan" (1883, Architecture Course, Kōbudaigakkō). Handwritten manuscript in Architecture Library, Faculty of Engineering, University of Tokyo.

Galison, Peter. *Image and Logic.* Chicago: University of Chicago Press, 1997.

Galison, Peter, and David Stump, eds. *The Disunity of Science: Boundaries, Contexts, and Power.* Stanford: Stanford University Press, 1996.

Gavin, Masako. *Shiga Shigetaka, 1863–1927: The Forgotten Enlightener.* Richmond, UK: Curzon Press, 2001.

Gifu Daigaku Kyōiku Gakubu. *Nōbi jishin (Meiji nijūyonen) anketo chōsa hōkoku.* Gifu, 1977.

Gifuken Gifu Sokkōjo. *Meiji nijūyonen jūgatsu nijūhachinichi daishin hōkoku.* Gifu, 1894.

Gooday, Graeme. "Teaching Telegraphy and Electrotechnics in the Physics Laboratory: William Ayrton and the Creation of an Academic Space for Electrical Engineering in Britain, 1873–1884." *History of Technology* 13 (1991): 73–111.

Gooday, Graeme, and Morris Low. "Technology Transfer and Cultural Exchange: Western Scientists and Engineers Encounter Late Tokugawa and Meiji Japan." *Osiris*, 2nd ser., vol. 13 (1998–99): 99–128.

Gray, Thomas. "On Instruments for Measuring and Recording Earthquake Motions." *Philosophical Magazine*, ser. 5, no. 12 (1881): 199–212.

Gwilt, Joseph. *An Encyclopedia of Architecture.* London, 1842.

Hagiwara Takahiro et al. "Kaku kenkyu kikan no rekishi." *Zisin* 34 (September 1981): 135–62.

Hamamatsu Otozō. "Jishin kansokushi." *Zisin* 34 (September 1981): 73–92.

Hara Tokuzō. "Josiah Conder and His Patrons." In *Josiah Conder: A Victorian Architect in Japan*, edited by Suzuki Hiroyuki, pp. 45–48. Tokyo: Bijutsu Shuppan, 1997.

Hashimoto Manpei. *Jishingaku koto hajime: kaitakusha Sekiya Kiyokage no shōgai.* Tokyo: Asahi Shimbunsha, 1983.

Hatsuda Tōru. *Shokunin-tachi no seiyō kenchiku.* Tokyo: Kōdansha, 1997.

Hattori Ichizō. "Destructive Earthquakes in Japan." *Transactions of the Asiatic Society of Japan* 6 (1877/78): 249–75.

Herbert-Gustar, A. L., and P. A. Nott. *John Milne: Father of Modern Seismology.* Tenterden, UK: Paul Norbury, 1980.

Hewitt, Kenneth. *Regions of Risk: A Geographical Introduction to Disasters.* London: Addison, Wesley, Longman, 1997.

Higuchi Jiro and Higuchi Yoichiro. Henry Spencer Palmer Museum. http://homepage3 .nifty.com/y/higuchi/ (accessed August 2004).

Hobbs, William H. *Earthquakes: An Introduction to Seismic Geology.* New York: D. Appleton, 1907.

Hoffman, Susanna, and Anthony Oliver-Smith. *The Angry Earth: Disaster in Anthropological Perspective.* New York: Routledge, 1999.

———. *Catastrophe and Culture: The Anthropology of Disaster.* Santa Fe, NM: School of American Research Press, 2002.

Hossain, Hameeda, Cole Dodge, and F. H. Abel, eds. *From Crisis to Development: Coping with Disasters in Bangladesh.* Dhaka: University Press Ltd., 1992.

Hovey, Edmund Otis. "Geological Society of America" (report). *Science* 29, no. 746 (1909): 623–39.

Huffman, James L. *Creating a Public: People and Press in Meiji Japan.* Honolulu: University of Hawaii Press, 1997.

Hughes, Thomas. *Networks of Power: Electrification in Western Society, 1880–1930.* Baltimore: Johns Hopkins University Press, 1983.

Ichiura Ken. "Jūtaku to kanshiki kōzō." *Kokusai kenchiku* 8, no. 3 (March 1932): 117–22.

———. "Kenchiku seisan no gōrika." *Kenchiku ʒasshi* (December 1937): 40–46.

Ikegami Ryōhei. "Ōmori jishingaku no nokoshitamono." *Zisin* 34 (September 1981): 37–72.

Ikeya Mataji et al. "Reproduction of Mimosa and Clock Anomalies before Earthquakes: Are They 'Alice in Wonderland' Syndrome?" *Proceedings of the Japanese Academy*, 74, ser. B (1998): 60–64.

Imamura Akitsune. *Jishingaku.* Tokyo: Dainihon-Tosho, 1905.

———. "Preliminary Note on the Great Earthquake of SE Japan on Sept. 1, 1923." In Imperial Earthquake Investigation Committee, *Seismological Notes* 6. Tokyo, 1924.

———. "The Great Earthquake in SE Japan, Sept. 1, 1923 with two appendices." In National Research Council of Japan, *Scientific Japan, Past and Present* [printed in connection with the Third Pan-Pacific Science Congress, Tokyo, 1926], pp. 141–76. Kyoto, 1926.

Imperial Earthquake Investigation Committee (IEIC). "Condensed Statement on the Construction of Earthquake Proof Wooden Buildings." *Publications of the Imperial Earthquake Investigation Committee in Foreign Languages* 4. Tokyo, 1900.

Inoue Katsugorō, ed. *Meiji daijjshin roku.* Tokyo: Heikyōshiken, 1891.

Inoue Shōichi. *Tsukurareta Katsura Rikyū shinwa.* Tokyo: Kōbundō, 1986.

———. *Hōryūji e no seishinshi.* Tokyo: Kōbundō, 1994.

Ishigawa Seibi, ed. *Meiji nijuyonen jūgatsu nijuhachinichi Aichi-ken daishin roku.* Nayoga: Aichi-ken Nagoya Sokkōjo, 1891.

Ishihara Ken, ed. *Nōbi sanjō jishin jikki.* Tokyo, 1891.

Itō Chūta. "On Japanese Architecture." In Japan Times and Mail, *Architectural Japan*, pp. 1–3. Tokyo, 1936.

Itō Tamekichi. *Nihon kenchiku kōʒō kairyōhō.* Tokyo: Kyōeki Shosha, 1892.

———. "Anzen kenchiku tetsugu oyobi kairyō kōzōhō." *Kenchiku ʒasshi* 74 (1894): 39–44.

———. *Mokkō jutsu kyokashō.* Tokyo: Shokko Gundan Sōritsu Jimusho, 1894.

———. *Shinshiki daiku hō.* Tokyo, 1934.

Jenkins, Frank. *Architect and Patron.* London: Oxford University Press, 1961.

Jerzombek, Mark. "Meditations on the Impossibility of a History of Modernity: Seeing beyond Art's History." In *The Education of the Architect: Historiography, Urbanism, and the Growth of Architectural Knowledge*, edited by Martha Pollak. Cambridge, MA: MIT Press, 1997.

Johnson, Alessa, ed. *Dreadful Visitations: Confronting Natural Disaster in the Age of Enlightenment.* New York: Routledge, 1995.

Jones, Caroline E., and Peter Galison, eds. *Picturing Science, Producing Art.* New York: Routledge, 1998.

Jones, H. J. *Live Machines: Hired Foreigners and Meiji Japan.* Vancouver: University of British Columbia Press, 1980.

Jones, Col. Lester E. "Science and the Earthquake Peril" (paper to be read March 17, 1926). Privately printed and bound, in Retrospective Collection of MIT Libraries.

Karatani Kojin. "Japan as Museum: Okakura Tenshin and Ernest Fenollosa." In *Japanese Art after 1945: Scream against the Sky,* edited by Alexandra Munroe, pp. 33–39. New York: Harry Abrams, 1994.

Katayama Ichirō, ed. *Nōbi shinshi.* Gifu: Katsunuma Takekazu, 1893.

Katō Yoichi. *Daijishin no jikkyō.* Nagoya: Morishima Mizutarō, 1891.

Katsugame Shigetarō, ed. *Nōbi shinsai zue hyōshi.* Tokyo, 1891.

Kawagoe Kunio et al. *Kenchiku anzenron (Shin kenchikugaku Taikei 12).* Tokyo: Shōkokusha, 1983.

Kawanabe Kusumi. "Josiah Conder and Kawanabe Kyosai." In *Josiah Conder: A Victorian Architect in Japan,* edited by Suzuki Hiroyuki, pp. 61–64. Tokyo: Bijutsu Shuppan, 1997.

Kawazoe Noboru. *Contemporary Japanese Architecture.* Tokyo: Kokusai Koryū Kikin, 1973.

Kaye, Barrington. *The Development of the Architectural Profession in Britain.* London: George Allen & Unwin Ltd., 1960.

Kenchikugaku Kenkyūkai. *Kenchikugaku kōhon.* Tokyo, 1905.

Kikuchi Dairoku. *Recent Seismological Investigations in Japan.* Tokyo, ca. 1904.

Kikuchi Kazuo. *Nihon no rekishi saigai. Meiji hen.* Tokyo: Kokon Shoin, 1986.

Kikuoka Tomoya. *Kensetsugyō o okoshita hitobito.* Tokyo: Shōkokusha, 1993.

Kishida Hideto. "Modern Architecture in Japan." In Japan Times and Mail, *Architectural Japan,* pp. 167–69. Tokyo, 1936.

Kitahara Itoko. *Bandaisan funka: saii kara saigai no kagaku e.* Tokyo: Yoshikawa Kobunken, 1998.

Kiyoshi Seike. *The Art of Japanese Joinery.* New York: Weatherhill, 1977.

Kizawa Noritoshi and Yamawa Yoshihiko. *Meiji shinsai shūroku.* Nagoya, 1891.

Kōda Rohan. *Gojūnotō.* Tokyo: Iwanami Shoten, 1953 (originally published 1891).

Koshino Takeshi. *Hokkaidō ni okeru shoki yōfū kenchiku no kenkyū,* Sapporo: Hokkaido Daigaku Toshokankakai, 1993.

Kotō Bunjirō. "On the Cause of the Great Earthquake in Central Japan, 1891." *Journal of the College of Science, Imperial University* 5, part 3 (1893): 295–353.

———. "The Scope of the Vulcanological Survey of Japan." *Publications of the Imperial Earthquake Investigation Committee in Foreign Languages* 3 (1900): 89–93.

Lancaster, Clay. *The Japanese Influence in America.* New York: W. H. Rawls, 1963.

Larabee, Ann. *Decade of Disaster.* Champaign: University of Illinois Press, 1999.

Larson, Margali S. *The Rise of Professionalism.* Berkeley: University of California Press, 1977.

Latour, Bruno. *Science in Action: How to Follow Scientists and Engineers through Society.* Cambridge, MA: Harvard University Press, 1987.

———. *The Pasteurization of France.* Cambridge, MA: Harvard University Press, 1988.

———. *We Have Never Been Modern.* Cambridge, MA: Harvard University Press, 1993.

Lavan. "Are the Japanese Workmen Slow?" *Scientific American Supplement,* no. 20 (May 13, 1876): 309.

Lears, T. Jackson. *No Place of Grace.* New York: Pantheon Books, 1981.

Lenox-Conyngham, Sir Gerald P. "Remarks." In National Research Council of Japan, *Proceedings of the Third Pan-Pacific Science Conference, Tokyo, Oct. 30–Nov. 11, 1926,* vol. 1, pp. 76–78. Tokyo, 1928.

Levy, Richard. "The Professionalization of American Architects and Civil Engineers, 1865–1917." Ph.D. diss., University of California, Berkeley, 1980.

Lo Ming-Cheng, Miriam. *Doctors within Borders: Profession, Ethnicity, and Modernity in Colonial Taiwan.* Berkeley: University of California Press, 2002.

Low, Morris. "The Japanese Nation in Evolution: W. E. Griffis, Hybridity, and the Whiteness of the Japanese Race." *History and Anthropology* 11 (1999): 2–3.

Majima Kenzaburō. "On the Construction of Earthquake-Proof Buildings" (English abstract). In National Research Council of Japan, *Proceedings of the Third Pan-Pacific Science Conference, Tokyo, Oct. 30–Nov. 11, 1926,* vol. 2, p. 1453. Tokyo, 1928.

Makino Masami. "Konkurito henbō ron." *Kokusai kenchiku* 8, no. 11 (November 1931): 433–42.

Mallet, Robert. *The Great Neapolitan Earthquake of 1857. The First Principles of Observational Seismology . . .* London: Chapman and Hall, 1862.

Markus, Andrew. "Gesaku Authors and the Ansei Earthquake of 1855." In *Studies in Modern Japanese Literature: Essays in Honor of Edwin McClellan,* edited by Dennis Washburn and Alan Tansman. Ann Arbor: Center for Japanese Studies, University of Michigan, 1997.

Marx, Erwin. *Die Hochbau-Constructionen: Des Handbuches der Architectur*, dritter theil, 2 band, 1 heft [Wande und Wand-Oeffnungen]. Darmstadt: Verlag von Arnold Bergstrasser, 1891.

Merchant, Carolyn. *The Death of Nature*. San Francisco: Harper & Row, 1980.

Mihashi Shirō. *Dai kenchiku-gaku*. Tokyo, 1915.

Milne, John. "Seismic Science in Japan." *Transactions of the Seismological Society of Japan* 1, part 1 (1880): 3–37.

———. "The Earthquake in Japan of Feb. 22, 1880." *Transactions of the Seismological Society of Japan* 1, part 2 (1880): 1–116.

———. "Notes on the Recent Earthquakes of Yedo Plain, and Their Effects on Certain Buildings." *Transactions of the Seismological Society of Japan* 2 (1880): 1–39.

———. "Suggestions for the Systematic Observance of Earthquakes." *Transactions of the Seismological Society of Japan* 4 (January–June 1882): 85–117.

———. "Seismology." *Kagaku ɀasshi* 20 (1883): 313–18.

———. "On the Earthquake Phenomena of Japan." *Report of the 54th Meeting of the British Association for the Advancement of Science* (London, 1885): 248–49.

———. *Earthquakes and Other Earth Movements*. New York: D. Appleton, 1886.

———. "On Construction in Earthquake Countries." *Minutes of the Proceedings of the Institution of Civil Engineers* 83, session 1885–86, part 1, paper 2108, pp. 278–320 (1886).

———. "Volcanoes of Japan." *Transactions of the Seismological Society of Japan* 9, part 2 (1886).

———. "Earthquake Effects[,] Emotional and Moral." *Transactions of the Seismological Society of Japan* 11 (1887): 91–113.

———. "Seismological Work in Japan." *Nature* (October 31, 1889).

———. "Preliminary Report on Earthquake Motion." *Transactions of the Seismological Society of Japan* 14 (1891): 1–42.

———. "Seismometry and Engineering in Relation to the Recent Earthquake in Japan." *Nature* 45, no. 1154 (December 10, 1891).

———. "Seismic, Magnetic, and Electrical Phenomena." *Transactions of the Seismological Society of Japan* 19 (1894): 23–29.

———. "A Catalogue of 8331 Earthquakes Recorded in Japan 1885–1892." *Seismological Journal of Japan* 4 (1895): 1–367.

———. *Seismology*. London: Kegan, Paul, Trench, Truber & Co., 1898.

———. "Seismological Observations and Earth Physics." *The Geographical Journal* 21, no. 1 (January 1903): 1–22.

Milne, John, ed. *Construction in Earthquake Countries.* Special issue of *Transactions of the Seismological Society of Japan,* vol. 14. Tokyo, 1889.

Milne, J., and W. K. Burton. *The Great Earthquake in Japan, 1891.* London and Yokohama: Standford, 1892.

Minear, Richard. "Orientalism and the Study of Japan." *Journal of Asian Studies* 39, no. 3 (May 1980): 507–10.

Miyata Noboru and Takata Mamoru, eds. *Namazu-e: jishin to Nihon bunka.* Tokyo: Satofumi Shuppan, 1995.

Miyawaki Hikozaburō, ed. *Daijishin jichi kenbunroku.* Nagoya, 1891.

Miyazawa Seiji. *Kin-gendai Nihon kishōsaigaishi.* Tokyo: Ikarosu Shuppan, 1999.

Monbushō (Ministry of Education). *Catalog of Objects Exhibited at the World's Columbian Exposition, Chicago, U.S.A., 1893, by the Department of Education, Japan.* Tokyo, 1893.

———. *Kogyogakkō kenchiku seizu kyoju yomoku.* Tokyo, 1904.

Montel, Alfredo. *Building Structures in Earthquake Countries.* London: Charles Griffin & Co., 1912.

Mori Takayuki, ed. *Jishinjuhō.* Nagoya, 1891.

Morris-Suzuki, Tessa. *The Technological Transformation of Japan: From the Seventeenth to the Twenty-First Centuries.* Cambridge: Cambridge University Press, 1994.

Morse, Edward. *Japanese Homes and Their Surroundings.* Rutland, VT: Charles E. Tuttle Co., 1972 (originally published 1886).

Muramatsu Teijirō. "The Japanese Construction Industry IV." *The Japan Architect,* no. 318 (January–February 1968): 139–46.

———. "Mokuzō kōzō no kindaika." In Nihon Kenchiku Gakkai, *Kindai Nihon kenchiku-gaku hattatsushi,* pp. 7–10. Tokyo: Maruzen Kabushiki Gaisha, 1972.

———. *Daiku dōgu no rekishi.* Tokyo: Iwanami Shoten, 1973.

———. *Nihon kindai kenchiku gijutsushi.* Tokyo: Shōkokusha, 1976.

———. *Nihon kindai kenchiku no rekishi.* Tokyo: Nihon Hōsō Shuppan Kyōkai, 1977.

———. *Waga kuni daiku no kōsaku gijutsu ni kansuru kenkyū.* Tokyo: Rōdō Kagaku Kenkyujo Shuppanbu, 1984.

———. "History of the Building Design Department of Takenaka Kōmuten." In Building Design Dept. of Takenaka Kōmuten, *Takenaka kōmuten sekeibu.* Tokyo: Shinkenchiku-sha, 1987.

———. *Yawarakai mono e no shiten: itan no kenchikuka Itō Tamekichi.* Tokyo: Iwanami Shoten, 1994.

Mutō Kiyoshi. "Gojūnotō and Earthquakes." In *Proceedings of the World Engineering Congress, Tokyo 1929*, vol. 7 (paper no. 668), pp. 269–91. Tokyo: World Engineering Congress/Kōgakkai, 1931.

————. "Seismic-Proof Construction." In Japan Times and Mail, *Architectural Japan*, pp. 201–7. Tokyo, 1936.

Nagoya-shi Bōsai Kaigi Jishin Taisaku Senmon Iinkai. *Nōbi jishin bunken mokuroku*. Nagoya: Nagoya-shi Shiminkyoku Saigai Taisakuka, 1978.

Nagoya Ukiyochinbunsha. *Meiji jishin shōhō*. Nagoya, 1891.

Naimushō Shakaikyoku. *The Great Earthquake of 1923 in Japan*. Tokyo, 1926.

Naitō Tachu. "Earthquake Proof Construction." In National Research Council of Japan, *Proceedings of the Third Pan-Pacific Science Congress, Tokyo, Oct. 30–Nov. 11, 1926*, vol. 2, pp. 1474–75. Tokyo, 1928.

————. "Building Construction after the Great Earthquake." In *Proceedings of the World Engineering Congress, Tokyo 1929*, vol. 7, pp. 95–101. Tokyo: World Engineering Congress/Kōgakkai, 1931.

————. "Quake Proof Structure." In Japan Times and Mail, *Architectural Japan*, pp. 210–14. Tokyo, 1936.

Nakajima Chōtarō et al. *Rekishi saigai no hanashi*. Kyoto: Shibunkaku Shuppan, 1992.

Nakajima Yoichiro. *Kantō daishinsai*. Tokyo: Yūzankaku, 1973.

Nakamura Tetsutarō, ed. *Nihon kenchiku ji*. Tokyo: Maruzen, 1904.

Nakatani Norihito. "Bakumatsu, Meiji kikujutsu no tenkei katei no kenkyū." Ph.D. diss., Waseda University, Tokyo, 1998.

————. *Kinsei kenchikuronshū*. Osaka: Henshū Shuppan Soshikitai Asetate, 2004.

Nakatani Norihito et al. " 'Zōka' kara 'kenchiku' e." *Kenchiku zasshi* 112, no. 1410 (August 1997): 13–21.

Nakayama Shigeru. "Japanese Science." In *The Encyclopedia of the History of Science, Technology, and Medicine in Non-Western Countries*, edited by Helaine Selin. Dordrecht, The Netherlands: Kluwer Academic Publications, 1997.

Nihon Kenchiku Gakkai. *Kindai Nihon kenchiku-gaku hattatsushi*. Tokyo: Maruzen Kabushiki Gaisha, 1972.

Nishiyama Uzō. "Wagakuni kenchikuka no shōrai ni tsuite." *Kenchiku zasshi* (April 1937).

Ogawa Masuo. *Tokyo shōshitsu: Kantō daishinsai no kiroku*. Tokyo: Koseido, 1974.

Oldham, R. D. "The Constitution of the Interior of the Earth as Revealed by Earthquakes." *Quarterly Journal of the Geological Society* 62 (1906): 456–73.

Ōmori Fusakichi. "Notes on the Great Mino-Owari Earthquake of Oct. 28, 1891." In *Publications of the Imperial Earthquake Investigation Committee in Foreign Languages,* no. 4, pp. 13–24. Tokyo, 1900.

———. "Seismic Experiments on the Fracturing and Overturning of Columns." In *Publications of the Imperial Earthquake Investigation Committee in Foreign Languages,* no. 4, pp. 138–41. Tokyo, 1900.

———. "Tokyo to daijishin no fusetsu." *Taiyō* 12, no. 4 (1906): 173–77.

———. *Jishin gaku kōwa.* Tokyo: Kaiseikan, 1907.

———. "Preliminary Notes on the Cause of the San Francisco Earthquake of Apr. 18, 1906." *Bulletin of the Imperial Earthquake Investigation Committee* 1, no. 1 (January 1907): 26–43.

———. "Preliminary Note on the Formosan Earthquake of Mar. 17, 1906." *Bulletin of the Imperial Earthquake Investigation Committee* 1, no. 2 (March 1907): 53–69.

———. "Note on the Valparaiso and Aleutian Earthquakes of Aug. 17, 1906." *Bulletin of the Imperial Earthquake Investigation Committee* 1, no. 2 (March 1907): 75–113.

———. "Notes on the Secondary Causes of Earthquakes." *Bulletin of the Imperial Earthquake Investigation Committee* 2, no. 2 (October 1908): 101–35.

———. "Preliminary Report on the Messina-Reggio Earthquake of Dec. 28, 1908." *Bulletin of the Imperial Earthquake Investigation Committee* 3, no. 1 (1909): 37–45.

———. "Note on the Form of Japanese Castle Walls." *Bulletin of the Imperial Earthquake Investigation Committee* 9 (1918–1921): 30–32.

———. "Measurement of the Vibration of Gojūnotōs, or 5-Story Buddhist Stupas (Pagodas)." *Bulletin of the Imperial Earthquake Investigation Committee* 9 (1918–1921): 110–52.

———. "Note on the Kansu Earthquake of Dec. 16, 1920." In Imperial Earthquake Investigation Committee, *Seismological Notes,* no. 1, pp. 4–9. Tokyo, 1921.

———. "The Omachi (Shinano) Earthquakes of 1918." *Bulletin of the Imperial Earthquake Investigation Committee* 10 (1922–28).

———. "On the Severe Earthquake of Dec. 8, 1921." In Imperial Earthquake Investigation Committee, *Seismological Notes,* no. 2, pp. 1–21. Tokyo, 1922.

———. "The Semi-Destructive Earthquake of April 26, 1922." In Imperial Earthquake Investigation Committee, *Seismological Notes,* no. 3, pp. 1–30. Tokyo, 1922.

———. "Earthquake Zones in and around the Pacific." *Bulletin of the Imperial Earthquake Investigation Committee* 11, no. 1 (March 1923): 28–32.

———. "Tokyo Observations of the Strong Earthquake on January 14, 1923." In Imperial Earthquake Investigation Committee, *Seismological Notes,* no. 4, pp. 1–19. Tokyo, 1924.

Opderbecke, Adolf. *Das Holzbau-Buch fur den Shulgebrauch und die Baupraxis.* Hannover: Verlag Th. Schafer, 1909.

Ouwehand, Cornelis. *Namazu-e and Their Themes: An Interpretative Approach to Some Aspects of Japanese Folk-Religion.* Leiden: Brill, 1964.

Paul, H. M. "Measuring Earthquakes." *Science* 4, no. 96 (1884): 516–18.

Perkin, Harold. *The Rise of Professional Society in England since 1880.* London: Routledge, 1989.

Perry, J., and W. E. Ayrton. "On a Neglected Principle that may be Employed in Earthquake Measurement." *Transactions of the Asiatic Society of Japan* 5 (1876–77).

Poole, O. M. *The Death of Old Yokohama.* London: George Allen and Unwin, Ltd., 1968.

Porter, Theodore. *The Rise of Statistical Thinking, 1820–1900.* Princeton: Princeton University Press, 1986.

Pownall, C. A. W. "Notes on Recent Publications Relating to the Effect of Earthquakes on Structures." *Transactions of the Seismological Society of Japan* 16 (1892): 1–18.

Pyle, Kenneth. *The New Generation in Meiji Japan: Problems in Cultural Identity, 1885–1895.* Stanford: Stanford University Press, 1969.

Raymond, Antonin. "Notes on Architecture in Japan." *Cultural Japan* 4, no. 2 (July 1936): 177–81.

Rebeur-Paschwitz, Ernst von. "The Earthquake of Tokio, April 18, 1889." *Nature* 40 (1889): 294–95.

———. "On the Observation of Earthquake Waves at Great Distance from Their Origin, with Special Relation to the Great Earthquake of Kumamoto, July 28th, 1889." *Transactions of the Seismological Society of Japan* 18 (1893): 111–14.

Reynolds, Jonathan. "The *Bunriha* and the Problem of 'Tradition' for Modernist Architecture." In *Multicultural Japan: Paleolithic to Postmodern,* edited by Donald Denoon, pp. 228–46. Cambridge: Cambridge University Press, 1996.

———. *Maekawa Kunio and the Emergence of Japanese Modernist Architecture.* Berkeley: University of California Press, 2001.

Richards, J. M. *An Architectural Journey in Japan.* London: Architectural Press, 1963.

Rose, Joshua. "The Japanese Government Building at the Centennial Grounds in Fairmount Park." *Scientific American Supplement,* no. 11 (March 11, 1876): 169.

———. "The Japanese at the Centennial." *Scientific American Supplement,* no. 25 (June 17, 1876).

Rosenberg, Nathan. "America's Rise to Woodworking Leadership." In *America's Wooden Age,* edited by Brooke Hindle. Tarrytown, NY: Sleepy Hollow Press, 1985.

Rosenfield, John M. "Western-Style Painting in the Early Meiji Period and Its Critics." In *Tradition and Modernization in Japanese Culture*, edited by Donald Shively, pp. 181–219. Princeton: Princeton University Press, 1971.

Rubinger, Richard. "Education: From One Road to One System." In *Japan in Transition: From Tokugawa to Meiji*, edited by Marius Jansen and Gilbert Rozman, pp. 195–230. Princeton: Princeton University Press, 1986.

Saeki Hōun. *Hitsū tansan Mino Owari*. Tokyo: Gominsha Sōritsu Jimusho, 1891.

Saita Tokitarō. "Earthquake Proof Construction in Japan." In National Research Council of Japan, *Proceedings of the Third Pan-Pacific Science Conference. Tokyo, Oct. 30–Nov. 11, 1926*, vol. 2, pp. 1438–39. Tokyo, 1928.

Sakashita Yukari. *Waza takumi hito Sakashita Jinkichi*. Takayama, 1994.

Sand, Jordan. *House and Home in Modern Japan: Architecture, Domestic Space, and Bourgeois Culture, 1880–1930*. Cambridge, MA: Harvard University Asia Center, 2003.

Sano Toshikata. *Kaoku taishin kōzō ron*. Tokyo, 1915.

———. "Recent Developments of Architecture in Japan." In *Proceedings of the World Engineering Congress, Tokyo 1929*, vol. 7, pp. 1–4. Tokyo: World Engineering Congress/Kōgakkai, 1931.

———. *Sano hakase tsuisōroku*. Tokyo: Sano Hakase Tsuisōroku Henshū Iinkai, 1957.

Sano Toshikata and Taniguchi Tadashi. *Taishin kōzō hanron*. Tokyo: Iwanami Shoten, 1934.

Sasamoto Shōji. *Saigai bunkashi no kenkyū*. Tokyo: Takashi Shoin, 2003.

Satachi Shichijirō. "The Future Domestic Architecture of Japan" (September 1879, Architecture Course, Kōbudaigakkō). Handwritten manuscript in Architecture Library, Faculty of Engineering, University of Tokyo.

Sawislak, Karin. *Smoldering City: Chicagoans and the Great Fire*. Chicago: University of Chicago Press, 1996.

Sekiya Seikei. "The Severe Earthquake of the 15th of Jan., 1887." *Transactions of the Seismological Society of Japan* 11 (1887): 79–90.

Sekiya Seikei and Y. Kikuchi. "The Eruption of Bandai-san." *Journal of the College of Science, Imperial University of Japan* 3, no. 2 (1889): 1–172.

Shapin, Steven. *A Social History of Truth: Civility and Science in Seventeenth-Century England*. Chicago: University of Chicago Press, 1994.

Shiga Shigetaka. *Nihon fūkeiron*. Tokyo: Seikyōsha, 1894.

Shigaken Kaigyōishi Kumiai Sōkai. *Gifukenka shinsai fushōsha kyūryō ryakki*. Hikone, 1892.

Shimizu Keiichi. "Meijiki ni okeru shotō-chūtō kenchiku kyōiku no shiteki kenkyū." Ph.D. diss., Nihon University, 1982.

Shively, Donald H. "The Japanization of the Middle Meiji." In *Tradition and Moderni-zation in Japanese Culture,* edited by Donald Shively, pp. 94–96. Princeton: Princeton University Press, 1971.

Smith, Carl S. *Urban Disorder and the Shape of Belief: The Great Chicago Fire, the Haymarket Bomb, and the Model Town of Pullman.* Chicago: University of Chicago Press, 1996.

Smith, Henry D., II. "Tokyo as an Idea: An Exploration of Japanese Urban Thought until 1945." *Journal of Japanese Studies* 4, no. 1 (Winter 1978): 45–80.

———. "The Edo-Tokyo Transition: In Search of a Common Ground." In *Japan in Transition: From Tokugawa to Meiji,* edited by Marius B. Jansen and Gilbert Rozman, pp. 347–74. Princeton: Princeton University Press, 1986.

Smith, Merritt R. "Becoming Engineers in Early Industrial America." STS Working Paper no. 13, Science, Technology, and Society Program, Massachusetts Institute of Technology, 1990.

Sone Tatsuzō. "A Thesis on the Future Domestic Architecture of Japan" (September 1879, Architecture Course, Kōbudaigakkō). Handwritten manuscript in Architecture Library, Faculty of Engineering, University of Tokyo.

Sprague, Paul E. "The Origin of Balloon Framing." *Journal of the Society of Architectural Historians* 40 (December 1981): 311–19.

Steinberg, Theodore. *Acts of God: The Unnatural History of Natural Disasters in America.* Oxford: Oxford University Press, 2000.

Stewart, David B. *The Making of a Modern Japanese Architecture.* Tokyo: Kōdansha Int., 1987.

Strange, Edward F. "Architecture in Japan." *Architectural Review* 1 (1897): 126–35.

Stratham, H. H. "Japanese Architecture." *Architectural Review* (October 1912): 177–88.

Sugimoto, Masayoshi, and David L. Swain. *Science and Culture in Traditional Japan.* Cambridge, MA: MIT Press, 1978.

Sunami Takashi. "Architecture of Shinto Shrines." In Japan Times and Mail, *Architectural Japan.* Tokyo, 1936.

Suyehiro Memorial Committee. *Scientific and Technical Papers of Suyehiro Kyōji.* Tokyo, 1934.

Suzuki Hiroyuki. *Victorian gothic no hōkai.* Tokyo: Chūō Kōron Bijutsu Shuppan, 1996.

Suzuki Hiroyuki, ed. *Josiah Conder: A Victorian Architect in Japan.* Tokyo: Bijutsu Shuppan, 1997.

———. *Itō Chūta o shite imasu ka.* Tokyo: Okoku, 2003.

Suzuki Hiroyuki, Reyner Banham, and Kobayashi Katsuhiro. *Contemporary Architecture of Japan, 1958–1984.* New York: Rizzoli, 1985.

Suzuki Hiroyuki and Hatsuda Tōru. *Zumen de miru: toshi kenchiku no Meiji.* Tokyo: Kashiwa Shobō, 1990.

Suzuki Hiroyuki and Yamaguchi Hiroshi. *Nihon no kindai gendai kenchiku shi [Shin kenchiku-gaku taikei],* vol. 5. Tokyo: Shōkokusha, 1993.

Suzuki Sakujirō, ed. *Aichi gifu daijishin no sanjōḍ* Nagoya, 1891.

Swain, David L. *Science and Culture in Traditional Japan.* Cambridge MA: MIT Press, 1978.

Tachikawa Tomokata. "Kōbushō yontō gishu Tachikawa Tomokata shoshin." In Nihon Kenchiku Gakkai, *Kindai Nihon kenchiku-gaku hattatsushi,* p. 14. Tokyo: Maruzen Kabushiki Gaisha, 1972.

Takahashi Yūzō. "William Edward Ayrton at the Imperial College of Engineering in Tokyo . . ." *IEEE [Institute of Electrical and Electronics Engineers] Transactions on Education* 33, no. 2 (May 1990): 198–205.

Takamatsu Tōru. "The Way Japan Joined Mechanized Civilization." In Tadao Umeseo et al., *Japanese Civilization in the Modern World.* Osaka: National Museum of Ethnology, 1998.

Takenaka Kōmuten shichijūnenshi Hensan Iinkai. *Takenaka Kōmuten shichijūnenshi.* Tokyo: Takenaka Kōmuten, 1969.

Taki Daikichi. "Future Architecture in Japan" (1883, Architecture Course, Kōbudaigakkō). Handwritten manuscript in Architecture Library, Faculty of Engineering, University of Tokyo.

———. *Kenchiku kōgi ron.* Tokyo: Kenchiku Shoin, 1890.

———. "Taishin kōzō." *Kenchiku zasshi* 7, no. 74 (1894): 51.

———. *Kenchiku kōgi roku.* Tokyo: Kenchiku Shoin, 1896.

Tamitsu Koji, ed. *Shinsai isō.* Tokyo, 1892.

Tanaka, Stefan. *Japan's Orient: Rendering Pasts into History.* Berkeley: University of California Press, 1993.

———. "Imaging History: Inscribing Belief in the Nation." *The Journal of Asian Studies* 53, no. 1 (February 1994): 24–44.

Tanakadate Aikitsu. "A Magnetic Survey of Japan." *Journal of the College of Science, Imperial University* 14 (1904): 1–180.

Tanakadate Aikitsu and Nagaoka Hantaro. "The Disturbance of Isomagnetics Attending the Mino-Owari Earthquake of 1891." *Journal of the College of Science, Imperial University* 5, part 3 (1892): 149–96.

Tatsuno Kingo. "Itariakoku isukiya-tō jishin kenchiku." *Kenchiku zasshi* 4, no. 43 (1891).

———. "Report on the Earthquake-Proof House." In *Shinsai yobō chōsakai hōkoku* 1, pp. 1–62. Tokyo: Imperial Earthquake Investigation Committee, 1893.

Tatsuno Kingo, Katayama Tōokuma, Nakamura Tsutarō, and Sone Tatsuzō. "Models of Buildings for the Seismic Experiments." In *Shinsai yobō chōsakai hōkoku* 2. Tokyo: Imperial Earthquake Investigation Committee, 1895.

Taut, Bruno. *Fundamentals of Japanese Architecture*. Tokyo: Kokusai Bunka Shinkokai, 1936.

————. *Houses and People of Japan*. London: John Gifford, 1938.

Tenabe Heigaku. "Technical Education in Japan." In Japan Times and Mail, *Architectural Japan*, pp. 170–72. Tokyo, 1936.

Terada Torahiko and Matazawa Takeo. "A Historical Sketch of the Development of Seismology in Japan." In National Research Council of Japan, *Scientific Japan, Past and Present*, pp. 251–310. Kyoto, 1926.

Thomas, Julia Adenay. *Reconfiguring Nature in Japanese Political Ideology*. Berkeley: University of California Press, 2002.

Tokyo Metropolitan Government. *Tokyo and Earthquakes*. Tokyo, 1995.

Toyama Minoru. "Dainihon Jishin Shiryo." *Reports of the Imperial Earthquake Investigation Committee* 46 (1904): vol. 1, pp. 1–606; vol. 2, pp. 1–595.

Traweek, Sharon. *Beamtimes and Lifetimes: The World of High-Energy Physicists*. Cambridge, MA: Harvard University Press, 1992.

Tredgold, Thomas. *Elementary Principles of Carpentry*. London: Lockwood and Co., 1870 (5th edition; originally published 1828).

Uchida Seizō. *Nippon no kindai jūtaku*. Tokyo: Kashima Shuppankai, 1992.

Udias, Augustin, and William Stauder. "The Jesuit Contribution to Seismology." *Seismological Research Letters* 67, no. 3 (May/June 1996): 10–19.

Umehara Chūzō. *Shin-u shinsairoku*. Osaka, 1891.

Usami Tatsuo. "Waga kuni no jishingaku no ayumi." *Zisin* 34 (September 1981): 1–36.

Usami Tatsuo and Hamamatsu Otozō. "Nihon no jishin oyobi jishingaku no rekishi." *Zisin* 29, no. 4 (December 1967): 1–34.

Utsu Tokuji. "Historical Development of Seismology in Japan." In *International Handbook of Earthquake and Engineering Seismology* (part B), edited by William H. K. Lee, Hiroo Kanamori, Paul C. Jennings, and Carl Kisslinger. San Diego: Academic Press, 2003.

Valensise, Gianluca, and Daniela Pantosi. "The Investigation of Potential Earthquake Sources in Peninsula Italy." *Journal of Seismology* 5 (2001): 287–306.

Vaughan, Diane. *The Challenger Launch Decision: Risky Culture, Technology, and Deviance at NASA*. Chicago: University of Chicago Press, 1996.

Viollet-le-Duc, Eugene Emmanuel. *Discourses on Architecture*. Boston: James R. Osgood & Co., 1875.

Wakabayashi, Minoru. *Design of Earthquake-Resistant Buildings*. New York: McGraw Hill, 1986.

Watanabe Masao. *The Japanese and Western Science*. Philadelphia: University of Pennsylvania Press, 1976.

Watanabe Toshio. "Josiah Conder's Rokumeikan: Architecture and National Representation in Meiji Japan." *Art Journal* 55 (Fall 1996): 21–27.

Watsuji Tetsuro. *Climate and Culture (Fūdo)*. Geoffrey Bownas, trans. New York: Greenwood Press, 1961.

Weisberg, Gabriel, and Yvonne Weisberg. *Japonisme: An Annotated Bibliography*. New York: Garland Publishing Co., 1990.

Wendelken, Cherie. "Living with the Past: Preservation and Development in Modern Japan." Ph.D. diss., Massachusetts Institute of Technology, 1994.

————. "The Tectonics of Japanese Style: Architect and Carpenter in the Late Meiji Period." *Art Journal* 55 (Fall 1996): 28–37.

Wichman, Sigfried. *Japonisme: The Japanese Influence in Western Art since 1858*. London: Thames and Hudson, 1981.

Winchester, Simon. *Krakatoa: The Day the World Exploded, August 27, 1883*. New York: HarperCollins, 2003.

Wood, Robert Muir. "Robert Mallet and John Milne—Earthquakes Incorporated in Victorian Britain." *Earthquake Engineering and Structural Dynamics* 17 (1988): 107–42.

Yamaguchi Seiichi. "Josiah Conder on Japanese Studies." In *Josiah Conder: A Victorian Architect in Japan*, edited by Suzuki Hiroyuki, pp. 53–56. Tokyo: Bijutsu Shuppan, 1997.

Yamashita Fumio. *Jishin yochi no senkusha Imamura Akitsune no shōgai*. Tokyo, 1989.

Yang, Daqing. *Technology of Empire: Telecommunications and Japanese Imperialism, 1930–1945*. Cambridge, MA: Harvard University Press, 2003.

Yokoyama Toshio. *Japan in the Victorian Mind: A Study of Stereotyped Images of a Nation, 1850–80*. London: Macmillan, 1987.

Yoshihara Yonejirō, ed. *Wayō jūtaku kenchiku zushū*. Tokyo: Kenchiku Shoin, 1910.

Yoshimoto Makiko. "Echigo mazedaiku." M.A. thesis, architecture. Hokkaido University, 1994.

Yuzawa Seinosuke. *Meiji Daijishin kenbunroku*. Tokyo, 1891.

INDEX

Page numbers in italics indicate figures.

"actor-network theory," 237*n*10
Adachi Yoshijuki, 34
Adas, Michael, 15
aftershocks, 128–35, 275*n*46
Akasaka Detached Palace, 267*n*17,
  292*n*28
Alcock, Sir Rutherford, 47, 49, 88
American Architect and Building News
  (journal), 46
Anglo-Japanese architecture project:
  Conder's reframing of, 142–43;
  Japanese skepticism of, 54–62; Western criticism of, 50–54. *See also* Conder, Josiah; Imperial Earthquake Investigation Committee; Japanese
  architecture; Kōbudaigakkō; Western
  learning
Ansei earthquake of 1855. *See* Great
  Ansei Earthquake (1855)
architectural history *(kenchikushi)* and
  Japanese style, 182–85
architectural profession: art and, 23–25,
  69–71, 94–95, 143, 164, 213, 233,
246*n*49; cultural status of, 19–28; science and, 25–28; search for Japanese
  style and, 182–85, 212; terms for architecture, 20–23. *See also* Japanese
  architecture
art: Japanese architecture and, 23–25,
  69–71, 94–95, 143, 164, 213, 233,
  246*n*49; nativist turn and, 94–95; vs.
  science, 69–71, 96–98, 107–12, 213–14
artisans. See *daiku*
Asahi shimbun (Tokyo newspaper), on
  Nōbi earthquake, 114, 115
Asakura Seiichi, 33
Ashio Copper Mine pollution scandal,
  236*n*3
Assam (India) earthquake of 1905, 165
Association of Japanese Architects
  (Nihon Kenchiku Kai), 180, 224; Conder and, 93; Itō and, 194–95
astronomy, 277*n*73
avant-garde. *See* modernism
Ayrton, W. E., 66–67

BAAS. *See* British Association for the
  Advancement of Science

Bandai-san eruption of 1888, 104–6, 105, 134

biology and architecture, 85–90, 231–32

Bosch-Ōmori seismograph, 170–71

Bridgens, R. P., 57

bridges, 228, 240n7; Nagara River railroad bridge, 121, 136, 137, 138, 165

British architecture: Britain as "earthquake country" and, 167–68; carpentry texts and, 203–16; two Britains and, 48–50

British Association for the Advancement of Science (BAAS), 102, 170, 283n41

Brunton, R. H., 40, 43–44, 57; Asiatic society paper by, 66; earthquake structures and, 86, 141; yatoi and, 80

Buckle, Henry Thomas, 82, 106

building regulations: Great Kantō Earthquake and, 222; Meireki Fire (1660) and, 265n80

the Bunriha, 214

Burges, William, 96

Burton, W. K., 135–39, 137

Cappelletti, Giovanni, 186, 192–93

carpentry: daiku and, 28–29, 45–48, 119, 138; Japanese architecture after Nōbi and, 182, 185, 202–11; Meiji-period technique, 35–37, 36–37; Western texts on, 203–11; Western vs. Japanese, 44–48. See also daiku; joinery; "Western carpentry"

cartographic method. See mapping

castles, 240n7, 273n38, 274n42; Fuji-san curve and, 146, 147, 149; Nagoya Castle, 121–22, 123, 124–25, 233

casualty figures, 283n47; in Great Kantō Earthquake, 220, 229; in Great Nōbi Earthquake, 273n31. See also comparative lethality rates

catfish imagery, 130, 216, 276n55

Cawley, George, 17, 57, 73; daiku practice and, 40–41, 43, 47–49; foreign

anxieties and, 84; Nōbi earthquake and, 149

Chamberlain, Basil Hall, 81–82

Chaplin, W. S., 71

Chastel de Boinville, Alfred, 73

Chicago Columbian Exposition of 1893: Conder's address to, 163; Hō-ō-den (Phoenix Hall) at, 164; Japanese architecture and, 17, 19, 150, 162–64; Japanese science and, 137, 163–64

Chisholm, Lawrence, 94

climate. See meteorology

clocks, 100, 101

comparative lethality rates, 172–74, 175–76, 284n53

compromise (setchū): Itō and, 186–90; Palace project and, 56; traditional architecture and, 31–38; wood-framed masonry and, 56–58. See also wayō setchū

concrete. See ferro-concrete

Conder, Josiah: "architecture" and, 23; art vs. science and, 214; binarisms and, 95–98; buildings designed by, 92, 93; carpentry and, 203–6; Chicago Exposition speech by, 150, 163; crack patterns and, 65–66; Dresser and, 50, 52, 55; foreign anxieties and, 84; Imperial Palace project and, 55, 56; Ischia debate and, 107–9, 111–12; Itō and, 190, 201; Japanese construction and, 40, 42, 52, 78–79, 150, 193, 201; Kōbudaigakkō and, 13–14, 19–21, 33, 93; Milne and, 65–66, 79, 94, 98, 107–9, 111–12, 117–20, 139–43, 147–48; Nōbi earthquake of 1891 and, 117–20, 139–43, 173; retirement of, 95; Tatsuno and, 61; Tokyo lectures of 1891–92, 139–43; zōkagaku course of, 13–14, 19–21, 27–28, 183, 200, 203–6

constructive science: Conder and, 78–79, 140–43; Lescasse and, 256n59; Milne and, 79–80, 102, 146, 162; Mount Fuji

earthquake of 1906 and, 175–76; Japanese architecture and, 180–211; Milne on, 117–20, 143–48; nationalization and, 130–35; in photography, 135–39, *137*, 145–46, 165; relief work and, 131–33, *134*; "return to normal" after, 128–35, 275n49; rural areas and, 117–20, 131; search for earthquake resistance and, 180–82, 185, 186–91, 191; Western views of, 148–50; in woodblock prints, 120–28, *124–27*

Great Sanriku Tsunami (1896), 160, 268n41

Gwilt, Joseph, 246n48

Hall, W. Silver, 119
Hashimoto Manpei, 129, 145, 152, 172
Hatsuda Tōru, 57
Hattori Ichizō, 101, 252n1, 268n41
Hayashi Tadahiro, 33–34
Hobbs, William H., 158
Die Hochbau-Constructionen: Des Handbuches der Architektur (German text), 206–8, *207*
Horiguchi Sutemi, 230, 295n59
Hōryūji pagoda, 53, 98

Ichiura Ken, 224, 293n41
IEIC. *See* Imperial Earthquake Investigation Committee
Ikegami Ryōhei, 294n46
Ikeya Mataji, 280n6
Imamura Akitsune: Ōmori-Imamura rift and, 217–20, 226–27; prediction of Tokyo earthquake and, 217–19, 221, 225–26, 292n24
Imperial Earthquake Investigation Committee (IEIC), 151, 160–62, 165–66, 224; earthquake resistance and, 181, 197–202; Itō Tamekichi and, 197–202
Imperial family and relief work, 131–33, *134*
Imperial Meteorological Observatory, 99

Imperial Palace project, 55, 56, 93
Imperial University. *See* Tokyo Imperial University
instrumental seismography, 71–80; European earthquake countries and, 168–71; Ōmori scale and, 154–59
international exhibitions, 44–48. *See also* Chicago Columbian Exposition of 1893
International Seismological Association, 170, 283n41
Inukai Tsuyoshi, 196
Ischia debate, 106–12
Ischian earthquake of 1883, 173
Ishii Keikichi, 163
isoseismal map, 154–59
Italy: climate of, 230; earthquake architecture in, 63–66; earthquake map of, *169;* Great Neopolitan Earthquake (1857), 108, 173; Ischia debate, 106–12; Mercalli scale, 156–57; Messina earthquake of 1908, 172–73; prediction in, 219
Itō Chūta, 180, 182–83, 186, 210, 212, 231, 232
Itō Hirobumi, 12, 93
Itō Tamekichi, 26, 185; IEIC and, 197–202; *Mokkō jutsu kyōkasho* (Wooden Work Manual), 192–97, 201; *Nihon kenchiku kōzō kairyōhō*, 187–91, 194–95; "Safe from Three Damages House," 186–90, *189*, 199; Shokkō Gundan and, 191–97, 200
Iwasaki family, 93
Iwasaki Yanosuke, 117

Japan: Its Architecture, Art, and Manufactures (Dresser), 50–52
Japan Architectural Institute (Nihon Zōka-Gakkai), 245n44, 286n16
Japanese architecture: after Nōbi earthquake, 180–211, 212–17; earthquake-proof carpentry, 208–9;

Japanese architecture *(continued)*
evolutionary metaphor and, 85–90,
231–32, 262n52; ferro-concrete in,
212–17; first-generation concerns and,
19–28, 212; Italian building practice
and, 63–66; modernism and, 230–32;
professionalism in, 245n42; resist-
earthquake regime in, 212–17, 233;
search for Japanese style and, 182–85,
212; strengthening of brick walls,
180–82; *wayō setchū* in, 31–38. *See also*
Imperial Earthquake Investigation
Committee; Kōbudaigakkō
Japanese carpentry. See *daiku;* Japanese
houses; joinery; wooden construction
Japanese culture: catfish imagery in, 130,
216, 276n55; depiction of earthquakes
in, 216–17; Japanese seismicity and,
229–31; portents in, 151–54; Western
views of, 43–44
Japanese houses: biological view of,
85–90; climate and, 296n66; hybrid designs of, 264n71; Itō and, 286n15; modernist views of, 230–32; *yatoi* views of,
40–44. *See also* wooden construction
Japanese literature: architecture in, 94;
daiku and, 35–37; earthquakes in,
82–83
Japanese seismology: after Great Kantō
Earthquake, 225, 226–33; as colonizing project, 174–77; Confucian explanations and, 144–45; depth of cultural
roots of, 177–79; as ethnography,
80–85; European vs. Japanese inscription and, 154–59; instrumental seismograph in, 71–80; as international science, 159–67; Italian seismology and,
63–66; Japanese architecture and,
213–17; Meiji state and, 98–103; Milne
and, 98–103, 167–71; Nōbi earthquake
and, 134–35; Ōmori-Imamura rift and,
217–20, 226–27; Ōmori legacy and,
165–67, 225–26; Ōmori scale in,

154–59; popularization of, 134–35;
portents and, 151–54; prediction and,
217–20, 225–26; terrestrial physics
and, 66–71, 161, 170, 282n24
Japanese style: architectural search for,
182–85, 212; transition from wood to
masonry in, 16–17
Japan Seismological Society. *See* Seismological Society of Japan
Japan Weekly Mail (newspaper): Ischia
debate and, 109, 110; nativism and, 92;
on Nōbi earthquake, 115, 117–20
jerry-building, 193–94, 198
Jiji shinpō (newspaper), 119, 120
joinery, 41, *42; daiku* technique, 41, *42,*
119; Itō and, 188–90, 197, 200
Jones, Lester E., 227

Kajima family, 32–33
Kajima Iwakichi, 57
Kaoki taishin kōzōron (Anti-Earthquake
Structural Theory for Buildings;
Sano), 213
Katayama Tōkuma, 19, 198, 267n17
Katō Hiroyuki, 82
Kawanabe Kyōsai, 97–98
Kelvin, Lord William Thomson, 73, 167,
261n26
kenchiku (architecture), as term, 22–23,
183
Kenchikugaku kōhon (textbook), 27
Kenchiku zasshi (journal), 19, 197, 200,
206–8, *207*
Kigo Kiyoyoshi, 56, 93, 95, 182, 183
Kikuchi Dairoku, Baron, 101, 144, 160,
170, 190, 200; on Japanese seismology,
160, 162; *Recent Seismological Investi-
gations in Japan*, 165, 209
Kikuchi Y. (geologist), 105
kiku-jutsu (carpentry technique) books,
35, 36–37, *36–37*
Kishida Hideto, 232–33
Kitamura Kōzō, 250n82

Rebeur-Paschwitz, Ernst von, 167, 283n40
reinforced concrete. *See* ferro-concrete
Reynolds, Jonathan, 214
rigidity, 41, 42, 214, 215. *See also* ferro-concrete; masonry
Rizzo, G. B., 283n47
Rōdō Kumiai (Laborer's Union), 196
Rokumeikan (building), 92–93, 266n6
roofs, 87, 187; aseismic properties and, 67, 140; IEIC designs, 288n52; Japanese vs. European, 140; of temples, 87; traditional Japanese systems and, 40, 41, 140. *See also* truss
Rossi-Forel scale, 154–56
Royal Institute of British Architects (RIBA), 20–21, 52, 97
Rubinger, Richard, 242n15
Ruskin, John, 27, 49

Safe from Three Damages House (Itō Tamekichi), 186–90, *189*, 199
Saigō Takamori, 12
Saita Tokitaro, 223
Sakamoto Naomichi, 33
sakan (plasterers), 57–58
samurai lineage: Japanese science and, 239n1, 242n15; Kōbudaigakkō and, 12–14
Sand, Jordan, 88
San Francisco earthquake of 1906: Ōmori and, 166, 171–72; Sano and, 212–13, 215
Sano Toshikata, 222, 223–24; ferro-concrete and, 212–17; on wooden framing, 296n65
Sanriku tsunami of 1896. *See* Great Sanriku Tsunami (1896)
Satachi Shichijirō, 16–17, 19, 21, 25
Satsuma clan, 12
science: architectural profession and, 25–28; architecture as biology, 85–90; art and, 69–71; Chicago Columbian

Exposition and, 163–64; Kantō earthquake and, 225; Nōbi earthquake and, 134–35, 139–43; *zōkagaku* and, 183. *See also* Japanese seismology
Science (journal), 102
Scientific American, 45
Seikyōsha (Society for Politics and Education), 91–92
seismicity of Japan, 39–44; after Nōbi earthquake, 160; foreign buildings as defenseless against, 162–64; public awareness of, 103–6. *See also* "earthquake countries"
seismograph, 64, *68*, 71–80, 260n24–25; Columbian Exposition and, 163–64; Ewing-Gray-Milne version of, 72–73; railroads and, 138
Seismological Society of Japan (Nihon Jishin Gakkai), 63, 64, 72, 95, 101, 160; foreign members of, 160, 258n2; founding of, 39–40, 63–64, 66; Milne's lecture and, 143–48. *See also* Imperial Earthquake Investigation Committee
seismologist *(jishingakusha)*, 135
Sekiya Seikei, 99, 153, 154; ethnography and, 83; foreign audience and, 105–6; IEIC and, 160; Nōbi earthquake and, 116, 129; prediction and, 219; public earthquake awareness and, 104, 105
Sentaro Kurasaki, 163
Shakai Seisakuha (Social Policy Faction), 290n10
Shiga Shigetaka: *Nihon fūkeiron*, 92, 106, 161
Shimizu family, 32–33, 287n41
Shimizu Kisuke, 57, 195
Shimizu Manautsuke, 33
shinbashira (central mast of pagoda), *68*, 178
Shinsai Yobō Chōsakai. *See* Imperial Earthquake Investigation Committee
shokkō, as term, 192

Tokyo-Yokohama earthquake of 1880, 64–66

tools *(dōgu)*, 29–31, 44

Toyama Minoru, 263*n*62

Toyohara Kunitaru, *124–27*

traditional Japanese construction: as architecture, 267*n*23; Conder's views of, 139–40; *daiku*-work and, 11–12, 13, 28–38, 231–32; Great Kantō Earthquake and, 231–33; Japanese views of Western learning and, 54–62; modernist views of, 230–32; Ōmori and, 177–79; pagodas and, 50–54; prefabricated housing and, 224–25, 232; resist-earthquakes regime and, 224; roofs in, 40, 41, 140. See also *daiku;* wooden construction

Transactions of the Seismological Society of Japan, 1894 cover of, *148*

Tredgold, Thomas: *Elementary Principles of Carpentry,* 203–6

triangle and earthquake resistance, 42, 186–87, 199

truss: carpentry knowledge and, 204, 206, 248*n*68; IEIC and, 199; Itō and, 186–87

tsunamis. *See* Great Sanriku Tsunami (1896)

United States: American carpentry, 190–91, 248*n*68; views of Japanese carpentry in, 44–48; wooden construction in, 243*n*22. *See also* San Francisco earthquake of 1906

University of Tokyo. *See* Tokyo Imperial University

Utsu Tokuji, 294*n*46

Verbeck, G. F., 71

Viollet-le-Duc, Eugène-Emmanuel, 15–16, 27

"volcano consciousness," 106

Wagener, Gottfried, 71

Waters, Thomas, 12, 65

water supply systems, 116, 227–28, 229

Watsuji Tetsuro, 230

wayō setchū (Japanese-Western compromise), 31–38, 56–58, 77–78, 249*n*76; joinery and, *42*

Wendelken, Cherie, 93, 183, 264*n*73, 287*n*28

"Western carpentry" *(yōfū daiku shigoto):* as academic specialty, 182, 185, 202–11; *daiku* and, 222; Itō and, 186–97

Western learning *(yōgaku):* American vs. European knowledge, 87–88; IEIC and, 197–202; Itō and, 186–97; Meiji government and, 12–14. *See also* Anglo-Japanese architecture project

Western views of Japan: Great Kantō Earthquake and, 227; Nōbi earthquake of 1891 and, 148–50; Sekiya and, 105–6. *See also* "earthquake countries"

woodblock prints: *namazu-e* (catfish pictures), 130, 216; Nōbi earthquake of 1891 and, 120–28, *124–27,* 273*n*35, 274*n*41

wooden construction, *207;* in America, 243*n*22; ants and, 175; Conder's view of, 40, 42, 52, 78–79, 150, 193, 201; earthquake cracks and, 259*n*20; fireproofing and, 88–89, 265*n*82; foreign views of, 40–44; Great Kantō Earthquake and, 222, 227–28, 293*n*40; Great Nōbi Earthquake and, 115, 118; masonry as advance on, 14–19; national character and, 296*n*65; seismic stability of, 64–65, 67–69, 78, 105–6, 155–56; traditional building practice and, 11–12, 14, 48. See also *daiku;* fire; Japanese houses; pagodas; traditional Japanese construction

"wood-framed masonry," 56–58, 89
worker corps. *See* Shokkō Gundan
World War II, reconstruction after,
   233
Wren, Sir Christopher, 15
Wright, Frank Lloyd, 222

"X" (pseudonym). *See* Conder, Josiah

Yamaji Aizan, 273*n*33
Yamao Yōzō, 12–13, 79–80, 101, 262*n*46
yatoi (foreign experts): British reform
   projects, 48–50; criticism of Anglo-
   Japanese project among, 50–54; divisions among, 50–54, 65–71, 76–80,
   89–90; Japanese roofs and, 187; Meiji
   government and, 13, 39–40; seismology as ethnography and, 80–85;
   "wood-framed masonry" and, 57. *See
   also* Kōbudaigakkō

yōfū (Western-style) architecture, 19–28
yokan (Western-style wings), 264*n*71
Yokohama: earthquake of 1880 in,
   64–66; Great Nōbi Earthquake (1891)
   and, 114–15
yonaoshi (world rectification), 130–31
Yoshimoto Makiko, 251*n*93

zairai-kōhō ("the way we now build"),
   202
zōkagaku (architecture): *kenchiku* and,
   183; as profession, 21–22. *See also*
   Japanese architecture; *kenchiku*
zōkagaku course at Kōbudaigakkō, 13–14,
   19–21, 27–28, 183, 200; carpentry in,
   203–6; Conder and, 13–14, 19–21,
   27–28, 183, 200, 203–6; student skepticism and, 58–61
zōkagaku-shi (architect): *daiku* and,
   21–22; as title, 20

Text: 10.25/14 Fournier

Display: Fournier

Compositor: Sheridan Books, Inc.

Printer and Binder: Sheridan Books, Inc.